Necker REFORM STATESMAN OF THE ANCIEN RÉGIME

Necker REFORM STATESMAN OF THE ANCIEN RÉGIME

Robert D. Harris

University of California Press

Berkeley • Los Angeles • London

University of California Press
Berkeley and Los Angeles, California
University of California Press, Ltd.
London, England
Copyright © 1979 by
The Regents of the University of California
ISBN 0-520-03647-7
Library of Congress Catalog Card Number: 77-93464
Printed in the United States of America

1 2 3 4 5 6 7 8 9

CONTENTS

In recent years historians of eighteenth-century France are becoming aware of a "Necker question." The question is whether the citizen of Geneva who became such a prominent figure in the government of Louis XVI has been treated justly by historians of the *ancien régime* and the French Revolution. Twentieth-century scholars have usually presented the Genevan banker as a mediocrity at best, a charlatan at worst. The contributor to the Lavisse history of France, Henri Carré, and the eminent historian of French finances, Marcel Marion, have both taken a dim view of his talents. The most frequently cited biography is that of Eugène Lavaquery, who, after stating that "Necker is the most important name in our history from 1776 to 1789," went on to denigrate harshly both his personal character and his ministerial career. In his book on Protestant bankers in France, Herbert Luethy generally accepted Lavaquery's opinions, although he admitted that some accusations were not well supported by evidence.

The portrait that emerges from the above authors is that of a Genevan who was inordinately vain, pathologically ambitious, faintly ridiculous, and wholly incompetent for the tasks to which he had been called. Worse, Necker is said to have made his fortune dishonestly, bankrupted the Company of the Indies by fraudulent financial operations, and ruined the monarchy by his expedients for financing the American War. He is portrayed as a reactionary mercantilist in economic doctrine who had the temerity to disagree with Turgot. He tried unsuccessfully to sabotage American independence. Above all, he is condemned for publishing his *Compte rendu* in 1781 that artfully concealed the true situation of the royal finances. Far from enjoying a surplus of revenue over expenditures as he boasted, the royal government was actually running a terrific deficit due to war expenditures. It was left to Calonne to reveal the true state of the royal finances before an Assembly of Notables in 1787. By then it was too late to save the royal government from bankruptcy, and the financial crisis led to the Revolution.

The difficulty with this portrait of Necker is how to account for his being "the most important person in France from 1776 to 1789." There is no question that he was one of the most highly respected of all the ministers of Louis XVI. He had a large following in public opinion of that day. Philosophes and crowned monarchs alike expressed their admiration for the character and "genius" of the foreigner who served the king of France with devotion and unselfishness. Here is a paradox that invites attention. Why should this individual who stood so high among his contemporaries have fallen so low in the opinion of historians?

This book is admittedly a rehabilitation. It was not intended to be when I began it some twelve years ago. At that time I was only aware of a "Necker question." But as I explored the sources it became apparent that the present-day image of Necker is too much derived from pamphlets printed anonymously by his enemies, mostly in 1780 and 1781. They were in fact "libels" sponsored by those whose interests had suffered from Necker's reforms, primarily financiers whose offices were abolished and profits curtailed, or *grands* who were incensed by Necker's reforms of the royal households. These libels do not stand up under critical investigation. In fact it is difficult to see how anyone could have taken them seriously.

But there is another source for the present-day image of Necker which cannot be dismissed so easily. The physiocrats and their sympathizers had little taste for the Genevan who had questioned the universality of their theories when applied to the administration of the kingdom. Turgot and Condorcet especially conceived an intense dislike for the Genevan banker. Because of Turgot's high stature among historians, there has been little interest in Necker's economic ideas, much less his views on the reform of the *ancien régime*. The principal purpose of this work is to present Necker's ideas on reform sympathetically, and to place his ministry in the general context of the reform movement in France following the Seven Years' War.

After beginning this task I became aware that others also had come to suspect the prevalent views about Necker. In 1963 J. F. Bosher wrote an article, "Jacques Necker and the Reform of the State," which raised the "Necker question" perhaps for the first time. In his book published in 1970, *French Finances, 1774–1795: From Business to Bureaucracy,* Bosher devoted a chapter to Necker's reform of the financial administration of the royal government, giving him high marks. Henri Grange had also published articles beginning in 1957 tending to show that the famous quarrel between Turgot and Necker in the Flour War of 1775 was not necessarily all to the glory of Turgot and the discredit of Necker. In 1974 appeared his comprehensive and sympathetic work on Necker's economic, religious, and political thought, *Les Idées de Necker.* My own manuscript was nearly completed when I became aware of the biography of Necker by Jean Egret that was published in December 1975, *Necker, ministre de Louis XVI.* It was not surprising that this scholar should turn his attention to the subject, for his studies on the magistrates and notables of the late *ancien régime* fitted him well for appreciating Necker.

The above works have been useful in writing this manuscript, and I hereby acknowledge my debt to their authors. At the same time I trust that their works will not render my own superfluous. I have restricted the topic to Necker's first ministry from 1776 to 1781, believing it to be a complete subject in itself. The problems and the general situation he faced in later ministries during the French Revolution were so different from those of his reform ministry that I believed it appropriate to leave that subject to another work.

Since I began this manuscript, a number of institutions and individuals have greatly helped me in both research and writing. I wish especially to thank the University of Idaho for granting me a sabbatical leave for the academic year 1975–1976, when the research and writing of the manuscript was largely completed. The Idaho Research Foundation (formerly the Research Council) awarded me three summer research grants from 1968 through 1974 that I gratefully acknowledge. Most of the research was done since 1965 at the Bibliothèque nationale and the Archives nationales in Paris. Both were pleasant places in which to work, and their staffs were always helpful and courteous. This was true also where briefer forays were made: the departmental archives at Châlons, Bordeaux, and Clermont-Ferrand; the Public Record Office and the British Museum in London; the Public and University Library in Geneva, the University Library at Lausanne, and the Historical Library of the City of Paris at the Hôtel Lamoignon. I should like to thank the University of Chicago Press for permitting me to use passages of two articles that were printed in the *Journal of Modern History*. The first was in the June 1970 issue: "Necker's *Compte rendu* of 1781: A Reconsideration." The second appeared in the June 1976 issue: "French Finances and the American War, 1777–1783." Above all, I should like to express my appreciation to the present proprietor of the Château de Coppet, Count d'Haussonville, who not only permitted me to examine the *pièces justificatives* of the *Compte rendu* in the library of the château, but has shown a friendly interest in my work. He read an earlier draft of the manuscript and made a number of helpful suggestions.

In writing this book I have also benefited from the advice of colleagues in the University of Idaho History Department, who have listened to papers I have read at different colloquia and conferences over the years, all on the rehabilitation of Necker. My seminar class in the spring semester 1975 read an early version of Chapter IV and made several suggestions for improvement that were used.

In the preparation of the final manuscript I am much indebted to Ted Stanton, editor of the *Daily Idahonian,* whose editorial pencil greatly improved it. Mrs. Dayle Williams has assisted me in typing earlier drafts of the manuscript. The final copy was typed by Mrs. Florence Anderson, who has been much more than a typist: her vast knowledge of style and form has aided many students and professors.

In the last pages of his *Compte rendu,* Necker acknowledged the great help he had received from "the companion of his life" in carrying out his reforms in social welfare. I have been as fortunate in my task of rehabilitating Necker. The academic life was new to my wife, Ethel, only seven years ago. But she has shared my enthusiasm in the adventures of research and has cheerfully adapted to living abroad, spending several summers and a sabbatical year away from home and family. It is to her that this book is dedicated.

Many terms are described in the text, and these descriptions can be located by using the index. Examples are: *fermes, régies,* liberalism, and enlightened despotism.

The terms listed below, both French and English, are not specifically defined elsewhere and may be puzzling to the reader. It was necessary to use some French words so often that I have not italicized them but treated them as English words. These are: anticipations, brevet, livre, rente, setier, and venal (used as an adjective for offices).

abonnement: an agreement whereby a region or corporate group settles for a tax by agreeing to pay a specified sum.

administrative monarchy: refers to the type of regime established by Richelieu and Louis XIV whereby intendants sent to the provinces by the royal council became the chief administrative officers, supplanting the traditional corps of officials.

ancien régime: I have preferred to use the French term, which means "former regime" (before the French Revolution) and not "ancient regime." "Old regime" can also be misleading.

anticipations: short-term loans of about three to six months made to the royal government by financiers, chiefly receivers general of the direct taxes and farmers general of the indirect taxes.

brevet: an order of the king that does not require the seal or registration.

caisse: the treasury of a financial company that handled some part of the royal finances.

decree-in-council: this is my translation for *arrêt du conseil,* an act of the royal council having the force of law.

élection: this is derived from the *élus,* officials who had fiscal and judicial functions in the provinces before the regime of intendants. The *élection* came to designate the geographical area administered by the subdelegate of the intendant. There were 178 *élections* in the *pays d'élections* in 1789.

generality: the geographical area administered by an intendant. There were twenty in 1789 in the *pays d'elections,* each named after the chief city in which its intendant resided.

grands: the highest-ranking aristocracy, such as princes of the blood and members of great noble families who held lucrative positions in the royal households.

lettres de cachet: sealed letters, in contrast to open letters (*lettres patentes*), emanating from royal authority acting upon individuals. These were often used by ministers of the government to exile or imprison dissidents.

lit de justice: the chair in which the king sat when he presided personally over a meeting of the Parlement of Paris, ordering it to register an edict against which it had remonstrated.

livre tournois: the monetary unit of the *ancien régime.* Sometimes the word franc was used in its place. It was equal to 20 sous; 12 deniers made one sou. Three livres made one écu. Twenty-four livres made one louis. The latter was roughly equivalent to the British pound sterling.

pays conquis: lands recently annexed to the French kingdom that were administered by intendants, as were the *pays d'élections.*

pays d'états: these were provinces coming under royal sovereignty after the regime of the *élus* had been established in the kingdom. The newly acquired provinces were permitted to keep their assemblies of estates, which had ceased to exist in the *pays d'élections.*

rentes: the oldest type of loan made by the French royal government. The name comes from the income received by the *rentier.* There were two types of such loans, rentes *perpetuelles* and rentes *viagères.* The capital was assigned to the government permanently, without any specific provisions for amortization. The perpetual rente earned for its owner a yearly income usually at 5 percent of the capital of the loan. The life rente earned a higher rate, usually 10 percent of the amount loaned, but it was paid only during the life of the person (*tête*) on which it was constituted. "Annuity" does not seem to me a satisfactory translation.

setier: a measurement for the quantity of grain equal to 288 liters.

sovereign courts: this refers to the entire structure of judicial tribunals of the *ancien régime:* the *parlements,* Courts of Aides, and Chambers of Account. The Paris courts had the largest area of jurisdiction, but there were in addition twelve regional courts for all three of the above.

taillables: those subject to the direct tax known as the *taille,* as contrasted to those exempt from it, the non-*taillables.*

venal offices: much of the government of the *ancien régime* was done by officials who purchased their offices and could bequeath them to heirs. The official class was distinguished from those who held their posts by commission and were dismissible by the ministers or the king. An example of the latter were the intendants, called *commissaires départis.*

Note: Throughout this book all translations from the French are my own.

Chapter I

THE BANKER

By an edict of October 22, 1776, dated at Fontainebleau, Louis XVI appointed Jacques Necker counselor of finance and director of the royal treasury. Ostensibly Necker was to serve as deputy to the newly appointed controller general, Louis Gabriel Taboureau des Réaux. In fact, Taboureau was without experience in financial administration and would be a figurehead, leaving management of the royal finances to Necker.[1] This arrangement endured scarcely more than eight months. Uncomfortable in his role, Taboureau resigned on June 29, 1777, and Necker was promoted to director general of finances.

This title had not been used since early in the century, and was revived to fit the peculiar circumstances of the individual called to the helm. For Jacques Necker was not a subject of the king of France but a citizen of the city-state republic of Geneva. He was a Protestant called to serve in the government of a country where the laws denying civil rights to Protestants were still unrepealed though not rigorously enforced. Moreover, his social origins, education, and experience contrasted sharply with that class of functionaries from which appointments to the highest positions in the government were normally drawn. These were the sons and nephews of prominent families, scions of magistrates who had served the government for generations and constituted that branch of the nobility called "the robe." The normal career of a member of the class was to begin as a *maître des requêtes* in the royal councils or the sovereign courts such as the Parlement of Paris. He could expect to advance to the rank of counselor, and from there perhaps to be sent to the provinces as intendant, before he could hope to be called to the highest posts in the government.[2] In contrast, Necker had been a commercial banker for nearly twenty years, and at the time of his appointment in 1776 was serving as resident minister of the republic of Geneva. Thus, his appointment was remarkable for three reasons: his nationality, his religion, and his social origin.[3]

1. Archives nationales (AN) K 161, no. 8, Necker to Maurepas, undated.
2. Vivian R. Gruder, *The Royal Provincial Intendants: A Governing Elite in Eighteenth Century France* (Ithaca, 1968), pt 1, pp. 1-94.
3. The title of controller general was not used after the resignation of Taboureau des Réaux until the advent of Calonne in November 1783. Necker could not receive that title

Necker's ascendency was unusual, but not unprecedented. Sixty years earlier another foreign-born Protestant without family background had acquired an even more powerful position in the economic life of the kingdom. The brief and ephemeral career of the Scotsman John Law from 1716 to 1720 left a profound impression on the French. It conjured visions of fanciful promotional schemes, unlimited printing of paper money given forced circulation, frenzied speculation, and final collapse. The ghost of "the System" haunted Necker throughout his first ministry. Every act that suggested a parallel with those of his Scottish predecessor sent a shudder through the conservative classes in French society. The epithet "charlatan" came easily to the lips of Necker's enemies, for he seemed to have Law's gifts for raising money by credit. The final result, they believed, could only be a collapse like that of 1720.

Yet the supposed similarity between John Law and Jacques Necker was entirely superficial. Indeed, there could hardly be a greater contrast. Law was an adventurer and a gambler, Necker prudent and cautious. The Scotsman's fertile imagination was brimming over with new schemes; the Genevan distrusted reverie and was concerned most with the feasible. Law became a French subject and a Catholic; Necker remained a devoted Protestant and never became a French citizen. Law constantly expanded his powers in the government; Necker believed in his first ministry that his responsibilities should be reduced. Law was interested in titles and rank, receiving the fittingly ephemeral title of Duke of Arkansas.[4] Necker cared little for such distinctions. Throughout his career he signed his name simply as "Necker." When he became director general of finances, some officials asked if they should address him as Monseigneur and were told he would be satisfied with Monsieur. Despite a legend propagated by a twentieth-century biographer, Necker showed little interest about his own forebears in the hope of finding blue blood in his veins. He was ambitious, certainly, but his ambition was not that of a social climber.

It was his older brother, Louis Necker, who was interested in the family history. Louis sought information about the family from cousins in Germany. His correspondence with them eventually came into the possession of the First Syndic of the Genevan government and is preserved in the manuscripts of the Historical Society in Geneva. At the end of the nineteenth century these letters were studied by the Genevan literary scholar Eugène Ritter, who was interested in the ancestry of Madame de Staël, Necker's daughter.[5] He found among the documents an unsigned and undated paper translated from the English into the French. The writer claimed to have discovered a certain Roger Necker, an Irish

because it required taking an oath before the Paris Chamber of Accounts, which his religion prevented him from doing. But there can be no doubt that in fact, if not in name, Necker exercised all the powers of the controller general's office from June 1777 until May 1781.

4. John Kenneth Galbraith, *Money: Whence It Came, Where It Went* (Boston, 1975), p. 25.

5. Eugène Ritter, *Notes sur Madame de Staël, ses ancêtres et sa famille* (Geneva, 1899).

nobleman from Armagh who had been companion at arms of William the Conqueror. The writer added that he would trace the lineage down to the present if he received a thousand pounds. There is no evidence that this dubious proposition was followed up. Louis Necker did inquire of his German cousins, one an expert on family history, if they knew anything about an Irish ancestor. They did not. The family history could not be traced earlier than the late sixteenth century, they said, and the ancestors were all in Pomerania at that time.

The matter of the Irish ancestry might have ended then had there not appeared in 1789, in far-off Regensburg, a small anonymous book written in German entitled *Familiengeschichte des Herrn von Necker.* The unknown author wrote near the beginning of the tract that "according to a letter written by Mr. Necker to his cousin in Pomerania, the family traced its origin from Armagh in Ireland." [6] In 1886 a German scholar wrote a brief essay about the origins of the Necker family and said that "perhaps the proud beginning of that letter was the finance minister's own words." [7] Several years later Ritter wrote that "undoubtedly" Jacques Necker was the author of that letter, but he gave no reason why he thought so. [8] If such a letter existed it would seem more likely that it was written by Louis Necker, more interested in family history than his brother. But Louis was seeking information from his cousins rather than proffering it, so it seems doubtful that he could have written it.

Ritter also surmised that the Necker coat of arms as recorded in the *Armorial genevois* was derived from the above-mentioned document of the English genealogist. If so, this also must have been the work of Louis Necker rather than of the minister of finance. A twentieth-century biographer, Eugène Lavaquery, found a motif in a coat of arms that can be seen today in the Museum of Public Assistance in Paris (painted on two large medicine jars donated by Madame Necker to the hospital she founded), which he believes was derived from the above-mentioned document. Based upon this evidence, a coat of arms of uncertain origin and an obscure work in German of unknown authorship, Lavaquery began his biography of Necker: "As his fortune grew, Jacques Necker saw fit to embellish his modest origins. . . ." Then follows the story of the companion of William the Conqueror and the coat of arms.

Necker, while adopting the coat of arms, never publicly claimed Irish origins until 1789. Then, at the culminating point of his career he judged it appropriate to reveal to the world, along with his own merits, those of his family. Such was the purpose of the German brochure which appeared anonymously in the first

6. *Familiengeschichte des Herrn von Necker, Königl. Französischen Staatsministers; Nebst beyläufigen Bemerkungen über seinen Karakter und seine Finanzoperationen* (Regensburg, 1789), p. 4.

7. J. Hermann, *Zur Geschichte der Familie Necker* (Berlin, 1886), p. 1.

8. Ritter, *Notes sur Madame de Staël,* p. 15.

months of 1789 at Regensburg. . . . This is, among others, one of the strongest expressions of his immeasurable vanity.[9]

The above passage is, among others, a good example of the evidence Lavaquery relied upon to make his most astringent observations about Necker's character. No reference to a noble Irish ancestry appears in any of Necker's writings. It is true that his grandson, baron de Staël, wrote that "the family to which Mr. Necker belonged was of Irish origin, his ancestors having had to flee during the religious persecution of Queen Mary."[10] It is not known where he got that bit of information. While his brother and his wife thought differently about the matter, Jacques Necker himself placed little value on noble lineage. In his essay on Colbert he expressed contempt for mercenary genealogists, "those servitors of the vanity of men." [11]

In any case, it is fairly well established that Necker's forebears were from Pomerania, and that from the late sixteenth century they were a family of pastors, city officials, and lawyers. Necker's father, Charles Frédéric Necker, was born in 1686 at Küstrin in the Brandenburg province of Neumark. Trained in law, he entered the service of George Louis, elector of Hanover, at the beginning of the century. When the elector became king of Great Britain, the fortunes of Charles Frédéric Necker advanced accordingly. He served for three years as secretary of the British ambassador at Vienna. In 1724 he received a pension from George I to maintain a boarding school for young English scholars at Geneva. Simultaneously the city government of Geneva offered him a chair at the Genevan Academy to teach the public law of the German Empire. He rose rapidly in Genevan society, receiving the rank of "bourgeois" within two years. In 1734 he became a member of the Council of Two Hundred, which conferred life membership, and from 1742 to 1747 he served a term in the Consistory.

Charles Frédéric Necker married the daughter of a prominent Genevan family, Jeanne-Marie Gautier. The family was of distant Huguenot origin, having fled France after St. Bartholemew's day and taken refuge in Geneva. The Gautiers traced their descent from Jacques Coeur, famous merchant and financier of Bourges in the fifteenth century. The mother of Jeanne-Marie Gautier was born Madeleine Gallatin. Jacques Necker was a distant cousin of Albert Gallatin, the American Secretary of the Treasury under Jefferson and Madison.[12]

Two sons were born to this marriage. The elder was Louis, known in later years as Louis de Germany. Like his younger brother, Louis was well endowed intellectually. In fact, he was considered the more brilliant of the two and was selected by his father for a university education and an academic career.

---

9. Eugène Lavaquery, *Necker: Fourrier de la révolution* (Paris, 1933), pp. 1-2.

10. Auguste de Staël, "Notice sur M. Necker," in Jacques Necker, *Oeuvres complètes de M. Necker publié par le baron de Staël, son petit-fils,* 15 vols. (Paris, 1820-1821), I, iii.

11. *Eloge de Colbert* (Paris, 1773), p. 4. It is in Necker, *Oeuvres complètes,* XV, 3-126.

12. The common ancestor was Marin Gallatin, who was born about 1546 and who died on October 4, 1625. See Albert Choisy, *Généalogies genevoises* (1947), p. 161.

Although trained in law, he became a professor of mathematics and physics at Geneva. He was a lifelong friend of D'Alembert and contributed a number of articles on natural science to the *Encyclopédie*. His university career was interrupted by a scandal in his private life that caused some notoriety at the time, and that seems to have titillated Voltaire, then feuding with the Genevan government over the question of theatrical presentations.[13] Louis left Geneva to enter the banking business in Marseilles, then in Paris, where he became a managing partner of the new firm that succeeded Thellusson, Necker and Company in 1772.

Jacques Necker was born in 1732 in Geneva. He was precocious, finishing his secondary education at age fourteen. He had a marked predilection for literature, and had the choice been his, he might have pursued the career in which his daughter achieved so much fame. But his father did not think highly of that pursuit and decided that Jacques would enter commerce. At eighteen he went to Paris to work in the banking firm of Isaac Vernet, a brother of a colleague of his father at the Genevan Academy. His keen intelligence was rapidly absorbed in matters of commerce and banking. He early assumed responsibilities in the absence of his employer, which at first appalled the elderly Vernet but then won his confidence. Vernet was childless; eventually he regarded the brilliant young assistant as a logical successor when he should retire.

In 1756, a few months before Necker's twenty-fourth birthday, Isaac Vernet did retire, and a new company was formed, Thellusson and Necker. Vernet remained a "sleeping partner" (*en commanditaire*), with a share in the profits, but active management devolved upon Jacques Necker and George-Tobie de Thellusson. The latter was the second son of Isaac Thellusson, prominent banker and resident minister of Geneva at Paris in the 1730s and 1740s, who had died the year before the founding of the new company. George-Tobie de Thellusson, inheriting a large fortune, must have contributed most of the capital for the new company. Necker's resources were much more slender. His most important contribution probably was his banking skill and his dedication to hard work.[14]

Thellusson, Necker and Company lasted until 1772, when it was dissolved and gave way to a new firm, Germany, Girardot and Company. Necker and Thellusson retired from active management and were succeeded by Louis Necker (who now adopted the name "de Germany") and Jean Girardot de Marigny, brother-in-law of Thellusson. According to his wife, Jacques Necker "completely severed all ties with the bank" at this time. However, Herbert Luethy has discovered the contract of the new company, which shows that Jacques Necker and George-Tobie de Thellusson remained sleeping partners in the bank and, in fact, contributed most of the capital, sharing profits proportionately.[15]

13. Herbert Luethy, *La Banque protestante en France de la révocation de l'édit de Nantes à la révolution*, 2 vols. (Paris, 1961), II, 235.

14. *Ibid.*, p. 230.

15. *Ibid.*, pp. 402-405.

The company came to an end automatically with the death of Thellusson in September 1776. The documents inventoried by Luethy show the liquidation of the Thellusson interest in the bank and its distribution among his heirs. There is no documentary evidence, however, of what happened to Necker's interest. In August 1777 a new firm, Girardot, Haller and Company, was formed in which Louis Necker withdrew from active management but remained a sleeping partner. Did Jacques Necker retain any interest at all in the new bank? We do not know. In the libel campaign launched against him in 1780 his enemies asserted that Girardot, Haller and Company was still very much "his bank" and that he was reaping inordinate profits from government loans he was able to funnel through this bank as minister of finance. Luethy seems ambivalent on this. While writing that "we have good reason to believe that Necker ceased to have any formal and effective association with the new contract," he then goes on to show that the libelists had good reason to believe otherwise. "If the new company had liquidated Necker's interest along with Thellusson's it would have retained very little capital." He then quotes the libelist J. M. Augeard to the effect that the new company was simply a smoke screen to cover Necker's devious operations.[16]

When Necker withdrew from active management of the company in 1772, his own references to his fortune show that it was completed at that time and altered very little afterward. Just how large his fortune was is uncertain. In 1778 he loaned 2,400,000 livres to the French government, which he later said "was the principal part of my fortune."[17] Two days after his appointment to the royal treasury in October 1776, the bookseller and diarist Hardy recorded that Necker made a public declaration of his wealth, giving it as three million livres.[18] In the absence of any creditable evidence to the contrary, there is no reason to dispute this.[19] Just how Necker's fortune was earned, in what type of banking activity, whether in secret collusion with the French government—or by obscure, sharp practices that he would later blush to admit, or by honorable and normal operations—has been discussed at length by Necker biographers. Evidence of the Necker bank operations is sparse, leading some authors to attach too great a weight to the libelous and anonymous pamphlets of Necker's enemies.[20]

However, some information is available about the operations of the bank from the time of Isaac Vernet through the Germany, Girardot period of 1777.

16. *Ibid.* Throughout his discussion of Necker, Luethy seemed strangely fascinated by the libels. While admitting their dubious nature, he often quoted from them, giving the impression that "there is no smoke without fire." See the comment of Henri Grange, *Les Idées de Necker* (Paris, 1974), p. 40, n. 9.

17. Necker, *Nouveaux éclaircissements sur le compte rendu,* in *Oeuvres complètes,* II, 363-364.

18. "Journal du libraire Hardy," *Bibliothèque nationale* (BN), MSS Français, 6682, fol. 288.

19. Compare Luethy, *La Banque protestante,* II, 370-371, who believed Necker's fortune was equal to Thellusson's, over 7 million livres; but this is pure conjecture.

20. See n. 35 below.

According to Necker's grandson, the baron de Staël, the bulk of the fortune was due to "large-scale speculation in the grain trade."[21] Speculation in this commodity was rampant in the eighteenth century. The yearly grain crop fluctuated severely, causing serious shortages in some areas and a surplus in others. The speculative fever was not limited to bankers. Many joined, including, it is said, hairdressers and servants.[22] But the banks with large capital resources were in the best position to scan the international market and to import grain from other countries into France. Léon Cahen believed that Necker acquired his knowledge about the grain trade by studying the archives of the Thellusson bank of the earlier generation.[23] Isaac Vernet also engaged in such operations. From 1747 to 1749 his firm was commissioned by the French government to buy grain "for the account of the king." The bank probably continued this type of operation under Thellusson and Necker. There is no evidence, however, that Necker's bank was involved in the contract between the controller general, Terray, and the Malisset group that provided fuel for the legend of the *"pacte de famine."*[24]

The Thellusson-Necker bank was called upon in the last years of Louis XV to make short-term loans to the royal government. This relationship began during the ministry of the duc de Choiseul, but was greatly expanded when abbé Terray was controller general from 1769 to 1774. Our only source of knowledge for this delicate subject is from baron de Staël's brief biography of his grandfather.[25] In January 1772, an agreement was signed by Terray with the bank for an advance of one million livres. That Thellusson-Necker had become an important source of credit for the royal government is indicated by an urgent letter addressed to Necker, quoted by de Staël: "We beg you to come to our assistance within the day. . . . We are on the eve of departure for Fontainebleau. Time is short and you are our only resource."[26] De Staël did not say that this message was sent by Terray, only that it was from "someone within the office of the *Contrôle-général.*" Nor was the letter addressed: "Dear Usurer," as reported in a recent work.[27] Indeed, according to de Staël's discussion of the terms of these loans, they were far from usurious.

In addition to granting such short-term emergency loans, Necker's bank became a broker for the marketing of long-term government loans, surveying the international market for investors. In Vernet's time a considerable proportion of the bank's clients had been Dutch. Thellusson and Necker added major Genevan

21. "Notice sur M. Necker," in Necker, *Oeuvres complètes,* I, x-xi.

22. Léon Cahen, "Le Pacte de famine et les spéculations sur les blés," *Revue historique,* 152 (May-August, 1926), 37.

23. *Ibid.*

24. Luethy, *La Banque protestante,* II, 374.

25. "Notice sur M. Necker," Necker, *Oeuvres complètes,* I, xx-xxi.

26. *Ibid.*

27. Lucien Laugier, *Un Ministère réformateur sous Louis XV: Le Triumvirat (1770-1774)* (Paris, 1975), p. 201.

creditors. The bank handled the cumbersome administrative chores involved in the ownership of those government obligations called *rentes.* The *rentier* was required to present himself at the Hôtel de Ville to receive annual interest payments. The bank took care of this and other matters for its international clientele, charging a commission of one-half percent of the capital invested. This was more routine and less speculative than the grain operations, but it was one area in which Necker seems to have become a specialist.[28]

The above nearly summarizes what is known of the origins of Necker's fortune. In 1780 a libel campaign was launched in an effort to discredit him and force him from office. Several stories were circulated about how his fortune had been created. It was said that, behind the facade of seeming indifference to money, he was secretly making huge profits from government loans; also, that exorbitant commissions were made by the bank, so that Necker was more than making up for his ostentatious refusal to accept a salary and other emoluments accruing to the finance minister.[29] Yet, in the absence of creditable evidence to the contrary, there is no reason to doubt Madame Necker's assertion in her 1787 essay that Necker "had lost all interest in making more money" when he retired from management of the bank in 1772.[30]

Two tales that circulated in the libel campaign of 1780 have been taken seriously by historians. One had to do with a supposed speculation in notes issued by the French government in Canada during the Seven Years' War; the other concerned Necker's handling of the finances of the Company of the Indies in the last years of its privileged trading monopoly in the area east of the Cape of Good Hope.

According to the first story, when France and England began discussing peace in 1762, the first secretary of the French Foreign Ministry, one Claude-Pierre-Maximilien Radix de Sainte-Foy, notified Necker through intermediaries that Great Britain was insisting that France honor notes issued to Canadians during the war. These notes had greatly depreciated in value. If France were to agree to reimburse them at par, their value would shoot up dramatically as soon as this became known, or so it was claimed. Radix de Sainte-Foy is said to have offered to keep Necker posted on the secret negotiations if the Genevan banker would agree to hand over to Sainte-Foy and his intermediaries one-third of any profits from speculation on the notes. Necker supposedly agreed. Taking advantage of the privileged information, he allegedly bought depreciated Canadian paper;

28. Luethy, *La Banque protestante,* II, 238-242.

29. [Jean-Marie Augeard], *Lettre de M. Turgot à M. Necker,* in *Collection complète de tous les ouvrages pour et contre M. Necker,* 3 vols. (Utrecht, 1781), I, 1-35.

30. Madame Necker, "Portrait de M. Necker fait en 1787," *Mélanges extraits des manuscrits,* 3 vols. (Paris, 1798), II, 372-404. This essay was read by Madame Necker to a gathering of friends in 1787. She did not publish it in her lifetime, contrary to Luethy's statement that "she published it in 1786"; see *La Banque protestante,* II, 401-402. This would mitigate the "indecency" which that author found in Madame Necker's comments about her husband. Furthermore, if she was mistaken in saying that "he severed all connections with his bank in 1772," she was still fundamentally right in her main assertion that Necker did not care to make more money after that time.

when news of the French guarantee was made public, Necker sold the notes, making a profit of 1,800,000 livres, which, however, he declined to share with his informants.

Like most stories circulated in the libel campaign, this was wildly improbable. To make such a profit so quickly would have been a spectacular event that must have left some evidence. In fact, the story is supported by no evidence other than the libel pamphlets. Furthermore, some available information contradicts the story. The "secret clause" about the Canadian notes was published in the treaty of 1763. It stipulated that the French guarantee applied only to those notes held by new Canadian subjects of Great Britain. This would have made speculation on them by international bankers difficult. The treaty of 1763 also was vague as to how the notes would be reimbursed. The Declaration stated that "the notes and letters of exchange would be exactly paid, according to a liquidation made at a convenient time."[31] It was not until 1766, according to the *Encyclopédie méthodique,* that Britain succeeded in getting compensation for the Canadians. But it was greatly reduced from the par value of the notes. The new British subjects held 7 million livres in letters of exchange, for which they received 55 percent of par value, and 34 million livres in notes (*ordonnances*), for which they received only 34 percent of par value. According to the authors of the libels, the depreciated paper that Necker is supposed to have bought up was worth from 40 to 50 percent of par value.[32]

There is scattered information from other sources about the ultimate fate of these Canadian notes. For example, the probate of the will of Isaac Vernet in 1772 listed about 300,000 livres of depreciated paper, which included Canadian notes.[33] Why did he not dispose of them at the same time Necker was said to have made his great coup? In the bankruptcy proceedings of Isaac Panchaud in 1770, his assets listed an item of 400,000 livres of *ordonnances,* letters of exchange, "and other Canadian paper coming from the banks of Quebec, Montréal and London" but which were given a value of only 15,000 livres.[34] It would not appear that anybody made a killing from Canadian notes! Yet the story has been constantly repeated in secondary works devoted to Necker's career since that time.[35]

31. George Frédéric de Martens, ed., *Recueil des principaux traités d'alliance, de paix, de trèves . . . depuis 1761 jusqu'à présent,* 8 vols., 2d ed., rev. (Göttingen, 1826-1835), I, p. 55.

32. *Encyclopédie méthodique: Finance,* 3 vols. (Paris, 1783-1784), I, 169-170. The libels are in the Utrecht publication *Collection complète de tous les ouvrages . . .* Several of them recount the speculation on Canadian notes, including the first one, "Lettre de M. Turgot à M. Necker."

33. Luethy, *La Banque protestante,* II, 231.

34. *Ibid.,* p. 424.

35. For example, René Stourm, *Les Finances de l'ancien régime et de la révolution,* 2 vols. (Paris, 1885), I, 36; Pierre Jolly, *Necker* (Paris, 1951), pp. 50-51; Luethy, *La Banque protestante,* II, 374-375. Luethy quoted Stourm as authority and wrote that, while "there is no authentic document" to support the story, Necker never contradicted it. This is not a valid argument because Necker did not deign to reply to such slanders.

Several years after Necker's association with the Company of the Indies, he was accused of having ruined the company through usurious loans from his bank, and through various other financial expedients that he is said to have imposed upon the company's directors. The seventh of the libel pamphlets of 1780, dated September 12, accused him of having defrauded the company. The pamphlet was entitled simply *Letter to Mr. Necker, Director General of Finances;* but in the collection of libels published at Utrecht in 1781, this pamphlet was referred to as the *Liégeoise,* presumably because it was printed in Liége. Both Metra and Bachaumont, two journalists of the day, reported that it was badly printed on poor-quality paper, "as if," wrote Bachaumont, "it were printed furtively in some remote corner of the country." It was unsigned, as were all the libel pamphlets attacking Necker in 1780. Bachaumont noted that the author presented himself as someone who had been intimately associated with the Company of the Indies; "everything is treated in such a lucid and knowledgeable manner," he wrote, "that the reader is convinced."[36] Metra, however, was not so carried away by it:

There has just appeared a new libel against Mr. Necker. . . . It accuses him of charlatanism, and maintains that he robbed the Company of the Indies during the period when he was banker. . . . In a word, it passes in review all his operations, in an outrageous manner, but by no means convincing to impartial and well-meaning people.[37]

The libel campaign sought to force Necker from office by generating panic over his financial policies. The author of the *Liégeoise* maintained that Necker's operations with the Company of the Indies in the 1760s strikingly resembled those he was now pursuing ten years later as director general of the royal finances. His "miserable financial expedients" drove the company into bankruptcy and were now doing the same to the royal government. The following passage from the *Liégeoise* is characteristic:

It will be remembered what state of languor the Company of the Indies, revived in 1764 by Mr. Necker's care, fell back into in 1767 under the same care. It was always in great need of funds at the moment of its expeditions to India. Several stopgap measures had already been exhausted when Mr. Necker engaged the Company to acquire its *piastres* at Cadiz, and to pay for them by means of a circulation of drafts drawn on his correspondents in several commercial cities of Europe. The bankers of Cadiz drew drafts of three months on bankers of London; the latter, on the expiration of the Cadiz drafts, reimbursed themselves on the bankers of Hamburg, the latter on those of Amsterdam, and finally the bankers of Amsterdam on the general cashier [of the company] at Paris; each operation took three months, that is, an entire year for the entire operation; the

---

36. Louis Petit de Bachaumont, *Mémoires secrets pour servir à l'histoire de la république des lettres en France depuis 1762 jusqu'à nos jours,* 36 vols. (London, 1777-1789), XVI, 63.

37. François Metra, *Correspondance secrète, politique et littéraire* . . . 18 vols. (London, 1787-1790), X, 202.

proceeds of the sale at L'Orient served to extinguish the final drafts, and so finally the *piastres* were paid for.

It can easily be seen that this bank circulation was ruinous for the Company; indeed, four commissions at ½ percent each, four courtages at one-eighth, that makes 2½ percent; add to that the difference in exchange rates, which for large sums cannot be evaluated at less than 6 or 7 percent per year; that makes 9 percent at least which this bank credit cost the Company. This was not all; these circulations demonstrated the uneasiness of the Company, they cast discredit upon it which is just what Mr. Necker wanted, one will see why: The following year a new expedition of *piastres* is necessary, the profits of the year are almost consumed by the payment of (the *piastres*) of the preceeding year; what to do? They consult, they calculate, they imagine, but nothing comes of it; it is necessary to have recourse to Mr. Necker, the savior of the Company, the guardian angel of the commerce of the Indies.

At first he saw only difficulties and dangers; but finally yielding to his unselfish love for the Company of which he felt that sooner or later he would be the victim: "Come," he said, "don't worry, you will have *piastres,* I promise you." It would have required little more for them to have erected a statue to him; they awaited with an anxiety which gratitude and admiration could scarcely contain for the inspired one to explain his means. Finally he declared that the Company could not itself make use of the means of the preceding year, but that, devoting himself entirely to it, he would use the credit of his bank in place of that of the Company, and that the price of *piastres* would be fixed at the same rate as the last ones, that is to say, about 10 percent above the current level. It is true that whether out of prudence or modesty, Mr. Necker did not have this recorded in the minutes, but, if my memory serves me correctly, it was deposited under three seals into the hands of Mr. Costard, secretary of the Company of the Indies, and must still be there if master Claude (otherwise called Valdec de Lessart) who for good reasons takes care of all such matters, has not disposed of it otherwise.

This bargain appeared to the greater number of Administrators, the duc de Duras, the marquis de Castries, the president Brisson and the always faithful Valdec, as a masterpiece of unselfishness, perhaps even of economy; however that may be, it was scarcely signed and deposited when Mr. Necker proposed to the Company a little project of a lottery [loan]; they protested that it would be impossible to find subscribers. "Well, it shall be myself who will subscribe to your lottery loan; yes, gentlemen, the same man who will furnish *piastres* without cash payment, will still give you money for your lottery notes." What an invaluable being, alas! They scarcely realize his worth. He has already assured the placement of his lottery in Geneva, and this money will serve to pay his *piastres* and secure him thereby a profit of 10 percent on ten to twelve million livres without having to open his purse.[38]

The above passage is only the beginning of the misdeeds charged to Necker's account by the author of the *Liégeoise.* Through the intermediary of his London

38. *La Liégeoise, ou Lettre à M. Necker, Directeur général des Finances,* in *Collection complète de tous les ouvrages,* I, 6-10, n. 1.

correspondents, the banking firm of Bourdieu and Chollet, Necker was said to have had the Company of the Indies exchange its drafts for Indian currency in the hands of English merchants in the East who could not legitimately exchange their rupees for English money. (The British East India Company had a monopoly of such exchange.) Necker supposedly had the company make this exchange at ruinous rates—fifty-four sous per rupee rather than the true market value of forty sous. The English merchants in India acquired an enormous number of drafts on the French Company of the Indies, which increased its distress, again supposedly to Necker's satisfaction. It gave him all the more opportunity to force his own short-term loans on the Company, his "miserable lottery loans," and all the other "happy expedients by which Mr. Necker sought to bring discredit [to the company], even at Paris."[39]

There is no evidence whatever to support these outlandish charges. Evidence available on the company's operations in the 1760s would certainly have given some indication of these fraudulent operations if they had in fact occurred. In March 1769, when the financial crisis was upon the Company, the stockholders appointed a twenty-member committee, including the syndics, directors, and other deputies, to study the financial predicament thoroughly. Ten more consultants, experts in banking and finance, were brought into the committee. Necker was not a member. He had been syndic from 1765 to 1767—his only official position, except as a stockholder—before the exclusive franchise was withdrawn in August 1769.

The findings of this committee were turned over to the controller general, Manyon d'Invau, and the intendant of finance who supervised the company, Charles-Robert Boutin. They in turn handed the report over to abbé André Morellet, prominent writer for the *économistes,* those who wished to abolish the exclusive privilege of the company in the East. In writing his memorial published in August 1769, Morellet had access to all the government's records on the company's affairs. Nowhere in this lengthy document, nor in his reply to Necker's trenchant, effective rebuttal, did Morellet allude to the kind of misdeeds charged by the *Liégeoise.* He would certainly have had strong motives for doing so, if any such evidence had come into his possession. On the contrary, he went out of his way to heap praise on the Genevan banker for his services to the company. "You enjoy," he said to Necker, "the greatest consideration of the Company, and the most merited; you have rendered it essential services; your counsels are respected by it."[40] Another opponent of Necker in 1769 was the comte de Lauraguais, a member of the group of stockholders who followed the leadership of the British-born banker Isaac Panchaud. Lauraguais, who was to become an enemy of Necker in the years of his first ministry, wrote lengthy

39. *Ibid.*
40. André Morellet, *Examen de la réponse de M. N[ecker] au mémoire de M. l'abbé Morellet sur la Compagnie des Indes* (Paris, 1769), p. 63.

treatises on company affairs during 1769 and later, and nowhere does he mention such practices as alleged by the *Liegeoise*.[41]

It is true that each expedition that sailed to India had to stop at Cadiz and load on Spanish silver piasters to balance its payments for the return cargo purchased in India. Only a portion of these payments could be made in European merchandise carried to the East. According to the foremost historian of the Company of the Indies, the Spanish piasters were melted down upon arrival at Pondichéry and recoined.[42] But this was simply an item of expenditure to be added to the balance sheet. Weber gave a complete accounting of the proposed expedition of 1769, which was canceled due to the suspension of the company's franchise. The outbound voyage was to have purchased merchandise amounting to 6.5 million livres and specie amounting to over 12 million livres. The rate of interest for financing the voyage was 6 percent. The total of expenditures for this voyage would have been 28.4 million livres, the total receipts 30.2 million.[43] As for the "miserable lotteries" and other Company of the Indies loans in the decade, they were all promulgated by edict of the king and their terms were well-known. The loan made in "perpetual rentes" in 1764 was at the rate of 4 percent. The life rente loan of 1765 was at the standard rate of 10 percent, including amortization. The lottery loan of 1767 was at 5.5 percent, redeemed in five years. The emergency loan of April 6, 1769, was indeed more onerous, due to the difficult situation of the company, but was still 7.75 percent rather than the 10 percent asserted by Morellet.

There would be no reason for taking the *Liégeoise* seriously if it had not become in recent years the chief evidence that Herbert Luethy has relied upon in establishing the thesis (the same as that of the writer of the *Liégeoise*) that Necker's service for the company was the apprenticeship for his career later as minister of finance for Louis XVI. In both cases he was the "clever banker" whose expediency ruined first the company and then the royal government.[44]

In the absence of direct evidence, Luethy believes the general circumstances of the Indies trade plus certain scattered pieces of evidence lend credibility to the assertions of the *Liégeoise*. The serious balance of payments problem, reflecting the fact that Europe imported much more from the East than she exported, placed the Company of the Indies in a difficult position: "It had to make its payments in Asia by passing through London."[45] There is evidence that Necker had close relations with the London firm of James Bourdieu and Samuel Chollet, and that this company took care of these exchange transactions for the company.

41. Louis de Brancas, comte de Lauraguais, *Mémoire sur la Compagnie des Indes* (Paris, 1769).

42. Henry Weber, *La Compagnie française des Indes (1604-1875)* (Paris, 1904), p. 490.

43. *Ibid.,* p. 502 n. 1.

44. *La Banque protestante,* II, 419.

45. *Ibid.,* p. 381.

J. B. Coquereau's account of a stormy stockholders' meeting on July 3, 1767, published in a polemic denouncing abbé Terray's financial administration, made it appear that the Company of the Indies was depending heavily on Necker's bank for credit. The author published in the same work some lengthy letters written by an anonymous stockholder who on one occasion assailed the terms of a bank loan subscribed by the company as extremely onerous. These two scraps of evidence can be more appropriately discussed in the context of company affairs during the 1760s.[46] Here it may be noted that Coquereau wrote the account of that stockholder's meeting several years afterward, and his misdating it by three years (he has it in 1764 rather than 1767) detracts from its authority. The letters of the stockholder, however, were obviously written by an eyewitness and have the appearance of authenticity. But the blast made in the sixth letter, dated April 4, 1769, about "those leeches the bankers" who supported Necker's proposal for an emergency loan, does not reflect the letter-writer's general estimation of Necker, which was very high; nor does his analysis of the causes for the failure of the company, which is penetrating (and similar to Necker's), indicate that it was due to exorbitant rates of interest on loans.[47]

The most important reason for Luethy's confidence in the *Liégeoise* is his belief that the author was Isaac Panchaud. If true, historians would indeed be required to take it seriously, for Panchaud was deeply engaged in company affairs then, and he was a brilliant and influential banker. But this London-born Swiss could hardly have been the author of the *Liégeoise*. The ideas and feelings expressed in that pamphlet are quite contrary to what is known about Panchaud. The writer of the libel was a conservative defender of the *ancien régime,* bitterly hostile to Necker's reforms. He seems to express the outraged feelings of officeholders and financiers whose offices were suppressed or whose profits were greatly reduced in the series of reforms that Necker undertook early in 1780. Panchaud was a reformer himself, especially in financial administration. He was an advisor of Turgot, the chief promoter in the founding of the Discount Bank in 1776. He was also an advisor of Joly de Fleury in 1781, and sought to have a sinking fund established. Like Necker, Panchaud believed the French could learn from the English about finance and banking. But the author of the *Liégeoise* was obviously a Frenchman who disliked and distrusted the international community of bankers to which Panchaud belonged. He especially disliked Genevan and English bankers, who, he believed, were defrauding the good-natured and compliant French king; and he thought all of Necker's government loans were usurious.

Panchaud did not share this belief; with the exception of Necker's life rente loan of February 1781, which, unlike his other loans, was exempt from the tax of the *dixième d'amortissement,* he thought the interest rates on Necker's loans

---

46. See Chapter II.
47. J.-B. Coquereau, *Mémoires concernant l'administration des finances sous le Ministère de M. l'abbé Terrai* (London, 1776), pp. 364-366.

were reasonable in the circumstances.[48] The author of the *Liégeoise* betrayed his ignorance about banking and credit when he wrote that life rentes placed on three or four lives was a revival of the discredited and onerous *tontines,* prohibited by law since 1771. According to that system the government was required to continue paying the annual rentes for the entire loan until the death of the last tontine-holder. Panchaud could not have been so ill informed about the distinction between the life rentes and tontines. Finally, it is obvious by the attempt to flatter the king and Maurepas that the author was offering himself as a candidate to succeed the Genevan as the king's finance minister, a post to which Panchaud could hardly have aspired.

The only reason for believing that this libel was written by Isaac Panchaud is a passing remark made by Bachaumont in his journal in 1785, five years after the printing of the *Liégeoise.* In his entry of February 1785, Bachaumont wrote:

Mr. Panchaud has spoken out against the libels, but he is not unaware of the use that can be made of them in case of need, for everyone attributes to him several pamphlets that were launched against Mr. Necker at one time, such as "Letter of a Liégeois" where the director of finances was, if not calumniated, at least wronged, mistreated, castigated.[49]

The inaccurate rendering of the title of the pamphlet and the general vagueness of the above entry do not lend it much authority.

Who was the author? There is no certain answer. But the brochure's style and content point to the intendant of Valenciennes, Gabriel Sénac de Meilhan. Certain passages are remarkably similar to Sénac's known publications.[50] The son of a court physician, he was a prominent figure in the literary salons of the period, having ambitions toward belles lettres. He received the usual training of the young magistrate and expected to rise in the royal government. Constantly thwarted, he never rose above the rank of intendant. He conceived a violent hatred for the Genevan banker, whose qualifications for the post of finance minister he thought much inferior to his own. The court page, Alexandre de Tilly, wrote in his memoirs that Sénac de Meilhan "was a man, who, for having written a few pages, often insignificant, but generally more witty than of substance, believed himself on the level of the greatest writers, and betrayed on every point a vanity that was almost stupid."[51] Much of Sénac's literary talent was devoted to writing violently mendacious libels against Necker. We will meet him again in later chapters. Of course, it cannot be known definitely if he was the author of the *Liégeoise,* but it appears probable.

---

48. Benjamin Panchaud, *Réflexions sur l'état actuel du crédit de l'Angleterre et de la France* (n.p., 1781), pp. 43-44.

49. Bachaumont, *Mémoires secrets,* XXVIII, 151.

50. See especially *Le Gouvernement, les moeurs, et les conditions en France avant la Révolution,* ed. Lescure (Paris, 1862), p. 226. Compare with *La Liégeoise,* p. 37.

51. Alexandre de Tilly, *Mémoires de Tilly pour servir à l'histoire des moeurs de la fin du XVIIIe siècle,* 3 vols. (Paris, 1828), I, 168.

In his memoirs, written late in life, André Morellet took notice of these slanders. He wrote that no one who knew Necker personally could believe any of them.

The desire for fame and distinction was his dominant motive, and this kept him from meanness of any kind. . . . He owed his fortune to the bank and to some advantageous operations with the Company of the Indies before he became a Director. . . . The profits of this type, however moderate the rate of interest, are always considerable when a large amount of capital is invested; and if these rates are at the market price only ignorance or malevolence could turn it into a crime.[52]

In the face of such testimony by an avowed ideological opponent, it would require serious evidence to prove that Necker's fortune was created by fraudulent means. The libels by themselves certainly do not constitute such evidence. Whatever may have been the failings of the Genevan banker, dishonesty was not one of them.

52. André Morellet, *Mémoires de l'abbé Morellet,* 2 vols., 2d ed. (Paris, 1882), I, 150. It will be remembered that Necker was not a director but a syndic of the Company.

Chapter II

NECKER AND THE
COMPANY OF THE INDIES

The French Company of the Indies was a joint stock company for foreign trade, having received its statute from the government in 1717. It was granted the exclusive franchise for carrying on French trade east of the Cape of Good Hope. No other subjects of the king of France were permitted to trade in those areas, which included India, Southeast Asia, and the Far East. Every autumn the ships of the company returned from the Indies to the French port of L'Orient, where their cargoes were sold at a gross profit ranging from 70 to 140 percent. The products brought back from the east consisted of such items as pepper, camphor, porcelain, cotton fabrics, glassware, and teakwood.

In return for its exclusive franchise and for government protection, the company was required to submit to government control. Prior to 1763 the king's commissioners, appointed from the *maîtres des requêtes* of the royal council, supervised the administration of the company. Below them were the directors, appointed by the king for long tenures from a list submitted to him by the stockholders. The syndics were supposedly experts in commerce and finance appointed for short terms who represented the stockholders' interests. In reality, syndics were often appointed from outside the assembly of stockholders.[1] The controller general exercised the right of presiding over stockholders' meetings. There was no doubt that the government considered the company its own agent, and that the interests of the state were paramount to all else in the conduct of its affairs.

Throughout the history of the Company of the Indies there tended to be friction between the stockholders and the royal appointees who governed the company. The stockholders had invested in the company's commercial ventures and were primarily interested in profits and dividends. The officials had the outlook of government functionaries, little concerned about efficiency of administration or margins of profit. "The radical vice [of the administration]," wrote one of the stockholders, "is the same as that of the State in general: Too great

1. Henry Weber, *La Compagnie française des Indes*, p. 447.

an expenditure, an administration little inclined to economy, and too timid."[2]
Necker expressed a similar view in his *Reply to Morellet* in 1769:

a form of administration which submits the management of the Company to a
commissioner of the king is opposed to the spirit of economy, or at least does
not sustain it, because the man who represents the government has no pressing
motive to be concerned about economy. . . .[3]

In time of war the company became, in the words of Necker, "the War Office
of the Department of the Indies." It maintained fortresses and armed ships and
participated in the fortunes of war. The Seven Years' War was disastrous to the
company. Its assets were diminished by 100 million livres; most of its commercial installations in the east were destroyed; much of its shipping was sunk by
the British fleet; and it incurred a heavy debt of 60 million livres, spent primarily
for its wartime operations. Of course, the government indemnified the company
in various ways. But separating the costs of government tasks from commercial
operations was often a fertile source of disagreement between government and
company.

The suffocating control of its commercial operations by the state was only
one of the dangers that beset the company. Also threatening after the mid-century was the rise of new economic doctrines which challenged the prevailing
precepts of mercantilism. According to the latter, what was good for the state
was good for the economy. In contrast, the new economic ideas extolled the
virtues of freedom of enterprise, freedom of trade, and condemned the vices of
government regulation of the economy and state-supported monopolies. The
beneficial effects of competition in a free market and the appeal to individual
self-interest—these were the new ideas which, should they become influential in
the government, would destroy the exclusive trading privilege of the Company
of the Indies. In 1747 Jean-Claude Vincent de Gournay became intendant of
commerce and began to expound his doctrines on free trade and removal of
government regulation of manufactures. It was Gournay who is said to have
coined the expression, "laissez-faire, laissez-passer." In 1758 Dr. François Quesnay published his *Tableau économique* and thereby initiated the rise of a sect of
doctrinaires who were known as the *économistes* in their own day but are called
"physiocrats" today. Although more interested in agriculture than commerce,
the *économistes* warmly seconded Gournay's attack on mercantilist ideas and his
principles of freedom of enterprise and perfect competition.

Necker became immersed in the affairs of the Company of the Indies for
about a decade following the end of the Seven Years' War in 1763. In fact it
would not be wrong to look upon this period as an apprenticeship for his later

2. "Lettres d'un actionnaire," in Coquereau, *Mémoires concernant le ministère de
Terrai,* p. 322.
3. Jacques Necker, *Réponse au mémoire de M. l'abbé Morellet sur la Compagnie des
Indes* (Paris, 1769), p. 37.

career as minister of finance, but not in the way alleged by the author of the *Liégeoise*. In the assemblies of stockholders he first expressed ideas on administrative reforms that characterized his thought on governmental reform as a whole. He confronted the same forces that were later his enemies when he became minister of finance: stubborn resistance to reform by government officials steeped in tradition and routine, and highly speculative theories of the *économistes* divorced from practical experience.

Necker's economic ideas and policies in the affairs of the company were to appear two-faced to doctrinaire minds, both of his own day and later. On one hand, he insisted on exclusive trade privileges for the company in the East, which naturally ranged him on the side of the mercantilists in the minds of the *économistes*. But equally, he insisted upon commercial autonomy for the company, freed from the cumbersome weight of government administration. For the conservative officials he was altogether too liberal. In the end, he did not succeed in his reform plans because both forces blocked it. The government gave some heed to his reforms—enough, he believed, to show what could have been accomplished if it had given his plans full support. But the *ancien régime* dragged down the company by the summer of 1769. The *économistes,* for their part, destroyed the company and with it the Eastern trade because of their opposition to the exclusive privilege, and their assumption, in the words of Vincent de Gournay, that with free trade a hundred ships would sail to the East each year instead of twelve.

Necker's influence in the affairs of the Company of the Indies was for the most part exerted in an unofficial capacity. He was a syndic for two years, 1765-1767, but withdrew from this office due to pressures of his private banking business. His main influence was as a stockholder, presenting memorials and plans of reorganization to the stockholders and serving on special commissions set up to investigate company operations. Such a commission was appointed immediately after the end of the Seven Years' War, in a general assembly held in August 1763. Necker was among six chosen by the assembly to study the position of the company following the devastation caused by the war.[4]

The stockholders were understandably disgruntled. Their stocks had dropped in market value from eighty livres per share to forty livres during the war, and they expected to be asked for an additional loan to enable the company to resume commerce in the East. The losses already suffered, and the likelihood of being asked to throw good money after bad, distinctly worried many prominent investors. In the new conditions that faced the company in the East, with the British undisputed masters in the Indian Ocean area and their own British East India Company aggressively pursuing the Indies trade, what were the realistic possibilities of a successful commercial French company? Would it not be best to renounce commerce altogether, transfer the Asian assets to the government,

4. AN Col. C² 47, folios 47ff.

and hope for an agreement that would pay creditors and give stockholders fair value on their stock?

This appeared to be the viewpoint of nearly half the stockholders at the August assembly, particularly the wealthier ones. They succeeded in getting the assembly in September to request that the government guarantee them sixty-four livres per share, to be paid in the form of bonds (perpetual *rentes*) at 4 percent interest.[5] The following February, however, the king refused to raise the stock above the market price, giving the stockholders two choices: liquidate at the market price of their stocks, or attempt to revive commerce in the Indies. It was at this juncture that Necker's role became important.

The Genevan banker first intervened in the assembly of stockholders on August 30, 1763. He had argued in favor of preserving the privilege and resuming commercial operations. He contended that commercial prospects were good, and that the company could operate at a profit and eventually pay dividends. But this would require time and money. It was necessary to borrow in order to continue commercial operations. The wealthier stockholders were cool to this. The comte de Guerchy wrote: "Mr. Neck [sic], a banker, read a very well written paper to support the loan, showing that, among other things, even if the stockholders lost, the state itself would always be the gainer, which is very consoling!"[6] Necker's August memorial is not available. But the following February he read a lengthy memorial that is preserved in the archives, detailing his ideas on reforms necessary to make the company commercially viable.

It was necessary, he said, to reorganize the company along commercial lines, so that merchants rather than government officials would determine policy. The stockholders must recover the right to appoint all the administrators, who would be responsible to them. "The stockholders, guided by their own interests would rarely make a mistake in their choice."[7] The term of each director should be limited to six or seven years rather than remain the customary life appointment. Directors should submit annual accounts of their operations to the assembly. The office of royal commissioners, who had exercised a preeminent influence in the company's affairs in the past and who were appointed by the king, should be abolished. With this reorganization the company would be governed by commercial considerations and interests alone.

His appointment to the stockholders' investigating committee in August 1763 gave Necker an intimate knowledge of the financial situation and the conditions under which the company operated. On April 17, 1764, he presented to the assembly a detailed account of the assets and liabilities of the company for the following year, 1765, and his reasons for believing the company was commercially viable. It would be necessary to borrow money to revive the company's

5. Jean Tarrade, *Le Commerce colonial de la France à la fin de l'Ancien Régime,* 2 vols. (Paris, 1972), I, 55-59.

6. AN Col. C^2 46, fols. 247ff.

7. AN Col. C^2 47, fols. 53-60, "Discours de M. Necker, banquier."

trade and, equally important, to cut costs that had no relevance for a commercial enterprise. "Amelioration" along with loans to restore the commerce of the Indies was the two-pronged policy of the Genevan banker; this was very similar to his policy as director general of finances during the American war.

Necker's memorial of April 17 contained concrete financial recommendations. The company would need to borrow 42 million livres in the next five years to restore its commerce in the Indies. By 1769 it should be making a profit of 5,140,000 livres, and in 1770 the stockholders should receive a dividend. It was a "highly speculative" plan, observed the unknown writer who in 1771 wrote a summary for the controller general of events concerning the company since the peace of 1763.[8] As it turned out, Necker's plan of 1764 proved too optimistic by far. In 1770, instead of declaring a dividend, the company gave up its Eastern commerce and turned over its assets to the royal government, making the kind of settlement many stockholders had envisaged immediately after the war. Why events turned out this way became a matter of controversy in 1769 and afterwards. Probably a historian cannot answer the question. What can be done is to present Necker's view of these events and of why his 1764 forecast was so far off, a subject generally ignored by the polemical works on Necker.

Vital to the success of Necker's revamping of the company was the attitude of the government. It would have to approve the reorganization of the company's structure, and recognize that much of the company's debt was incurred by performing some of its functions. It should expect to assist the company financially for that reason.

The government proved surprisingly conciliatory on the reorganization, at least in 1764, but somewhat niggardly on financial assistance. On June 20, 1764, the controller general told the stockholders of the king's decision on proposals submitted to him by the committee appointed by the stockholders the previous August. Louis XV would grant a new constitution making the company exclusively a commercial enterprise. Company stockholders, directors, and syndics were invited to present their plan to the king specifying the articles of the new constitution. Immediately following this report Necker read another memorial to the assembly setting forth the concrete proposals of the investigating committee. The assembly approved Necker's memorial and had it printed. It became the basis for the edict of the royal government promulgated in August 1764, setting up the reformed Company of the Indies.

Necker now was beginning to be known outside the circle of bankers and company leaders. In the entry of his *Correspondance* for July 15, 1764, Grimm mentioned him for the first time:

Mr. Necker of Geneva, head of one of the most powerful banks in Paris, read at the last general assembly of the Company of the Indies a memorial in the name of the deputies of stockholders, among whom he is numbered. This memorial, which was printed, traces the new plans of administration upon which the

8. See the document "Compagnie des Indes," in AN Col. C² 106, fols. 71-100.

Company proposes to continue its commerce. The plan appears to have been well thought-out, and it has just been adopted by the Company. Mr. Necker is a man of great intelligence and merit. In sketching at the end of his memorial the portrait of a true merchant, he drew, without realizing it, his own portrait.[9]

The edict of August 1764 was intended to meet only immediate needs in restoring the company's commercial operations. The ultimate statutes governing the company were to be decided later, when deputies of the stockholders could present their definitive proposals to the king. This was finally done in 1768, and the definitive statutes were the letters patent of June 1768. Meanwhile, the preamble of the edict of 1764 noted with satisfaction the success of the new administration in restoring commerce with the Indies. "We desire that the said Company of the Indies be and remain a commercial company, that it alone shall direct its affairs and its commerce." The edict reconfirmed the exclusive privilege of the company east of the Cape of Good Hope. It exhorted the company to "expand this commerce which is confided to it with a zeal which its importance deserved," and urged that its leaders bring to their task "the wisdom and economy which alone can make its operations useful to our State and to the property of those of our subjects who have an interest in it."[10]

The August edict also mentioned how the new administration was formed. A new board of nine syndics was chosen, presumably by stockholders. The new syndicate then appointed five new directors. The *Royal Almanach* for 1765 dropped the names and offices of the royal commissioners, which had been listed in the 1764 *Almanach.* Evidently the company was in entirely new hands. Directors were either of the merchant class or had served in the company at lower echelons of administration. Necker's name appeared in the list of new syndics.

In the next three years the new management continued to be concerned primarily with commerce and financial matters, particularly with liberating the company from its wartime debts. But it carried out reforms as well. In his *Reply to Morellet* in 1769, Necker referred to "different economies established since 1764 up to the end of June, 1768 . . . in a time when a thousand thorny matters turned attention from commerce."[11] With respect to purely commercial affairs the company seems to have made an impressive recovery during these years. Its foremost historian, Henry Weber, writes:

Its commerce increased remarkably; the number of ships outfitted for the Indies rose from five to fifteen in four years; the value of its outbound cargo rose from 600,000 livres to 7.5 million livres; its return voyages increased also from six to fifteen ships and the profits rose from 600,000 livres to 11 million livres. In the last year of its privilege it realized a profit of 8,238,000 livres.[12]

9. Friedrich Melchior Grimm, *Correspondance littéraire, philosophique et critique par Grimm, Diderot, Raynal, Meister, etc.,* 16 vols. (Paris, 1877-1882), VI, 38-39.

10. AN AD IX 385, no. 166.

11. *Réponse à Morellet,* p. 37.

12. *La Compagnie française des Indes,* p. 502.

Weber adds, however, that the plans for the expedition for 1769, which were dropped because of the halting of commercial operations that year, did indicate a precipitate decline in profits, to 1,760,000 livres. But he observes that the financial problems that led to the suspension of the privilege by the government could not have been due to purely commercial reasons. "Its commercial activity at least was satisfactory at that time and its rapid recovery justified expectations that in a few years it would attain the greatest period of prosperity it had enjoyed in the past."[13]

Yet despite this seeming success, in 1767 the company entered into a prolonged crisis, illustrated first by tumultuous stockholder sessions and finally by a financial crisis that led to the revocation of its privilege in August 1769. Among stockholders, there had always been a strong minority who remained steadfastly skeptical about Necker's optimistic plan of April 1764. They believed that the company was not viable commercially, and that stockholders should seek a satisfactory liquidation as soon as possible. Above all, they were reluctant to see the administrators obtain more loans. In 1764, stockholders were called upon for a loan of 13.7 million livres out of their own pockets. Another "appeal" to them was always a possibility. An additional loan of over 10 million in "perpetual rentes" at 4 percent was issued in 1764. The following year the directors asked and received permission to issue a loan in life rentes yielding a capital of 8.8 million livres. Now, in April 1767, the directors asked assembly approval of a loan of 12 million livres in the form of a lottery loan paying an interest of 5.5 percent to be redeemed in five years. The assembly was becoming restive. If the company was thriving, why were these loans necessary? Necker's explanation in his *Reply to Morellet* was that the company was forced to liquidate a wartime debt of 60 million livres. This was rightfully a royal debt, he thought, which eventually the government would recognize and pay off. Necker believed throughout this crisis that the financial difficulties stemmed from assuming burdens of sovereignty that should not be required of a commercial company.

The years after 1767 were not propitious for seeking help from the royal government, itself drifting helplessly toward the quasi-bankruptcy of 1770. Furthermore, some in the government thought the company was an encumbrance on the government rather than vice versa. They believed the royal government had paid the company much more than any sovereignty costs. The company's request for more assistance when commercial operations were thriving created suspicion that something was radically wrong with the company rather than the government.

It was not the first time the Company of the Indies had faced financial woes amid seeming prosperity. In 1755, on the eve of the Seven Years' War and at the end of one of its most prosperous periods, it faced obligations requiring a loan of 55 million livres. According to a memorial drawn up by the intendant of

13. *Ibid.*, p. 503.

commerce, Vincent de Gournay, for the controller general, there seemed to be no possibility of finding such a loan. To continue, the company needed government assistance. Gournay advised against further aid. The company's financial troubles, he believed, were not momentary but endemic. He blamed poor administration, itself the result of monopolistic trade. His proposal to the controller general in 1755 was to withdraw the exclusive privilege of the Eastern trade from the Company of the Indies, to open up those areas to free trade among private shippers and merchants. This would expand commerce enormously, he argued; instead of twelve ships making the annual voyage to the East there would be a hundred. Competition would assure the French market a much larger quantity and variety of Asian products at a much lower price.[14]

Gournay's memorial had no consequence because of the coming of the war. The government aided the company to tide it over the crisis. But in the postwar period, it seemed likely that the ideas of Gournay would find a receptive audience among the king's ministers if the company sought more assistance. Indeed, during the sixties the ideas of free enterprise, abolition of trade restrictions, the virtues of individual self-interest, and the spur of the profit motive in expanding the economy gained favor in the government. The all-powerful foreign affairs minister, the duc de Choiseul, was said to look with favor on the ideas of the *économistes*. In September 1768 Manyon d'Invau became controller general, replacing Laverdy. He was a known disciple of Vincent de Gournay.

By the spring of 1767 there were three discernible views about the company: that of the *économistes*, who wanted to abolish the exclusive trading franchise; that of those who wanted to liquidate the company, but only on conditions that would guarantee the property of stockholders; and that of those who thought the company could continue successfully if greater reforms were instituted, and if the royal government would help tide it over the present financial crisis, which, it was believed, was due primarily to expenditures that rightfully belonged to the government. The latter was Necker's view.

It has been mentioned that the edict of August 1764 did not fix permanently the statutes of the company. This was to be done by permitting stockholders to make proposals to the king through their directors and syndics. On April 4, 1767, the administration of the company presented its proposals to the assembly. A committee of thirteen deputies was appointed to study these proposals and to report to the assembly at the next meeting, on July 3, 1767. At this meeting the directors found themselves faced with a revolt, the reasons for which are not clear. It is evident that the leadership installed in June 1764 no longer enjoyed the confidence of a substantial number of stockholders, probably because of financial policies of the administration. There was also suspicion that the new leaders of the company, like the old, were too subservient to the

14. Vincent de Gournay, "Observations sur le rapport fait à M. le *Contrôlleur-général,* par M. de S. le 26 juin, 1755, sur l'état de la Compagnie des Indes," in supp., Morellet, *Mémoire sur la situation actuelle de la Compagnie des Indes.*

government. There was concern that the new statutes proposed by the directors were reactionary, that they would place the company once again under tutelage of the government and take away the authority of the assembly of stockholders.

The tumultuous assembly of July 3 was presided over by a syndic, Marion, who soon lost control of the proceedings, as everyone began shouting at once. At this point, according to the account of J. B. Coquereau, Necker made himself heard above the din "by force of lungs" and admonished the assembly: "If you change the administration the Company will cease as of tomorrow, for its payments are only being sustained by my bank."[15] The insurgents succeeded in electing a new slate of administrators. But the arrival of the controller general, Laverdy, brought an end to the revolt. After scolding the delegates for "behaving as if they were living under the laws of England," Laverdy set aside the act of the assembly and confiscated the minutes of the meeting.

This was the end of the revolt. At the next meeting, held March 12, 1768, and presided over by Laverdy himself, the proposals of the thirteen deputies (who seem to have been reduced to twelve according to the minutes of the meeting printed by Coquereau) were again submitted to the assembly. The meeting seems to have been decorous. The opposition was somewhat mollified by the decision to permit each stockholder to write a memorial to the king on what the permanent statutes of the company should be. The assembly agreed to allow the controller general to draw up the statutes based upon the recommendations of the deputies and the individual memorials, a decision viewed with considerable disgust by the writer of the *procès-verbal,* who obviously shared the views of the opposition.

Coquereau's account of the meeting of July 3, 1767, is not trustworthy for a number of reasons. First, he misdated the meeting by three years (July 3, 1764), so he must have written about the event long after it happened. The correct date is given in the summary of events concerning the Company of the Indies written in 1771.[16] In the latter account of the meeting of July 3, no mention is made of Necker's intervention as reported by Coquereau. Such a statement would have been entirely out of character for Necker, who was usually prudent and circumspect about what he said—a handicap for him in the salon, but not in the business world. Furthermore, the statement attributed to him, "The Company is dependent on my bank for its payments," was not true. The company was not in a desperate financial situation in 1767. The lottery loan of 12 million livres was easily placed. Weber writes: "The loan was a great success, being rapidly subscribed to, which was impressive proof of the credit it had established and the skill of its new administration."[17] Coquereau's "memoirs" were a violent attack on abbé Terray's financial ministry, indeed a libel, and none of the libels in this period can be accepted without reserve. Yet, this need not reflect upon

15. Coquereau, *Mémoires concernant le ministère de Terrai,* p. 305.
16. AN Col. C² 106, fols. 71-100.
17. *La Compagnie française des Indes,* p. 571.

the value of the "Letters of a Stockholder" that Coquereau published in his book: the unknown writer was obviously not only present at the meetings of the assembly of stockholders, but was a person with a gift of expression and a good knowledge of company affairs.

The new statutes of the company were promulgated by letters patent on June 1768.[18] Some reforms accomplished since the edict of August 1764 were confirmed, but in other respects the final statutes were a disappointment to the reformers and amounted to a reaction. The six syndics were to be elected by the general assembly of stockholders for terms of six years. There were to be six directors, also chosen by the stockholders, but for life tenures. They were to receive a salary of 15,000 livres a year. The king reserved the right to choose syndics and directors from a list of five or six candidates nominated by the general assembly. But the royal commissioners who had dominated the administration of the company under the pre-1764 regime were not restored. A very important concession to the reform was the article greatly strengthening the institution of the deputation. This committee, appointed by stockholders, was given the powers of an inspectorate. It could investigate all operations of the company and had access to all records.

Militant stockholders were not pleased with the life tenures of the directors, nor with the fact that those appointed by the syndics in 1764 were considered permanent. Only five were appointed, and one had resigned since then, so in the assembly convened August 31, 1768, the stockholders were able to select two new directors, the king making the final choice from a list of seven names. One member of the assembly suggested that the other four stand for election by the assembly. They refused. It was evident that the reform had not gone as far as desired in making the directorate responsible to the stockholder assembly. It appears that Necker shared this opinion, which was expressed in his *Reply to Morellet* more than a year later. Weber believed that most of the syndics were not satisfied with the new statutes:

The reform was put into execution in 1765, three years, therefore, before the appearance of the letters patent, and the promoters were Necker, the marquis de Castries, the marquis de Sancé, and the duc de Duras; yet, all the modifications they desired were not accepted by the royal government, so Necker treated the reform as incomplete.[19]

Another reason for dissatisfaction was Laverdy's insistence that he preside over the meetings of general assemblies of stockholders, among whom he was becoming distinctly unpopular. In the meeting of August 1768, for example, he ruled against those who sought to have the four directors stand for election. This meeting brought more bad news to stockholders. The next expedition to be sent to the Indies would require 21 million livres to outfit, but only 7 million would be on hand. It appeared that a loan of 14 million might be required, unless, the

18. AN AD IX 385, no. 170.
19. *La Compagnie française des Indes,* p. 450, n. 2.

directors and the controller general hinted, certain resources that they could not divulge might be available. There were vehement protests against such secrecy. Some stockholders contended they had a right to be informed of the exact situation of the company's finances, but Laverdy again ruled against them.

It was a matter of some satisfaction for the dissidents, among them the writer of the "Letters of a Stockholder," when Laverdy resigned as controller general the next month, September 1768. Evidently they did not know about the economic ideas of his successor, Manyon d'Invau, for the writer of the "Letters" was impressed by the manner in which Manyon conducted the next general assembly of stockholders on March 14, 1769. "He demonstrated as much gentleness, conciliation, and politeness as his predecessor did sullenness, harshness, and despotism."[20]

The meetings of March 14 and March 29, 1769, were calm and harmonious, despite the disquieting news about finances. According to the new statutes, the next meeting should have been called in January 1769, but it was delayed until March 14. On that date the directors explained that they had been unable to determine the exact situation of the company's finances, and that the inquest was still incomplete. But, they said, the finances were in much more serious condition than had been revealed previously. An 18-million-livres loan was needed to operate until November. By then, presumably, the profits of the yearly sale at L'Orient would ease the situation. But payments that the company could not meet were falling due as early as May.

Eight members were appointed to investigate the matter and report to the assembly on March 29. They found that it was not 18 but 21 million that had to be borrowed. Three of the deputation, led by Isaac Panchaud, recommended that the company abandon Indies commerce and become a discount bank. Panchaud thought the company was financially weak and its prospects dim. He placed little hope in the future of French commerce in the Indies, due to political instability in the subcontinent and the towering preeminence of the British East India Company. He was eager to see establishment of a discount bank, which he thought might eventually provide for France a strong institution similar to the Bank of England. Necker did not agree with Panchaud's gloomy view, believing the Indies trade fundamentally profitable. The question of the company's future should not be taken up, he told the assembly, until they had ascertained the intentions of the king, who had founded the company for state interests. Since Necker blamed the financial crisis on the company's assumption of some of the state's burdens, he was convinced that, if the king wanted the company to continue commerce with the East, he would extend a helping hand.[21]

The majority of the stockholders refused to permit the company to give up its privilege and discontinue commerce. But then they had to decide how to meet the impending financial obligations. It was agreed that the deputies,

20. Coquereau, *Mémoires concernant le ministère de Terrai,* p. 334.
21. *Ibid.,* pp. 348-349.

syndics, and directors would form an ad hoc committee to study the matter thoroughly and to make recommendations to the general assembly on April 3. The first payment that would have to come from those means was due April 15.

On April 3 the committee chairman said it had decided to propose a short-term lottery loan of 11 million livres to tide the company over until autumn. Proceeds from the sale at L'Orient would pay this loan in full by the following February. But, he continued, after that decision had been made, a long letter was received from the controller general, Manyon d'Invau. The letter said that Louis XV had read the minutes of the March assemblies. The king in-structed the controller general to write and tell the deputies to make an accurate study of the company's financial condition; to consider carefully the advantages and disadvantages of continuing commerce; that whatever decision was reached must safeguard the rights of property and of creditors; that he would not approve of a temporary short-term loan, or a lottery loan of life rentes, but would insist on a long-term loan guaranteed by a mortgage; that the only property that remained to be mortgaged was the stocks of the stockholders, which, according to the edict of 1764, could not be done unless the stockholders gave their approval. Finally, the king said that, if the company was unable to continue commerce, he would suspend its privilege and permit free trade to individual merchants in the Indies, and that he would look with favor on the company's transforming itself into a discount bank.

The document expressing the king's wishes was, of course, written by Man-yon d'Invau, the disciple of Vincent de Gournay. It was a sufficient answer to Necker's trial balloon. There could be no hope of royal assistance. The stock-holders overwhelmingly rejected the proposal that they mortgage their stocks. The writer of the "Letters" believed that this decision meant the end of the company. Necker then proposed a short-term loan, the same, evidently, that the ad hoc committee had accepted earlier, hoping that the king could be persuaded to change his mind and give the company an opportunity to meet its most pressing obligations. Panchaud, still working for the dissolution of the company and its conversion into a discount bank, vehemently opposed Necker's loan, calling it a "ruinous expedient." However, the assembly approved the loan by a great majority, and the king did reverse himself and authorize the loan by an edict of April 6.

Panchaud proposed as a substitute for Necker's loan an appeal for a voluntary contribution by stockholders, and offered a contribution himself, as did some others. This proposal was refused by the assembly, much to the indignation of the writer of the "Letters of a Stockholder," who exploded against "those leeches, the bankers . . . without modesty or brow," who did not care about the welfare of the Company but only their own exorbitant profits that they were making at its expense, "who did not blush to come out openly for the project of Mr. Necker."[22] But he also said that Necker's project was passed "by acclama-

22. *Ibid.,* pp. 356-357.

tion." How much importance should be attached to this passage is a matter of some consequence, since it seems to support allegations made in 1780 that Necker had bankrupted the Company by ruinous financial expedients. But the idea expressed in this passage is an isolated one, not appearing elsewhere in the letters. In August the writer looked upon Necker as the great defender of the company and of stockholders' interests. In his seventh letter, written after the stormy meeting of April 3, the writer provided a thoughtful analysis of the reasons for the financial failure of the company, and said nothing about exorbitant interest rates.[23] It would appear that this outburst against bankers was the sort of *boutade* that one might expect in the excited atmosphere of the meeting of April 3. In any case, the short-term lottery loan was not usurious in the circumstances. The interest was 7.75 percent, not 10 percent, as is sometimes said, because the loan ran for only ten months.[24]

The ad hoc committee next turned to raising a long-term loan of 30 million livres. It asked the king to "unite himself with the company" by granting a new contract for 30 million. Of this, 14 million would liquidate the debt the king owed the company; the remaining 16 million would be granted to the company as indemnity for the infringement of its privilege and "by way of donation and protection."[25] This was the card that Necker wanted to play. The long and intimate partnership between the company and the royal government certainly indicated that in this emergency the king would extend his "protecting hand." But now it was a forlorn hope. On July 20 company administrators received from the government a copy of abbé André Morellet's treatise *On the Present Situation of the Company of the Indies,* which had been printed at the king's expense. On July 24, a letter from the government invited them to reply to Morellet's attack by July 29. Simultaneously, the ad hoc committee received a copy of Morellet's treatise and a proposal to suspend the privilege of the company. The government hoped to have the suspension approved by the committee, consulting only the prominent stockholders, and avoid a general assembly. But the committee insisted on convoking the full assembly of stockholders on August 8, 1769.

André Morellet was one of the foremost publicists for the *économistes.* Like Turgot, he was influenced both by the commercial ideas of Vincent de Gournay and the agrarian school of the physiocrats who became so influential during that decade. A perfectly honest and sincere person, an able writer, he had become

23. *Ibid.,* pp. 365-370.
24. Necker, *Réponse à Morellet,* p. 38.
25. Coquereau, *Mémoires concernant le ministère de Terrai,* p. 373. The debts owed by the king to the company were listed in an *état* drawn up by the ad hoc committee, and were included in abbé Morellet's book *Mémoire sur la situation actuelle de la Compagnie des Indes.* The government apparently made exceptions to the exclusive privilege of the company, for example, by permitting private traders to import silks from Nanking. This was contested by the company and revoked. See the *procès-verbal* of the stockholders' meeting of March 14, 1768, written by Coquereau.

completely captivated by a doctrine, indeed, a dogma. Theory took precedence over facts. The confidence with which he assailed the figures and accounts drawn up by the ad hoc committee was effectively ridiculed by Necker at the August 8 meeting, much to the delight of the assembly of stockholders. Despite this passage at arms, Morellet was an habitué of the salon of Madame Necker and remained on good terms with her husband, leading some to suspect that the famous debate was staged like a bogus wrestling match. But the treatises published by both protagonists leave no doubt about the genuineness of the ideological combat.

Morellet was a close friend of the controller general, Manyon d'Invau, who turned over to him all the records and accounts that could be useful, including those of the ad hoc committee. Morellet made a seemingly strong and persuasive case for suppression of the exclusive trading franchise. He asserted that the capital assets of the Company of the Indies had declined steadily since its reorganization in 1725, that it had been a constant drain on the royal finances, that its troubles were due to bad administration, the high costs of its establishments (warehouses, depots, fortresses, and so forth), and the wars in Europe and Asia. He appeared to think that the wars were a consequence of the company's activities; that it was to serve the economic interests of the stockholders of the company that France was drawn into continual wars with Great Britain. He wrote that the nation would be better off without the exclusive trading monopoly, and stockholders would benefit by ending an unfortunate venture that had devoured so much of their capital as well as that of the king and the nation.

Morellet assailed at every point the financial statements drawn up by the ad hoc committee. He claimed the committee estimated its physical assets on the basis of original cost, leaving out depreciation; it inflated the number of black slaves owned by the company, and also their price (1,000 livres each), since most were aged or infirm; it computed into the assets the exemption from paying the *dixième* on company loans, a privilege the king had granted and could, therefore, take away! A good example of Morellet's calculations was the item of liability arising from several lawsuits pending against the company. No figure was given for them by the ad hoc committee. Morellet wrote that the total claims amounted to 16 million livres, and "we suppose that the final liquidation of all these different objects will be reduced to around six million livres." Therefore, Morellet corrected the committee's balance sheets by adding that amount to their liabilities.

Another type of account the administrators sent to the controller general was the estimate of the profits to be made by sending twelve ships to the East in the autumn of 1769. It had computed the profits of the outbound cargoes at 35 percent and the return cargoes at 75 percent. Morellet admitted that "nothing is so difficult to establish or so arbitrary as the estimation of these profits," but did not hesitate to affirm that the profits would only be 25 percent on the outbound cargoes and 70 percent on the return cargoes. Therefore, he concluded that the company would not make a profit at all on that expedition but would lose 1,380,000 livres.[26]

At the general assembly of August 8, the stockholders were told by the controller general of the king's decision to suspend their exclusive trading privilege. The assembly was called upon to decide on three matters: whether to continue commercial operations, whether the company would be able to provision the Isles of France and Bourbon in the Indian Ocean, and what dispositions they could make to assure the investments of creditors. The government's action was keenly resented by all the stockholders, including the minority who followed Panchaud. The decision to suspend the privilege was made in secret without consulting either the administration or the assembly of stockholders. The comte de Lauraguais, a follower of Panchaud, wrote a much more bitter and hostile reply to Morellet than did Necker. But the latter's *Reply to Morellet* was read to the assembly and made Necker the hero of the hour. His memorandum was ordered published by the assembly at its expense. Our eyewitness, the letter-writer, records the scene:

It was at that moment that Mr. Necker took the floor and read a memorial in reply to that of the abbé Morellet. I could not describe to you, sir, the impression made upon the assembly by this discourse, the most eloquent I have ever heard! Every face which had been downcast in gloom and bitterness now looked up with hope and confidence. Indeed, this memorial, in its brevity, discussed the most essential points of that of the abbé Morellet; it unmasked the errors which this author had paraded as truths; it demonstrated the inaccuracy of his statements, the fallacy of his calculations, the sophistry of his reasoning, and overthrew his system from top to bottom. It completely repudiated his assertions insulting to the Company. It established in a manner most luminous and irrefutable that not only had the Company of the Indies rendered the greatest service to the State, far from being a burden to it, but that the stockholders had made enormous sacrifices for it, far from having increased their individual fortunes at its expense.[27]

To refute Morellet's accusation that the company had always been a drain on the government, Necker pointed out that it was an institution created by the state, for state interests rather than for the interest of the stockholders. The state, after the reorganization of 1725, completely dominated its operations. Funds granted by the king to the company were neither controlled by the stockholders nor granted for their particular interest. These funds were used for the goals of the state, either for warfare or for expenditures that were properly those of the sovereign, not of a commercial company. Examples were: developing the Isles of France and Bourbon; constructing ports, roads, arsenals, churches, hospitals, and other public buildings; paying the salaries of judges and

26. Morellet, *Mémoire sur la situation actuelle de la Compagnie des Indes.*
27. Coquereau, *Mémoires concernant le ministère de Terrai,* p. 381.

other public officials in the Indies; and maintaining troops under arms. Necker's argument was amply demonstrated by the documents published by Morellet. The assets of the company included artillery, small arms, munitions, hospitals, arsenals, and so forth.

The stockholders, Necker said, had sacrificed for the state by forgoing dividends and continually making loans out of their own pockets to keep the company from bankruptcy. Company assets had deteriorated over the century, but this was due to the consequences of war. For example, when the king surrendered his stock to the company in 1764 to help it back to its feet after the ravages of the war, this amounted to about 15 million livres in cash. But the war debt the company paid off from 1764 to 1769 amounted to 60 million livres. That the company should be blamed for the war was patent nonsense. "The war was carried into the Indies by express order of His Majesty, and all the economic operations [of the company] were directed by a special committee of the government, so that for several years the Company of the Indies was nothing but the War Office of the Department of the Indies."[28]

As for Morellet's challenge of the figures in the ad hoc committee's financial statements, Necker did not enter into a detailed discussion. It was, after all, up to the deputies to defend their accounts, to which he had not had access. But he made several witty observations about Morellet's "corrections," much to the enjoyment of the assembly. His eye fell on the abbé's appraisal of the true value of the property on the Isles of France and Bourbon, which had been ceded to the king: a huge figure of several millions, which Morellet gave right down to the last livre. By what magical means had he been able to transport himself to those islands and weigh so minutely every last rifle and uniform? He noted also that the "corrections" were all adverse to the company's assets. It was strange that the deputies had made no errors in the opposite sense. As a matter of fact, he noted some; for example, the deputies included as liabilities "debets" which it could reasonably be calculated would never be presented for payment.[29]

Necker argued that the company's commerce in the Indies had always been profitable except during the Seven Years' War. Between 1725 and 1756 the profits of exports to the Indies had been 35 to 45 percent, that of imports from the Indies 90 to 140 percent. Maritime losses had amounted to only 3 percent. Morellet had averaged the profits and losses between 1756 and 1769, which indicated an average loss. Necker showed that if the years of peace only were tabulated, the record would indicate a gain of 11 million livres from 1764 to

28. Necker, *Réponse à Morellet,* in *Oeuvres complètes,* XV, 151.
29. *Ibid.,* passim. That such errors were possible is illustrated in the report made by the deputy L'Heritier to the assembly in the April meeting. He found that the deputies had added twice a liability of 4 million livres. Thus the balance of assets over liabilities was 57 million livres rather than 53 million livres, as originally reported (Coquereau, pp. 353-354). Luethy mistakenly wrote that this bookkeeping error was "adverse to the Company"; *La Banque protestante,* II, 390, n. 24.

1769. It was not a spectacular profit, but Necker thought it should be encouragement for continuing the reform begun in 1764.

He thought the most important reform would deal with the organization of the joint stock company itself. The stocks were sold in small denominations, and were owned anonymously. Stockholders had a right to attend the annual meetings and vote, but then they sank back into anonymity. What was needed, Necker said, was to associate the proprietors of the company more directly with its administration. There should be no divergence of interest between the owners (the stockholders) and the administration. If the owners, impelled by the profit motive, controlled the company, it would bring about much greater economy (*amélioration*) than had been accomplished from 1764 to 1769. It would also ease the financial situation and the problem of credit. If lenders knew that the company was in the hands of the proprietors, desiring to operate at a profit, they would open their purses much more easily, and at lower rates of interest. Company management should be aboveboard, without the secrecy that characterized past administrations, too much under the control of the government.

It is publicity which quiets the fears of the lender and draws capital from the most distant countries. It was an administration established somewhat on these principles that was desired in 1764. But as we were forced by diverse circumstances not to alter the nature of the stocks or to assure a fixed income to them, neither the spirit of property nor the necessary liaison between the stockholders and the administration could be established. Yet, what confidence had not the Company of the Indies obtained as a consequence of its constitution, from 1764 to 1768, a period when its administrative regime had been totally changed! What considerable credit had it not acquired after an unfortunate war which had destroyed all its establishments, and which had left it nothing but enormous debts to liquidate![30]

The record was not one to be ashamed of, and the rapid recovery of the company from the devastation of the Seven Years' War demonstrated what could be done if private enterprise and the "spirit of property" were given an opportunity. Necker's conviction that proprietors dominated by the profit motive should control the company was one he shared with the *économistes*. Why did he not go along with them all the way and admit that, if the cost of doing the government's work was responsible for the financial plight of the company, then logically the company should separate itself from the government? The principles of the *économistes* were true in the abstract, he said, but they were not equally applicable in every situation. The circumstances of trade in the Indies required close cooperation between government and proprietors. It called for a monopolistic company, having the exclusive franchise of trade. Individual shippers could not purchase goods as cheaply in the East as could one company doing all the buying. The Indies trade required large capital outlays

30. *Réponse à Morellet,* in *Oeuvres complètes,* XV, 180-181.

that only a company enjoying a trade monopoly could command. The assumption that free trade in the Indies would "send a hundred ships around the Cape of Good Hope each year instead of a dozen" was a hypothetical expectation, resting upon abstract ideas rather than experience.

In his rebuttal to Necker's memorial, Morellet admitted that only time could resolve the debate about the efficacy of free trade principles in the Indies.[31] The suspension of the privilege lasted for sixteen years. In 1785 the royal government decided that free trade in the Indies had been weighed and found wanting. The preamble of the decree in council of April 14, 1785, might have been written by Necker, so exactly did it express his arguments of 1769. In fact, the preamble was written by his arch-enemy, Charles-Alexandre de Calonne.

His Majesty, by the study which has been made for him regarding the exports from his kingdom and the imports from Asia, has recognized that competition, useful for other branches of commerce, can only be harmful in this [area] ; that indeed, experience has shown that cargoes from Europe, not being coordinated, are not proportioned to the needs of the places where they are sent.

The result was that European shippers tended to drive down the prices of goods exported to India and drive up the prices of goods purchased there. Furthermore, what was purchased without centralized direction resulted in a surplus of some goods and a shortage of others.

The preamble of the decree in council continued:

Considering that in addition to the inconvenience deriving from a lack of coordination is the impossibility of private shippers providing the means sufficient to finance a trade so far, with so many risks, and which requires a long period, His Majesty is convinced that only a privileged company, having the necessary resources, credit, and protection can usefully carry out trade in the Indies and China.

In restoring the privileged trading company, the government sought to explain why the privilege had been suspended in the first place, and the reasons for the financial plight of the company in 1769:

The political tasks, the expenditures of sovereignty, and the encumbrance of a too complicated administration having been the principal causes for the losses suffered by the former Company, it has seemed desirable that the new [company] be entirely free from [these obligations], that nothing should distract its attention or its funds from the objects of commerce, and that it be freely governed by its own proprietors.[32]

Other sources agree with the above analysis for the failure of the free trade policy. The editor of the *Encyclopédie méthodique: Finances,* although gener-

31. *Examen de la réponse de M. N. au mémoire de M. l'abbé Morellet sur la Compagnie des Indes* (Paris, 1769), p. 3.

32. "Arrêt du conseil d'état du roi portant établissement d'une nouvelle Compagnie des Indes. Du 14 avril 1785." AN AD IX 385, 3d bundle, no. 20.

ally sympathetic to the ideas of the *économistes,* and particularly to Morellet, had to admit in 1784 that, in comparing commerce in a five-year period under the privilege with five years under free trade, "the advantage seemed to be on the side of the Company, and would indicate the necessity of the exclusive privilege."[33] The trade with China was a little better, "but by no means conclusive for free trade." The editor concluded that the commerce of the Indies did not seem to be made for liberty, at least under the conditions of that time, and that "it was impossible that in the end, free trade would not be abandoned." The editor's analysis for the failure of free trade was similar to that expressed in the decree in council of 1785: the necessity for large ships, requiring a heavy capital outlay, and a two-year time span for the expeditions to be completed and profits realized. The commerce of the Indies was "beyond the capacity and the means of individual merchants." And yet, the editor did not wish to see the restoration of the company. He thought that a consortium of merchants supported by the government could be the solution.

The twentieth-century historian of the "last Company of the Indies" agrees with the above analysis of the period of free trade:

In France local rivalries, the lack of a spirit of cooperation among merchants impeded the formation and growth of a financial organization capable of competing with the British East India Company. Therefore, towards 1780 the government began to be concerned about the numerous bankruptcies caused by entering a commercial arena without sufficient preparation. Only the shippers who had treaties with the English could survive. But our exchange rate steadily worsened. Therefore, the liberal thesis lost ground daily, and there was unanimity in favor of the restoration of the privileged company for commerce in India and the Far East.[34]

So much agreement from such diverse sources would seem to indicate that Necker's analysis in 1769 of the financial situation of the company was not mistaken, and that his criticism of the free trade thesis was borne out by experience. At least his *Reply to Morellet* hardly seems to deserve the derision that has been heaped upon it by Luethy.[35]

Necker's ties to the company did not end with the termination of its privilege. He was elected deputy by the assembly at its meeting of January 23, 1770. By that date, Manyon d'Invau had been succeeded as controller general by abbé Terray, who as a former syndic of the company had been intimately involved in its affairs. The hope that he would restore the privilege was short-lived. He presided over the meetings of stockholders with the firm hand of a Laverdy, convinced as was his predecessor that stockholders were not competent to run the company.

33. *Encyclopédie méthodique: Finances,* "L'Inde," II, 577.
34. M. J. Conan, "La Dernière Compagnie française des Indes: Privilège et administration," *Revue d'histoire économique et sociale,* 25 (1939), 37-38.
35. *La Banque protestante,* II, 394.

But while refusing to restore the privilege, the abbé did remove the road-blocks to a solution of the company's financial difficulties. In January 1770 the king granted a contract of 30 million livres that he had refused the preceding year, enabling the company to issue a lottery loan of life rentes (also refused by Manyon d'Invau) to meet its most pressing obligations. In April 1770 the final contract—in which the company turned over its assets in the East to the government, which assumed its debts—was made with the king. The company continued to exist, occupying its headquarters at 9, rue des Petits-Champs, in the same locality as the *contrôle-général*. But it no longer engaged in commerce. It was absorbed in liquidating its obligations, which, even if assumed by the government, were administered by the company.

The proposal of Panchaud to convert the company into a discount bank was not pursued; it is not known why. Panchaud went bankrupt the preceding September and was no longer involved in company affairs. But his follower, the comte de Lauraguais, was named a deputy at the same time as Necker. The latter was by no means opposed to a discount bank. Panchaud finally succeeded in getting such a bank established in the last months of Turgot's ministry, and Necker strongly supported the bank throughout his own ministry.

If Necker's role in the affairs of the company during the decade after the Seven Years' War did not necessarily demonstrate his "superior genius for the first time," as claimed by Madame de Staël, it did reveal his thinking about reform as a whole. He believed in the liberal maxims that business enterprise should be left to businessmen, that the vigilant eye of self-interest is the best guarantee of efficient operation. But at the same time he distrusted the specula-tions of the doctrinaires. In that respect, his intervention in the affairs of the company provide an overture to his career as reform minister in the government of Louis XVI.

Chapter III

THE FORMATION OF AN AMBITION

Whatever may be the judgment of Necker's role in the affairs of the Company of the Indies, this was the means by which he became known to the public. By 1768 his reputation was such that the government of Geneva considered him its most distinguished resident in France and appointed him minister to the court of Versailles. It was a critical period in the relations between the small city-state republic and its powerful neighbor. Geneva was entering a time of political turbulence that culminated in the crisis of 1782, bringing with it armed intervention by both France and Piedmont. Such an event was already threatening in 1768, and it seems due to Necker's influence with the duc de Choiseul that it was prevented.[1]

The new position aided Necker's rise to power because it brought him into contact with a far wider and more influential circle of acquaintances than was usual for a private banker, even one of the more prominent bankers in Paris. One quality of the successful statesman that Necker did not mention in his essay on Colbert (intended to portray the ideal statesman), was the ability to ingratiate oneself personally with the powers that be. In an absolute monarchy this consisted of the king, his chief minister, and also, according to the Montesquieu-formed political thought of the day, public opinion. Necker succeeded with all three. He established such strong personal ties with the duc de Choiseul that, when the Genevan government grew dissatisfied with Necker's handling of a particular matter and attempted to send a special envoy, Choiseul refused to receive him. He said he recognized only Necker as the spokesman for the affairs of the republic.[2] Necker maintained good though not as close relations with Choiseul's successor, the duc d'Aiguillon. In 1776 he formed a strong friendship with the comte de Maurepas, mentor of the young king, Louis XVI. When this friendship began to deteriorate after the first years of Necker's ministry, he was supported by the king himself until May 1781. He was also favored by the respect and support of the young queen, Marie Antoinette.

1. For a thorough discussion of Necker's role as diplomat, see Edouard Chapuisat, *Necker (1732-1804)* (Paris, 1938).
2. *Ibid.*, p. 42.

With regard to public opinion, Necker almost surely was the most successful minister of the second half of the eighteenth century in cultivating a large following. If this following cannot yet be called "popular" (it was to become so in the July days of 1789), it was extensive among those who made and unmade reputations: the philosophers, poets, artists, journalists, and their audiences. Of course, he had vehement enemies, but his circle of admirers and friends was remarkable for one who was not only a foreigner without social rank, but also not very gifted in the qualities that made for advancement in the salons and social circles of the day. This vogue for Necker—"necromania" his enemies called it—is a puzzling though incontestable phenomenon.

It is certain that any explanation must include the role of Madame Necker and her salon. Yet this raises another question, for scarcely less surprising than the appointment of the Protestant citizen of Geneva to the post of finance minister was the position of influence so quickly won in the social and cultural life of Paris by this village girl from the Vaud. Like her husband, Suzanne Necker was born and remained a devout Protestant throughout her life. Yet she established friendship and extensive correspondences with several leading figures of the French Enlightenment. Grimm, Diderot, Buffon, d'Alembert, and Bernardin de Saint-Pierre were among habitués of her salon; even the absent Voltaire corresponded from Ferney with her. Sainte-Beuve remarked that "in order to enumerate all whom Madame Necker received at her salon in Paris or at Saint-Ouen it would be necessary to list the elite of France."[3]

Suzanne Curchod was born in 1737 at the village of Crassier in the Jura Mountains a short distance from Lausanne. Her father was pastor in the Reformed Church at Crassier. Her mother's family, named d'Albert de Nasse, came from the nobility of Dauphiné and had taken refuge in the Vaud to escape the anti-Protestant laws in France. It was from her mother that Suzanne received her beauty. Her education—unusual for a woman even in that day—was handled by her father. At sixteen she could express herself fluently in Latin; she also learned Greek and English, and was well grounded in philosophy, mathematics, and the natural sciences.

If her education resembled that of John Stuart Mill, Suzanne's youth was not so austere. She was a popular leader in the young people's literary society in Lausanne. Numerous admirers preparing for the ministry flocked to her home, ostensibly to help her father with his pastoral chores, in reality hoping to win the hand of "the beautiful Curchod." She was tall and slender, with an abundance of blonde hair, sparkling blue eyes, and a lovely complexion. She impressed people by her gaiety, spontaneity, and simplicity of manners.[4]

3. C.-A. Sainte-Beuve, *Causeries du lundi,* 15 vols., 3d ed. (Paris, 1850–1862), IV, 240.

4. Empress Maria Theresa wrote to her ambassador in Paris in 1780 that "the Genevan painter, Liotard, was here a few years ago for I wanted to see his paintings. Among them I was particularly struck by one of a pretty girl, with a book in her hand, in an interesting pose. It was a portrait of Madame Necker, which I still often look at with pleasure"; Florimond-Claude de Mercy-Argenteau, *Correspondance secrète entre Marie-Thérèse et le comte de Mercy-Argenteau,* ed. A. d'Arneth and A. Geffroy, 3 vols. (Paris, 1874), III, 406.

Among her admirers in 1757 was the eighteen-year-old Edward Gibbon, sent to Lausanne by his Anglican father to be weaned from the Catholicism to which he had succumbed while at Oxford. One menace parried, the son presented his father with quite a new one: Gibbon fell in love with the beautiful Curchod and, on his own, became engaged to her. It may have seemed a strange choice for Suzanne, for Gibbon was far from physically attractive—according to his portraits in later life, at least. In a letter to a friend, Suzanne described her first impressions of Gibbon: "His physiognomy is so spiritual and singular that I do not know anyone who resembles him. It is so expressive that one always discovers something new in him."[5] Perhaps it was a striking personality, a wit, and an education similar to her own that accounts for the attraction.

Before returning to England in 1758 to obtain his father's consent to the match, Gibbon let his fiancée know that his mission would be difficult. In fact, the elder Gibbon refused to sanction the proposed marriage. The powerful presence of the father and a no-less-willful stepmother decided the matter. "I sighed as a lover, I obeyed as a son," the eminent historian records in his memoirs.[6] For Suzanne it was not so easy. In an anguished letter she asked him if he really intended to end their engagement. She had told him before his departure that she did not want to marry him against his father's will and that she was prepared to wait, either until the father relented or passed on, for he was now elderly. A long and painful period passed before she became reconciled to their definitive separation. This, together with her father's death in 1760, seems to have ushered in the periodic illnesses and precarious health that stalked her throughout life.

Suzanne faced these blows with fortitude, becoming a tutor to children in Lausanne and Geneva. She was fortunate in the protection of Paul Moultou, well-known Genevan literary figure, pastor, and lifelong friend of Rousseau and editor of his *Confessions.* At Moultou's home Suzanne met Madame de Vermenoux, who had come from Paris to Geneva to consult a famous physician. Madame de Vermenoux, who belonged to the Parisian aristocracy, was rich, young, and beautiful, widowed, with a small son. Pleased with Suzanne's company, she engaged her as her son's tutor. Thus Suzanne came to Paris in 1764.

A sister of Madame de Vermenoux had married George-Tobie de Thellusson, Necker's banking partner. Through this relationship Necker had become acquainted with the beautiful widow and asked her to marry him; she had declined, although apparently not definitely. While she liked and admired him, marriage to a commoner would have meant giving up her noble rank. In any case, it was as a suitor that Necker continued to frequent the house of Madame de Vermenoux and in April 1764 met Suzanne. Necker is described at this time

5. Gabriel-Paul Othenin de Cléron, vicomte d'Haussonville, "Le Salon de Madame Necker," *Revue des deux mondes,* 37 (January-February 1880), 62.

6. Edward Gibbon, "Memoirs of My Life and Writings," in vol. I of *The History of the Decline and Fall of the Roman Empire,* 6 vols. (New York, n.d.), p. 112.

as "a bit stout in figure, but his physiognomy was well-formed and pleasing, and he had beautiful eyes."[7] It was a brief courtship. The marriage of Suzanne and Jacques Necker took place in November 1764 in the chapel of the Dutch embassy in Paris. They did not inform Madame de Vermenoux of the marriage until after the event, either because they thought she would be displeased, or, as a letter by Suzanne to her indicates, because they feared that Suzanne's departure from the household would be painful. As it turned out, their fears were groundless. Madame de Vermenoux remained a close friend of the Neckers until her death in 1785.[8]

It was an extraordinarily happy marriage, for the Neckers remained devoted to one another throughout the turbulent years that followed. Suzanne died in 1794, her husband survived her by ten years. There were some clouds on the idyll, due primarily to Madame Necker's precarious health and to the couple's differences over the upbringing of their only daughter, who was born in 1766.[9] But their loyalty and mutual admiration became proverbial, for neither sought to conceal it.[10]

At the time of the marriage, Necker's bank was located in the Marais district of Paris, in the narrow street Michel-le-Comte. Prior to retiring in Geneva, Isaac Vernet had owned apartments around the corner, on Beaubourg Street. Necker probably had lived in the Vernet household when he first came to Paris. For new quarters for his bride and himself, he rented apartments in the Hotel Hallwyl next to his bank. Here their daughter, Anne-Louise-Germaine, the future Madame de Staël, was born on April 22, 1766. Soon after this the Neckers moved to the Hotel Leblanc on Clery Street, which they purchased; this remained their town residence until they moved into the residence of the controller general in

7. D'Haussonville, "Le Salon de Madame Necker," p. 91.

8. Edouard de Callatay, *Madame de Vermenoux* (Paris and Geneva, 1956).

9. B. d'Andlau, *La Jeunesse de Madame de Staël (de 1766 à 1788) avec des documents inédits* (Geneva, 1970).

10. It need not be exaggerated, however, as it seems to me Luethy has done. See *La Banque protestante,* II, 372: ". . . henceforth he [Necker] had invariably at his side his indefatigable minister of propaganda who never again permitted him to descend from the pedestal upon which she had placed him, and it is from the date of this 'union of Genius and Virtue' which begins to orchestrate the concert of mutual panegyrics which will not cease to inflate itself even to nausea." As noted in Chapter I, n. 30, above, it was in 1787, several years after the first ministry, that Madame Necker composed her essay "The Character of Mr. Necker" and read it to a group of friends. It was not published until after her death, in 1798. The 32-page essay was included in a three-volume collection of her varied writings, edited by Necker. One does not get the impression in reading these volumes of an excessive adulation of her husband. In his *Compte rendu au roi* of 1781, which was published in February of that year, Necker mentioned in passing the hospital work of his wife and indeed eulogized her for it. It was no doubt unusual for a minister of the royal government to mention his wife in such a formal document, but it was also unusual for a minister's wife to have accomplished what Madame Necker did. It would require an extraordinarily delicate mechanism to be turned to nausea by this, particularly in view of the antidotes that lay at hand in the much greater quantity of libels directed against the Neckers.

July 1777. Always concerned about his wife's health, Necker purchased a country retreat for a summer residence, first the Villa Madrid at Neuilly, then a magnificent château and park at Saint-Ouen overlooking the Seine. This became the favorite residence of the Neckers and their numerous guests.

Immediately after their marriage, Madame Necker began the formation of her salon. In three or four years it had become one of the foremost societies of its kind in Paris.[11] Her success was phenomenal, considering that it took Madame Geoffrin more than twenty years to form her salon. Why Suzanne initiated this project has been a subject of controversy. Some have accepted the opinion of Marmontel, one of the first writers to be invited to her salon, who said that she was primarily interested in advancing the ministerial ambitions of her husband.[12] "She had enough ambition for two," writes Luethy. But Othenin d'Haussonville disputes this view, pointing out that Suzanne was always attracted to literary and philosophical societies, of which she had been an active participant in Lausanne.[13] One attraction of Paris that had helped draw her from Switzerland was the fame of Parisian salons. Her interest in and knowledge of literature and philosophy were more than superficial, as Voltaire recognized when he called her "the beautiful Hypathia," after the famed Hellenistic philosopher and commentator of Plato and Aristotle, who lived in Alexandria in the early fifth century.

It was a seemingly incongruous society, this gathering of French philosophes presided over by the daughter of a Swiss pastor, who remained steadfastly loyal to her Protestant religion. In fact, Suzanne did not relish free discussion of atheism and Christianity, and on one occasion she burst into tears during a lively exchange with Grimm—much to her mortification. While she befriended the philosophes, she pitied them their lack of Christian faith. What, then, attracted them to the Friday evenings of "Sister Necker" (as Grimm called her), assuming that it was something more than a Protestant dinner? They seem to have admired their hostess for her learning and wit, but also for something in that day called "elevation": a quality that was the direct opposite of vulgarity, of course, but meant something even more refined and noble.

These were the years of the vogue for Rousseau. The wife of the Genevan banker seemed to be the very model of Julia, the heroine of Rousseau's sentimental novel, *La Nouvelle Héloïse*.[14] Diderot's admiration for Madame

11. D'Haussonville, "Le Salon de Madame Necker," *Revue des deux mondes,* 38 (March-April, 1880), 66.

12. Jean-François Marmontel, *Oeuvres complètes de Marmontel,* 19 vols. rev. ed. (Paris, 1818-1820), II, 132.

13. D'Haussonville, "Le Salon de Madame Necker," p. 66.

14. Dupont de Nemours in a letter to the hereditary prince of Baden compared Madame Necker to Julia. He is quoted in Jean Egret, *Necker: Ministre de Louis XVI* (Paris, 1975), p. 22. Paradoxically, it appears that Madame Necker did not relish this particular novel or its heroine, although she was a close personal friend of Madame d'Houdetot, supposedly the actual model for Julia.

Necker indicates that he was himself by no means immune to the rising tide of sentimental morality. When Suzanne first sought to have him come to her "Fridays" he wrote to Sophia Volland roguishly: "You know what a vain person I am. There is a Madame Necker here, a pretty woman with a keen mind, who is crazy about me. She's persecuting me to come to her house."[15] If Diderot had mistaken ideas about Madame Necker's motives, he was quickly disabused. She became for him "the woman who possesses all that the purity of an angelic soul adds to the delicacy of taste." When he presented a copy of his novel *Salons* to her, he wrote a lengthy letter of apology for the "many impertinent things" she would read in it. "It is really too bad," he wrote, "that I never got to know you sooner. You would certainly have inspired me with a taste for purity and delicacy which would have passed into my books."[16]

Although Suzanne was unquestionably successful in attracting the leading intellectual and literary figures to her Friday evening meetings, the opinions of her skill as hostess of a salon were not always favorable. Some praised her conscientious effort to draw out of each participant his own special talent, her attentiveness to see that everyone was satisfied with the evening.[17] But Marmontel, one of the first writers invited, judged her severely as a hostess, although he was fond of her personally and wrote her flattering, indeed gallant, letters. He wrote in his memoirs that she had none of the graces of a French hostess. "Without taste in her apparel, without ease in her manner, without charm in her politeness, her mind, like her countenance, was too posed [*ajusté*] to be graceful." On the other hand, he wrote that "a charm more worthy of her was that of decency, of candor, of kindness ... Her feeling [*sentiment*] was perfect."[18] Writing in the nineteenth century, Sainte-Beuve seemed to accept Marmontel's judgment. "At Paris Madame Necker was always a transplanted flower."[19] The spontaneity of her youth was transformed into the self-discipline of an adult who tried too hard to please. The impression she made of being "posed," however, may have been due to a physical handicap that has become known to historians only recently: she was completely deaf in her right ear.[20]

Necker was ill-prepared by his education (his formal education ended when he was fourteen) and his profession to take an active part in salon conversation. He attended but left the leadership to his wife. Evidently he was not a good listener either, for he is described as frequently absorbed in his own thoughts. One should not take too literally the statement of Madame Necker in her 1787 essay that Necker "read nothing," for his printed works show that he read widely. She meant that his thoughts were formed more by reflection than by

15. D'Haussonville, "Le Salon de Madame Necker," p. 87.
16. *Ibid.*, p. 94.
17. Callatay, *Madame de Vermenoux,* p. 92, citing the memoirs of Madame de Genlis and Madame Angiviller.
18. Marmontel, *Oeuvres complètes,* II, 130.
19. Sainte-Beuve, *Causeries du Lundi,* IV, 240.
20. B. d'Andlau, *La Jeunesse de Mme. de Staël,* p. 29.

reading. His self-absorption was apt to give the impression of prideful disdain for others. Marmontel believed this a mistaken impression, that Necker's aloofness in the salon was not pride or arrogance but simply good judgment and awareness of his own limitations in that milieu. "He spoke abundantly and well on subjects that he knew, but maintained a prudent reserve on other subjects."[21] Madame du Deffand, who, despite failing eyesight, was a most perceptive observer of character, wrote in letters to Walpole that in the salon "Necker was very much at ease [fort naturel] and very gay." She mentioned his "frankness, good humor, gentleness and kindness," but added that he "spoke little" and was "often distracted." She found he lacked that particular quality so necessary in salon life of entering into another's thoughts and helping develop them to fruition. She said that he was therefore "useless" [stérile] for the salon.[22]

On the "character of Mr. Necker," much was written in his own time and immediately after his death. The portrait ranges from the adulation of his wife and daughter to more restrained but still highly favorable accounts by his grandson, baron de Staël, and such friends of many years as J. H. Meister, to vitriolic descriptions by political enemies such as Sénac de Meilhan and Auget de Montyon. Of all these accounts, perhaps the most faithful was both a physical and a moral portrait written by Meister shortly after Necker's death in 1804.

Mr. Necker's physical aspect had something about it too remarkable not to be described. He had a large head and a long face. It was especially the forehead and the chin which exceeded ordinary proportions. His brown eyes, although rather small in proportion to the other features of his face, had at once a great deal of gentleness and vivacity. His glance was keen, pleasant, and spiritual, although with a singular penetration, and also often with deep melancholy. The design of his eyebrows, high above his eyes, gave a very striking impression of boldness and originality. The expression of this feature played a large part in the play of his physiognomy, especially in moments of deep concentration, or in movements of prideful disdain. The mouth was small, too small relatively for the wideness and length of his cheeks, but the movement of his lips often had a great deal of finesse and gracefulness. After the age of thirty he became fat and stout; in the last years of his life his corpulence, particularly in his legs, became frightful. At first glance his carriage and movement seemed to suggest an extreme heaviness, and yet on further observation, one was astonished to observe so much measure, gentleness, and adresse.[23]

Meister's moral portrait was as finely etched. Necker's most prominent characteristic was a keen sensitivity and "the most refined and delicate feeling in every relationship." Associated with this trait was a deep sympathy for suffering or pain in others. "Public misfortunes affected him as strongly as a personal

21. Marmontel, Oeuvres complètes, II, 134.
22. Marie Anne du Deffand, Correspondance complète, 2 vols. (Paris, 1865), II, 494, 559.
23. Jacques-Henri Meister, "Sur M. Necker," Mélanges de philosophie, de morale et de littérature, 2 vols. (Geneva, 1822), II, 61-63.

misfortune, and the least pain of those he cherished caused him deep concern, making him capable of the most earnest, gentle and tender attention."[24] But also, he had a gift for seizing the comic and the ridiculous in situations and persons. Meister asserted that nothing except the comedies of Molière ever made him laugh so heartily as Necker's witty sallies against the pompous and the pretentious. Baron de Staël confirms this trait in his grandfather: "The most conspicuous feature of his personality was a piquant gaiety, a good-natured joking, of which others as well as himself were alternatively the butt."[25]

It is certain that descriptions of Necker depicting a bitter, morose, Alceste-type personality are far from the mark. Those who knew him best mention his good nature and sense of humor. Baron de Staël remembered from his own childhood how Necker liked to play with his grandchildren. The bailiff of Bern, Charles-Victor Bonstetten, records an incident when he was dining alone with the Neckers. Madame Necker left the dining room momentarily and the young daughter and Necker immediately flew into a merry romp, only to be seated with composed faces when Madame Necker returned—except that Necker's wig was on backwards![26] On the other hand, the sunniest dispositions are susceptible to cloudy spells, and there is evidence that Necker was not immune. Traveling evidently did not agree with him, and once when they visited Madame Necker's friends in Geneva, she felt it necessary to write to them afterward and apologize for the somewhat less than genial mood of her husband.[27]

Two characteristics have often been ascribed to Necker: pride and ambition. There can be no question about his high regard for his own abilities or that the dominant motive of his life was to place those special talents in the public service. The question is whether he was proud to the point of self-sufficiency, or ambitious to a degree approaching a pathological condition, as asserted by some authors.[28]

An observation on his pride made by the biographer of Madame de Vermen-oux is worth noting. He thought that Necker's physical appearance may have given people the impression of a man of inordinate pride. Madame du Deffand, with her sight nearly gone, could not have been influenced in this way, and her analysis of Necker's character may have been nearer the truth.[29] She did not see in him the proud, arrogant person that some others did. "He is certainly convinced of his superiority," she wrote Walpole, "but that does not make him either self-sufficient or pedantic."[30] In the summer of 1776, when it became

24. *Ibid.*, p. 70.

25. Baron de Staël, "Notice sur M. Necker," in Necker, *Oeuvres complètes*, I, v.

26. Callatay, *Madame de Vermenoux*, p. 126.

27. Fédor Golovkin, ed., *Lettres diverses recueillies en Suisse* (Geneva, 1821), p. 307.

28. See, e.g., Marcel Marion (*Histoire financière de la France depuis 1715*, 6 vols. [Paris, 1914-1929], I, 292), who was very much influenced by [Antoine-Jean Auget de Montyon], *Particularités et observations sur les ministres des finances les plus célèbres depuis 1660 jusqu'en 1791* (Paris, 1812), pp. 196-266.

29. Callatay, *Madame de Vermenoux*, p. 126.

30. Du Deffand, *Correspondance complète*, II, 559.

known that Necker was under consideration for appointment to the *contrôle général,* she wrote that "he has capability without presumption, generosity without ostentation, prudence without guile, it would be a very good choice to appoint such a man, but his religion is an insurmountable obstacle."[31]

The testimony of Necker's wife and daughter has usually been discounted because they both seemed so unreserved in their adoration of his "character" and "genius." Naturally such a close relationship would preclude a detached and objective appraisal; yet to reject their observations altogether would be to deprive the historian of useful evidence. After all, the testimony of those closest to a person could be more frank, and more truthful, than that of disgruntled political or personal enemies. Madame Necker and Madame de Staël were both intelligent and perceptive observers of character. If Madame Necker put her husband on a pedestal, she could take him down on occasion, as when she wrote the following about him in a letter to a friend in Geneva shortly after her marriage.

Imagine a person so enchanted with his superiority that he cannot see my own, so convinced of his perspicacity that he is always being hoodwinked, so per-suaded that he unites all the talents to the highest point of perfection that he disdains seeking other models. . . . I have reason to believe however that the innocent remedy which this letter will make him swallow will cure him in time of this insupportable malady.[32]

This was written with her husband watching over her shoulder. That Necker could accept such reprimands in good grace does not suggest a person of prickly vanity who could not support the least personal criticism, as described by Auget de Montyon.[33]

Madame de Staël's judgment of Necker's pride was that it was only one side of the coin. The other side was timidity and diffidence. In her essay "On the Character of Mr. Necker," written shortly after his death, she wrote:

He spoke eloquently whenever he was keenly aroused, when a powerful idea, or even more, an elevated feeling moved him. But to the very end of his life I often observed a great deal of timidity in him. I often saw his noble face blush when it chanced that attention was turned upon him by some recitation. His power did not really come into play until he was struggling against difficulties worthy of that power. He grew with the circumstances; he was proud against the strong; reassured by danger; he had at once the most noble pride and the most genuine modesty. No one could as much as he oppose injustice with all the dignity of his conscience. But in the midst of his friends, especially vis-à-vis himself, he measured himself constantly against his ideas of perfection of all kinds. I passed

31. *Ibid.,* p. 565.
32. Quoted in d'Haussonville, "Le Salon de Madame Necker," pp. 64-65.
33. "In consequence of this explosion of amour-propre any disagreement with his opinions appeared to him an injury, and any criticism was in his eyes, a crime which made him furious . . ." Montyon, *Particularités et observations,* p. 205. This is clearly inaccurate. Necker maintained good relations with a number of people with whom he disagreed, among them André Morellet and Dupont de Nemours.

my life pleading with him against his lack of faith in himself, against the imaginary reproaches that he made toward himself on occasions when he had exerted his greatest talents and virtues. Such was his character since his earliest youth.[34]

Necker's was not the pride of a small man, the "mass man" as described by José Ortega y Gasset, self-satisfied, complacent; but rather, it was the pride of one constantly straining for perfection, and constantly aware of falling short of his goal.

What was his goal, what was the object of his ambition? He did not care for wealth and what it could buy. He did not collect art treasures, or porcelain or furniture or manuscripts. According to Madame Necker, he left her in complete charge of the family budget and all purchases. Neither did he care for the trappings of power: the deference, the privileges, the little things that often compensate those in high positions for the burdens and vexations of office. As finance minister he did not constantly strain to expand his power; quite the opposite, as we shall see, he sought to decentralize the functions of the finance minister. He did insist on having the authority needed to carry out his reform program. He did not suffer easily being thwarted by those in his own department. The great importance he attached to "amelioration" led him to scrutinize expenditures of other departments. When he felt that his policies were endangered, and that they absolutely required it, he requested from the king admission to the High Council. When this was refused he resigned. The ambition of Necker, however great it may have seemed to observers at that time and since, was intimately bound up with his goals as a reform statesman. This shifts our attention from the person to his conception of the role of the statesman and the policies he believed most important in the French monarchy of his day.

It has been noted that Necker retired from active direction of his bank in 1772. From that date his goal was evidently a career in the government. The appearance a year later of his *Eloge de Colbert* was widely recognized as his bid for the post of finance minister, as well as his reform program if appointed. He entered the book in competition for the prize of eloquence annually offered by the Académie française. The Academie conferred the prize on the *Eloge de Colbert* after it was read to them by d'Alembert in August 1773, although it did not yet bear Necker's name. But, as the reviewer wrote in the *Correspondance littéraire* of Grimm, Diderot, and Meister, "everybody knew that the author was Mr. Necker, the resident minister of the Republic of Geneva."[35]

The review was probably written by Meister, who heaped fulsome praise on the author, emphasizing his originality and "genius." There was some effort to apologize for and explain the stylistic shortcomings. It was written in the space

34. Anne-Louis-Germaine de Staël-Holstein, "M. Necker: De Son Caractère et de sa vie privée," in *Mémoires sur la vie privée de mon pere, suivies des mélanges de M. Necker* (Paris, 1818).

35. Grimm, *Correspondance littéraire*, X, 281.

of six weeks; the author's expression tended to fall short of the ferment of his ideas. He was not trained as a writer, and it was the "originality of his genius which makes his expression seem so feeble and sterile." The unhistorical nature of the treatise was also commented upon. It was not the product of historical research, but rather of a profound mind that was able to grasp a few links in the chain to discern the whole. If Necker attributed to the great Colbert certain ideas that manifestly he did not have, it was because "political economy has evolved since his day and Mr. Necker was simply describing what Colbert would have thought if he were writing a century later." This kind of exercise seemed quite legitimate to the writer of the *Correspondance littéraire*. It was, after all, recognized to be Necker's bid to accede to the finance ministry, an ambition the writer of the review warmly supported. The essay on Colbert was "the result of meditation of a citizen and a statesman who has profoundly reflected on the duties of an administrator, a subject which he understands by reason of his own vision and experience."[36]

Other commentators were not so enthusiastic. The loyal Madame du Deffand was greatly attracted to it, although she sometimes complained that Necker's writing as well as his discourse "had too much metaphysics in it." She insisted that her correspondents, Horace Walpole and Voltaire, write her their impressions of the *Eloge de Colbert*. Neither seemed eager to do so, and it required some prodding. Walpole wrote that he found the *Eloge* "to be the work of a man of very fine intellect and of good will, but not very eloquent." He found certain passages "too emphatic."[37] While the author avoided much of the "grandiloquent nonsense" of the day, sometimes he indulged too much in the fashionable rhetoric that is never found in good authors. Nor was Walpole convinced that Colbert was as great a minister as Sully. Voltaire welcomed the defense of Colbert, whom he thought unjustly maligned by the *économistes*. But he wrote Madame du Deffand that he "found as much bad as good in it, as many obscure phrases as clear ones, as many malapropisms as words that were exact, as much exaggeration as truth."[38] In the final analysis, Voltaire thought it was the best work on Colbert to date, and it was, after all, not an easy subject for winning the prize on eloquence. In a letter to Paul Moultou, Voltaire was less reserved in his praise of the essay:

It is being said that the author of the *Eloge de J. B. Colbert* might some day succeed his hero. I should like to see it, for the rarity of the event as well as for the honor of Geneva. This is the second citizen who has carried off the prize in one of our academies. But J. Jacques only resembles that dog of a Diogenes, whereas the other has some appearance of becoming a minister of state.[39]

36. *Ibid.* p. 282.
37. *Correspondance de Madame du Deffand,* II, 349-350, n. 2.
38. *Ibid.,* p. 365.
39. François-Marie Arouet de Voltaire, *Oeuvres complètes,* 52 vols. (Paris, 1877-1885), XLVIII, 454-455.

Whatever its stylistic shortcomings, the *Eloge de Colbert* is an important document in Necker's political and ministerial career. It provides an introduction to the themes he was to expound later. It also indicates the nature of his ambition, for he unveiled himself in it. It was not really a historical work but belonged to a genre long familiar in the "mirror of princes" literature, although in this case it was ministers rather than kings who were the subject. Colbert was the model minister, the archetype. But Necker was looking at himself, not Colbert, and for this reason the essay is of interest for his own career as reform statesman.

The essay begins with a description of what an ideal minister should be, then shows how J. B. Colbert fit that model. "If men are made in the image of God," Necker wrote, "then the minister of finance, next to the king, must be the man who most closely approaches that image."[40] Like the master of the world, the minister of finance must govern without effort, or at least appear to do so. As the Supreme Being assures the harmony of the universe, so the finance minister directs passions toward the public welfare and state power. It is he who must bring under his purview the rights of men and those of the nation, to mediate between the individual who does not want to pay taxes and the needs of society that require taxation. Finance administration is the hub of all parts of the government. It decides what proportion of the national income will be devoted to defense, it must advise the directors of foreign policy what language will be in accord with the powers of the state.

Finally, it is the administration of finances which envelops in its care the interest of the entire people: because it is by a just and intelligent taxation that it fosters economic development; it is by a wise distribution of government expenditure that the tribute of the citizen accomplishes its purpose, and gives him in return for his taxes increased security, order, and tranquility.[41]

Obviously, more than ordinary talents are required for the minister of finance to achieve this. Five basic qualities were stipulated. First was compassion: a sympathy that included all in the realm, not overlooking the poor and those in the most remote provinces. The second was virtue, a sacrifice of the minister's own interests for the public interest. This included not only sacrifice of pecuniary interests, but of private affections and public acclaim, for he would often need to deny friends favors, and would have to pursue unpopular policies. The virtue of the minister was based on the firm foundation of religious faith, for it is the concept of God "who holds in His hands the first ring of this chain, which allows us to glimpse the harmony of the universe, and by this magnificent example, gives us an idea of order, and an ardent desire to please Him." Third was "genius," by which Necker meant intellectual and mental faculties of a high

40. Jacques Necker, *Eloge de Jean-Baptiste Colbert. Discours qui a remporté le prix de l'Académie française en 1773* (Paris, 1773), p. 9.
41. *Ibid.,* pp. 9-10.

order. The administrator cannot go by the rules, or learn his task from books. His glance at a situation is intuitive, a power given to him by nature. The fourth prerequisite of a great statesman was what Necker called "character," one to which he attached high importance. A man could be brilliant, as were some ministers he could name, but if his character were frivolous or inconstant, this brilliance would be of no use. It is character that makes genius effective, that translates great thoughts into great accomplishments. It, too, is a natural gift and cannot be learned. Finally, the fifth requirement of the great minister was the understanding of men—an ability to choose able subordinates, to discern a person's character and capabilities at once.

Having drawn the portrait of the ideal minister of finance, Necker turned his attention to Jean-Baptiste Colbert: the man, his ideas of statecraft, and what he had accomplished. "He defended the public interest against private interests, society against the individual, the future against the present." This certainly required character; and Necker compared Colbert in this respect to his predecessor, Nicolas Fouquet, who was lamentably lacking in resistance to the importunate requests of courtiers, whatever other engaging qualities he may have possessed.

Necker wrote that Colbert was primarily concerned about economic growth and the material well-being of the population. Government fiscal policies could contribute greatly to those ends. Taxes should weigh as lightly as possible on the population, and should be administered equitably. He noted Colbert's attempt to establish a uniform land survey as a basis for the assessment of the *taille,* but admitted that the project had floundered. "Happy will be the administrator who can free the peasants from the arbitrary assessment of officials," he wrote, no doubt envisaging his own future program. Very important for the equitable administration of the taxes was a careful attention to simple rules of accountability. Severe and rigorous enforcement of these rules was the only remedy against corruption and abuse of the fiscal powers of the government. Here Colbert's record was unimpeachable.

Other ways in which Colbert fostered economic growth were by abolishing internal restraints on trade in the area of the Five Great Farms and by building roads and canals, such as the great Languedoc canal linking the Mediterranean to the Atlantic. Colbert deplored the tendency of the French bourgeoisie to invest its capital in public office rather than in the economy, and sought to discourage it by reducing both the number of venal offices and their profits. This significantly reduced interest rates, which promoted industrial and agricultural growth.[42]

Necker defended Colbert from the criticism often made of him by the *économistes* in the eighteenth century: namely, that he did not sufficiently appreciate the benefits of freedom of enterprise, or of economic individualism and competition. Colbert was aware of the benefits of all those principles,

42. *Ibid.,* p. 30.

according to Necker, but "he tempered them with a spirit of wisdom." He did not believe that a country could achieve economic progress simply by relying on the laws of nature. France was well-endowed by nature, but so were some of the most backward countries in Africa. Economic progress required the guiding hand of the administrator. Necker believed a fully developed economy was one in which all the land was cultivated, and which in turn supported national industry and manufactures. Exports should consist of manufactured goods, or luxury products; imports should consist of grain or other agricultural products, or raw materials. This in turn would permit a larger population, which for Necker was the gauge of an economy of "happiness" (*bonheur*). To bring about this result required some intervention in the economy by the government.

Colbert's policies, according to his apologist, were not dictated by some doctrinaire set of principles. Here Necker lashed out at the "rhetoricians," by which he meant the *économistes*—those who believed one could learn great principles by analysis, by division, by separation, by erudition. "No," he wrote, "these principles must be seen at a glance, they must be enveloped in one's thought." The genius, in contrast to the erudite, grasps these principles by "the rapidity of his combinations, which gives to his mental operations the character of instinct." This very Bergsonian idea was not well received in the Age of Reason by such exemplars as Turgot and Condorcet. The above passage in the *Eloge* must have been the source of the sobriquet by which they always referred to Necker in their correspondence: "M. l'Enveloppe."

Later pages of the *Eloge de Colbert* dwelt again on the character and personal life of a great minister. These passages had a significance for Necker's later career unsuspected at the time. The great minister will inevitably have powerful enemies. He should not allow their attacks to agitate him, but should rather look upon them as "fire which will purify his heart as it does gold, which causes the grosser metals to separate from it." The great minister does not deign to reply to slanders, an "elevated soul" does not notice them.

Returning to Colbert's career, Necker said that "the war came, and upset all Colbert's plans of administration and his economic system."[43] Like Necker's own ministry, Colbert's was one of good intentions thwarted by circumstances. Necker said that Colbert opposed the Dutch war; but his history was not impeccable. Colbert apparently did not oppose that war, though he had expected it to be a short one.[44] There is no question, however, that the six-year war in the 1670s did undermine much of Colbert's constructive work. Should a minister whose advice is not heeded by the king resign, or continue in the government? Necker justified Colbert's decision to remain at his post. He had a better chance of persuading the king to adopt a policy of moderation and prudence by staying in the government than by resigning.

43. *Ibid.*, p. 59.
44. Henri Sée, "Que faut-il penser de l'oeuvre économique de Colbert?" *Revue historique*, 152 (May-August 1926), 181-194.

The final pages of the *Eloge* rose to lyrical heights, as befitted an essay competing for the prize of eloquence. The great minister does not care for personal wealth, or any of the pleasures that are the concern of ordinary men. His pleasure is derived from achieving his goal for the country. There is no greater joy than the satisfaction of having used the powers of the office of finance minister to better the lot of the people of the nation. There is no greater reward than being able to say at the end of the work day: "Today I lightened the rigor of the tax burden, I protected those who were subject to the caprices of authority, I contributed to the general welfare by eliminating a useless expenditure for ceremony."[45]

Such was the character, such was the ambition. The style of the essay was indeed too emphatic, too declamatory, which none of Necker's later works were. It was, nonetheless, a genuine expression of his thought and feeling, rather than an exercise in rhetoric. One may compare this early essay with Necker's introduction to *On the Administration of Finances in France,* published in 1784, about three years after the end of his first ministry. The two works are consistent. His ideal minister was unchanged. He admitted that the thirst for *gloire* and the esteem of the public was his dominating passion, but he found no need to apologize for this, "the most pardonable of passions."[46] These remarks, if somewhat self-congratulatory, were true. Those authors who have seen a "pathological character" in his ambition would need to show why it was so, and what ill effects it may have produced. If Necker's ambition was a disease, one is reminded of George II's reply to the warning that General Wolfe was mad: "Then I wish he would bite all my other generals!"

A final trait of Necker's character should be mentioned, since it is not often commented upon. He was remarkably lacking in rancor. His enemies could wound him, but they could never arouse in him a ferocious will to crush them, or to seek vengeance. Some who knew him well felt him too forbearing, and insufficiently aware of evil. As a youth the comte de Ségur, son of the secretary of state for war, often visited the Necker household and became well acquainted with the family. His testimony, written many years later, after the French Revolution, is pertinent:

The most hateful envy could not by any pretext deny to Mr. Necker the noblest character, an elevated soul, a strong love for the public good, intentions that were always pure, extensive knowledge, and a brilliant eloquence. But he was on the other hand, like the king, stronger on principles than in action. Both judged men as they ought to be rather than as they are, were too easily persuaded that it was only necessary to want the good in order to have it. They did not know the logic of passion; they did not know that with most men nothing is more opposed to their interest rightly understood than their egotism. . . . Being admitted to the intimacy of Mr. Necker and his wife even though still young, I

45. *Eloge de Colbert,* p. 69.
46. Necker, *De l'Administration des finances en France,* in *Oeuvres complètes,* IV, 96.

can assert that never could one listen to him without being touched by his feelings, and struck with respect for his character. One breathed in this household an air of simplicity and virtue, completely foreign to the brilliant court and the corrupt capital.[47]

The lack of misanthropism in the Genevan banker was probably a trait he shared with the century itself: the world of the philosophes, the sentimental novelists, and the encyclopedists. It was the "springtime of the modern world," as Carl Becker has described the eighteenth-century Enlightenment, a century of optimism.

Necker was a man of his own time also in sharing to a greater extent than has been realized the outlook of the liberal economists. At the conclusion of the *Eloge* he offered some notes on political economy. He spent the next two years expanding them and preparing his second book for publication. The particular circumstances in which *On the Legislation and Commerce of Grain* appeared attracted much greater attention to it than to his first book. It was here that Necker openly challenged the doctrines of the *économistes*.

47. Louis-Philippe de Ségur, *Mémoires: Ou Souvenirs et anecdotes,* 3 vols. (Paris, 1825-1826), I, 110-111.

Chapter IV

NECKER AND THE *ECONOMISTES*

On several occasions while serving the Company of the Indies, and also in his essay on Colbert, Necker took issue with the disciples of Dr. François Quesnay, whose *Tableau économique* was published in 1758. A pioneer contribution to economic theory, the *Tableau* portrayed the production and distribution of economic wealth very much as would a physician's diagram of the circulation of blood. The intricate chart, the "zig-zag," showed that wealth was produced by the "productive class" of farmers or cultivators who tilled the soil directly. It was distributed by the "distributive class," the landed proprietors who had leased the land to the producers, and who received from them in the form of rent the surplus over and above the costs of production. Then the *Tableau* showed the transformation of surplus wealth into nonagricultural goods and services by the "sterile class" of merchants, artisans, manufacturers, and professional people. A peculiar feature of the physiocratic doctrine was its insistence that the source of all wealth was from agriculture. Other types of activity were no doubt beneficial and desirable, but they did not create new or surplus wealth above the costs that went into the production of their goods and services. Only agriculture created new wealth, instead of merely transforming it from one kind into another.

Another peculiar feature of the system was the special status it gave the landlord or proprietor class. By what right did this class receive the entire surplus, called the "net product"? Because they had provided the original capitalistic investment in the land. The proprietors were not a parasitic class, but vitally necessary for the well-being of the entire circulatory system. They had the vision, enterprise, responsibility, and character to initiate agriculture in the beginning. From their disposal of the net product, agriculture would be continually expanded through new capital investment in land. From the net product of the proprietors should come all the tax revenue for the government. It was the surplus wealth in their hands that provided all the higher refinements of civilization: art, science, universities, and the liberal professions, all of which did not even transform wealth from one kind to another but simply consumed it. Therefore, a wealthy, prosperous proprietary class was vitally necessary for the well-being of the nation. What was good for the proprietors was good for all.

Necker's much publicized opposition to the "sect," as the disciples of Quesnay were called, was not because he was a conservative in economic thought. His writings show that he had absorbed several of the ideas of the *économistes*. Where he differed was in his instinct for placing experience above theory. General laws and grand principles might be true, abstractly considered, but they were subordinate to common sense and the wisdom of practical life. The kinds of problems statesmen dealt with could not be resolved by economic theory alone. There were moral, psychological, and social aspects to be considered as well.

For their part, the *économistes* could not admit any doubts about the timeless and universal truth of their doctrine. One of the most vigorous protagonists of the sect, the marquis de Mirabeau, affirmed that "since the beginning of the world there had been only three great inventions which have given stability to political societies: writing, money, and the *Tableau économique.*"[1] Small wonder that Quesnay's followers reacted furiously against the doubter! Because of Necker's defense of the Company of the Indies, his praise of Colbert, and his treatise opposing unlimited export of grain in 1775, he was denounced by the *économistes* as a defender of the old order of economic thought and practice that they were out to destroy. That order, they said, consisted of a stifling regulation of the economy by the government in the supposed interests of consumers; a Colbertist supervision of industry in the interests of the state; and commercial policies dictated by what Adam Smith called "the mercantile system," which is known to historians as "mercantilism."

The *économistes* were the first to attach the mercantilist label to Necker, and the myth has been perpetuated by historians.[2] This despite the fact that specialized studies of his economic thought have shown that he cannot be so labeled. Until recently the most thorough study, done by Vacher de Lapouge, concluded that anyone who believed Necker was a mercantilist could not have read his books: "when one examines the few significant passages closely one sees that the mercantilism of Necker is reduced to a general tendency of his mind; but as for the principles themselves of that system and their practical consequences very little remains."[3] As to what school of economic doctrine Necker

---

1. Victor de Mirabeau, *Philosophie rurale,* I, 52-53, as quoted by Adam Smith in *An Inquiry into the Nature and Causes of the Wealth of Nations* (New York, 1937), p. 643.

2. Luethy, *La Banque protestante,* II, 381; see also Gustave de Molinari's comments in his ed. of Necker's "Sur La Législation et le commerce des grains," in *Mélanges d'économie politique,* 2 vols. (Paris, 1848), II, 225, n. 1. Molinari describes Necker's system as "mercantilism with some variations."

3. Claude Vacher de Lapouge, *Necker économiste* (Paris, 1914), p. 229. The foremost doctrine of mercantilism was the importance of foreign trade and the inflow of bullion into a country due to a favorable balance of trade. The most powerful country, economically, was the one with the greatest amount of treasure in the form of gold and silver. According to the mercantilists, the state should control foreign commerce in order to induce that flow of bullion. One need only read the first chapters of Necker's treatise on the grain trade to see that he was not a mercantilist. While admitting that gold and silver was one form of state

might belong, the same author was at a loss to say. In the final analysis he thought Necker was not very significant in the history of economic doctrine, being a pragmatist above all else. This was the general conclusion of two other scholars who had made a special study of Necker's economic thought.[4]

This negative verdict has been challenged in recent years by Henri Grange in an exhaustive work devoted to Necker's thought. Grange believes Necker had a much keener perception of social and economic forces than has been recognized. Necker, he says, anticipated some of the insights of Karl Marx (which the latter duly acknowledged), in particular the theory of surplus value created by the workers and appropriated by the owners of the means of production.[5] Necker discerned what in the nineteenth century came to be called the "iron law of wages," that is, that a great number of workers competing against each other makes it possible for the owners of the means of production to hire them at a bare subsistence wage. Necker saw the fallacy of the physiocratic assumption that what was good for the landowners was good for everyone; he knew the reality of the grim class struggle between workers and proprietors. In his 1775 treatise on the grain trade he spoke up vigorously for the poor.

Above all, Grange sees Necker as the herald of state intervention in the economy to protect the weak from the strong.[6] As for mercantilism, he denies that Necker could be associated with that doctrine because his view of the state was not mercantilist. He did not see the state as representing the interests of the prince only, but that of all the citizens. In this sense, Grange acknowledges that Necker's thought approached that of the liberal economists. But he correctly points out that Necker rejected the liberal doctrine of natural law as the basis for private property rights. Those rights, Necker maintained, were created by society, and society had the right to alter them in the interests of all the people—a principle that would seem to place him in the camp of the utilitarians or even of the socialists. Indeed, Grange shows that Necker left the imprint of his ideas on the Swiss predecessor of Marx, Sismondi.[7] In any case, it appears from Grange's study that Necker's economic and social ideas were neither conservative nor reactionary, but well ahead of his time.

---

power, he thought the population of a country was much more important. Nothing in Necker's writings indicates that he gave more importance to foreign trade than to agriculture. His ideal economy was a highly developed national economy in which agriculture, commerce, and industry were evenly balanced. To build a national economy he favored moderate protective tariffs. His economic thought in this respect bears some resemblance to such nineteenth-century national economic systems as those favored by Henry Clay in the United States, Friedrich List in Germany, and Sergius Witte in Russia. What put Necker clearly outside the thought of the mercantilists was his conviction that the state cannot control the flow of wealth. Money flees the strong arm of the government that tries to grasp it by force and settles in countries that are liberal and moderate.

4. Fr. von Sivers, "Necker als Nationalökonom," *Jahrbücher fur Nationalökonomie und Statistik*, 22 (1874), 17-27. Berta Kraus, *Das Okonömische Denken Neckers* (Vienna, 1925).

5. Henri Grange, *Les Idées de Necker* (Paris, 1974), p. 94.

6. *Ibid.*, pp. 162-200.

7. *Ibid.*, pp. 248-252.

While credit must be given Necker for these advanced ideas, he was far from being a socialist. He firmly believed that property rights, even if not sacred, were still to be protected by the state, and that they were the bulwark of the social order. He did not think the great inequalities of wealth could ever be eradicated; the poor would always be with us. He did acknowledge that the English popular classes enjoyed the most favored material conditions of any people in Europe, and he thought this was due in part to the influence of the institution of parliament. Certainly he hoped that his own provincial assemblies would ameliorate the lot of the poor. But that the poor themselves could organize and participate actively in political life in France seems never to have occurred to him before and during his first ministry. Their only hope for protection against the harsh regime of the landlords was the benevolent intervention of the sovereign, seconded by his minister.

If Necker was neither a mercantilist nor a protosocialist, then what was he? Are we to conclude that economic ideas really had little influence on him and that he was simply a pragmatist? But the well-known dictum of John Maynard Keynes cannot be forgotten: "Practical men, who believe themselves to be quite exempt from any intellectual influences, are usually the slaves of some defunct economist."[8] When we search Necker's early writings for sources of influence, it appears inescapable that the most important were those whom he is supposed to have despised, namely the economic liberals themselves, even the *économistes*. In his practical application of economic ideas to concrete problems it was the liberal policies that he adopted.

It might be well to pause at this juncture to consider the term "liberalism," an expression that evokes such varied ideas and feelings. Among the left parties in the political spectrum of continental Europe today, the word "liberalism" seems to stand for a doctrine that in reality amounts to special pleading for the property-owning classes. The slogans of liberalism fit only too well the material interests of landlords and captains of industry. Along with this is a callous indifference to the sufferings of the exploited working classes caught up in the toils of the economic system. In this view, liberalism stands for unbridled egotism.

Quite a different meaning is conveyed to most people of Anglo-Saxon background. To them liberalism represents a way of thinking that is innately hostile to dogmatic certitude. Truth is always tentative, subject to change in the light of new experiences. Flexibility and accommodation to the opinions of others is characteristic of the liberal mind, and this often manifests itself in a willingness to compromise. In government it means the toleration of a loyal opposition, restraint and moderation in the exercise of power. Freedom, of course, is the great slogan of liberalism: freedom of speech, press, conscience, assembly, and of enterprise, so long as such freedom does not infringe upon the

8. John Maynard Keynes, *The General Theory of Employment, Interest and Money*, p. 383, as cited by D. C. Coleman in *Revisions in Mercantilism* (London, 1969), p. 17.

rights of others. Liberalism means a distrust of concentrations of power, whether in the state or in the private sector of the economy. As much as possible the individual and society should be free of government interference. But where circumstances require intervention the government should be prepared to intervene. Even in those circumstances, the liberal statesman recognizes that what the government can accomplish is limited. The choice of means is very important, and the means chosen are considered only temporary and exceptional. Society and the individual operate best under their own initiative. Unwise and incautious intervention can be harmful to the freedom of the individual and the best interests of society.

It is clear that Necker shared the ideas of the second definition of liberalism given above, not only in his economic thought but in his views on government and society. "Society is founded on the moderate reciprocity of concessions and sacrifices," he wrote in the *Eloge de Colbert.* "It is by this prudent harmony that men find happiness, peace, and security in union."[9] In the introduction of his treatise on the grain trade he listed three interest groups in French society, "three classes of men with distinct pretensions: the landlords, the merchants, and the people." By the latter he meant the workers dependent upon manual labor for their livelihood. Landlords wanted to dispose of their grain harvests on the most advantageous terms, and so they invoked the principle of property rights. The merchants wanted to buy and sell their grain in the environment most conducive to their operations, so they invoked the principle of freedom of trade. The working class wanted its food supply guaranteed by government control of the grain trade, so they invoked the principle of humanity. All these desires and claims were legitimate. But no principle can be absolute, because the desires of the landlords, merchants, and workers are sometimes contradictory. There must be compromise, adjustment, and conciliation, and this was the role of the government.[10] What Necker sought to do in his book on the grain trade was to find some practical guidelines that would meet the desires of all three classes. His insistence that the government must assure the minimum subsistence of the workers by whatever intervention is necessary was the central thesis of the book. It was this that aroused against him the fury of the *économistes.*

It may seem surprising in our industrial age that so much of the debate over economic principles in the second half of the eighteenth century revolved around the grain trade. Even at that time some began to wonder if so much attention given to a single commodity was not becoming excessive. Voltaire took note of the popularity of the subject:

Towards 1750 the nation, satiated with poetry, tragedies, comedies, operas, novels, romances, with moral reflections even more romanesque, with theological disputes on grace and convulsions, began finally to reason on the subject of

9. *Eloge de Colbert,* p. 38.
10. "Sur La Législation et le commerce des grains," in Gustave de Molinari, ed., *Mélanges d'économie politique,* II, 212-213.

grain. Vineyards were forgotten in order to talk only of wheat and rye. Many useful things were written about agriculture, read by everyone except farmers. People surmised, on coming out of the Opéra-Comique, that France must have an enormous amount of grain to sell. Finally the cry of the nation obtained from the government in 1764 the liberty to export grain.[11]

Despite Voltaire's bemusement, there were good reasons why grain became the favorite topic of conversation in the salons and in the journals. No other commodity brought out so clearly and dramatically the issues involved between the liberal economic schools and the traditional habits of thinking about economic problems. Bread was the staple in the diet of the greatest number of people. Where so much of the population earned barely a subsistence, a rise in the price of grain could have dramatic consequences, arousing the deepest fears of the multitude. Panic over threatened bread shortage and high prices had prompted disturbances throughout the eighteenth century in various regions of France. Governments, ministers, and lesser magistrates were always concerned about the bread supply. Harvests could vary widely from one year to the next. In lean years the shortage of the basic staple for the population could become acute. In bumper harvest years the surplus could cause a precipitate drop in grain prices, depressing not only the agricultural sector but the rest of the economy.

It was the latter aspect of the question that most attracted the attention of the physiocrats. For some years before 1764 the country had experienced good harvests and low prices, resulting in the stagnation of agriculture. This depression, the physiocrats argued, was due to the overanxious, regulative government, which, always fearful that the food supply would run out, sought to guarantee adequate supplies by pursuing policies that hindered the free circulation and production of grain. There were a number of regulative policies traditionally used by governments, both in the medieval city-state and the monarchical states. One was to supervise closely the people who entered the grain trade. Middlemen were apt to be suspect, since it was notorious that fabulous profits were sometimes made buying in a market where grain was plentiful and holding it off the market until it became scarce. Therefore, commerce in grain was strictly regulated. Merchants must have official authorization to enter the trade; they could not purchase grain crops that were still unharvested; they were required to retail grain at centralized, official marketplaces; if the price reached a dangerous level the government would seek to control prices; merchants were forbidden to export grain outside the kingdom. In times of scarcity the government might encourage imports from outside through subsidies; it might also maintain its own grain storage.

The physiocrats argued that, in its fear of high prices, the government's regulation of the grain trade contributed to the dearth rather than alleviated it. The goal of government policy, they said, should be comparatively high grain prices and a plentiful supply. The two goals were not contradictory. If complete

11. Voltaire, *Oeuvres complètes*, XVIII, 11.

freedom of enterprise were permitted to both producers and distributors, the profit motive could be relied upon to expand the area under cultivation. High prices would continue despite the plentiful supply because the merchants could export the surplus to foreign markets. Such had been the result of English policy, where free export was allowed. Free export alone would guarantee a price level that would be within the means of the indigent classes and still encourage farmers to expand production. Rising agricultural prices would encourage capital investments in the land and improve agricultural techniques. In this respect England, too, where landlords resided on their estates and took a personal interest in improved methods of production, was leading the way.[12]

Due to the increasing fame and influence of the "sect," the government of Louis XV was led in 1763 to embark upon a system of free trade in grain. The declaration of May 25, 1763, authorized free transport of grain among the provinces; anyone who wished could engage in the trade without official authorization. An edict the following year permitted the export of grain outside the country as long as the price did not exceed 30 livres the *setier.*[13]

Unfortunately, nature did not deal kindly with her friends the physiocrats. The last years of the 1760s were poor years agriculturally, and serious crop failures occurred in 1770 and 1771. Shortages threatened, and the d'Aiguillon ministry, whose finance minister was abbé Terray, restored government controls. Terray's law of 1770 did not ban free interior trade, but did resume some traditional restrictions. Export outside the country was forbidden; grain merchants had to register; officials who received the king's money were forbidden to speculate with it in grain; and grain could not be sold anywhere except in the public and official market places. In addition, Terray stored grain by letting out government contracts to private persons for that purpose—the contracts that became unjustly famous in the legend of the "pacte de famine."[14]

Four months after the beginning of the new reign, in August 1774, came the "St. Bartholemew of ministers," the dismissal of the unpopular d'Aiguillon ministry and the beginning of the great reform ministry of Turgot. This disciple of both Vincent de Gournay and the Physiocrats promulgated the most important and far-reaching of all the acts inspired by the *économistes,* the decree of September 13, 1774. In a lengthy preamble Turgot set forth clearly and simply, "so that the most ignorant village priest could explain it to his parishioners," the principles of free trade in grain. He attempted valiantly to combat the popular prejudice against grain merchants and the notion that shortages were due to dishonest speculators and monopolizers.

It is the variation of the seasons and the regions that causes differences in the grain harvests. This inequality must be evened out by permitting freedom of

12. Georges Weulersse, *Le Mouvement physiocratique en France de 1756 à 1770,* 2 vols. (Paris, 1910), I, 384.

13. For official decrees, edicts, and declarations of the royal government concerning the grain trade, see François André Isambert et al., eds., *Recueil général des anciennes lois françaises,* 29 vols. (Paris, 1822-1827), XXIV.

14. Léon Cahen, "Le Pacte de famine de les spéculations sur les blés," pp. 32-43.

trade between provinces and stockpiling between time periods. Therefore, the transport and the storage of grain, after its harvest, are the only means of preventing shortages of bread.[15]

Transportation and storage, he said, can be carried out most efficiently by private enterprise spurred by the profit motive. It is foolish for government to attempt to fix and hold prices at a certain level. Prices are determined by the supply at harvest time. When there is a poor crop in one province, the consumers must expect to pay more for transporting the grain from other regions in the kingdom or other countries; consumers in the shortage-stricken area must also expect to pay for storage of the grain brought to them. The price mechanism is the only way that private enterprise will bring grain to the stricken area, and therefore the rise in grain prices is not due to evil monopolizers, but is the very means by which the shortage of grain and the crisis of subsistence will be met. "Not only is the rise in grain prices inevitable, but it is the only possible remedy for the shortage, by attracting the commodity to the province through the profit motive."

Government intervention in meeting this crisis, according to Turgot, is always costly and inept. By subsidizing the import of grain from outside, or by maintaining government warehouses, the government deters private entre-preneurs who cannot compete with the financial power of the royal treasury. The government always operates at a loss, and therefore the taxpayers have to pay for its ineptness. "It is by commerce alone, and by free commerce, that the inequalities of the harvests will be corrected."

Turgot's decree of September 1774 condemned the principles of abbé Terray's act of 1770. To require grain merchants to be licensed was to subject them to the arbitrary powers of officials; the prohibition of buying and selling grain outside regular, authorized markets was an inconvenience for both buyer and seller. It inhibited large grain operators from buying great quantities of grain for shipment to provinces in need. Finally, grain merchants must be assured that their calculations would not be upset by the blundering operations of the government.

The decree of September contained four articles. The first restored the declaration of May 25, 1763, permitting anyone engaged in the grain trade to buy and sell anywhere he chose, "even outside the market place." The second prohibited the king's officials from interfering with the operations of grain and flour merchants. The third declared that the government would stay out of grain operations and would not maintain storages, subsidize imports or exports, or engage in similar operations. Finally, the decree declared freedom of grain imports into the kingdom and freedom to export the same foreign grain outside the kingdom. The decree of September 1774 did not, however, restore freedom of export for French grain, as did the law of 1764.

15. Gustave Schelle, ed., *Oeuvres de Turgot et documents le concernant, avec biographie et notes,* 5 vols. (Paris, 1913-1923), IV, 201ff.

Again, as in the 1760s, the experiment in freedom turned out badly, due primarily to the poor grain harvest in the summer of 1774. In the spring of 1775, grain shortages became serious in the provinces north and east of Paris. Prices rose to the critical level, threatening to advance beyond the capabilities of the day laborers. Popular demonstrations began in the Aisne and Oise river valleys and in the region immediately around Paris. The disturbances took the form of popular protests against the high prices of flour and a demand that the government fix a ceiling for grain and flour.

Turgot was reluctant to give up the experiment with the principles of his decree. He and his advisors suspected the genuineness of the popular movement. It seemed too well organized, and was thought to be financed by highly-placed opponents of the ministry, the prince de Conti being most suspect. This "conspiracy theory" of the Flour War of 1775 has persisted among the admiring biographers of Turgot. Recent work on the subject has shown that it rests upon no solid evidence.[16] Nevertheless, Turgot and his advisors were convinced that the situation called for firmness. They thought there should be no relenting and no concessions made to popular demands, which, even if they were not insti-gated from above, were only an expression of ancient prejudices and super-stitions regarding commerce and grain.

Necker had turned his attention to the question of the grain trade and of government policy for some time before the spring of 1775. He had sought to present a manuscript to Turgot personally to get his approval for its publication. The controller general declined to receive it, telling its author icily that he could publish anything he wished. André Morellet witnessed the incident and saw Necker leave the controller general's office "wounded, but not crushed."[17] Necker proceeded to have the work, *On the Legislation and the Commerce of Grain,* published in the spring of 1775, as the grain riots were mounting in intensity. Turgot and his friends could only look upon publication of the book at that time as a demagogic appeal to the populace. Upon receiving a copy, Turgot wrote the following note to Necker on April 23:

I have received, sir, the copy of your work which you left at my door. I thank you for this courtesy. If I had decided to write upon this subject and had wished to defend the opinion which you hold I would have awaited a more peaceful moment when the question would have interested only persons able to judge it without passion. But on this point, as on others, people have different ways of thinking.[18]

In his reply, Necker protested the insinuation that his book was intended to arouse the populace against the ministry:

16. Edgar Faure, *La Disgrâce de Turgot* (Paris, 1961), pp. 293-318. George Rudé, *The Crowd in History. A Study of Popular Disturbances in France and England, 1730-1848* (New York, 1964), pp. 26-31.

17. André Morellet, *Mémoires,* I, 237.

18. *Oeuvres de Turgot,* ed. Schelle, IV, 412-413.

It was the twelfth of March when my book was given to the printer, which is proven by the date on which the censor passed it; at that time there was not the least scarcity of grain anywhere. If that which has appeared since then, in some areas, had seemed to you or the keeper of the seals a reason to suspend publication of this work, and if you had let me know, I would have respectfully deferred to your wishes. But an abstract work, moderate in its ideas and circumspect in form could not have, it seems to me, any influence on passions. I hope you will pardon me, sir, the earnestness with which I defend myself from the reproach you seem to make to me. It is painful enough for me to differ with you in your thinking about some matters of political economy. I should not like you to have other grievances against me. Your opinion in this respect is keenly felt. . . .[19]

Such protestations were futile in stemming the fury of the *économistes.* Several prominent members of the "sect" joined in the denunciation of Necker and his book. On May 14, Bachaumont referred to an article which had appeared, written anonymously but obviously by an *économiste,* in which there was "more personal invective than reason"; the article was by Condorcet.[20] In July other *économistes* and their sympathizers entered the fray, among them Voltaire, the abbé Baudeau, and the abbé Morellet, Necker's erstwhile opponent on the question of the Company of the Indies. The correspondent Metra also took note of the furious attack of the *économistes* on the author of *On the Legislation and the Commerce of Grain.* Metra himself thought the "author presented his ideas with a moderation which, in the present century, is no slight merit." He remarked in July that the refutation of Morellet "undertook to demonstrate that the rules this anti-*économiste* lays down for the administration of the grain trade and the reasoning by which he supports them leads to the same liberty he combats."[21]

The observation was a good one. Unlike most of the *économistes,* Morellet was a personal friend of Necker's and often a guest at Madame Necker's "Fridays." He did not share the contempt Turgot, Condorcet, and the abbé de Véri held for the Genevan banker. His judgment of Necker's book was fair. There was much more liberalism in it than the traditional policy of government regulation. Necker had accepted practically all the concrete recommendations in Turgot's September decree.[22] He recognized that merchants and speculators in grain perform a useful and necessary service, buying in one region where there is a surplus and transporting the grain to a province suffering a dearth, and also purchasing large stocks of grain at harvest time and storing for the lean winter months. Necker expressly repudiated Terray's law of 1770: the requirement that

19. *Ibid.*
20. Bachaumont, *Mémoires secrets,* VIII, entry for May 14, 1775.
21. Metra, *Correspondance secrète,* I, entry for April 20, 1775; II, entry for July 1, 1775.
22. It is at the beginning of pt. 2 of "Sur La Législation et le commerce des grains" that Necker begins the following discussion: pp. 281ff in Gustave de Molinari's ed.

grain merchants be officially registered, that receivers of the king's revenue be prohibited from entering the grain trade, and that grain not be sold except at public markets. His reasoning for opposing these measures was the same as Turgot's.

Nobody recognized better than Necker, with all his experience as a grain speculator, how it is that officious governments can inhibit the private initiative of grain merchants in performing their essential functions. Arbitrariness, he wrote, is the worst vice of officialdom. Whatever policies the government does adopt, they should be clear and consistent, well thought-out, so that private entrepreneurs and merchants can confidently plan their operations. Provincial administrators should not regulate the grain trade; this is the proper function of the royal government alone. The government should not presume to fix prices of grain; this would be futile, since so many variable factors influence the price. Government intervention in the grain trade, especially stockpiling grain, is not in the best interests of the country. This should be left as much as possible to private initiative. The government should not generally subsidize imports or exports, for this can throw speculators into disarray. Nor should bonuses be given to foster interior circulation of grain. The best grain policy, Necker wrote, would require the least intervention by the government, and the fewest exceptions. The worst would be to oscillate between total liberty and total regulation.

Where he sharply disagreed with the *économistes* was in rejecting their absolute faith in the autonomy of natural laws in the economic sphere. He refused to trust the fate of millions of poor people to the highly theoretical postulates of undoubtedly brilliant minds, such as those of Quesnay, Mirabeau, and Turgot. There is no general principle, he argued, which, though sound in itself, is not subject to abuse. For example, while one category of merchants undoubtedly performs the beneficial functions noted above, this is not true of all merchants, or in all situations. The popular distrust of monopolizers and speculators had some justification in fact. Liberty of commerce could be abused in situations in which collusion among speculators could raise the price of grain artificially, without any justification in the market.

Here Necker spoke from knowledge and experience, not theory. He recognized that a few speculators with vast capital can narrow the scope of competition; they can use psychological techniques to create panic among buyers and drive up the price of grain. A modern author has shown that during the eighteenth century a strong gambling spirit seemed to affect the population. An extraordinary number of people went into grain speculation.

In the space of fifty years the number of middlemen quadrupled at Troyes, and increased ten-fold at Châlons; at Etampes one met among their number a hairdresser and a servant. . . . Between 1765 and 1774 an intensive speculative movement appeared which must have provoked the most legitimate apprehensions of the people.[23]

23. Cahen, "Le Pacte de famine," p. 37.

Necker believed the government must intervene to protect consumers from those merchants whose only interest is to force the price of grain upward artificially through collusion. It was necessary to find a balance between true liberty, that which is beneficial, and the abuse of liberty. This is the role of the government, and particularly of the minister of finance. It was not so much a theoretical task as a practical one.

What practical guidelines did Necker write for the instruction of his readers, among whom he had hoped to find Turgot? If there was to be any fundamental law at all he thought it should be a prohibition on export of grain outside the country. This was due to the special circumstances regarding France, notably her population, which was the largest in Europe. Less populated countries such as England or Holland could risk a more liberal export policy. National character also was a factor. He seemed to think the French psychology was particularly prone to panic whenever a grain shortage was suspected. But export should not be completely prohibited if there was unquestionably a surplus. Determining if there was a surplus was difficult. He thought the best guide would be the market price. If the grain price fell at or below 20 livres the setier, the government could permit export, but only in the form of flour, not grain. Additional precautionary measures would require bakers to maintain a month's reserve stock during the critical period of the year.

With regard to the internal commerce in grain, Necker was much more hesitant to infringe upon the freedom of the merchant and the proprietor. Only when the price of grain reached and surpassed 30 livres the setier would he begin to restore controls, and then moderately and cautiously. The government would require grain to be sold at public marketplaces. But if the merchant could show by affidavit that he intended to ship grain to another province, even that restriction would not be imposed, and he would be permitted to purchase grain outside official marketplaces. When the grain price rose enough to threaten the subsistence of the working class, the activities of speculators would be brought under scrutiny, for their usefulness to the public ceased. Large grain purchases which were not transported would probably be for only one purpose, to reap windfall profits from the suffering of the people.

It needs to be emphasized that Necker is said to have made his own fortune from speculation in grain, and he certainly understood the merchant's viewpoint. He took cognizance of the argument that since freedom of trade is such a great good, its abuses must be accepted along with its benefits, and that it is illusory to suppose one could be had without the other. He wrote:

Freedom is almost always beneficial to commerce, because most transactions being useful or at least harmless to society, to submit them to regulation would be to substitute the apathetic eye of the administrator for the active and zealous attention of self interest; it would be to trace out for merchants the path which they could find very well for themselves, and in which the decision depends upon an infinite number of calculations, quite beyond the legislator; the latter can place barriers at known precipices, but within that common enclosure he must allow each one to go his own way.[24]

The barrier that Necker would place on complete freedom of domestic trade (when the price rose above 30 livres the setier) was certainly liberal if one peruses the tables of grain prices during that century compiled by Ernest Labrousse. The average price of wheat from 1710 to 1789, declining from its peak in the years of the War of Spanish Succession, never again surpassed the 30 livres per setier mark until the catastrophic harvest of 1788. Of course, there was great variation according to regions. The price in Provence was often above 30 livres the setier, which was exceptional. In 1778 there was a spurt to 30 livres in the southwest. In other provinces, however, the price rarely surpassed that barrier.[25] It is clear that if Necker's guidelines for internal commerce had been adopted, grain merchants would have suffered little regulation from 1775 to 1788.

Such was the essay that subjected the Genevan banker to a storm of abuse from the pens of the *économistes* in the spring and summer of 1775. It was a strange reaction on the part of the "sect," for Necker's book was indeed moderate and circumspect in its proposals, as the author claimed in his letter to Turgot. His principal point was to oppose a general law permitting freedom of export such as that of 1764. But that law had never been revived by Turgot, so the main argument in Necker's book was rather academic as far as any current policy was concerned. Furthermore, even with respect to the law of September 13, 1774, Turgot himself made several exceptions. Paris was not included in the law, and regulation continued there. Turgot contracted with the Leleu Company to stockpile grain near Paris. He offered subsidies to grain merchants to see that ample supplies were available in Champagne during the coronation ceremonies in June 1775. In the Flour War he provided additional funds for establishing charitable workshops to aid the indigent. In fact, on the administrative level far removed from the clash of doctrines, Turgot's policy was not very different from that of Necker during the latter's first ministry from 1776 to 1781. As will be seen, Necker did not revoke the act of September 13, 1774, and continually referred to it as the basic law on the subject in his correspondence with intendants.

Furthermore, Necker's aim as far as the price level was concerned was the same as that of the *économistes*. He also wanted a "good price" for grain to encourage agricultural expansion. He was not a deflationist. On the contrary, he believed that the steady but moderate rise in the price level during the century aided economic development of the country. In fact, this moderate inflation led

24. "Sur La Législation et le commerce des grains," p. 277.
25. Ernest Labrousse et al., *Histoire économique et sociale de la France,* 2 vols. Vol. II: *Des Dernier Temps de l'âge seigneurial aux préludes de l'âge industriel (1660-1789)* (Paris, 1970), p. 392, 401-405.

him to think that the government debt was not too alarming, because the inflation contributed in some measure to its amortization. Nor did the moderate inflation harm workers, because wages would necessarily follow prices. What was dangerous was the sudden spurt in the price of grain due to the vagaries of the season or other accidental causes. In that case wages could not follow the price of subsistence. Necker wanted to even out the sharp fluctuations by control of exports. He believed that the "good price" for landowners could be achieved by less dangerous means than absolute freedom of export. He advocated the elimination of internal restrictions on trade, such as the rights of *péages,* and *leyde*—taxes that private persons levied on goods passing through waterways, roads, and markets.

So we are brought back to the question: why did Necker's book cause such a furor? It seems to have been due to his insistence that the government must take responsibility to assure the minimum subsistence of the working class, "the most numerous class of the king's subjects." Necker was appalled by the pronouncement of the Parlement of Toulouse, at that time a fervent believer in the doctrines of Quesnay, that "the king does not owe his people subsistence."[26] Better to let the people starve, the magistrates seemed to say, than to infringe upon the sacred rights of property or to meddle with the natural laws of economics! It was a dangerous doctrine and Necker felt instinctively that, if it should prevail in the king's council, the consequences could be catastrophic. He understood as few did the deep-seated conviction in the population that the price of bread cannot be allowed to rise above the critical level.

As in the case of the Company of the Indies, events after 1775 surely vindicated Necker's position. Hardly any government today refuses to take responsibility for the supply of grain. Both liberal and socialist democracies take charge of importing grain and stockpiling it when there is a shortage. The activities of speculators are supervised, and those contrary to the public interest are curtailed. Even in a wealthy exporting country like the United States criticism can be aroused by the rise in bread prices caused by gigantic grain exports such as those to Soviet Russia in 1972.

In recent years, studies have been made on the question of subsistence in the last years of the *ancien régime.* One by R. B. Rose describes the constant schism in opinion on subsistence in the last quarter of the eighteenth century in France. The leaders were all imbued with the principles of free trade, which even Jacobins were reluctant to give up. But the popular classes insisted it was the government's responsibility to control the cost of living.[27] In June 1787 the ministry of Loménie de Brienne passed an edict granting free and unlimited export of grain throughout the kingdom. Early the following summer France experienced the worst crop disaster of the century, due to drought followed by

26. "Sur La Législation et le commerce des grains," p. 269.
27. R. B. Rose, "The French Revolution and the Grain Supply," *Bulletin of the John Rylands Library,* 39 (September 1956), 171-187.

hail storms. Incredibly, the Brienne ministry continued to permit unlimited export of grain throughout the summer of 1788. It was not until October, a little more than a month after he was recalled to the government, that Necker succeeded in repealing the law of June 1787. Historians agree that the crop failure and severe grain shortage had an important influence on events in 1789.

In his chapter devoted to the physiocrats in *The Wealth of Nations,* published in 1776, Adam Smith remarked:

That system which represents the products of land as the sole source of the revenue and wealth of every country has, so far as I know, never been adopted by any nation, and it at present exists only in the speculations of a few men of great learning and ingenuity in France. It would not, surely, be worth while to examine at great length the errors of a system which never has done, and probably never will do any harm in any part of the world. I shall endeavor to explain, however, as distinctly as I can, the great outlines of this ingenious system.[28]

Unlike Keynes, the Scottish philosopher may have seriously underestimated the harm that can be done by a "few men of great learning and ingenuity." It was not only on the question of subsistence for the working class, but on the general reform movement in France preceding the Revolution that the inflexibility of the Physiocrats revealed itself. Here also Necker was at loggerheads with the doctrinaires.

28. New York, 1937, p. 627.

Chapter V

THE REFORM MOVEMENT
IN FRANCE, 1763-1781

The five years of Necker's first ministry (1776–1781) were part of a general reform movement of about twenty years' duration carried on by the finance ministers of France following the disastrous defeat of the Seven Years' War. Necker's ministry can be seen as the culmination of this movement. The reaction against reform began immediately with his successor in 1781. Joly de Fleury and Calonne were basically hostile to the reform.[1] "Reform movements," like other historians' constructions, need to be defined. They may be said to exist when an important number of people in positions of power and influence are convinced that change is essential. When sovereigns, their ministers and generals, the wealthy, the intellectual and artistic elites—those whom one would ordinarily expect to be perfectly satisfied with the status quo—begin to advocate and support reform, it is evident they have been moved by some powerful force.

The outcome of the mid-eighteenth-century wars between France and Great Britain jolted the complacency of many such people in France. Great Britain obviously was surpassing her rival in several important ways. The traditional valor and proficiency of the French in arms was no longer decisive. In overseas settlements in North America, in the commercial exploitation of the colonies, in technological and industrial innovation, in development of a more productive agriculture, France was making progress, but was being outdistanced by her rival. Above all, the Seven Years' War had revealed unmistakably the fiscal helplessness and incompetence of the French government in comparison with the British. Great Britain had about one-third the population and land area of France, yet the British were able to finance the war by loans on a scale that baffled the French. "British public credit is one of the wonders of the world," wrote Isaac Panchaud in 1781.[2] The eighteenth-century wars were financed by the British

---

1. It is usually thought that Calonne was a reform minister. For a contrary view, see J. F. Bosher, *French Finances, 1770-1795: From Business to Bureaucracy* (Cambridge, 1970), p. 145. Concerning the reform of the central administration of finance, at least, Bosher says Calonne was a "major opponent."

2. Benjamin Panchaud, *Réflexions sur l'état actuel du crédit de l'Angleterre et de la France*, p. 5.

largely through loans, rather than by increased taxation.[3] The French government during the Seven Years' War attempted to imitate the British example, with disappointing results. Government loans were marketed with difficulty even though offered at very favorable terms to investors. Taxes were increased hastily and incautiously, chiefly at the expense of classes traditionally exempt. But this did not improve the credit posture of the government, and it aroused determined resistance in the sovereign courts, especially the Parlement of Paris. There is probably little doubt that financial matters as much as the fortunes of battle led France to the conference table and the humiliating peace settlement of 1763. In its ability to finance war by credit, the British government had achieved what in modern parlance is called a technological breakthrough.

Of course, finances had always been a crucial element in European warfare since the rise of the professional standing armies at the beginning of the modern age. But the conditions of the eighteenth-century duel between France and Great Britain placed greater importance on money than ever before. These were largely naval wars fought in several theaters: the Mediterranean, the North Sea, the Atlantic, the Caribbean, and the Indian Ocean. If one were to plot on a graph the increase of funds appropriated in wartime by France and Great Britain, the line for naval expenditures would curve sharply upward, far above that for land armies. Naval war had become hyperbolic, to use the expression of a present-day author describing "total war" in the twentieth century.[4]

It was realized that a government's credit was directly related to its regular, annual income. The major source of income was from taxes. But this posed another anomaly for French statesmen. Writing in 1776, Adam Smith noted that England supported a tax burden of about 10 million pounds sterling (around 240 million livres tournois), "without its being possible to say that any particular order is oppressed." France had a population and land area roughly three times that of England; her land was fertile in resources, her geography favorable to trade, her population as industrious and intelligent as that of England. Then why should a tax burden of 15 million pounds sterling (360 million livres tournois) be such a hardship? There was no question in Smith's mind but that it was. "The people of France . . . it is generally acknowledged, are much more oppressed by taxes than the people of Great Britain."[5]

Fiscal reform was the primary, although not the only objective of the twenty-year reform movement in France following the Seven Years' War. The economic theories of Quesnay and his disciples were motivated first of all by a concern for the fiscal problems of the royal government.[6] Henri Bertin, controller general from 1759 to 1763, was the first of the finance ministers to be

3. J. E. D. Binney, *British Public Finance and Administration, 1774-1792* (Oxford, 1958), p. 106.

4. Raymond Aron, *The Century of Total War* (Boston, 1955), p. 19.

5. Adam Smith, *The Wealth of Nations,* pp. 856-857.

6. J. Conan, "Les Débuts de l'école physiocratique. Un Faux Départ: L'Echec de la réforme fiscale," *Revue d'histoire économique et social,* 36 (1958), 45-63.

influenced by the theories of the physiocrats. His successor, Clément-Charles Laverdy, came to the post from the Parlement of Paris; he is usually thought to have been an opponent of the movement, but recent studies have revealed his importance as a reform minister.[7] The financial ministry of Joseph-Marie Terray (1769–1774) is said by some to have been the most important of all the ministries for financial reform during the twenty-year period.[8] But most historians today would probably single out Terray's successor, Anne-Robert-Jacques Turgot, as the most brilliant and promising reform statesman of the *ancien régime.* His fall from power in 1776 is often said to have been "the last chance for the *ancien régime* to reform itself without revolution." Due to the towering eminence of Turgot, the ministry of Jacques Necker, who came to the *contrôle général* six months after the fall of Turgot, has not been taken very seriously. The opinion of Marcel Marion has tended to rule on this matter as on so many others. In the first volume of his financial history of France, Marion wrote:

Between the vast projects of Turgot and the mean expedients of the Genevan banker, the difference is so great, and the opposition so clear cut, that it is an outrage to truth to associate the latter, devoid of any general ideas and incapable of rising above petty details, among the statesmen who attempted to prevent a violent revolution by peaceful means.[9]

The injustice of these remarks will be apparent to anyone who takes the trouble to read Necker's ample writings on reform. These will be discussed in the following chapter. But it can be remarked here that it is a peculiar position from which Marion judges the reform ministers. It is doubtful that any of them were consciously attempting to prevent a violent revolution, which few anticipated in those years. It is true that there were popular disturbances, and that both Turgot and Necker were concerned about the alienation of public opinion from the administrative monarchy. Both sought to heal the schism by fiscal reform. But whether reform might have prevented the Revolution is so hypothetical that some have called it a false question.

The reform ministers in this period differed among themselves in their analysis of the problems of fiscal reform and their approach to it. But they had the same objective in mind: namely, to put the royal finances on a sound basis. Their thinking about methods had much in common. They all believed it essential to balance ordinary government expenditures with regular, dependable income.[10] This required slashing expenditures wherever possible, particularly for

7. Maurice Bordes, "La Réforme municipale du contrôleur-général Laverdy et son application dans certain provinces," *Revue d'histoire moderne et contemporaine,* 12 (October-December 1965), 241-270.

8. Marion, *Histoire financière de la France,* I, 259-279; Lucien Laugier, *Un Ministère réformateur sous Louis XV,* pp. 161-343.

9. Marion, *Histoire financière de la France,* I, 294.

10. For Terray's views, see his "Mémoire présenté au Roi par M. l'abbé Terray au mois de juillet 1772 à Compiègne," in Charles-Joseph Mathon de la Cour, *Collection de comptes rendus,* 2d ed. (Lausanne, 1788), pp. 69-89.

the court and the royal households, which seemed to be out of control. It was necessary to abandon all the ruinous expedients that had compounded the financial embarrassment of the royal government rather than alleviated it: the creation of superfluous offices, the excessive dependence on the class of financiers who granted short-term loans (anticipations) to the government, the exorbitant terms of the long-range loans. Above all, it was imperative to reform the tax system itself, which had become so patently inequitable that there was a veritable rebellion among the taxpayers, "a civil war between the government and its subjects," as Turgot was to phrase it.[11]

Yet there were differences among the reform ministers over how to realize their common aims. Two contrasting policies may be discerned that were perhaps more tendencies than clear-cut policies. One may be called the reform of enlightened despotism, its opposite the reform of liberalism. Both are troublesome terms when it comes to precise definition. But in general the ministers of enlightened despotism believed that the administrative monarchy could best carry out the reforms. The enlightened, energetic, public-spirited finance minister, seconded by no less capable intendants in the provinces, was best able to carry out the needed reforms. Obstacles to reform lay primarily in the strongly entrenched privileges and exemptions from taxation enjoyed by the nobility, the church, and numerous categories of the third estate. The reformers of enlightened despotism believed this resistance could only be overcome by using all the powers of absolute monarchy. The pained outcries of those suffering from this method would have to be ignored.

The alternative view held by liberal reformers was that the administrative monarchy could not carry out any lasting reform by sheer force. It was necessary to appeal to the enlightened portion of the nation, to "public opinion" as it was understood at the time, if reforms were to be effective. Support for the reform movement must come from outside the government as well as from the minister and the intendants. Those to be enlisted, later called "the notables," were not restricted to any one class; they were to consist of liberal nobles, leaders drawn from the professions, from the bourgeois class of the cities; in short, public-spirited citizens from all estates were to make up the assemblies of notables at both the national and the provincial level. They would act in an advisory role, lending moral support of the public to the efforts of the reform minister.

The financial ministry of Joseph-Marie Terray and the judicial ministry of chancellor René-Nicolas de Maupeou in 1770-1771 probably best illustrate the successes and failures of enlightened despotism. Terray found the government facing bankruptcy. He resolutely slashed expenditures by writing off government obligations to its creditors, transforming *tontines* into ordinary life rentes, reducing interest rates on other types of obligations, reducing pensions paid by

11. Turgot, "Plan d'un mémoire sur les impositions," in Pierre-Samuel Dupont de Nemours, ed., *Oeuvres de M. Turgot: Précédées et accompagnées de mémoires et de notes sur sa vie, son administration et ses ouvrages,* 9 vols. (Paris, 1808-1811), IV, 208.

the government as much as 30 percent, and suspending reimbursement on all loans, including "anticipations" of the Receivers-General (*rescriptions*) and those of the General Farms (*billets*). He appropriated the revenue assigned to the Sinking Fund to pay for current expenditures. These methods were effective, however ruthless. When his successor, Turgot, came to the finance ministry in August 1774, he found that the budgetary situation, in the words of a present-day biographer, was "no longer dramatic."[12]

The judicial reform of chancellor Maupeou was no less ruthless. Recalcitrant judges of the Parlement of Paris and other sovereign courts saw their offices liquidated and the system of venality for their replacements abolished. Among the courts that ceased to exist and whose members were exiled during the regime of Maupeou was the Paris Court of *Aides,* the traditional court of last resort for all litigation concerning royal finances. The powers of remonstrance and of obstruction of royal legislation were firmly curtailed. Appellate courts were instituted in which not only venality but gifts (*épices*) to judges by litigants were outlawed. Maupeou's reform was a harbinger of the National Constituent Assembly.

Yet despite their efficiency and benevolence, the historian cannot but be struck by the intense hostility of the public toward the Terray-Maupeou ministry. R. R. Palmer writes:

To the modern observer today nothing is clearer than that the Bourbon monarchy, in the generation before the Revolution, seriously attempted to solve the basic problem of French society, the existence of special privileges based on legal stratification or hierarchy; and nothing is more remarkable than that the French public, bourgeois and intellectuals, seldom saw this to be the issue. . . .[13]

It was not only those classes, but porters and stall-holders at the Halles who cheered the return of the Parlement of Paris in October 1774, six months after the beginning of the new reign.[14] It appears that Louis XV himself, prior to his death in April 1774, had come to consider the Maupeou reform a mistake and was preparing for the return of at least some magistrates of the Parlement of Paris.[15]

Some historians, no doubt the majority at present, believe there was no course between enlightened despotism and revolution. The basic contradiction they see in what is described above as the liberal reform is that the notables were the chief beneficiaries of the system of privilege; therefore, they could hardly be expected to agree to what had to be done, namely, abolish their tax exemptions. So strongly has this view prevailed that many are hardly aware of the existence of an alternative method of reform to that of enlightened despotism. Regardless

12. Faure, *La Disgrâce de Turgot,* p. 151.
13. R. R. Palmer, *The Age of the Democratic Revolution: A Political History of Europe and America, 1760-1800* (Princeton, 1959), I, 89.
14. J. H. Shennan, *The Parlement of Paris* (Ithaca, N.Y., 1968), pp. 319-320.
15. Jean Egret, *Louis XV et l'opposition parlementaire* (Paris, 1970), p. 228.

of the merit of the liberal reform program, it is worth investigating, whether it confirms the prevailing view or alters it. The reason for taking up the subject here is that Necker was the foremost of the liberal reformers.

It is possible that what public opinion wanted in the third quarter of the eighteenth century in France did not match exactly what historians of the French Revolution have wanted for it. Efficiency and energy in the governmental administration, development of the modern state, free enterprise, economic growth, the building of canals and the enlargement of seaports—these were no doubt good things that the administrative monarchy in the reform era attempted to implement. But public opinion also talked about such matters as "justice," "liberty," and the "rights of the nation." Above all, public opinion seemed to stress representation and what is now called politicization, that is, the right of citizens to take an active part in the management of their affairs rather than leaving them to agents of the royal government. Maupeou's work, and that of Terray also, however admirable, greatly increased the power of the intendants in the provinces, and of the ministers of the king. It ignored the Parlement of Paris' view that, in the absence of other means of representation in the *pays d'élection,* the sovereign courts were the natural protectors of the people against the arbitrary authority of the king's ministers and intendants. Neither Maupeou nor Terray ever thought the government should seek ways to appease this demand for representation or to recognize the need to permit the king's subjects to contradict the intendant and his agents. The fact was that the educated portion of the nation—"public opinion," whatever might have been its source in the second half of the eighteenth century—was not disposed to accept despotism, however enlightened or benevolent.

Perhaps the best spokesman for liberal reform before Necker was the first president of the Paris Court of Aides, Chrétien-Guillaume Lamoignon de Malesherbes. He had written a number of remonstrances since the beginning of the 1760s that protested abuses of power by the administrative monarchy, including both the intendants and the General Farms that administered the indirect taxes. In these remonstrances some of the reactionary themes of the parlements were espoused, but just as often the cause of the poor and defenseless was their object. As a magistrate, Malesherbes became well known for his defense of victims of *lettres de cachet:* innocent persons arrested by agents of the General Farm on suspicion of salt or tobacco smuggling and buried for months in the notorious *cachots* of Paris prisons. Today Malesherbes is best remembered for his advocacy of civil rights for Protestants and Jews and for his defense of the encyclopedists and of freedom of the press and of expression. Yet this unquestioned liberal was bitterly hostile to the Maupeou reform and led the Court of Aides into determined resistance to it in the spring of 1771. The result was the dissolution of the court and exile of its magistrates, who shared the fate of the Parlement of Paris. The Court of Aides returned with the Parlement of Paris in October 1774. Malesherbes resumed his office as first president, and began again writing remonstrances.

In April 1775, he read to the Court of Aides a remonstrance that a short time later was published against the express order of the keeper of the seals, Hue de Miromesnil. It was written for and addressed to the young king, Louis XVI, who had come to the throne about a year before. The remonstrance was written in as simple and readable style as possible to keep the attention of the person to whom it was directed. It was as good a document as any to reveal the thought of a person who rejected enlightened despotism, but was nevertheless enlightened.[16]

Malesherbes wrote that Oriental despotism was historically alien to the French and totally unfit for them in their present stage of civilization. He defined despotism as a regime where there is no defense of subjects against the arbitrary will of the sovereign, where there is no remedy against injustice. Frenchmen had always considered themselves free men, even under the most absolute of monarchies, for a monarchy holds three defenses against despotism: written laws available to all; a court system independent of the government and providing a right of appeal from judgments of lower courts; and finally, restraints on judges themselves by public opinion. A highly educated and sensitive people, such as the French, would vigorously protest flagrant acts of arbitrary power or patent injustice toward individuals.

The liberty of Frenchmen, Malesherbes continued, had been jeopardized by events beginning in the previous century. Most important was the cessation of meetings of the States-General and the various provincial assemblies in all but a few of the provinces. Even in the latter, the *pays d'états,* the powers of the assemblies have been more and more restricted, he said. When the assemblies of estates ceased to convene, the king had said that the sovereign courts of magistrates would stand in their place as the defender of French liberties. But jurisdiction of these courts has constantly diminished as more and more classes of cases move to the royal councils or are decided by intendants. In the *pays d'élections* the *élus,* who formerly administered the *élections,* are now brought under the authority of the intendants. Communities or communes at the primary level are under the authority of the intendant's subdelegate. An example of the despotic use of administrative power was the initiation of the royal *corvée* in 1738 by the controller general, Philibert Orry. This was not promulgated by any official act of the king or of the royal council, nor registered by the *parlements.* Orry simply wrote a circular letter to the intendants authorizing them to conscript peasant labor for road and bridge construction.

The worst part of this growth of administrative jurisdiction, Malesherbes maintained, has been its secrecy, both in hearing cases and in making decisions. So much of the work of justice has devolved upon the ministers and the intendants that they cannot possibly keep abreast of it. The result is that decisions involving the fortunes and the lives of citizens are decided by underlings—unknown, faceless, authoritative secretaries (*commis*). No publicity is

16. [Chrétien-Guillaume Lamoignon de Malesherbes], *Protest of the Cour des Aides of Paris: April 10, 1775,* ed. James H. Robinson, trans. Grace R. Robinson (Philadelphia, 1899).

given to their hearings or their decisions. The subdelegate of the intendant has no formal status; everything he does is over the signature of the intendant. Yet those people actually do most of the work in provincial government. The same is true in the central government, where the responsibilities of the controller general have increased enormously, but he is unable to give personal attention to more than a small fraction of the business that passes under his signature. Especially singled out by the remonstrance were the six intendants of finance who decided most of the judicial cases that came before the council of finance. Each was assigned a particular category of cases, and he decided them alone, without any contradiction being permitted.

The remonstrance of 1775 attacked not only the administration of the controller general and his intendants, but also that enormous bureaucratic apparatus, the Royal General Farms. The remonstrance alleged that the company leasing the General Farms made enormous profits, at the expense of both the king and the taxpayers. Some indirect taxes collected by the company were themselves harmful to the well-being of the population, but the manner of enforcement made them especially odious. It was the tax derived from the government's salt monopoly (the *gabelle*) that came under particular attack in the remonstrance. The artificially high price of salt maintained in the provinces under the regime of the *grandes gabelles* tended to deprive the population of a necessary and healthful item of diet. The bitterest remarks of the remonstrance described the arbitrary and brutal methods by which the company of the General Farms exacted this tribute. While the price was excessively high in the provinces controlled by the *grandes gabelles,* it was at its natural market level in bordering provinces entirely free of the *gabelle.* The disparity created a powerful temptation to smuggle free salt into the provinces of the *grandes gabelles.* The General Farms company, by contract, had the administrative means of enforcing the payment of the salt tax and policing the frontiers of the *grandes gabelles* provinces with its own agents, organized into military companies. According to the remonstrance, this police power was used without restraint, and without guarantees of justice for those caught in the net. Inspectors had the right to enter any home and search for contraband salt.

Since there was a continual war between those engaged in contraband and the General Farm, many suspects were arrested. "If, during one of these visits, the agents believe they have discovered a fraud, they draw up an indictment, which, if signed by two agents, places the burden of proof on the accused to escape punishment." The agents were permitted to arrest suspects by *lettre de cachet,* that is, authorization to imprison them without explanation, without any right to counsel or to be taken before a magistrate. The penalties for contraband were ferocious: life sentences to the galleys were frequent; high fines were imposed, and informers were given a share of the proceeds. This use of private informants was a fertile source of miscarriage of justice, according to the remonstrance.

Again, as in the administration of justice by the intendants and the minister of finance, the General Farms' greatest evil was its secrecy. The arrested had no right to a public trial, to counsel, or of appeal. The Court of Aides was normally the court of appeal for those accused of violation of the fiscal laws. But much of its jurisdiction was now assumed by the royal council, or by the intendants. Even if the accused had rights of counsel, the sinuosity of the tax laws and regulations permitted any abuse on the part of the *commis*. Because the law and regulations governing the royal taxes were both unknown to the public and of extreme complexity, the ordinary person had no defense against "the caprice, the haughtiness and the insults" of the agents of the Farm.

Turning its attention to the direct taxes collected by the royal government, the remonstrance expressed grievances similar to those in the case of the indirect taxes. The royal council fixed arbitrarily the sums to be levied. The assessment among the generalities, *élections*, and parishes was done secretly, so no one knew what his neighbor paid. The remonstrance condemned the exemptions from the *taille* enjoyed by the nobility. Fiscal privileges may have had some justification in a remote feudal age when the nobles served the king gratuitously in his army, but that excuse had long ceased to exist. The other two taxes, the *capitation* and *vingtième*, did not legally exempt the nobility. Yet in actual practice, "the poor and helpless are harassed on the pretext that it is in the interests of the king; and the powerful are favored and winked at against the interests of the king." Ministerial despotism was the natural ally of the rich and powerful. The ministers often had interests in granting favors to this class, but none at all in the welfare of the poor. It was the king who was the natural ally of the people against the clandestine and arbitrary power of the ministers.

How to restore this natural alliance between king and people was the principal concern of the remonstrance of 1775. "The surest means, the simplest and the most natural, and that which is in conformity with the constitution of this monarchy, would be [for the king] to listen to the Nation itself assembled, or at least to permit assemblies in each province." Through the establishment of representative provincial assemblies the evils of the fiscal system could be remedied:

We ask that all the taxes without exception, which are levied each year in the provinces may be there considered—not only the *taille* and the accessories, but the *capitation*, the *vingtième*, the sums levied for the building of the presbyteries, and even the militia and the *corvée*.[17]

No details were given on the organization of these assemblies, but the remonstrance indicated that they should be representative, that the people should have a right to name their deputies.

Such was the great remonstrance of the Court of Aides of 1775. When James Harvey Robinson published an English language translation of it in 1899, he remarked that "the rare pamphlet here reprinted furnishes us with a singularly clear and authentic picture of the French government before the Revolution."[18]

17. *Ibid.*, p. 43.
18. Introduction, *Protest of the Cour des Aides of Paris*, p. iii.

Four years later Marcel Marion published an article denouncing the remonstrance as "demagogic and irresponsible," maintaining that it was nothing but special pleading for the privileged classes and the tax-exempt.[19] This is surely a partisan view. Undeniably, much of the protest about "despotism" from the sovereign courts and particularly the Parlement of Paris was so motivated. But to insist that all such protests were nothing but conservative resistance to the laudable reform efforts of the administrative monarchy is to blot out from our view a large part of the reform movement. Marion's lack of sympathy for liberal reform, indeed his complete denial of it, explains his contempt for Necker. No document written by another hand expressed so well Necker's own ideas on reform as the great remonstrance of 1775.[20]

What might have given Marion pause was that the author of the great remonstrance, Malesherbes, was a good friend of Turgot. In July 1775, only a few months after he had written the remonstrance, Malesherbes entered the government as secretary of state for the king's household. The king was induced to make this appointment by Turgot. Malesherbes strongly supported Turgot's six edicts in February 1776, which the Parlement of Paris as strongly opposed. In the above-cited article Marion argued that Turgot rejected most of the theses of the remonstrance, and suggested that the document may not have expressed Malesherbes' ideas either! Equally dubious was Marion's view that Turgot was a worthy successor of abbé Terray in carrying out the reform of enlightened despotism. Contrary to a long-held assumption, Turgot did not oppose the return of the Parlement of Paris in October 1774.[21] There is much that is obscure about Turgot's political thought, for he wrote very little on that subject.[22] Yet he probably was not a proponent of either enlightened despotism or liberalism in the manner of Malesherbes. He was unique in the history of the reform movement and must be treated separately.

Turgot was an *économiste,* and his reform bore the heavy imprint of the "sect." He did not like labels and sometimes protested that he was neither an *économiste* nor an *encyclopédiste,* even though he made many contributions to the *Encyclopedia* on economic matters. It is true that he was as much influenced by the ideas of Vincent de Gournay as those of Quesnay. Turgot was never a good sectarian. He was much less inclined to be doctrinaire and inflexible when it came to practical applications of his theories than were his friends and advisors. He was hardly touched by the political philosophy of the marquis de Mirabeau and Mercier de la Rivière, with their enthusiastic endorsement of enlightened despotism. He was less doctrinaire than his lifelong disciple and

19. Marcel Marion, "Turgot et les grandes remontrances de la cour des aides (1775)," *Vierteljahrschrift für Social und Wirtschaftsgeschichte,* I (1903), 303-313.

20. Pierre Grosclaude, *Malesherbes: Témoin et interprète de son temps,* 3 vols., (Paris, 1961), II, 323.

21. Faure, *La Disgrâce de Turgot,* p. 143.

22. Gerald J. Cavanaugh, "Turgot: The Rejection of Enlightened Despotism," *French Historical Studies,* 6 no. 1 (Spring 1969), 31-58.

collaborator, Dupont de Nemours. Nevertheless, Turgot accepted the basic theses of the *économistes:* the belief that economic expansion was the major goal, and the notion that agriculture alone produced a clear profit, and that the proprietors who rent land were the disposers of surplus wealth.[23]

It was this idea of clear profit that determined the *économistes'* attitude toward the government's fiscal system. Since the proprietors alone received the net revenue (what remained after paying all costs of production), then it was axiomatic that the government should look to that class as the only source for tax contributions. The *économiste* tax policy was simple and categorical: a tax on the net income of proprietors should be the single source of government revenue. It was demonstrated in the "zig-zag" that only the proprietors could pay taxes anyway. Both direct and indirect taxes were ultimately paid by the recipients of the net profit from agriculture, the only "true income." But it made a great deal of difference to the health of the economy how the government siphoned off its share of the national income. By its fiscal policy, the government could greatly foster or seriously hinder economic growth. The key person in the *Tableau économique* of Quesnay was the one who farmed the land directly—who leased the land from the proprietor, invested capital in improvements, and thereby increased production. These were the true entrepreneurs of the agricultural revolution. The latter expression was not yet coined, but it was the English "farmer," the equivalent of the French *fermier,* who was the model of the physiocrats. In the ideal economy of the physiocrats, almost all arable land was under cultivation of this enlightened class of exploiters of the soil. It will be remembered that the proprietor class also provided capital for longer-range development of agriculture, and thus justly received the clear profit in the form of rent. But the short-term capital investment was the most crucial in France, and this was provided by the *fermiers.*

It followed from this analysis that it was extremely important for the government to protect and encourage the investment of capital in the land. The dissatisfaction of the physiocrats for the existing fiscal system was evident. The farmers were subject to the *taille* and paid it directly to the tax collectors. It was true that they deducted this tax as an expense of cultivation, and that it therefore was subtracted from the rent they paid proprietors. But the evil of the *taille* was that it was levied on the farmers with no regard to capital invested in the land. Since the *taille* was arbitrarily assessed, the farmer who invested in improvements was apt to attract the attention of the tax gatherers, especially if there was a shortage in collection and the principle of collective liability had to be invoked. Only the richer farmers could invest in capital improvements, and they were often the victims of the arbitrary system of administration of the *taille.* The uncertainty of what his assessment would be in the coming year made it difficult for the farmer to calculate his operations. Sometimes the risks of

23. Edgar Faure, "Turgot et la théorie du produit net," *Revue d'histoire économique et sociale,* 39 (1961), 283ff.

heavy assessment were computed in the terms of the lease, and the proprietor bore the risk. But usually the farmer was inhibited in the extent of agricultural expansion he was willing to undertake.[24]

Other types of taxation also thwarted the entrepreneur. Sales taxes, excise taxes, and transit duties impeded the free flow of commerce. Freedom of trade was a prerequisite for the *Tableau économique* to function properly. Land sale taxes and various registration taxes were levied against capital rather than profits and therefore hampered economic growth. Not only royal taxes but also the church's tithe and various forms of seigneurial dues were also paid by the farmers out of gross revenue. Church revenue, like royal revenue, should come directly from the proprietors. As for the various feudal dues still levied by the owners of fiefs, the physiocrats wanted to eliminate them all, either by purchase, if these dues were a form of property, or by abolition without indemnity if they were considered to have originated by abuses of personal power.

The preoccupation of the *économistes* with the "single tax" meant that they did not seriously consider reform of the *taille* or the indirect taxes. These were not to be reformed, but abolished. As a consequence, little was accomplished in Turgot's ministry with respect to those taxes. The collective liability of the parish for the full amount of the *taille* was abolished by Turgot in 1775. There is evidence that he was interested in the reform of the *vingtième,* and initiated a plan carried out later by Necker.[25] But nothing was accomplished in the direction of a single land tax.

Exactly how this fundamental revolution in the fiscal system was to be carried out can be seen in the "Memorial on Municipalities" written by Dupont de Nemours in late August 1775. Turgot had asked his friend and collaborator to draw up a plan for representative assemblies of landowners who would take over from the intendants and their agents the function of assessing the royal taxes. The memorial was written about a month after Malesherbes entered the government as secretary of state for the king's household. It does not appear that Malesherbes was consulted about the writing of the "Memorial on Municipalities," but it did contain one of the important requests of the remonstrance of the Court of Aides published in April, namely that the taxes be administered by the taxpayers themselves instead of by intendants, subdelegates, commissioners of the *taille,* and controllers of the *vingtième.* The memorial provided for a complete recording of landed income, the universal cadastre sought by Bertin in 1763. It would eliminate the arbitrary system of assessment and collection of the *taille* and the *vingtième.* The accurate recording of the wealth in landed income of the different parishes, *élections,* and generalities would make it possible for the "municipalities" to apportion the burden in accordance with the taxpaying ability of each.

24. Turgot, "Plan d'un Mémoire sur les Impositions," Dupont, ed., *Oeuvres de Turgot,* IV, 207ff.
25. See Chapter XI.

To what extent the "Memorial on Municipalities" reflected faithfully Tur-got's ideas is uncertain. When he received the work in September, Turgot wrote Dupont saying that it was somewhat more explicit and detailed than he had intended, and he proposed that they revise it in October. Whether this was done is not known. The text that has come down to us is that of Dupont, together with some notes on what points Turgot wished revised.[26] But there can be little doubt that the document's basic outline was approved by Turgot. He had reflected for fifteen years on how to establish such a system of representative assemblies. Condorcet, another loyal collaborator of the controller general, wrote that the ideas in the memorial were Turgot's ideas.[27]

While the principal objective of the municipalities was fiscal reform, the memorial of Dupont expressed ideas of broader scope. It was not enough to eliminate inequitable and arbitrary assessment of taxes that hindered economic growth. It was also necessary to reform the public's attitude toward taxation. Education of children was still largely a church function; this meant that the French were raised as Christians but not as citizens. They had little understand-ing of what they owed the state in return for its benefits; there was little sense of patriotism or attachment to the royal government or the nation. Loyalties were largely local, confined to the family or the parish or province. Turgot and Dupont de Nemours proposed a national educational council that would assume complete responsibility for education, directing all universities, colleges, and lesser schools, down to the schoolmaster to be placed in each parish. Instruction would be uniform and the same textbooks would be used. This national council would also supervise letters and make certain that writers and poets used their talents not frivolously but usefully, to inculcate virtue and patriotism. The king was promised that such an institution would "lead to the formation in all classes of society of virtuous and useful men, with pure hearts, a sense of justice, and who would be public-spirited citizens." Like much of the literature of the "sect," the "Memorial on Municipalities" had a strongly utopian flavor. It promised fabulous results if the king would adopt the scheme. "In ten years' time the nation would be unrecognizable. . . . In enlightenment, in good morals, in zeal for your service and that of the fatherland [the French] would surpass all other people who exist or who have ever existed."[28]

After this introduction the memorial turned to the subject of the "munici-palities" and their organization. These representative assemblies of landowners were to be created on four levels. The primary assemblies would be at the parish level, the secondary assemblies at the *élection* level, and the third assemblies at the capital city of the province or generality; the dome of the edifice would be the "great municipality of the kingdom," a national assembly of landowners.

26. Dupont de Nemours, "Mémoire sur les municipalités: Septembre 1775. Au Roi," *Correspondance inédite de Dupont de Nemours et du marquis de Mirabeau avec le margrave et le prince héréditaire de Bade,* ed. Carl Knies, 2 vols. (Heidelberg, 1892), I, 245ff.

27. *Oeuvres de Turgot,* ed. Schelle, IV, 676.

28. Dupont de Nemours, "Mémoire sur les municipalités," p. 249.

The function of these assemblies would be to receive from the royal council the sum of tax revenue to be levied, and then to distribute it among the generalities, *élections,* and parishes. They would also assume responsibility for social welfare and road maintenance at the local level. Nothing was said in the memorial about the intendants, or about the permanent administrative bodies that would carry out the decisions of the assemblies.

The representation in all assemblies was based strictly on landownership, determined with arithmetical precision. Each seat in the primary assembly would represent a landed income of 600 livres. Large landowners would control a number of seats determined by their income divided by 600. Small landowners whose composite income equaled 600 livres would select a deputy. The parish assembly would send deputies to the *élection* and the latter to the assembly of the generality; the national assembly would consist of deputies from the generalities. The rationale for basing representation on landed income was strictly physiocratic. Society was divided into those who paid wages and salaries and those who received them. The landowners alone disposed of the net product; all others, even merchants, professional people, bankers, artists, scholars, were hirelings, ultimately, of the landed proprietors.

The prejudice in favor of landed proprietors seemed to be even more deep-seated than economic theory alone might suggest. Only landowners were truly citizens because only they had a permanent interest in society and the state. All others were birds of passage. The artisan, the merchant, the day laborer, were here today and gone tomorrow. Even the owner of a building in the city who received rent from it was not really a citizen, because the building depreciated in the course of a century. The rent from buildings represented interest income from invested capital, not true rent. Only the land beneath the buildings should be considered in determining the representation of urban citizens in the assemblies. The urban landowners should possess land valued at 18,000 livres in order to have a vote in the parish assemblies. The memorial noted with satisfaction that the number of Parisians who could qualify would not be more than forty. In the assembly of the *élection,* each parish and city would be restricted to a single deputy, with the exception of the capital cities of provinces, which would be allowed two deputies, and Paris, which would be allowed four. But it was stated that this was a concession to prejudice rather than reason. The assemblies of the provinces and the "national municipality" would take no notice at all of the cities. When one thinks of the role Paris was to play in the coming Revolution, this passage of the memorial verges on the comic.

In his biography of Turgot, published in 1811, Dupont de Nemours maintained that Turgot had intended to present this plan of provincial assemblies before the royal council in the autumn of 1775 so that it could be used for assessing taxes the following year. Unfortunately, said Dupont, the popular disturbances of the Flour War in the spring of 1775 delayed implementation of the plan for another year. Dupont wrote that Turgot definitely planned to introduce the plan in October 1776, and only his fall from power in May prevented it.[29] Realistically, what chance was there that the king, Maurepas, the royal council, the Parlement, the privileged orders, and the landowners would all have accepted the plan in 1776? In February of that year the royal council presented Turgot's six edicts to the Parlement for registration. This required a *lit de justice,* for Parlement refused to sanction them otherwise. The most objectionable of the edicts abolished the royal *corvée* and levied a surtax on the *vingtième* to pay for the construction and maintenance of roads. The Parlement insisted that the nobility, subject to the *vingtième,* should not be required to pay for the *corvée,* that this cost should be borne by the *taillables* alone. Turgot's edict on the *corvée* was registered in a *lit de justice* but never implemented. His own position had been seriously undermined with Maurepas and the king by the opposition he had aroused. He was dismissed from his post on May 12, 1776. His successor, Bernard de Clugny, revoked the edict on the *corvée* but left the matter of its reform to the intendants of each generality. In view of these events it is difficult to see how the proposals of the "Memorial on Municipalities" could have been implemented in 1776. The plan for provincial assemblies that Calonne proposed to the Assembly of Notables of 1787 was based on that of Dupont and Turgot. Historians have usually condemned that Assembly for rejecting the plan, but it certainly had good reasons for doing so. Such a schematic, doctrinaire plan could hardly have worked, in the unlikely event that it had been accepted. That Dupont de Nemours could still believe in 1809 in the essential soundness of the scheme is only one more indication that minds captivated by the *esprit de système* are so often unteachable by experience.

It needs to be reiterated that Turgot himself was not a narrow doctrinaire ruled by the *Tableau économique* of Quesnay. He believed in the capitalistic expansion of industry as well as of agriculture. He was more democratic than the "Memorial on Municipalities" would indicate, for he believed that nonproperty-owners should have some means of representation. He was an encyclopedist as well as an *économiste.* That meant he was a true liberal in the modern understanding of that somewhat ambiguous term: he believed in freedom of expression, in the free exchange of ideas as well as of goods. Unlawful and unnecessary constraint on the individual from whatever source, public or private, was repugnant to him. Nor can he be accused of rushing headlong into reform without concern for the difficulties and the formidable opposition he would encounter. His *économiste* friends were frustrated by his hesitations. Even Maurepas expressed dissatisfaction at the slow pace of reform. During his debate early in 1776 with the conservative keeper of the seals, Hue de Miromesnil, on the *corvée,* Turgot wrote: "I know as well as anyone the need to make changes slowly according to the pace which public opinion and the course of events permit."[30] There is evidence that he was not nearly as ready to submit the project on municipalities to the council as Dupont would have us believe. According to the testimony of abbé de Véri, Turgot distrusted the widespread

29. Dupont de Nemours, ed., *Oeuvres de Turgot,* I, 198.
30. *Oeuvres de Turgot,* ed. Schelle, V, 6.

clamor for the institution of provincial assemblies because he thought the demand came from the privileged classes who wanted to use them to serve reactionary interests rather than those of reform. He was aware that in the English provinces of North America colonial assemblies quickly formed a solid union against the British government. The same could happen in France if provincial assemblies were established throughout the kingdom. Turgot was no republican, nor did he want to limit the power of the absolute monarchy. Therefore, the municipalities would not be permitted to question the tax quotas they received, nor to attempt to negotiate a fixed sum, nor to settle *par abonnement* as had the *pays d'état,* the clergy, and some princes of the blood. Turgot's municipalities would apportion the tax burden, not question it. Such was the conservative nature of his governmental reform.

Yet, with all those qualifications, it remains true that Turgot's reform program bore the unmistakable mark of the "sect." There was the belief in the single tax on landed income, the confidence in the economic analysis of the "net profit," and above all, a mind steeped in theory and little inclined to compromise with recalcitrant reality. His inability to meet minds that did not accept the above principles was commented upon by those who knew him well and observed him during his ministry. Abbé de Véri noted that "nature had refused him the art of persuasion. . . . A perfectly enlightened mind, profound knowledge, an integrity without blemish, the most complete unselfishness," such were Turgot's virtues, according to Véri. On the other hand, the abbé remarked: "Inflexibility in his opinions, the lack of tactfulness in accommodating his ideas with his equals, are his failings. Nobody is perfect."[31] More serious than the impression produced upon his equals by such failings was that made on the king. In the summer of 1775, Véri reports the king saying, after a meeting of the royal council with regard to the controller general: "You have heard him: only his friends have merit, and only his ideas are any good."[32]

Neither Turgot's ideas nor his friends served him well during the twenty months of his reform ministry. His *économiste* friends kept urging reforms beyond what he thought was prudent, and the result justified his apprehensions. Malesherbes, who was not an *économiste* but whom Turgot insisted be appointed secretary of state for the king's household, turned out to be a weak administrator. His famous confession after his ministry was probably true: "Mr. Turgot and I had derived all our knowledge from books; we had too little experience of practical affairs."

The principal achievement of Turgot as reform statesman was the freeing of the commerce of agricultural products, chiefly grain and wine, from traditional restrictions. Necker thoroughly approved of this policy and continued it during his ministry. The desirability of fostering freedom of exchange within the boundaries of the kingdom, of eliminating internal transit and customs barriers, was a policy in which the two reform statesmen were of one mind.

31. Joseph-Alphonse de Véri, *Journal de l'abbé de Véri,* ed. Jehan de Witte, 2 vols. (Paris, 1928-1930), I, 253.

32. *Ibid.,* p. 319.

Chapter VI

THE INTENT AND STYLE OF NECKER'S REFORM

Like Turgot's reform ministry, Necker's must be viewed from two perspectives: what he wanted to accomplish and what he achieved. Necker was painfully aware of the discrepancy in his own case. In writing about his first ministry after his departure from office in May 1781, he burst out: "Ah, what might have been accomplished in other circumstances! The heart aches to think about it. I labored during the tempest, keeping the ship afloat, so to speak. The days of peace belonged to others."[1]

France did not officially enter the American War until 1778, but preparations had begun almost at the time Necker was appointed director of the royal treasury in October 1776. As far as the finances were concerned, the following year was "a full year of war."[2] The needs of war obviously took precedence over reform, but in some cases the two went hand in hand. Necker was convinced that the direct taxes could not await reforms that he initiated before the end of 1777. He believed that the tax burden on the people had reached its peak of endurance, and that if war needs should force a rise in taxes, a reformed fiscal structure would be absolutely necessary. Even so, he thought a tax increase should be the very last resort. Of the triple negatives with which Turgot admonished the king in 1774, "no new taxes, no bankruptcy, no loans," Necker wholeheartedly endorsed the first two. But in wartime it was not possible to abide by the third. He believed, however, that the costs of war loans could be met by reducing regular, "ordinary" expenditures and thereby preventing a recourse to additional taxes.

In wartime it was vitally necessary not to tamper with the fiscal system in any way that might cause a momentary diminution in revenue. Reform of most indirect taxes, he thought, would have to await the end of the war. But this did not prevent him from drawing up detailed plans which he was anxious to put into effect as soon as the war ended; he alluded to them briefly in the *Compte rendu* of 1781. In the *Administration of Finances in France*, published in 1784, he described these projects fully. Like Turgot, Necker wrote lengthy preambles

---

1. Necker, *De L'Administration des finances en France*, in *Oeuvres complètes*, IV, 96.
2. Necker, *Compte rendu au roi*, in *Oeuvres complètes*, II, 9.

to all his reform edicts, royal decrees, and declarations, explaining to the public the reasons for each particular measure. His published works, the preambles to royal acts which he authored, and the important "Memorial on Provincial Administration" written in 1778 provide a fairly clear picture of his reform program.

To say that the Genevan banker had "no general views (*vues d'ensemble*)," as Marion has asserted, that he was only a man of "petty expedients," surely does scant justice to the effort Necker put into those projects. It is true that for those minds fascinated by the a priori postulates of the *économistes,* Necker's reform plans might seem uninspiring. In the fourth book of the extensive treatise on fiscal reform published by Guillaume-François Le Trosne in 1779, the author apologized to his readers for the detailed and dreary exposition he had just made of the fiscal system. "Knowledge of the evils that exist is necessary in order to know how to apply the remedy," he explained. But now that they had been through the desert, Le Trosne assured his readers, they were on the threshold of the Promised Land; for the remedies he was about to reveal were wonderfully simple. The good news was already contained in book one of his treatise, where he had set forth the *Tableau économique* of Dr. Quesnay:

However ancient, however numerous are the evils, one will be delighted to see they can have a remedy as certain as it is prompt in the principles I set forth in the first book; and one will be astonished at the facility with which it is possible to regenerate a Nation in an instant, and to make it pass from the most painful state to a state the most prosperous. I dare say that one will find these means so simple that one will no longer look upon the reform as presenting insurmountable difficulties in themselves. They present no more than those which come from the opposition of particular interests; and no one can deny that sovereign authority does have the necessary power to overcome them.[3]

It is worth noting in the above passage both the miraculous cure if the nostrums of the *économistes* were applied, and also the readiness to use the instrument of enlightened despotism if there should be any resistance to them. Le Trosne set forth in meticulous detail how indirect taxes could be abolished and a single land tax on proprietors established in five years. The additional land tax would be light, only a third *vingtième* need be added to the two in existence, plus direct taxes on salt marshes and vineyards. (The latter were to make up for the abolition of the *gabelle* and the *aides.*) There would be slashing cuts in the ordinary expenditures of the royal government. The budget for the king's household would be cut in half, from 40 to 20 million livres. Pensions granted by the king would be reduced to 8 million livres. The king's debts would be pared by one-fifth in an operation similar to that of abbé Terray in 1770. In this way the debt would be entirely eliminated and the expenditures greatly reduced, and the taxes would all come from the net product of agriculture. Le Trosne set

3. Guillaume-François Le Trosne, *De L'Administration provinciale et de la réforme de l'impôt* (Basle, 1779), p. 277.

forth this project with detailed figures that he admitted were often conjectural. In fact, he was badly informed about the king's ordinary revenue and expenditures.

It was against such authors that Necker had to compete in setting forth his own reform program to the public. "I will hazard the observation," he wrote in 1784, "that in no country is exaggeration in reform projects quite so seductive as in France, and at the same time, no country where the carrying out of reforms more resisted."[4]

The leitmotif in Necker's writings and in his acts as reform minister could be expressed in a single word: confidence. The goal of all his reforms was to build confidence and trust between the royal government and the people. This was a goal which he shared with Turgot and Malesherbes. The population received benefits from the state in the form of a civil order that guaranteed personal and property rights. The beneficiaries of this order should expect to contribute taxes for it. But they also had a right to be assured that the government would raise no more in taxes than necessary to fulfill the purposes of the state, and that taxes would be levied equitably and without undue cost in their collection. This was manifestly not the case in the France of the *ancien régime,* and the disaccord between taxpayers and government was patent.

Turgot and Necker approached the problem from opposite ends. If the "Memorial on Municipalities" reflected Turgot's ideas, he was much concerned about the ignorance of the taxpayers and their inability to understand why they should pay taxes. Necker believed the government should put its fiscal house in order first. He had a much greater respect for public opinion in the France of his day than did his rivals in the reform movement. One of Turgot's *économiste* friends, Trudaine de Montigny, wrote that "in the public there is neither reason nor principle," reflecting a general attitude of the "sect."[5] Necker looked up to public opinion rather than down on it. He recognized it as an awesome power that had grown up in the eighteenth century along with the expansion of commerce, education, and enlightenment. He was convinced that public opinion had become so powerful in France that it could no longer be ignored even in the most absolute of monarchies. There was no reason, however, why the king could not win the support of this important new force. In fact, there was no alternative. The royal government would either rule with the support of public opinion or attempt to rule against it. He agreed with Malesherbes that the French people in the second half of the eighteenth century were too intelligent, too well educated, too *sensible* to submit to despotism. "Especially in France," Necker wrote in *The Administration of Finances,* "it would be a great and dangerous error to base political power on despotism. It is a scythe which burns the crop, while on the other hand confidence fructifies and expands all means of power and wealth."[6]

4. *De L'Administration des finances,* in *Oeuvres complètes,* IV, 407.
5. Cited by Faure in *La Disgrâce de Turgot,* p. 421.
6. *Oeuvres complètes,* IV, 61.

It is probable that this leitmotif, confidence, was inculcated in Necker during his years as a banker. Few professions brought home so clearly the basis for confidence and the consequences of a lack of it. The use of credit on a large scale by governments was a relatively new phenomenon, accompanying the expansion of commerce in the eighteenth century. Necker wrote that the most powerful of governments was not strong enough to coerce investors. Capital belonged to no country. It crossed the frontiers of strong-armed regimes that attempted to grasp it, and it settled in countries whose governments were moderate and liberal. The only way owners of surplus capital could be induced to invest it was to demonstrate to them that the borrower would return their money intact along with interest. The worst policy was for a government to default on its obligations to creditors.

In his writings Necker often condemned the policies of abbé Terray, although without naming him. Nothing good could be accomplished by violating the rights of property, liberties, and immunities granted to subjects by acts of the royal government. The legacy of Terray's ministry was to cast a pall over the government's credit during the years of the American War. Necker's achievement in financing that war by credit can only be appreciated by an awareness of the damage Terray dealt to the confidence of investors. But his policies may have been necessary at the time, however unfortunate. The moral Necker drew from the experience of 1770 was that a capable finance minister would never permit the government to reach an impasse that required such remedies. Abuse of privileges was another matter. But even in those cases where privileges had been granted imprudently the government could only revoke them through negotiation, and with the consent of their holders. Reform would have to be carried out without despotism. This was the difficult task Necker set for himself.

In winning the confidence of the public, Necker placed great importance on the personal role of the minister of finance, as might be expected of the author of the *Eloge de Colbert.* In France, which lacked a House of Commons where orators could lead public opinion, it was government ministers who performed that role. They could not avoid the limelight; they were, perforce, actors on the public stage. Therefore the personal character of the finance minister, the preeminent official in the domestic government of the country, was all-important. Honesty, openness, unstinting devotion to the public interest, unyielding opposition to unmerited grants from the public treasury—these were the traits of character that Necker thought indispensable.

Only by making himself known to the public could the minister act out this role of leadership. The function of personal publicity was not to glorify the minister but to inform the public of all his operations. Every act of the public official should be published along with a preamble stating its purpose. Particularly in finance, the government should take the public into its confidence. Necker understood that one reason for the power of British public credit was the practice of the British government of submitting its annual budget to Parliament and then publishing it. As will be seen, Necker was the first finance minister of the French government to publish the annual revenues and expenditures, in the famous *Compte rendu* of 1781.

Today these ideas may seem platitudinous, but they were not in the France of the *ancien régime*. One need only read some of the political pamphlets of the time to see that each one of Necker's principles was contradicted and declared to be a dangerous innovation. A prominent magistrate published a lengthy commentary in 1785 on Necker's book on French finances that had appeared the year before. The author, President de Coppons, declared that secrecy, not publicity, was the true principle of the French monarchy.[7] Another writer asserted in a memorial to the king with regard to the publication of the *Compte rendu:* "It will be a long time before Your Majesty heals this wound inflicted upon the dignity of the throne."[8] As for Necker's insistence on mitigating the tax burden on the people through economy of expenditures, it was argued by Calonne, Besenval, and others that such a mean-spirited policy might be suited to a small city-state republic like Geneva but was totally incompatible with the grandeur of the French monarchy.[9] Necker's dramatization of his policies was seen as cheap publicity-seeking. In his biography of Turgot, Dupont de Nemours lauded the modesty of his hero, who maintained a noble reticence about his amelioration of the finances rather than boast about them—an obvious reference to Necker and his *Compte rendu*.[10]

For some reason, historians have tended to perpetuate the image of Necker created by his enemies, that of the Genevan banker ridiculously out of place in the government of Louis XVI. But such a historical assessment would be plausible only if Necker were like one of those pitiable comedians who, despite their most earnest efforts, evoke no response from the audience. This was certainly not Necker's situation. He was the most admired and respected minister of his age. His ideas fell on fertile soil, not only in France but throughout Europe. Visiting royalty sought him out. Czarevitch Paul of Russia and Emperor Joseph of Austria were guests at his estate at Saint-Ouen. After Necker's dismissal in 1781 some sovereigns, among them Joseph of Austria and Catherine of Russia, seriously considered inviting him to serve in their governments. In London, Edmund Burke and other members of Parliament expressed their admiration of his management of French finances. Within France, Necker's success in winning a large sector of the public to the support of his policies was unquestionable. Except for the *économistes,* the philosophes generally ap-

7. Président de Coppons, *Examen de la théorie et pratique de Monsieur Necker dans l'administration des finances de la France* (N.p. 1785.) BN L[b] 39.6290.

8. Jean-Louis Soulavie, *Mémoires historiques et politiques du règne de Louis XVI,* 6 vols. (1801), IV, 149. According to Soulavie the author of the memorial was Vergennes. But this seems highly improbable, given the absurdities in the article and that it does not square with the opinion Vergennes expressed about Necker in his correspondence.

9. See Chapters XII and XIV.

10. Dupont de Nemours, "La Vie et l'oeuvre de M. Turgot," *Oeuvres de M. Turgot,* I, 279.

plauded his reform efforts. Voltaire was a firm supporter of the Genevan, with the one exception of his sharp attack on Necker's book on the grain trade. After that incident, Voltaire resumed his former policy of publicly praising Necker, much to the displeasure of Condorcet.[11] At the time of Voltaire's return to Paris shortly before his death in 1778, Madame Necker took a prominent part in the ceremonies honoring this literary giant of the century. Diderot, Grimm, Buffon, and many other writers of the age were steadfast supporters of Necker. The widespread bewilderment and dismay at Necker's dismissal in 1781 had no counterpart when Turgot left office in 1776. Even more striking a contrast to Necker's position in public esteem was that of abbé Terray, who was finance minister for about the same length of time as Necker and for whom the public had a pronounced aversion.

Necker's leadership in educating the public and using publicity to explain the purposes of royal acts was important in healing that breach between king and people about which he and Turgot were so much concerned. But the institutional changes envisioned by Necker were, after all, the crux of the matter. The best way to cultivate patriotism and loyalty to the royal government was to enlist the people in the government itself. By "the people" Necker did not mean the broad mass, although he had none of the contempt for the multitude so often expressed by the philosophes and the *économistes*. He would enlist the energies and the devotion to public service of those at the local level from whatever walk of life they might be found, whether they were prelates, nobles, retired military officers, lawyers, merchants, or other professionals. It was in this class—the "notables"—that Necker saw the best hope for rallying the most enlightened and influential element of public opinion to support reform. The response of those who took part in the two provincial administrations that Necker established in 1778 and 1779 bore out his expectations.[12]

An important characteristic of Necker's reform was the importance he placed on searching for exact information regarding the social and economic conditions of the kingdom. In the historical writing on the eighteenth century, there has been a school of thought represented by Hippolyte Taine that sees the philosophes as heirs of the classical spirit, with its absorption in general, abstract ideas and its lack of interest in concrete facts. This view has rightly come under fire in recent years, and it can be admitted that Taine exaggerated his point; nevertheless, it would seem to fit the *économistes* to some degree. Necker may be wholly absolved from this failing. A considerable part of his time and effort as finance minister was taken up in the quest for information: for facts and figures on taxation, population, agricultural production, and trade statistics. Much of this information was used in his 1784 treatise *On the Administration of Finances in France*. This work was a phenomenal publishing success for its time, indicating that the reading public was not so given to abstract theories and contempt for

11. Grange, *Les Idées de Necker,* pp. 30-32.
12. See Chapter XI.

factual data as were some of the authors. In any case, Necker had the advantage over such doctrinaire minds as Le Trosne in having exact information at his fingertips. When he proposed a tax reform he was able to stipulate the precise amount of revenue it would yield, and exactly how a reduction in revenue might be compensated for in other parts of the administration.

A conviction that Necker shared with all reform ministers was that the royal government spent too much without justification or need. These excesses were due to abuses in the granting of pensions, the maintenance of useless offices, and the extravagance of the court and the royal households. But a proportion of such expenditures and the reason for the mounting royal debt was due to "great errors in foreign policy" that had led to the mid-century wars. Necker did not believe the finance minister could be indifferent to foreign policy and could not see why he should be excluded from the High Council, where the ultimate decisions were made on war and peace. He argued that it was important for the ministers in the highest policy-making council to be informed about the state of the finances and the economy in arriving at their decisions. No doubt he assumed that if his colleagues were as conscious as himself of the economic sacrifice involved they would be more hesitant to engage the country in reckless gambles. War made no economic sense to Necker at all. In the *Compte rendu* of 1781 he told the king and the nation that:

There is no conquest, there is no alliance which is equal to what Your Majesty will one day gain from the development of his own resources: the expansion of agriculture and of industry by the equitable repartition of taxes, the growth of credit by the wise administration of finances.[13]

It is obvious that Necker did not share an idea sometimes expressed in the twentieth century, that the royal government was "a poor state in a rich country." If the king of France was poor after gathering a harvest of about half a billion livres annually from his people, the fault was not because the taxes were not heavy enough, but because the king's finances were badly managed. Of course Necker agreed that the wealthy and the privileged did not pay their fair share of the tax burden. But that matter could not be corrected until the royal government set its own financial house in order. The sovereign courts continually harped on this theme; and Necker believed that until the ministers of the government began to take seriously these complaints, it would not be possible to shake the powerful hold of the *parlements* on public opinion. The ministers of enlightened despotism were too often concerned only with increasing the king's revenue. Necker believed that reform was not possible unless the people were persuaded that its object was tax equality. During his ministry, he and his agents of reform, including the provincial assemblies of Berri and Haute Guienne, found the population deeply suspicious of any alteration in the existing fiscal system. They could not imagine a change that was not for the purpose of increasing their

13. *Compte rendu au roi,* in *Oeuvres complètes,* II, 91.

burden rather than equalizing it or removing its evils. Therefore, Necker's reluctance to raise new taxes in his first ministry was not due simply to a thirst for glory, as is so often said; it was a fundamental part of his reform program.

A final general feature of Necker's thinking about the reform of the *ancien régime* was his belief in the limitations of the effectiveness of the royal government. "The will of the sovereign cannot be effective in the details of execution," he wrote in the *Administration of Finances*.[14] The success or inability of laws to make changes depended very much on the habits, the mores, the customs of the people. For example, the *vingtième* tax was in theory to be paid by all property owners regardless of class status except the clergy, who had settled for it by special agreement. In fact, the wealthy and noble landowners did not pay their fair share. The intendants were sometimes to blame, since they were inclined to deal leniently with the powerful.[15] The same was true of the *capitation* tax.[16] The deeply-rooted repugnance of the nobility for paying direct taxes to the royal government was not to be eradicated by simple decree. It would require time and persistent effort. It was in the provincial assemblies that Necker hoped to establish throughout the kingdom that the nobility would be confronted with the need for a more equitable fiscal system. He believed that their attitude could be changed by argument, by discussion. Such was the tactic of liberal reform as contrasted to that of enlightened despotism.

It was mentioned at the beginning of the chapter that Necker drew up detailed plans to reform indirect taxes at the end of the war. These concerned chiefly the government's salt and tobacco monopoly and the customs duties (*traites*). Necker believed these reforms would have to be initiated by the royal government. With those exceptions, most of his reform program was to have a regional basis rather than be dependent on the efficacy of the central government. He never had the penchant for uniformity that was so characteristic of the reform projects of the *économistes*. Diversity was a fact of life in the France of Louis XVI. Each region, each province had its unique features, whether economic, geographic, cultural, or social. What would have been a suitable method of financing road construction in one region might not have been so in another.

14. *De L'Administration des finances,* in *Oeuvres complètes,* IV, 166.

15. In correspondence with the intendant of Bordeaux in 1779, Necker refused the request of the duc de Duras to write off 16,500 livres of back taxes on the *vingtième,* levied since 1774, which he had not paid. Necker sternly rebuked the controller of the *vingtième* of the generality, one M. de Fontenay: "I am surprised at the servility in which the force of habit, I may even say, the abuse of power, has plunged the director and the controller of the *vingtième*; I request you to recall them to their duty, and make them sense that their functions require them to serve the interest of the king and that of the taxpayers. All requests, without distinction, must be subjected to a scrupulous and impartial discussion." Archives departmentales de la Gironde, C 3138, no. 4.

16. [Dupont de Nemours], *Procès-verbal de l'assemblée baillivale de Nemours pour la convocation des états généraux avec les cahiers des trois ordres,* 2 vols. (Paris, 1789), I, 218-226. Dupont estimated that the *taillables* paid one-eleventh of their revenue for the *capitation,* the non-*taillables* one-ninetieth of their revenue for the same tax.

The same was true in administering the other direct taxes—the *taille, capitation,* and *vingtième*—and the excise and sales taxes. Necker maintained that grand designs in carrying out reforms on a national level had come to grief in the past. In his book *On the Administration of Finances,* he mentioned specifically the attempts of Bertin to form a general cadastre in 1763 and Turgot's attempt to abolish the *corvée* in 1776, replacing it with a national administration for road construction. "Experience has come to support the opinion I have formed of the inappropriateness of general laws for the reform of a great part of the taxes."[17] His substitution for the royal government was to be the provincial assemblies and their administrations.

More than two years passed after he entered office before Necker first proposed to the king the initiation of a provincial assembly in the generality of Bourges in the Berri. This would be in the nature of an experiment, a "pilot plant." If it turned out well, Necker planned to extend the institution gradually to other generalities and eventually throughout the kingdom. The project came to him as a result of his experience as finance minister rather than as a preconceived idea. There was no mention of this institution in the *Eloge de Colbert,* nor in any of his writings prior to 1778. There were, of course, many other proposals for local assemblies in the literature of the day. The *économistes* had long called for them. Although Dupont's and Turgot's "Memorial on Municipalities" was not published until 1787, the marquis de Mirabeau had written extensively on the subject. Le Trosne's treatise mentioned above contained an elaborate blueprint for a system of provincial assemblies. It will be remembered that the use of local assemblies for fiscal reform and administration had been a principal demand of the remonstrance of the Court of Aides in 1775.

What seems to have led Necker to consider this particular institution was his reform of the *vingtième* in 1777, and his serious quarrel with the Parlement of Paris over it in May 1778. At that time Necker wrote and submitted to the king his "Memorial on the Establishment of Provincial Administrations," which was not intended to be made public, at least not at once.[18] Necker called the king's attention to the serious disaffection of his subjects regarding the fiscal system. He said the tribute extracted from the people had reached the limit of endurance, and that criticism of the government fiscality was widespread. The *parlements* were assuming the role of defending the people from the rapacity of the government.

17. *De L'Administration des finances,* in *Oeuvres complètes,* IV, 389.
18. In the entry of Grimm's *Correspondance* for September 1777—which date surely must be a printing error, since Necker's memorial was not written before 1778—the editor (probably Meister) wrote that he had received a copy "under the seal of the most strict secrecy." But he went on to quote excerpts from Necker's essay, which included some of his most important criticism of the regime of the intendants and also the role of the *parlements.* It would seem that Necker did want to get some of his ideas expressed in the essay before the public in September 1778. See Grimm et al., *Correspondance littéraire,* XI, 529-534.

The result of this is a troubled and confused murmuring which provides steady fuel to the ambition of the parlements to meddle in administration. Their desire to do so is becoming more and more evident. And they are behaving like all corps who want to acquire power, speaking in the name of the people, calling themselves the defenders of the rights of the nation; and it cannot be doubted that even though they are not fitted for this role either by education or by pure love for the good of the state, they will speak up on every occasion so long as they believe themselves supported by public opinion. Therefore it is necessary either to take that support from them or prepare for repeated battles which will disturb the peaceful reign of Your Majesty and lead inevitably either to erosion of authority, or to extreme measures of which the consequences would be incalculable.[19]

Necker explained to the king just what was wrong with the existing fiscal system, echoing, whether intended or not, many complaints of the remonstrance of the Court of Aides three years earlier. It was not so much the total weight of the tax burden (although Necker always insisted it was too heavy) as the inequitable partition of that burden among the generalities, *élections,* parishes, and individual taxpayers that was the source of the public's grievance. The injustice of the *corvées* was too patent and glaring for them to be allowed to continue. Arbitrary tax assessment must be replaced by regular, standard procedures that would enable the taxpayer to predict what his contribution will be. The judicial system must be reformed to provide justice for those wronged by financial officials. Finally, steps must be taken to counteract the alarming spread of general indifference toward the well-being of the state. This implied a public relations program to publicize government operations and to make possible active participation of the citizens in provincial government.

It was necessary to show why the intendants were unsuited to carry out these tasks. They were already overburdened with responsibility. Even if they conscientiously devoted all their efforts over many years to the task, they could never be effective in all the details of local government. The result was that much of their work and many decisions were left to their subdelegates. The latter did not have an independent status and were inclined to be "timid before the powerful and arrogant toward the weak." Necker made the same observation about his own post of finance minister. Altogether too many responsibilities had devolved upon this office, so that it was impossible for the minister to discharge all of them. The result was that the minister's subordinates, secretaries (*commis*), wielded great power without commensurate authority. It was they who had brought about this situation, always persuading the minister that his powers and functions should be increased, knowing that it would be to their own benefit. As for the intendants, Necker assured the king that he was not attacking them as persons, but only pointing out the nature of that post. It was usually temporary;

19. [Necker], "Mémoire au roi, sur l'éstablissement des administration provinciales, mai, 1778," *Oeuvres complètes,* III, 364-365.

the appointees considered it as a step up on the ladder and rarely expected to devote their careers to it.[20] The consequences of all these characteristics was the paradox of the intendants being unable to exercise their power adequately and effectively at the same time that it was formally absolute. The king's subjects in the provinces had no way of contradicting or disputing the decisions of the intendant. If they appealed to the royal council or the minister of finance, the latter could only refer the matter back to the intendant. The conclusion that Necker drew for the king from all these observations was that the widespread complaint about the "despotism" and the "arbitrariness" of the intendants had some basis in fact, and that the government must find some remedy for the evil. The intendants were to be maintained as the chief executives in the generalities, and their functions were spelled out in Necker's memorial, unlike that of Dupont and Turgot, which did not mention them at all.

It was not surprising that the intendants were displeased by Necker's memorial when it was published without his consent in 1781. Some of his most powerful enemies were intendants, who entered the pamphlet campaign against him in 1780 and 1781. Two of them perhaps most closely fitted the unflattering description drawn by Necker. The intendant of Valenciennes, Gabriel Sénac de Meilhan, and the intendant of Lille, Charles-Alexandre de Calonne, both took a condescending view of their post in the provinces and felt that their rightful place was occupied by the director general himself.

In his memorial, Necker also explained to the king why the *parlements* were unsuited for the role of mediator between the king and the people, a role they constantly claimed. In doing so, he again seriously offended a powerful group when his memorial was published. Necker's purpose in creating the new provincial government was to heal the serious alienation of the king's subjects from the royal government. By inviting the notables to participate in the provincial assemblies, he hoped to appeal to the latent sense of patriotism and spirit of public service he believed existed in that class. The *parlements,* he thought, did not truly reflect those qualities. They were concerned primarily with their own interests, not with those of the nation. Their objections to his reform of the *vingtième* was an example. He noted that the Parlement of Paris always protested those taxes which affected its own fortunes, but never bothered about others. For example, they were keenly sensitive about import duties on goods brought into the city of Paris, but not at all about high tariffs on the frontier of the nation, which did not affect them. Furthermore, Necker asserted that the magistrates of the Parlement of Paris were not qualified to review fiscal measures of the royal council. Their training and background fitted them for registering laws and remonstration against conflicts in laws, traditional functions that

20. Ardascheff listed 83 intendancies during the period 1774 to 1790. One can see that 36 intendancies were 5 years or less, 58 were 10 years or less, 69 were 15 years or less, and only 14 were over 15 years. Pavel M. Ardascheff, *Les Intendants de province sous Louis XVI* (Paris, 1909), pp. 465-467.

Necker did not intend to take from them. But the provincial assemblies would be far more capable interlocutors with the royal government on fiscal matters, because it was they who would assess and collect the taxes and who would have the most intimate familiarity with economic and social conditions in the province.

The question naturally comes to mind: would not these local assemblies of notables become just as recalcitrant, as egotistical, as dangerous to royal authority as the *parlements?* There was already the example of the assemblies of the *pays d'états,* especially the Estates of Brittany which, during the 1760s, threatened to join forces with the sovereign courts to confront the government with a united resistance of the nation. It will be remembered that Turgot hesitated to implement the "municipalities" because he feared the possibility of such an outcome. Necker clearly realized this danger and commented upon it at length. It must be remembered that his comments were for the king only; he did not intend for them to be made public.

First of all, the functions of the provincial governments were clearly defined by Necker. They would assess and collect the direct taxes, take charge of road construction and maintenance, and do whatever seemed feasible to further the economic development of the province. They should also have the power to levy taxes for local purposes. The assembly would meet once every two years for a session of no more than one month. Between sessions a bureau of administration appointed by the assembly, consisting of about one-fourth of its members, would execute the decisions of the assembly. But neither assembly nor bureau could make any expenditures without the king's consent. The intendants were permitted to observe the operations of both assembly and bureau. They would continue to exercise the police power in the province or generality. The assemblies would receive the quota of tax money to be raised from the provinces from the royal council and could not question the regular, annual quota. If it were necessary to ask for more tax revenue from the province, the assembly would be permitted to make observations to the king "in order to enlighten but never to thwart the king's will." This would seem to give the advisory function of the remonstrance to the provincial assembly. Necker did not seem to fear this because of his basic conviction that taxes should not be raised anyway.

He pointed out that the new assemblies would differ entirely from both the sovereign courts and the assemblies of the *pays d'états.* The king would have created the assemblies himself and could immediately disband them in case of disobedience. They would not be venal officers, as were the magistrates of the *parlements,* and therefore nothing could impede the king's dismissal of members of the assembly, whatever their noble rank. In other words, the royal power over the notables of the provincial assembly would be much greater than it was over the officers of the sovereign courts. The new assemblies would not resemble those of the *pays d'états* because the latter owed their existence to treaty rights acquired at the time the province was annexed to the kingdom, and the king was therefore bound to respect those rights. But there would be no such restrictions on his power over the new provincial assemblies. With such powers, Necker asserted, only the most flagrant errors of statecraft could bring about the feared union of the new provincial governments with the sovereign courts and the assemblies of estates.

When the "Memorial on Provincial Administrations" was published in 1781, neither the intendants nor the magistrates were happy about the manner in which Necker had treated them. Both vehemently criticized the memorial, but for opposite reasons. The *parlements* maintained that the director general was attempting to eliminate the only effective defense of the nation against despotism, namely themselves, and that he intended to strengthen the arbitrary powers of the royal government over the nation rather than limit them. The intendants on the other hand maintained that Necker was organizing powers independent of their control, and to undermine the intendants was to undermine the monarchy. Both positions, although clearly contradictory, have been repeated by Necker's critics of his provincial administrations since that time. In 1787, when the comte de Mirabeau published Turgot's "Memorial on Municipalities," his associate at that time, Brissot de Warville, wrote an appendix comparing Necker's provincial assemblies to those of Turgot. Brissot scathingly denounced Necker's "hypocrisy," alleging that his assemblies, instead of checking despotism, would bolster it, contrary to his professed purpose. On the other hand, in 1812, when Auget de Montyon published anonymously his tract on controllers general, he saw in Necker's assemblies the seeds of revolution, maintaining that they were subversive of royal authority.[21]

Neither points of view did justice to the subtlety of Necker's thought. However much he admired English institutions, he never intended to limit the absolute powers of the French monarchy, at least not during his first ministry. It is not surprising that Edmund Burke found in the Genevan a kindred spirit. For Necker believed also that national customs and habits were tougher than abstract systems or written constitutions: what was good for England or Holland might not necessarily be good for France. It is true that English examples influenced his thinking on reform in France. But there was a limit to what could be borrowed. National character and customs determined that limit.

While he consistently defended French absolutism, Necker just as consistently opposed despotism. He saw the same distinction between the two as did Malesherbes. As long as the absolute monarchy respects the laws guaranteeing both personal and property rights, as long as it permits the right to appeal—if there is publicity given to governmental measures, if public opinion can act as a check on usurpative and despotic acts, then the French monarchy could be both absolute and liberal, or "moderate," as was Montesquieu's expression. For both Malesherbes and Necker the word despotism did not conjure the image of a

21. Samuel Dupont de Nemours, *Oeuvres posthumes de M. Turgot: Ou Mémoire de M. Turgot sur les administrations provinciales mis en parallèle avec celui de M. Necker* (Lausanne, 1787); [Auget de Montyon], *Particularités et observations*, pp. 250ff.

crowned tyrant or even of arbitrary power wielded by a minister. The true despot was the subaltern who exercised the absolute powers of the king irresponsibly. Necker told Louis XVI that the chief purpose of the new provincial administrations was to liberate the peasant population from those who oppressed them. And these were not the intendants who were far away, or the ministers and the king who were even more remote, but the swarm of petty officials who administered the government's fiscal system and who were only too near the taxpayers:

Subdelegates, officers of the *élection,* managers, receivers and controllers of the *vingtièmes,* commissioners and collectors of the *taille,* officials of the *gabelles,* inspectors, process-servers, *corvée* bosses, agents of the *aides,* the *contrôle,* the reserved imposts; all these men of the fisc, each according to his character, subjugates to his small authority and entwines in his fiscal science the ignorant taxpayer, unable to know whether he is being cheated or not, but who constantly suspects and fears it.[22]

Despotism weakened the authority of the royal government, rather than strengthened it:

Royal power does not consist in detailed administration. By attempting to regulate everything to the minutest detail the government encounters resistance; it attempts to impose arbitrary decision by decrees in council; opposition consolidates, and the minister is apt to be the first to advise backing down. . . . To avoid compromising authority too often one must not be so anxious to use it ceaselessly; one becomes exhausted in its futile deployment, and one lacks power just at the time that it is necessary to maintain it.[23]

These remarks were probably made with reference to the crown's relations with the sovereign courts during the previous half-century. Retrospectively, the above passage would seem to be an apt description of the later years of the reign of Louis XVI. Those words should be as famous as Turgot's admonition to the king at the time of his dismissal in 1776: "Do not forget, Sire, that it was weakness that led Charles I to the block."[24]

Necker's method of implementing the new provincial administrations was typical. He did not propose to establish them all at once. His plan was to begin with one province and learn by experience. He would allow the local notables who attended the assembly considerable latitude in deciding on its organization and rules. The *économistes* who wrote about provincial assemblies made elaborate blueprints; in Le Trosne's treatise, for example, it was stipulated that "there would be two banquets, one at the beginning of the session and one at the end; they will be paid from the expense account of the local administration

22. Necker, "Mémoire sur les Administrations provinciales," *Oeuvres complètes,* III, 339-340.
23. *Ibid.,* p. 347.
24. Faure, *La Disgrâce de Turgot,* p. 499.

and a charge of six livres per person."[25] Yet they neglected such essential matters as the role of the intendant and the executive commission between sessions of the assemblies.

With due respect to the "vast projects" of Turgot and the *économistes*, it may well be asked if they accomplished nearly as much as what Marion called the "mean petty expedients" of the Genevan. The opponents of Necker seemed to believe that if their entire blueprint were not enacted all at once, any piecemeal reform was bound to be ineffective. Thus, Le Trosne: "All parts of administration are held together by links; and any reform which one may propose in one part is ineffective if the disorder is left in another part."[26] Calonne made a similar observation in his memorial to the king in November 1786, asking for the convocation of an Assembly of Notables:

In great affairs there is but an instant which sometimes separates the abyss of misfortune from the heights of prosperity. If in the present situation one is reduced to partial and successive operations, not one will be able to succeed and reach its goal. These measures which are proposed to you are essentially bound together and inseparablé. Their effectiveness lies in their totality; their utility is indivisible; their success depends on their concurrence.[27]

He repeated the same thought before the Notables in his opening address to that body on February 22, 1787. When such options are placed before deliberative assemblies, is it any wonder that the proposed reform will be rejected, especially when it contains such dubious propositions as did that of Calonne?

It may be asked if the reform program of the *économistes,* far from being the only true reform proposed, did not actually cause the failure of all reforms. Their doctrines were baneful not only to the reform movement but to the Revolution itself, for they were adopted with uncompromising logic by many leaders of the National Assembly and by the Girondins. Among the latter were Brissot de Warville and Condorcet.

Necker's method had the merit of being founded on experience rather than theory. It was slower, but surer, and won substantial support in public opinion— something neither Terray, Turgot, nor the *économistes* succeeded in doing. It remains to be seen, however, if Necker's reform ministry was something more than "a few sentences in preambles," as alleged by the writer of the *Liégeoise.* We will turn to the actual accomplishments of the four-and-a-half years of Necker's first ministry.

25. Le Trosne, *De L'Administration provinciale*, p. 565.
26. *Ibid.*, p. v.
27. Quoted in Hans Glagau, *Reformversuche und Sturz des Absolutismus in Frankreich: 1774-1788* (Munich, 1908), pp. 353-354.

Chapter VII

ESTABLISHING ORDER IN THE FINANCES

Exactly how Necker came to be entrusted with the finances of the government of Louis XVI is a subject about which few details are known. Because of his role in the affairs of the Company of the Indies and his two publications in 1773 and 1775, he was very much in the public eye. Madame du Deffand wrote to Walpole at the time of Turgot's dismissal from the controller generalship on May 12, 1776, that there was much talk about Necker succeeding Turgot, but she thought his religion would be an insurmountable obstacle.[1] When it became known on October 22, 1776, that Necker was to be appointed counselor of finance and director of the royal treasury, a new position that had been created for him, the news did not seem to surprise the public. Philosophes and encyclopedists (except for the *économistes*) seemed to welcome the appointment as a sign of growing religious tolerance. The writer in Grimm's *Correspondance littéraire* thought the appointment was some consolation for reverses suffered by the philosophe movement earlier in the year due to the dismissal of Turgot, the death of Mademoiselle de Lespinasse, and the illness of Madame Geoffrin.

Only the elevation of Mr. Necker can console us for these misfortunes. The confidence which His Majesty has deigned to bestow on this illustrious foreigner is an honor to letters, which have helped to make him known. And the triumph which merit has gained on this occasion over vain prejudice can no doubt be regarded as a sign of the progress which enlightenment and reason have made in France.[2]

Other journalists were more reserved in their praise of the Genevan. Metra remarked about "the turbulent and systematic genius of this Mr. Necker," and predicted that "we will probably see new upheavals (*révolutions*)."[3] Metra supposed, for one thing, that Necker would be in favor of paper money. Inevitably people thought of another "illustrious foreigner" who had been placed in charge of the royal finances sixty years earlier. No matter how emphatically Necker repudiated any kind of "fiat money," his appointment

1. Du Deffand, *Correspondance complète,* II, 565.
2. Grimm, *Correspondance littéraire,* XI, 367.
3. Metra, *Correspondance secrète,* III, 383-386.

raised the spectre of another "system" with paper money being given forced circulation.

On the death of Bernard de Clugny in October, there were a number of aspirants to the vacant post of controller general. One was Cromot du Bourg, superintendent of the household of Monsieur, brother of the king. Monsieur had vigorously urged the appointment of this ambitious but mediocre official. Another candidate was the farmer general and official in the queen's household, Jean-Marie Augeard, one of the most unsavory financiers of the day. Then there was the intendant of Valenciennes, Gabriel Sénac de Meilhan, the perennial candidate for the post.

The latter launched the story so often repeated since then in secondary works to explain exactly how Necker advanced himself to the position so ardently sought by Sénac himself. According to this story, Necker's ambition surpassed his avarice, for he did not hesitate to give enormous bribes to influential but needy courtiers. One Alexandre-Jacques Masson, born in 1741, the son of an iron manufacturer, had acquired some property in the Loire valley with the name of Pezai, and thereupon gave himself the title of "marquis de Pezai." Enormously ambitious and brimming over with self-confidence, he wrote memorials to several crowned heads of state in Europe, generously offering them advice on diverse matters. Pezai became the military instructor of the dauphin, Louis-Auguste, before the latter came to the throne as Louis XVI. His father had known Maurepas when the latter was secretary of state for the navy, since the elder Masson supplied military goods to the armed forces. According to Sénac de Meilhan, Necker bribed Pezai to lay before the king his memorials on finances and promised to acquit an old debt of doubtful legality claimed by his father, should Necker become finance minister. In this way, Necker is supposed to have hoisted himself into the office. His first act was said to have been a payment to Pezai of 300,000 livres from the royal treasury. "Such was Necker's first economy," wrote Lavaquery sarcastically.[4]

It is hardly necessary to say that this scenario is based upon no reliable evidence. At best there is only hearsay evidence, such as the memoirs of the Paris lieutenant general of police Jean-Charles-Pierre Lenoir. Years afterward, Lenoir wrote that Maurepas had told him at the time of Pezai's death in 1777 that it was through Pezai's influence that Necker became finance minister.[5] Even the hearsay evidence is contradictory. According to Lenoir, it was Maurepas who dispatched a courier to the Loire on news of Pezai's death in order to sequester his papers. But abbé de Véri wrote that Necker personally ordered the impounding of these papers.[6] It is known that Necker was acquainted with Pezai and corresponded with him, for some of Pezai's letters were preserved in the Coppet

4. Lavaquery, *Necker: Fourrier de la révolution,* p. 114.

5. Robert Darnton, "The Memoirs of Lenoir, lieutenant de police of Paris: 1774-1785," *English Historical Review,* 85 (July 1970), 532-559.

6. Abbé de Véri, *Journal de l'abbé de Véri,* II, 72-73.

archives. But nothing in those letters alluded to the transaction reported by Sénac de Meilhan, which must certainly have been his own invention. There is no hint in the letters of Pezai that he believed Necker to be in his debt.[7] It is possible that it was through Pezai that Necker became acquainted with Maurepas. But according to the prince de Montbarey it was the duchesse d'Anville, a relative of Maurepas and good friend of the Neckers, who introduced the Genevan banker to the mentor.[8] Another source has it that Maurepas' brother-in-law, the duc de Nivernais, a warm admirer of Necker, suggested to Maurepas that the Genevan be made director of the royal treasury.[9]

It appears certain that the key person Necker had to cultivate was the mentor rather than the king, and no shady, underhanded means were required for him to do this.[10] As long as he had the support of Maurepas, he could carry out reforms in the face of hostility of officials and financiers. Losing that support sometime in 1780 marked the beginning of the end of Necker's ministry.

Much depended, therefore, on the character of this person who was seventy-five years old when Necker entered the government. Jean-Frédéric Phélypeaux, comte de Maurepas, was the son of a prominent minister of Louis XIV: Louis Phélypeaux, comte de Pontchartrain. The father had been controller general in the last decade of the previous century. Early in the following reign he retired as secretary of state for the navy in order to make way for the accession of his son to that post. Jean-Frédéric de Maurepas held the office until 1749, when he was dismissed for having failed to show proper respect to the king's mistress, Madame de Pompadour. The circumstances of his disgrace redounded to his credit at the time of the death of Louis XV, for the young king who came to the throne was determined that the regime of the mistresses would end. Also, the fact that Maurepas was not affiliated with either of the two rival factions at court, the followers of the duc de Choiseul or those of the duc d'Aiguillon, may have contributed to his selection by Louis XVI as his chief advisor. It is possible that his godson, the marquis de Pezai, who was an intimate of Louis-Auguste when the latter was dauphin, may have had some influence in the new king's choice of his mentor.

Long years of exile from Versailles had ingrained in Maurepas the dread of suffering a second disgrace. His dominant passion as mentor was to retain his paramount influence with the young king and the queen-consort, Marie Antoinette. He had the seasoned courtier's highly refined sense of detecting the slightest threat to his supremacy, of being able to maneuver craftily to undermine a suspected rival. He rarely operated aboveboard or openly opposed a

7. Pierre-Henri, marquis de Ségur, *Au Couchant de la monarchie,* 2 vols. (Paris, 1913), II, 34-35.

8. Alexandre-Marie, prince de Montbarey, *Mémoires,* 3 vols. (Paris, 1826-1827), II, 245.

9. Guy-Marie Sallier, *Annales françaises depuis le commencement du règne de Louis XVI jusqu'aux états-généraux* (Paris, 1813), p. 13.

10. The letters of Necker to Maurepas before the former's appointment to the royal treasury are in AN K 163.

dangerous rival, but worked secretly behind the scenes. The method by which he undermined both Turgot and Necker was similar in its clandestineness. In the case of Turgot, it was "a secret war, carried out by psychological means, a war of attrition in the mind of the king."[11] In Necker's case Maurepas undermined the prestige of the director general by secretly protecting the anonymous libel campaign launched in 1780.

In fairness, it should be added that Maurepas was not without some qualities of statesmanship. His record as secretary of state for the navy was a good one. In those years he is described as possessing "a lively intelligence, a quick mind, having been nourished since his youth in affairs of state."[12] He brought Vincent de Gournay into the government to be intendant of commerce in 1747. Without the concurrence of Maurepas it would not have been possible for Turgot, Malesherbes, or Necker to have entered the government at all. He must have been open to some ideas of the philosophes and encyclopedists. Nothing indicates that Maurepas was a confirmed conservative as were some of his ministerial colleagues, notably the keeper of the seals, Hue de Miromesnil, and the secretary of state for war, the prince de Montbarey. He was, moreover, known for his never-failing sense of humor and his devastating wit, although some complained that he "treated great matters facetiously, and small matters gravely." His hospitality during his long exile at his estate of Pontchartrain was proverbial, and the number of his friends was legion. Nor was he grasping in a financial way, as were so many ministers of the *ancien régime.*

Maurepas was also primarily responsible for restoring the old *parlements* to their former positions, undoing the work of chancellor Maupeou. This meant that the new reign had to learn to live with those corporations of magistrates, whose stature in public opinion had been greatly enhanced. The events of the previous reign and the remonstrances of the Parlement of Paris against Turgot's six edicts in early 1776 indicated that the administrative monarchy faced a difficult time. Maurepas must have sensed this and was, therefore, amenable to suggestions Necker presented in a memorial in July 1776. In it the Genevan outlined the fiscal policy he thought the government should pursue. He noted that, according to a *Compte rendu* by the controller general, Bernard de Clugny, the government had a deficit of 24 million livres of ordinary expenditure beyond ordinary income. Necker believed the ordinary deficit was probably nearer 27 million livres.

The memorial was written in the month in which the British colonies of North America formally declared their independence from Great Britain. The French government had already decided upon naval rearmament. The possibility that France would be drawn into another major war with its traditional enemy was clear. Under these circumstances, Necker told Maurepas, it was vitally

---

11. Faure, *La Disgrâce de Turgot,* p. 480.

12. "Journal manuscrit du règne de Louis XVI par le conseiller au parlement Lefebvre d'Amécourt," BN MSS français, nouv. aquis. 22111, fols. 47-48.

necessary to strengthen the government's credit. The tax burden was at its extreme limit and without reform could be increased only with difficulty; and wartime would not be a favorable moment for reform. The cost of naval rearmament, and of war, should it come, would have to be paid through loans. Yet the government's credit was weak, due primarily to the harsh fiscal measures of 1770. The government must assure prospective investors that they could rely upon payment of interest and amortization through the regular, ordinary revenue of the government. This meant that the 27 million deficit would have to be eliminated, and more than that, a surplus of 10 million livres of regular income over regular expenditures assured, if the government were to be in a favorable position to issue future loans. Therefore, the immediate task of the finance minister, Necker wrote, should be to achieve that 10-million-livre surplus.[13]

How could the king's ordinary income be increased by 37 million livres? This was the crux of Necker's proposal. The Parlement of Paris and the Court of Aides had often asserted in their remonstrances that the government's financial needs could be met by cutting unnecessary expenditures, by eliminating waste, by more efficient organization of the royal finances. Necker believed this feasible, and he showed how it could be done. The prodigality of the preceding reign and its lack of concern for economy had been notorious. This could no longer be accepted complacently. It was necessary to eliminate useless offices, to reduce pensions and other gifts of the king and the queen, to control spending by the royal households, to diminish the profits of the financiers, the treasurers, the tax farmers, and all other officers who handled the king's revenue. Savings could be made by attention to details, by careful drawing up of new contracts with financial companies, and by stricter accounting of the king's finances.

To the credit of both the king and Maurepas, they understood Necker's policy and were willing to support it. Many others were not able to see how a war could be financed without raising taxes. The prince de Montbarey earnestly tried to persuade his kinsman, the comte de Maurepas, that anyone who maintained that the war could be financed without new taxes was necessarily a charlatan.[14] The abbé de Véri, supposedly an intelligent observer of the scene, remained steadfastly skeptical throughout Necker's ministry that his "amelioration" could possibly finance a war. Naturally, this widespread opinion was given added impetus by the libels of Necker's enemies. They compared him to a dental surgeon who plied his trade on the street and sent hawkers around to shout, "No pain, gentlemen, no pain!" As a matter of fact, Necker's policy was not painless. It merely shifted the pain from overburdened taxpayers, already victims of an unjust fiscal system, to great nobles who held lucrative offices in the royal households and the opulent class of financiers, both of whom had been

13. Our only knowledge about this July 1776 memorial to Maurepas is Necker's discussion of it in his *Mémoire au mois d'avril 1787,* in *Oeuvres complètes,* II, 177-180.

14. Montbarey, *Mémoires,* II, 311.

fleecing the government for years and who believed that such theft was a sacrosanct institution. By 1780, their screams were being heard in numerous pamphlets that began to appear denouncing the director general.

Despite the appeal Necker's July memorial undoubtedly had for Maurepas, there were still serious obstacles to appointing him controller general when Bernard de Clugny died on October 18. How would the French clergy accept a Protestant in such an important position in the domestic life of the country? Although Necker never mentioned the matter, a number of writers at the time spoke of serious legal obstacles. A minister of state and any magistrate who decided legal cases was required to take an oath before the Paris Chamber of Accounts; an oath could only be in the Catholic form. It was Necker, evidently, who proposed to Maurepas that a figurehead be appointed to the *contrôle général* and that he, Necker, be named to some legally subordinate office but given the functions of finance minister. Necker even suggested the individual to occupy that honorific position, and his proposal was adopted.[15] A royal edict of October 22 appointed one Louis-Gabriel Taboureau des Réaux as controller general, and Necker was named director of the royal treasury. One of the prominent journalists of the day, Pidansat de Mairobert, wrote that "Mr. Taboureau has been chosen, and to overcome his resistance, motivated by the fact that he knows nothing about finance, he has been given a sort of deputy for this part in the person of Mr. Necker."[16] As for the new controller general, the same writer remarked that "Mr. Taboureau is gentle, simple, human, of precarious health, lacking in that energy which is the source equally of heroic actions and great crimes."[17]

Some observers thought the arrangement could hardly endure. The comte de Lauraguais, who had worked with Necker in affairs of the Company of the Indies, remarked that he knew the Genevan well and that he was not a good bedfellow. Madame du Deffand was pleased to see her friend appointed to this new post, but doubted if Necker would remain in office very long because the opposition to him would be too great.[18] The French clergy, however, accepted the appointment with good grace, and some of the firmest supporters of Necker's reforms were in the high prelacy.

The opposition that Necker had to face immediately after his appointment to the royal treasury was within the *contrôle général* rather than outside it. Taboureau himself was not as pliable as hoped; but the most serious obstacles to innovation were found in the six venal offices of intendants of finance, and below them the first secretaries of bureaus (*commis*) and the intendants in the generalities. Necker brought work habits that were foreign to both officers and

15. Letter of Necker to Maurepas, AN K 163, no. 8.
16. [Mathieu-François Pidansat de Mairobert], *L'Espion anglais,* 10 vols. (London, 1779-1784), IV, 263.
17. *Ibid.,* p. 386.
18. Du Deffand, *Correspondance,* II, 576.

commissioners in the government of the *ancien régime.* He came to his desk punctually early in the morning, worked steadily for long hours, and expected the same of subordinates. He had a great appetite for details, poring over reports of his *commis,* ordering inquests for more information. This type of activity was considered beneath the dignity of a great minister, and earned him the contempt of observers like the abbé de Véri. In his first months in office he was constantly thwarted by both officers and commissioners. His letters to provincial intendants requesting that they send him information and statements about finances received the reply that they would not do so unless ordered by the controller general.[19] His attempt to get information on internal customs barriers was treated with haughty disdain by the intendant of finance to which he had addressed the request, Jean-Charles Philébert Trudaine de Montigny, eminent friend of Turgot and adherent of the sect.[20]

The six intendants of finance had acquired a seemingly unshakable position in the ministry of finance. All bureaus came under their supervision. They belonged to the high magistrature class; their offices were venal, and very lucrative. According to an unsigned memorial to Maurepas, dated June 22, 1777, each intendant cost the king more than a million livres per year due to their emoluments and to a generous allowance for office expenses. "The same duties could be performed, and much better, with an economy of six or seven hundred thousand francs," it was asserted.[21] The intendants of finance paid their secretaries from these funds, and this meant that the *commis* of the departments were not very responsive to directives from the finance minister. It was clearly an impossible situation from Necker's standpoint. At the end of June 1777, he succeeded in getting the consent of Maurepas and the king to abolish all six intendancies of finance and to replace them with four secretaries holding their posts by commission, and freely appointed and removable by the minister of finance. Taboureau des Réaux opposed this measure and offered his resignation. Necker resigned simultaneously, but was immediately appointed director general of finances, a post which had not been used since early in the century. Taboureau's resignation was accepted. Necker and his family moved into the quarters of the controller general at 9, rue des Petits-Champs. The Genevan banker was now completely in charge of French finances in fact if not in name.

As for the six intendants whose offices were abolished, the capital value of their charges was reimbursed on November 1, 1777.[22] Each of them retained the rank of counselor of state, or was granted it if he did not already possess it.

19. *L'Espion anglais,* IV, 397.

20. J. F. Bosher, *The Single Duty Project: A Study of the Movement for a French Customs Union in the Eighteenth Century* (London, 1964), p. 105.

21. "Note de 22 juin 1777," AN F[30] 110A, no. 5. Michel Antoine suggests that this *mémoire* may have been written by Pezai; see his book *Le Conseil du roi sous le règne de Louis XV* (Geneva, 1970), p. 421, n. 152.

22. Pierre-Jean-Baptiste Nougaret, *Anecdotes du règne de Louis XVI* (Paris, 1780), p. 214.

Necker initiated a policy that he continued throughout his first ministry, of giving preference in new appointments to those whose charges had been abolished. Three of the former intendants of finance were immediately appointed to a special commission set up to handle all legal tax cases appealed to the king's council. According to a recent study of this commission, it had existed in embryo during Turgot's ministry and was a response to one of the complaints in the remonstrance of the Court of Aides of 1775; namely, that individuals in the *contrôle-général* were permitted to decide such cases.[23] The commission of three, acting as an administrative court, was a boon to Necker because it freed him from judicial duties that the ministry of finance had accumulated for over a century, largely as a result of the expansion of powers of the provincial intendants. It also apparently solved the embarrassing matter about the oath, which was not required of him so long as he did not exercise judicial powers.

The ministerial shakeup of June 1777 was of tremendous importance for the advancement of Necker's reform program. He was now unquestioned master in the *contrôle-général,* and could appoint loyal subordinates who not only favored his reforms but shared his ethic of hard work and diligent application to details. One of his most important lieutenants was Bertrand Dufresne, who took Necker's former position as director of the royal treasury. An administrative genius of enormous energy and devotion to duty, he was Necker's foremost assistant, and he resigned from the finance ministry when Necker was dismissed in May 1781. He returned to the ministry along with Necker in the summer of 1788. Another able administrator was Michel-François Dailly, who was placed at the head of the department that administered the direct taxes, and who also lost his position when Necker was succeeded by Joly de Fleury in 1781.[24]

Besides making Necker master in his own department of finances, the result of the acts of June 1777 was to increase his authority in other departments that spent the king's revenue. This was essential if he were to carry out his reforms with the goal of putting the government's credit on a sound basis. The powers of the finance ministry over the agencies that collected the king's revenue were fairly effective by the third quarter of the century, at least as far as controllability was concerned, due in large measure to successful reforms of the duc de Noailles in the early years of the reign of Louis XV. But wastefulness and lack of control over expenditures were notorious in the great spending departments. These were, first of all, the two military departments, war and navy, and the royal households, beginning with the king's domestic household (as distinguished from his military household), the queen's household, and the households of the princes, the two brothers of the king. It was in these departments that Necker's reforms were most stubbornly resisted, and where his most dangerous enemies

23. Aline Logette, *Le Comité contentieux des finances près le conseil du roi (1777-1791)* (Nancy, 1964), p. 59.

24. J. F. Bosher, "The *premier commis des finances* in the Reign of Louis XVI, *French Historical Studies,* 3 no. 4 (1964), 475-494.

were to be found at the time Maurepas withdrew his support from the reform minister. As long as Necker enjoyed that support, he was able to make considerable progress toward his goal.

The most obviously wasteful departments were the king's domestic household and those of the queen and the princes. Ordinary expenditures of all these households totaled 32 to 36 million livres annually. It was commonly accepted that not all that amount was really spent to "maintain the splendor of the throne." Much of it went to purveyors of goods and services who demanded excessive profits, venal officials in the households who received enormous emoluments for little work in return, and simple diversion of funds, as in the case of Radix de Sainte-Foy, superintendent of finances in the household of the comte d'Artois.[25] Furthermore, the royal households were the final refuge of an unemployed aristocracy, who held many purely honorific positions and received exorbitant sums they considered only fitting to their rank. Many historic names were to be found in this group. It required more than ordinary courage to risk affronting them. During his brief term as secretary of state for the king's household, Malesherbes drew up an excellent plan of reform but never got so far as to show it to the king.[26] Necker believed this was one of the first government departments where reform should be attempted. He was not a republican and did not dispute the principle that in a monarchy the sovereign must be maintained in a certain state of "splendor." What he questioned was the necessity of the taxpayers' maintaining the splendor of crafty merchants, insolent officials, financiers, and an idle aristocracy.

Purchases by the royal households were customarily made high above market prices; Necker believed this was due to the negligent manner of payment rather than outright fraud. Payments were as much as four years in arrears. This gave the sellers of goods and services an excuse to charge inflated prices. The same nonchalance was observed in the payment of salaries and interest on offices in the royal households. An enormous debt-in-arrears had been built up. In the preamble of the regulation of December 22, 1776, Necker announced a new regime in the administration of the king's domestic household. The debt-in-arrears would be liquidated within six years. Henceforth, all purchases by the king's household would be paid for in monthly installments and acquitted within a year's time, and in cash rather than promissory notes. The bureau officers who made purchases were required to submit their proposals to the director of the royal treasury at the beginning of the year so that all expenditures of the household could be known. Finally, all heads of bureaus who made purchases for the household were asked to submit to the director of the royal treasury, within two months of publication of the declaration, a plan of economy for their particular sections. It is probable that Pidansat de Mairobert was correct in reporting the lack of compliance with the last provision. The king's domestic

25. For a discussion of Sainte-Foy, see Chapter XII.
26. Grosclaude, *Malesherbes,* I, 339.

household proved to be, along with the naval department, the most recalcitrant of the spending departments. Further reform of the household had to await the strengthening of Necker's position in the government as a whole.[27]

On the same day that the above directive was passed by the government, another regulation was published initiating a new system in administering pensions granted by the king. This had also been a flagrant abuse of the previous reign. There was no question but that many pensions were well deserved: retired soldiers who had served the country well, meritorious service of a civilian nature, the desire of the king to encourage pursuits in the arts and sciences by awarding grants, all these were legitimate. It was rather the abuse of pensions that cried out for reform. The source of the abuse, according to Necker, was in the secrecy of the system. No single bureau was in charge; every department had the right to grant pensions, and the lists were not published. A skilled courtier could draw several pensions from different departments without anyone knowing it. The most notorious of these secret pensions were the *croupes,* granted by the Royal General Farms and other financial companies according to terms in their contracts with the government. The word *croupe* means the rump of the horse behind the saddle, where additional riders are taken on by the horseman. Originally, it had no scandalous connotation, because the *croupier* was one who helped the tax farmer raise the money to purchase a share in the contract. Therefore, the *croupier* was a "rider" who had a legitimate right to a portion of the profits of the partner, the horseman. But from this innocent beginning it became the practice of the king, or the finance minister or other powerful persons, to grant a pension secretly to individuals who had nothing to do with the financial company's operations. Beautiful ladies of the theater sometimes received these favors, but more often they went to relatives or persons who disposed of powers to grant *croupes.* Abbé Terray was the most notorious practitioner of this abuse.[28] Turgot condemned the practice but had little opportunity to reform it.

In the regulation of December 1776, Necker stated clearly his pension reform goals. Eventually all pensions should be paid by the royal treasury and based upon a single brevet that would be published. All recipients of the king's grace would be listed in alphabetical order and the amount they received indicated. Yet this act showed that he would proceed cautiously. No existing pensions would be touched; they would continue to be paid as in the past by each department. But all new pensions would be paid by the royal treasury at the end

27. Volume III of Necker's complete works (*Premier Ministère de M. Necker*), edited by Baron de Staël, contains many of the edicts, decrees, and other acts written by Necker in the name of the king. For the regulation of December 22, 1776, concerning the king's household, see pp. 200ff. The preamble is omitted but the specific provisions are printed in Isambert et al., eds., *Recueil général des anciennes lois,* XXIV, 280; *L'Espion anglais,* IV, 403-406.

28. Pierre Roux, *Les Fermes d'impôts sous l'ancien régime* (Paris, 1916), pp. 627-628.

of each fiscal year. All requests for pensions must be submitted to the king in December of each year. A special fund would be set up to liquidate pensions in arrears. The practice so notoriously indulged in by abbé Terray of arbitrarily withholding a percentage of pensions for the benefit of the treasury would be discontinued. Finally, this act stated that only those involved in the administration of finances would receive any benefits from future contracts to be made with *fermiers* and *régisseurs.* This meant the future elimination of *croupes* of any kind.[29]

It was not until 1778 that Necker felt strong enough to carry through to completion his administrative reform of the pension system. By letters patent of November 8, 1778, all pensions after January 1, 1779, would be paid by the royal treasury. Treasurers of the different departments were forbidden to pay pensions, and the chambers of accounts were not to receive any account for pensions by such treasurers. There was one exception: retired soldiers and company grade officers would continue to be paid as before by the treasurer general of the war department. For all pensioners the manner of payment was simplified. Formerly it was necessary to have a special *ordonnance* from the department. Now only a simple receipt from the *ordonnateur* of the department had to be presented to the royal treasury for payment. A list of all pensioners would be published each year. The consolidation of all pensions under the royal treasury brought about some startling statistics. In the *Compte rendu* of 1781 Necker listed this item of expenditure at 28 million livres. "I doubt if all the other governments of Europe together pay one-half that sum," he remarked—an astonishing statement to publish. It was clear that he believed the reform of the pensions had only begun.[30]

These initial attempts to reform the administration of the king's domestic household and the pension system reveal the fundamental problem Necker faced in establishing financial order: the sheer lack of information about the royal finances, both income and expenditures. Receivers of the king's revenue, as well as its spenders, were venal officers who handled the king's finances along with their own private business, and often the funds of the two enterprises were inextricably mixed. The revenue-collecting agencies were the Royal General Farms and smaller *fermes* and *régies* that contracted to collect the indirect taxes and earned a profit from it. Direct taxes were collected by the receivers general of the generalities. The *financiers,* as those who handled the king's money were called, not only collected the tax money, but spent a part of it for the king. They paid the expenses of collection and also turned funds over to some other spending agency. For example, a considerable part of the revenue collected by the General Farms was transferred directly to the Hôtel de Ville, then used to

29. Necker, *Oeuvres complètes,* III, 52ff; Isambert et al., eds., *Recueil général des anciennes lois,* XXIV, 281-283.

30. Necker, *Oeuvres complètes,* II, 36; Isambert et al., eds., *Recueil général des anciennes lois,* XXV, 450-451.

pay *rentiers,* creditors of the government. That money bypassed completely the royal treasury.[31]

The financiers were treated with consideration because they were the source of the government's short-term loans, called *anticipations.* The royal government needed credit because of the time required to collect taxes. The *taille,* for example, took at least two years to harvest for each fiscal year. The government had to spend that money before it could be collected, and anticipations permitted it to do so. It was with the farmers general and the receivers general that the government contracted for most of these short-term loans. They were, in effect, advances to the government of loans from the private fortunes of the financiers, based upon a specific tax source as security.

Raising and spending money by anticipation made the government's accounting system extremely complicated. Each officer who handled the king's money, a *comptable,* was required to keep records of his transactions and make a detailed account for each fiscal year (*exercice*). When completed it was sent to the Council of Finance. Because of arrears in the collecting of revenue, and also delays in the spending of it, several years were required before all these "true accounts" (*états au vrai*) could be completed and the council of finance could draw up a general account for the fiscal year. This was then sent to the Paris Chamber of Accounts for detailed verification. By that time the "true account" had become highly fictitious in describing the total amount of money received and spent by the royal government for a fiscal year. It had no relation at all to a *compte rendu* detailing the ordinary revenue and expenditure. It was the practice to assign a certain amount of anticipations received in a given fiscal year retroactively to previous fiscal years, and some portion was assigned to future years. Each fiscal year, then, spent funds drawn from previous and future fiscal years by way of anticipations. Exactly what purpose was served by such a bewildering system remains a mystery. But as a result of the juggling of anticipations, the *état au vrai* of a fiscal year did present a balanced account of expenditures and revenues, though it was completed several years after the passing of the fiscal year.[32]

The Paris Chamber of Accounts and the regional chambers did not attempt to make a global account of all revenues and expenditures for a fiscal year. Their function was to guard against malversation of the king's funds. Each financier who handled the king's money was accountable to them. How efficient they were in that task is uncertain. The king's funds, as stated above, were often mixed with the private fortunes of the financiers, so that whenever an office was abolished, or a *comptable* went bankrupt, it was often a delicate matter to sort out the king's money from that of the accountable officer. It happened not

31. For a description of this semiprivate-enterprise system of financial administration, see Bosher, *French Finances,* chap. 4.

32. For a fuller description of the *état au vrai* drawn up by the Council of Finance and sent to the Chamber of Accounts, see Chapter XIV, concerning the *Compte rendu* of 1781.

infrequently that the officer owed the king rather than vice versa, and that the king was paying high rates of interest for the use of his own money. It is understandable why such a complex and wasteful system of financial administration would appear intolerable to the mind of an experienced banker.

Necker turned his attention first to the departments that spent the king's money, for they exhibited the worst features of waste and lack of control. These were the departments of war, navy and colonies, and foreign affairs, and the royal households. In each department there was a treasurer general who received the funds from the royal treasury for his department. But each bureau or section within the department also had its own treasurer, another venal officer. Often there were two or more treasurers for each office, who served in alternative years. Each office of treasurer also gave rise to other offices attached to them, called "controllers," who kept an account of funds received and spent. The sums assigned to the departments were usually so large as to leave considerable discretion to the spending department. The finance minister had no way of supervising or even knowing about the final disposal of these funds. The treasurers themselves looked to the department or section heads for their emoluments of office, rather than to the royal treasury, and were therefore independent of the will of the finance minister.

The treasurers were not only free of control by the minister of finance, but their offices had evolved since the beginning of the eighteenth century from a mere agency for spending royal funds to a semiprivate bank, performing functions very similar to those of the farmers general and the receivers general.[33] Profits of the larger treasury offices, such as the treasurer general for the navy, were enormous. Only a very wealthy person, or at least one who had wealthy parents or relatives to help furnish the funds, could purchase the office. The treasurer general received the standard interest of 5 percent on the capital value of his office, also a large salary and a commission of all the funds that passed through his hands. Since such large sums were involved, the opportunities for profit were monumental. Great fortunes were built up in a short time, like that of Maximilien Radix de Sainte-Foy, who was treasurer general of the navy for only three years in the 1760s. During the first years of Necker's ministry, this office was held by Claude Baudard de Sainte-James, who possessed one of the greatest fortunes of his time. Since treasurers were wealthy it was inevitable that the government would look to them for loans. They were authorized to pay for government supplies and other disbursements with their own promissory notes. The war and naval departments made particular use of this in wartime to pay for supplies in remote parts of the world where it was not convenient to pay in cash. In this way was formed what the financial statements of the *ancien régime* called "the debt in arrears," or simply "the war debt." These notes were similar to modern war bonds. The government did not pay annual interest for them, as it

33. Henri Legohérel, *Les Trésoriers généraux de la marine: 1517-1788* (Paris, 1965), p. 175.

did for anticipations. The interest was acquitted in a lump sum at the time the notes were redeemed. It was understood that they would be redeemed sometime after the war, when the government's finances permitted.

Necker's first major reorganization of financial administration was the decree-in-council of October 18, 1778, which provided "for the establishment of a new order for all the treasuries of expenditure." The preamble referred to the existence of numerous treasuries (*caisses*) which were not under the purview of the finance minister. The inconvenience of this situation was that funds lay idle in these treasuries when they could be used to meet more current expenditures in other departments in the same localities. Centralized direction of all the *caisses* by the finance minister would keep the funds circulating—and more economically than at present, when money was often sent from a province to Paris and then back to the same province.

The decree of October 18 required all treasurers to furnish whatever information the finance minister might request about their *caisses*. Each treasurer was to keep accurate daily accounts of expenditures and revenues and to send at the end of the year the total account to the Chamber of Accounts. At the end of each month an account was to be sent to the director general of finances, with an indication at the bottom of the exact amount in the *caisse*. Very important in this law was the stronger control the director general was to have over all treasurers. The latter could no longer issue notes on the credit of their *caisses* without his authorization. The emoluments of the treasurers would be paid by the royal treasury beginning with the next fiscal year, rather than by the department that spent the money. When treasurers' offices became vacant the replacements were to be made by the king on recommendation of the director general of finances, "since all *caisses* are emanations of the royal treasury."[34]

That the major spending departments would submit gracefully to this increased control by the director general was not to be taken for granted. Passive resistance was to be expected, as had occurred in the king's household. One month after the decree of October 18 came Necker's first bold stroke against the spenders in the two military departments, that of war and of the navy. The preamble of the edict of November 1778 explained that surplus offices of treasurers and controllers had come into existence purely as a means of raising money by the sale of those offices. The conditions allowed the officers were onerous for the royal finances and unjustified.

We have seen that their number is too great, and that the commissions which the treasurers exact are too high; that furthermore these commissions being proportionate to the amount of money paid out, in circumstances where we have the greatest need to economize, the accountable officers have been able to make fortunes out of all proportion to their services.[35]

34. Isambert et al., eds., *Recueil général des anciennes lois*, XXV, 439-441.
35. Necker, *Oeuvres complètes*, III, 73.

This edict abolished twenty-nine offices of treasurer and controller in the department of war and that of navy and colonies, replacing them with a single "treasurer-payer general" for each of the two departments and a single controller for each. The former remained a venal office whose purchaser paid a capital of one million livres, of which he would receive interest at 5 percent per annum in addition to a salary of 30,000 livres. But the system of commissions by which the treasurer could withhold as his own profit a certain percentage of the funds spent was abolished. This brought about a reduction in the lucrativeness of the treasurers' offices. A special study of the treasurers general of the navy shows that the income of this office dropped from 40 percent per annum of the capital value of the office to 8 percent, as a result of Necker's reform of November 1778. [36] The two new controllers would not be venal officers but would hold their posts by commission, appointed by the minister of finance. The latter's strengthened hold over the new treasurers was indicated by the fact that their salaries and all other emoluments thenceforth were to be paid by the royal treasury rather than by themselves.

This act of November 1778 was something more than a request for information that the financial officers could comply with or ignore as they saw fit. It was a serious thrust at their interests. The correspondent Metra reported in his entry of December 1:

Mr. Necker has dealt a severe blow to the financiers by the suppression of the treasurers-general and by the consolidation of their *caisses,* but the operation has the approval of all reasonable persons. However, I would have wished that it had not been executed so suddenly in order that bankruptcy might be avoided by several of these financiers who, in the praiseworthy practice of putting the funds in their *caisses* to use, have found them practically empty when it is necessary to render their accounts. These bankruptcies touch a number of people who have placed their money in notes of these financiers.[37]

It appears that the director general, who was a seasoned banker himself, appreciated their plight, and a year later had the king authorize a declaration giving these accountable officers, whose charges were abolished, three years in which to clear themselves with the chambers of accounts. In some cases an even longer period was permitted. [38]

Early in 1779 Necker turned his attention again to the department in greatest need of reform, where useless offices abounded: the royal households. It was

36. Legohérel, *Les Trésoriers généraux de la marine,* p. 317. Twenty-seven is sometimes given as the number of offices abolished by this edict, but it appears from later sources that there were four instead of two controllers of the treasuries for artillery and engineering mentioned in the original edict. The correct list is given in Necker's 1779 memorial to the king cited in n. 39 below.

37. Metra, *Correspondance secrète,* VII, 151.

38. Necker, *Oeuvres complètes,* III, 90.

here that he had to face the most serious resistance to reform. Early in 1779 he wrote a lengthy memorial to the king proposing a similar consolidation of *caisses* for the royal households to that accomplished in the war and naval departments. Knowing this would be strongly resisted by those close to Louis XVI, Necker set forth his reasoning at some length and marshaled all his arguments to gain the support of the monarch. He pointed out that the suppression of offices the previous November had not created as large a sum to be reimbursed as feared, because the capital of these offices was balanced, in large part, by funds the accountable officers were found to owe the royal government. Furthermore, he pointed out that economy was not the chief reason for this reform. The important matter was to bring order to the king's finances, to know precisely where and how the money was spent. The lack of order produced an unfortunate impression on public opinion, which always tended to exaggerate the financial abuses in the royal households. Furthermore, the demagogically inclined *parlements* could always win public support against new loans and tax proposals because of ignorance of the true situation. In order to counter this threat of the sovereign courts, Necker said it was necessary for the government to put its finances in order. He was clearly concerned about new loans and probably new taxes that would be necessary to raise the 80 million livres for extraordinary expenditures already decided upon.[39]

The memorial also stated forthrightly to the king the difficulty Necker experienced in getting the spending officials of the royal households to comply with his directives on accountability:

At this time I should not conceal from Your Majesty that although the decree-in-council of 18 October last expressly stated that all payers and treasurers would be held to furnish all information to the minister of finance that he might require, and notably to send him each month a statement of their accounts of receipts and expenditures, yet the treasurer of the *grand écuries* and that of the *menus plaisirs* [sections within the king's household], upon order of their chiefs, have refused to furnish these statements and although I have done everything possible to throw a veil over such insubordination in order not to discredit the finances and normal business, however this resistance has pierced through, and those who have known about it have believed that order is impossible to establish, and the good too difficult to accomplish. I do not think so yet because I know the support which Your Majesty gives to views of order and reason. I must add however that whatever may be these views, in order to accomplish them the minister of finance must not be afraid to make powerful enemies in carrying out his duty; in this respect I venture to say that an uncommon opportunity is to be grasped. Thus, the character of the monarch, the zeal of the servant, the urgent necessity of circumstances, public opinion in general, everything invites this reform of the treasuries.[40]

39. "Mémoire de M. Necker," AN F[30] 110A, no. 1.
40. *Ibid.*

The memorial succeeded in winning the king's consent. An edict of July 1779 abolished nineteen offices of treasurers and controllers in the households of both the king and the queen, and substituted in their place a single treasurer-payer general for both households. The capital value of the new office was one million livres, on which interest at 5 percent would be paid, and a salary was stipulated of 20,000 livres.[41]

According to Metra, Necker's analysis of the situation to the king was borne out by the reception of this edict by the public. In his entry for July 26, 1779, Metra noted:

There has just appeared a royal edict, suppressing all the treasurers of the king's household and that of the queen, and which creates a single Treasurer-Payer-General for the expenditures of Their Majesties. . . . The preamble of this edict, which is a masterpiece of beneficence and honesty, has delighted and enchanted all minds and hearts. . . . But since this is only a preliminary of several measures of economy proposed for the queen's household and those of the brothers of the king, Mr. Necker finds himself confronted with the ill humor of those who continually resist his parsimony.[42]

Earlier in the year, in February 1779, the treasurers in the department of roads and bridges were also consolidated into a single office. In October a similar reform eliminated about a dozen offices in the Swiss leagues, the postal administration, and the Paris police.[43]

By the autumn of 1779 Necker had made important progress in establishing control over the treasuries of the spending departments. But this was only in the interests of accountability. It was now possible for him to know what money was spent, but he still had no voice in deciding how much and in what manner it should be spent. These were the decisions of the *ordonnateurs* of the spending departments. Since Necker was convinced that all were wasting the king's money, a showdown was looming.

In the meantime his goal of establishing order in the finances was far from complete. The above-mentioned acts of the royal government concerned only the spending departments. In October 1779 Necker attempted to establish a comprehensive accounting system for all the king's revenue and expenditures. The preamble of the declaration of October 17 explained clearly his intentions:

The registers and the accounts of our royal treasury where one would naturally expect to find the totality of our revenues and expenditures in the most exact detail present in this respect insufficient knowledge and incomplete information. A portion of the tax income is neither turned into the royal treasury nor even known by it; and of various kinds of expenditures customarily being paid by other treasuries there is no trace at all in the royal treasury. . . . We have felt that it would be a considerable advantage to establish a form of accountability

41. Isambert et al., eds., *Recueil général des anciennes lois,* XXVI, 118-119.
42. Metra, *Correspondance secrète,* VIII, 185-186.
43. Necker, *Oeuvres complètes,* III, 86.

whereby all income and all expenditures would pass through the royal treasury, not always in cash but in the form of receipts in a way that opening the registers of the royal treasury one could clearly see the exact relationship of our ordinary revenue and expenditures for each year, and separately, the amount of extraordinary income and expenditures.[44]

The declaration required each accountable officer to send a receipt of all income or expenditure to the royal treasury during the year. Of course, the problem of tax arrears and retardation of payments persisted. But Necker's goal was to narrow the gap so that accounts at the end of the year would be as current as possible, as in the case of the expenditures of the king's household and the payment of pensions. The act of October 17, 1779, must have been the origin of the *Compte rendu* that Necker published in February 1781.

These reforms were remarkable both for their boldness and their moderation. Necker was scrupulous about the interests of those affected.[45] Where the total capital of the abolished offices could not be redeemed in full, interest continued to be paid on the remainder. As Metra reported, the reforms were reasonable, and no doubt public opinion shared that view. But the financiers hostile to any reform joined the ranks of Necker's enemies and took an active part in the libel campaign of 1780. Their opposition was all the more reprehensible in view of the war in which the country was engaged, which threatened to strain the royal finances as never before.

44. Necker, *Oeuvres complètes,* III, 45-46.
45. *Ibid.,* pp. 122-124.

Chapter VIII

FINANCING THE AMERICAN WAR

It is often said that France's participation in the war of the American Revolution caused her bankruptcy some six years later and precipitated the French Revolution. Necker has been blamed for this crisis because of the methods he chose to finance the war from 1777 to 1781. He refused to raise taxes, relying entirely on loans, leaving the bill to his successors, as it were. [1] According to the comte de Mirabeau the loans Necker issued "must be considered the most costly, the most badly organized, the most ruinous France has ever been forced to pay."[2] Especially condemned were the life rentes (*rentes viagères*), which were said to be catastrophic for the royal finances. This was mainly due to the ingenious longevity formula elaborated by certain Genevan bankers based upon the life expectancy of Genevan girls, the "immortals of Geneva," as they were called. It is further alleged that the Discount Bank founded by Turgot in 1776 became, under Necker's administration, the chief vehicle for marketing loans. Select bankers were permitted to monopolize the credit facilities of the bank, borrowing cheaply at the same time they marketed the rentes at a very high cost to the government.[3]

All of the above allegations originated in the libel campaign launched against Necker in 1780. There was a demagogic appeal to the widespread distrust of the international banking community in France, to which Necker had belonged before becoming minister of finance. Coupled with this was a virulent xenophobic attack directed at Genevans. It is against this background that the above list of indictments must be seen. As in the case of the Company of the Indies, we are not limited to the libelous pamphlets for evidence. Were Necker's loans more onerous, more "ruinous" than the loans of his predecessors and successors? The loan edicts were all published, and a reading of them today does not bear out such an assertion. As for the infamous life rentes, how do we know that a

---

1. Stourm, *Les Finances de l'ancien régime,* II, 204-223; Charles Gomel, *Les Causes financières de la révolution française,* 2 vols. (Paris, 1892-1893), I, 255; and Marion, *Histoire financière de la France,* I, 295ff.

2. (Honoré Gabriel de Riqueti), comte de Mirabeau, *Lettres du comte de Mirabeau sur l'administration de M. Necker* (n.p., 1787), pp. 8, 22.

3. Luethy, *La Banque protestante,* II, 461.

disproportionate number of them were placed on young lives? What evidence is there that these loans brought about the bankruptcy of the monarchy? Marion simply made this assertion without offering proof. It is true that the French loans were offered at a higher rate of interest than the British loans. It was one of Necker's goals to lower the rate for the government as well as for the private sector of the economy. But the legacy inherited from the previous reign could not be overcome immediately. Nevertheless, Necker claimed that he had funded all his loans by ordinary, regular revenue. Marion dismissed this claim summarily as "imaginary calculations," but without making any investigation of the subject.[4]

It cannot be denied that the American War placed a serious burden on French finances, as any war would. But it is necessary to get a precise idea of what that burden was. It is usually said that the war cost France about 2 billion livres. This is surely an exaggeration, perhaps derived from Marion's misreading of a manuscript in the Joly de Fleury collection. A table of war expenditures by the two military departments, war and navy, for the years 1776 through 1782 exists in that collection of manuscripts. The table lists the gross expenditures of the two services for each of the seven years, arriving at a total of 1,507,522,239 livres.[5] To that figure was added the "war debt" of the two services—a sum of 225 million livres of notes to be redeemed after the war. This gave a total gross expenditure of 1,732,522,239 livres. The unknown writer of the document pointed out, however, that this figure included the ordinary expenditures of the two departments that were not war costs, since they would have been spent even in peacetime. The annual ordinary expenditures were based upon the *Compte rendu* of 1781: 29.2 million livres for the navy and 85.6 million livres for the war department, making a total of 803.6 million for the seven-year period. The writer subtracted that sum from the gross expenditure and concluded: "One will see that the extraordinary expenditure occasioned by the war will have amounted, by the end of 1782, to 928,922,239 livres."

In the first volume of his financial history of France, Marion wrote that, according to the above table, the war and naval departments "spent extraordinarily" 1,507.5 million livres, to which he added the 225 million in arrears. Since that document did not include war costs for 1783, Marion concluded that the American War must have cost the French government somewhere between 1.8 and 2 billion livres.[6] It is obvious that he misquoted the document. It is true that there were other extraordinary costs incurred outside the two military departments that should be added to the total sum, along with the extraordinary costs of the military services in 1783. But these additions could not have made the total cost of the war much more than one billion livres.[7]

It might still be asked if the addition of one billion livres to the debt was not

4. Marion, *Histoire financière de la France,* I, 321, n. 1.

5. BN MSS Joly de Fleury, 1440, fol. 182.

6. Marion, *Histoire financière de la France,* I, 303, n. 2.

7. See my article "French Finances and the American War, 1777-1783," *Journal of Modern History,* 48, no. 2 (June 1976), 233-258.

sufficient to bring about the financial crisis of 1787-1788. That could be true if it is assumed that Necker's claims to have funded his loans were not genuine. On the face of it there seems to be no reason to think that a war cost of one billion livres spread over a period of eight years could not have been absorbed by the French government. The economy of the nation was buoyantly expanding, and this was reflected in the steadily rising income of the royal government from indirect taxes. Furthermore, England spent over twice the amount France did, and managed its debt satisfactorily.

Admirers of Turgot have held him up as a shining contrast to the Genevan because he advised the French government against intervention in the American affair, on the ground that the royal finances would not permit it. In a famous memorial on foreign policy he contended that the independence of the colonies was inevitable and French intervention unnecessary. Economics alone showed that empires founded on mercantilist principles were bound to give way to bonds of association based upon freedom, both economic and political. [8] The ideas of the *économistes* in foreign policy betray the same a priori contempt for facts as their economic theory. They assume that economic interests invariably determine foreign policy, that questions of prestige, of balance of power, of the thirst for domination are of no importance. All that is required is for governments to recognize their own enlightened self-interest to bring an end to unprofitable empires. It was only four years before Turgot wrote this memorial that the three most "enlightened" sovereigns of the age carried out the first partition of Poland, not, it appears, for economic reasons.

French foreign policy at the time of the first partition of Poland was still paralyzed from the consequences of the Seven Years' War. France was unable to aid effectively a traditional ally. But her successful participation in the American War marked the return of her influence as a power to be reckoned with. It may be said that the financial recovery from the depredations of the previous reign went hand in hand with the restoration of France's role in international affairs.

The architect of the revival of French foreign policy was Charles Gravier, comte de Vergennes. No one ever called him a genius, as so many did Necker, but Vergennes was a skilled diplomat with a long period of experience. The astuteness with which he timed the stages of French intervention in North America was no minor feat. First he authorized secret material assistance to the insurgents, then diplomatic recognition when it appeared by the end of 1777 that the new nation was militarily viable, followed by formal alliance in 1778 and the sending of an expeditionary force when it became necessary. All this was coordinated with his European policy of coaxing Spain into the war in 1779, fostering the League of Armed Neutrality in 1780, and preventing the eruption of a new German war in central Europe. No less skillful was Vergennes's handling of the intricate relations between France and the American ally. For the war in North America was also a civil war, with all the complexities created

8. Faure, *La Disgrâce de Turgot,* pp. 532-534.

by that situation and the inherent dangers for the outside power who inter-venes.[9] Vergennes managed to preserve the alliance from both the threat of some Americans to desert and make a separate peace and from those in France and Spain who were willing to negotiate a peace settlement falling short of complete independence for the American colonies.

Vergennes's diplomatic skill would have been useless if France had not found the means of financing naval rearmament and an expeditionary force. It was axiomatic that this could only be done via loans. Even if new taxes were imposed they could not be collected immediately and would only guarantee the new loans. This was seen in the financial ministry of Necker's successor, Jean-François Joly de Fleury, who increased both direct and indirect taxes but nonetheless had to issue more loans. While the terms of Necker's loans and his hesitancy in raising taxes may be a subject for discussion, the fact that he made use of loans is not open to debate. There was simply no alternative. The British government also financed its war costs entirely by loans.[10]

Contrary to a prevalent view, Necker had no fondness for loans per se. "The ability of borrowing to finance war has become baneful to nations," he wrote in 1784.[11] In the *Compte rendu* of 1781 he had remarked that public credit was a relatively new invention that "humanity would have been better off without." Yet if the enemy seizes this new weapon, the king of France must also. It was a necessary evil. In peacetime he thought the finance minister should strive to reduce the debt as much as possible; extraordinary expenditures should be met by taxation, not loans.

Whether to impose additional taxes or borrow, and impose only what is neces-sary to cover the interest on the loan comes to pretty much the same thing. . . . But there are moral considerations which must determine the preference. When the needs are considerable and pressing, and there is credit, loans must be used because raising a large sum by new taxes would be difficult and would cause convulsions. But for moderate needs, one must always prefer taxation, not only to simplify operations and make it easier to balance the finances, but also to build up public credit and reduce the interest rate by the sparing use of loans. [12]

Whether a government could raise massive sums through loans was by no means certain. The memory of the Seven Years' War was a fiscal as well as a military nightmare. Loans were marketed with great difficulty even though offered at extremely favorable terms to investors. All the government could do under such circumstances was to increase taxes precipitately, and this indeed produced "convulsions." The Parlement of Paris refused to register new taxes, or did so only under strong protest. It was a financial impasse rather than the inferiority of her arms that led France to the humiliating peace settlement of 1763.

9. René de la Croix, duc de Castries, *La France et l'indépendance américaine* (Paris, 1975), pp. 207ff.
10. Binney, *British Public Finance*, p. 106.
11. Necker, *Oeuvres complètes*, V, 125.
12. Quoted in *Encyclopédie méthodique: Finances*, I, 44.

Quite different was the financial posture of the enemy. Since the Revolution of 1688, England had been undergoing what the author of a recent work calls "a financial revolution." [13] The establishment of the Bank of England in 1694 as a semipublic institution and the expansion of its activities in the eighteenth century, along with certain fiscal practices such as the Sinking Fund, had made possible a public debt on a scale undreamed-of in former times. How was it that a country only one-third the size of France, with one-third its population and much less endowed with natural resources, could equip armies, build navies, and fight wars in several theaters of the world, all by the use of credit? How to explain the rise of this awesome power, and how to provide France with the same weapon was a foremost preoccupation of the new government of Louis XVI as a new war with the traditional rival loomed.

Necker undertook to instruct Maurepas, the king, and the public on the nature of this credit. It was not really mysterious, he said, since it depended only upon the integrity of the borrower and the confidence he inspired in the lender. Trust could only be built up over a period of time by sound administration. "The genius of good administration," he wrote in the *Compte rendu,* "consists only of prudence, order, and good faith."[14] Confidence in the government could be cultivated by giving publicity to the government's finances. Publication of the British budget each year and its submission to Parliament provided information to creditors about its financial situation.

Ultimately, Necker believed the power of British credit was explained by the character of the country's institutions. In his treatise on the administration of finances, published three years after his first ministry, when he was out of office and could give freer rein to his anglophilism, he paid high tribute to the British constitution:

The strong bond between citizens and the state, the influence of the nation on the government, the guarantee of civil liberty to the individual, the patriotic support which the people always give to their government in times of crisis, all contribute to making the English constitution unique in the world.[15]

But he was not a republican, or even in favor of a limited monarchy for France during his first ministry. He thought the principle of absolutism was not inconsistent with trust and confidence between the royal government and the nation. This required, however, a complete renunciation of those fiscal habits so much in evidence in the previous reign, "where obligations were constantly defaulted upon, and the government was reduced to borrowing at onerous rates which even so did not produce the desired funds." [16] It was no mean achievement for Necker to borrow 530 million livres during his first ministry, to market the loans without any difficulty, to maintain the circulation of money without

13. P. G. M. Dickson, *The Financial Revolution in England* (London, 1967), pp. 3-14.
14. Necker, *Oeuvres complètes,* II, 25.
15. *Ibid.,* IV, 170-171.
16. "Mémoire de M. Necker," AN F[30] 110A, no. 1.

inflation, and to leave the credit of the government "stronger at the end of the war than it had ever been in the peace which preceded it," as Necker's successor, Joly de Fleury, exclaimed in some wonderment in 1783. [17] How was he able to carry out this feat?

The crux of Necker's fiscal policy was close attention to the relationship of fixed expenditures to fixed income, or according to the expression most often used, those revenues and expenditures termed "ordinary." If the ordinary accounts were balanced, the government's credit posture was favorable for borrowing. "The wealth of the sovereign," he wrote, "does not consist of a capital fund, but of annual revenue." [18] The foundation of credit for the monarchy was the king's annual revenue, which could be safely depended upon to come into his coffers. The ordinary expenditures of the royal government were equally fixed and certain. They were determined by decision of the king and council at the beginning of the fiscal year. If there were "cost overruns," the excess must be placed in the category of extraordinary expenditures. Of course, if such overruns became habitual, then the ordinary expenditure would be raised, as was done for the naval department. In the *Compte rendu* of 1781 Necker noted that the navy's normal peacetime expenditure was 31 million livres (29,200,000 livres after deduction of pensions, which began to be paid by the royal treasury rather than the treasurer general of the naval department). But he remarked that the king was expected to increase this sum for the future peacetime navy. This was done during the decade of the 1780s, becoming fixed at 45 million livres in the *Compte rendu* of 1788.

What distinguished the accounts termed "ordinary" from those that were "extraordinary" was their degree of certainty. "The ordinary revenues and expenditures are as well known at the beginning of the year as at the end of the fiscal year," he wrote in 1787.[19] And again, "the fixed revenues and expenditures have a positive and distinct character which cannot be mistaken."[20] Extraordinary expenditures were those contingent on unforeseen circumstances. Furthermore, maintaining the distinction between the two types of accounts was not just a matter of convenience; it went right to the heart of Necker's fiscal policy. He insisted on the moral importance of distinguishing the ordinary from the extraordinary accounts:

Ordinary expenditures must be balanced by fixed and constant revenues. It is a great error, both politically and morally, not to observe the proper distinction between this type of expenditure and needs that are extraordinary, because there is danger of raising permanent taxes to the level of temporary expenditures. It is necessary therefore to provide for extraordinary and momentary needs by resources that are also extraordinary and momentary; and if one chooses the recourse of loans, the interest on the loan must be classified among the ordinary expenditures.[21]

17. BN MSS Joly de Fleury, 1441, fols. 45-47, 70.
18. *De L'Administration des finances*, in *Oeuvres complètes*, V, 98.
19. *Mémoire au mois d'avril, 1787*, in *Oeuvres complètes*, II, 209.
20. *Ibid.*, p. 272.
21. *Nouveaux Éclaircissements sur le compte rendu*, in *Oeuvres complètes*, II, 345.

If creditors were assured that the government could meet its fixed charges on its debt from ordinary revenue, they would have no reason to fear a default. Necker was as emphatic as he could possibly be that interest charges were part of ordinary expenditures. In the *Compte rendu* of 1781 he wrote: "The most unjust as well as the most dangerous of all fiscal policies is to borrow money without having assured the interest payments on it, either by economy or by increasing revenue." [22] It would be a serious blow to credit if the government should be forced to suspend interest payments on both rentes and on debts that were exigible. Rentes had been the traditional type of obligation, enabling the government to escape the church's ban on usury. The rentier turned over his capital to the government in return for an annual payment, which was not called interest, but a rente, since the capital was not expected to be returned to the rentier. The rentes could be either perpetual, at the standard rate of 5 percent, or they could be life rentes, in which a higher rate of interest was paid but only during the life on which the rente was constituted. An exigible debt, in contrast to the rente, was one in which the government borrowed money and promised to return the principal through some agreed-upon plan of amortization, as well as paying the annual interest.

The finance ministers of the eighteenth century were agreed that both rentes and interest on the exigible debt should be considered ordinary expenditures. But there was some difference among them about the amortization payments on the exigible debts. During the Seven Years' War, those payments were suspended. In Loménie de Brienne's *Compte rendu* of 1788, he listed all such payments as extraordinary expenditures. It was not considered such a serious matter if the government were to suspend amortization payments, as Loménie did in August 1788, on certain exigible loans. Necker, however, believed in general that amortization payments should be classified as ordinary expenditures, and his *Compte rendu* of 1781 listed 17 million livres in such expenditures. But on the two lottery loans, that of December 1777 and October 1780, he listed only the interest charges as ordinary expenditure and considered redemption payments extraordinary. He reasoned that those payments depended upon future lottery drawings and lacked the "positive" character of ordinary accounts. His enemies who attacked the credibility of the *Compte rendu* naturally seized upon that apparent inconsistency with glee. But they chose to ignore the fact that Necker had done rather well in paying 17 million livres for amortization when it was usually thought unnecessary in wartime.

The great drama of Necker's first ministry was whether he would succeed in keeping the ordinary accounts balanced, as new war loans were piled on ever more loans. Would he be able to balance the ordinary accounts of the royal

---

22. *Compte rendu au roi,* in *Oeuvres complètes,* II, 4. In view of the number of times Necker expressed this principle so clearly, it is astounding to read in Gomel that "according to Necker the loans would feed themselves so that it was not necessary to create new tax revenues to meet the interest and amortization of each loan, and that these expenditures could be charged to the proceeds from the loans"; Gomel, *Les Causes financières de la révolution,* I, 254.

finances through improvement of administration, the elimination of waste and inefficiency, the reduction of costs of collecting taxes, the reduction of pensions and gratifications, and all the other measures that came under the heading of ameliorations? Would he be able to escape, in the end, the recourse to new taxes? It was by no means a foregone conclusion.

The starting point of his budgetary operations was the *Compte rendu* of his predecessor, Bernard de Clugny, which had indicated an ordinary deficit earlier in the year of 24 million livres. In December 1776, Necker presented his first statement on the finances to the king, showing that the ordinary deficit had been reduced to 20.5 million livres by that time. [23] A year later, on December 1, 1777, he submitted a second financial account showing that during 1777 the ordinary deficit had been lowered to 5.5 million livres. The year following, on November 30, 1778, a third statement showed that the ordinary deficit had finally been erased.[24]

These accounts were not published, but in the preambles of all his loan edicts Necker informed the investing public about the state of finances, both the amelioration he had carried out and the new extraordinary needs that would require loans. In the preamble to the edict of November 1778, his first large issue of life rentes, he announced that "we have succeeded in balancing our ordinary expenditures with ordinary revenues." But he referred to the heavy war expenditures, especially for the navy, and assured creditors that if it were necessary to impose new taxes to maintain the balance of ordinary accounts he would not hesitate to do so. [25] It turned out to be unnecessary. How he was able to do this by economizing on expenditures and increasing the ordinary yield of revenue without additional taxes will be the subject of the following chapter. Here we will examine the type of loans issued during Necker's ministry, and the cost of those loans to the government. What truth was there in the allegations that those loans "were the most ruinous that France had ever been forced to pay," and that the Genevan had planted a fiscal time bomb in the royal finances that detonated some six years after his first ministry?

It is undeniable that France's credit at the beginning of the American troubles in 1776 was inferior to that of the British government. Throughout the American war the British borrowed at a lower rate of interest than the French. Necker inherited rather than created this situation, and he had to make the best of it. France could not offer on the open market its traditional perpetual rente at 5 percent. The actual rate of interest on the free market for government notes was 6-2/3 percent. This was a legacy of the reign of Louis XV and particularly the

23. AN F[30] 110A, no. 52.

24. *Ibid.*; see also in the same carton the "Compte de l'année 1778." Compare "Etat actuel des recettes et des dépenses ordinaires du roi," December 1777, AN F[4] 1082, no. 20, and "Récapitulation des pièces présentées au roi du 21 novembre 1778." "L'Etat actuel des recettes et des dépenses de sa majesté," *ibid.*, no. 26.

25. The edict of November 1778 was printed by de Staël in Necker, *Oeuvres complètes,* III, 17-23.

"partial bankruptcy" of abbé Terray in 1770. In order to refund the government's obligations, Terray issued a loan in February 1770 of 160 million of perpetual rentes at 4 percent. During the years of the American War, these 4 percent notes remained at about 60 percent of face value on the open market. Therefore, it was possible for the investor in government rentes to purchase these 4-percent notes on the open market at reduced value and have a claim against the government at face value. This meant, in effect, that he could earn an interest of 6-2/3 percent.[26]

The royal government could borrow money at 5 percent through the credit facilities of the "intermediate corps," such as the city of Paris, the clergy, and the provincial estates, and by exacting loans from officials. Necker borrowed nearly 161 million livres from these sources, representing about 30 percent of his total loans.[27] Most of these loans were exigible, and amortized over a period of years. It is a great error to say, as some authors have, that Necker did not know of any other type of amortization except the life rentes.[28] On the contrary, only 35 million out of his total of 530 million livres of loans were perpetual rentes without any provisions for amortization.[29] The redemption payments for the loans of the *pays d'états* were usually 5 percent, making a total charge of 10 percent per annum. Five percent was the legal interest rate, and there could hardly be any criticism of those loans. Necker's successor, Joly de Fleury, also used the credit facilities of the intermediate corps, but it was obvious in late 1781 and all of 1782 that they were becoming exhausted.

It was necessary for the royal treasury to enter the open market for loans. Two techniques were used by Necker to induce the owner of surplus capital to invest it in government securities; neither was a novelty, both having been used in the previous reign. One was the lottery loan, the other the *rente viagère,* or life rente. The lottery loan appealed to the gambling instincts of the investor. It offered him the opportunity to win favored securities by taking his chances on the great wheel at the Hôtel de Ville, where the drawings were held. The most he could lose would be by placing his capital at a mediocre rate of 4 or 5 percent. Necker's first lottery loan was issued in January 1777. It was a combination of perpetual rentes at 4 percent and life rentes placed on one or two lives. The initial capital was given as 24 million, 18 million of which were perpetual rentes. However, the figure carried in later accounts of the government debt shows that the initial creation of life rentes was 9.8 million, rather than 6 million livres in capital. The annual cost of the life rentes was 1,090,000 livres, or an average interest of 11.1 percent. These rentes were obviously the prize sought by the

---

26. "Mémoire sur un emprunt de 80 million, janvier, 1782," BM MSS Joly de Fleury, 1448, fols. 175-176. See also Necker, *Oeuvres complètes,* V, 486.

27. The figure includes loans of the *pays d'états*; loans from officials and financiers, not counting anticipations; and the loans from the clergy, from the Saint-Esprit in 1780, and from Genoa.

28. See, e.g., Luethy, *La Banque protestante,* II, 471.

29. See Table 1, at the end of this chapter.

investor. The annual cost of the perpetual rentes was 720,000 livres, or 4 percent. Paul-Edme de Saint-Cyran, who published tables converting life rentes into perpetual rentes in 1779, gave the average cost of the loan of January 1777 at 6 percent.[30]

Two other lottery loans were issued by Necker, one in December 1777, the other in October 1780. Both were exigible debts, amortized over a period of seven and nine years respectively. The inducement for investors was bonuses (*primes*) for certain bonds (*billets*). Since the interest payment was included in the redemption and the bonus payments, the average cost of these loans is difficult to give, and the experts disagree. Necker, it will be remembered, did not calculate the redemption payments on these two loans as an ordinary expenditure. He carried the interest cost in the *Compte rendu* of 1781 at 5 percent. In his history of the French public debt Adolphe Vührer gave the total cost of the 1777 loan as 6 percent and that of the 1780 loan as "a little less than 7 percent." He added that "this ingenius form of loan, which produced a considerable sum, was in reality the most advantageous the treasury could have adopted."[31] It would appear, indeed, that the average cost of the three lottery loans was well below the 6-2/3 percent that was the market price of the rentes of 1770.

The same can be said of the much-decried life rente loans issued by Necker in his first ministry. Here also, abbé Terray left a heavy legacy. In June 1771 Terray issued a life rente loan in the hope of attracting Dutch investors (so it is called the Loan of Holland) by offering life rentes at 8 percent on one life and 7 percent on two. The bait was to permit investors to purchase the rentes in depreciated French government paper (including the 4-percent notes of 1770). Half the purchase price could be met by this depreciated paper, which the government honored at face value; the other half was paid by the investor in cash. This meant that the actual cost to the government was around 12 percent.[32]

30. Paul-Edme Crublier de Saint Cyran, *Calcul des rentes viagères sur une et sur plusieurs têtes* (Paris, 1779), seconde partie, pp. 21-22.

31. Adolphe Vührer, *Histoire de la dette publique en France,* 2 vols. (Paris, 1886), I, 270.

32. Marion, *Histoire financière de la France,* I, 264, n. 2; Luethy, *La Banque protestante,* II, 488. In looking at the figures of the Loan of Holland in the tableau of life rentes published by the Hôtel de Ville in 1789, Laugier compares that loan with one of Necker's life rente loans, that of November 1779, which had a capital of 67,150,000 livres and an annual payment in rentes of 6,571,958 livres (Laugier, *Un Ministère réformateur,* p. 200, n. 6). He asserts that the Loan of Holland "was less onerous to the treasury" than the loan of November 1779. If one looks at the figures, that would seem to be true: the Loan of Holland had a capital of 119,793,000 livres, paying annual rentes of 9,397,469 livres, or 7.84 percent. In contrast, the interest rate of the life rente loan of November 1779 would appear to be 9.78 percent. But Laugier overlooked two important matters. First, the capital of over 119 million livres received by the government from the Loan of Holland was only half in cash; the other half was in depreciated government paper, which, however, the government accepted at face value. As has been shown above, the actual cost of the Loan of

Even such favorable terms failed to attract Dutch investors. The original amount of the loan was a capital of 26.78 million livres, with rentes of 2 million livres. By December 1774, less than one-fourth this amount had been subscribed to by Dutch and Genevan investors. In October 1771, half the initial amount authorized by the loan of June was transferred from Holland to Paris and offered to French investors. It appears to have stagnated until the beginning of the new reign; then it was rapidly extended far beyond the original amount of 2 million livres of rentes. In Turgot's *Compte rendu* of 1775, it appears that life rentes of the Loan of Holland had reached 8 million livres, four times the amount authorized in the original act of June 1771. Apparently it was after the subscription had reached that sum that Turgot closed the loan, in March 1775.[33] In 1789 the rentes of the letters patent of June 1771 had reached 9.39 million livres, with a capital of 119.79 million livres having been received by the government. But it must be remembered that this capital was only half in cash, the other half being in depreciated paper. This was the most burdensome of all life rente loans in 1789.[34]

There is a great deal of mystery about how this enormous extension of the Loan of Holland took place. Evidently the Paris Chamber of Accounts vehemently protested these secret extensions of the loan.[35] The editor of *L'Espion anglais* believed that another secret extension that took place in 1776 was made by Clugny. Herbert Luethy has placed the responsibility for this on Necker, claiming that on October 31, 1776, Necker reopened this loan secretly and allowed selected Genevan and Bernese bankers to purchase 323,850 livres of life rentes with a nominal capital of over 4 million livres. By backdating the rentes to February 1, 1776, Necker made it possible, according to Luethy, for his friends to realize an interest rate of 13 percent.[36] But the evidence he produces for this grave charge is not convincing. The receipts of all the rentes he refers to are

Holland to the French government was about 12 percent. The proceeds from the loan of November 1779 were all in cash. Furthermore, the life rente loan of November 1779 was subject to the 10-percent tax known as the *dixième d'amortissement,* from which the Loan of Holland was exempt. That meant in reality that Necker's life rente loan in 1779 was sold to investors at the interest rate of 9 percent on one life and 8 percent on two lives. See "Tableau des rentes viagères de l'Hôtel de Ville de Paris," in Marion, *Histoire financière de la France,* I, 472-473.

33. Mathon de la Cour, *Collection de comptes rendus,* p. 146. The date of the loan is not given in Turgot's *Compte rendu* of 1775, but the terms are indicated: 8 percent on one life, 7 percent on two lives. Only the Loan of Holland had those terms.

34. This was certainly the opinion of the Paris Chamber of Accounts. In registering the letters patent of 18 December 1774, which fixed the capital of the Loan of Holland, the Chamber addressed the king: "The king is humbly beseeched to order that the said loan will not exceed the sum of two million in life rentes authorized by these letters, and to consider that such an onerous loan can only be prejudicial to the interest and the economy of his finances"; AN P 2739, "Plumitifs de la chambre des comptes," March 29, 1775. The Chamber never made any objection to Necker's loans.

35. *L'Espion anglais,* IV, 400 and passim; V, 235, n. 1.

36. Luethy, *La Banque protestante,* II, 496ff.

dated February 29, 1776. On nine of the receipts it is stated that they were registered by decree in council of September 14, 1776. It will be remembered that Necker was not appointed to the treasury until October 22.[37]

It was the author of the *Liégeoise,* the seventh of the libels published against Necker in 1780, who first made the charge that Necker had permitted Genevan bankers to subscribe to life rentes at ruinous terms for the government. He wrote:

They subdivide the risk among thirty different lives; that is to say, that a Genevan who wishes to purchase 3000 livres of life rentes, acquires 100 livres on each of the 30 lives of girls from ten to twelve years of age; each [contract] should last at least 70 years before the obligation of the state is extinguished.[38]

Necker's life rente loans were offered the investing public at a standard rate of interest "for all ages" of lives upon which the rentes were constituted. The assumption was that the average life would be a median age between five and sixty years; according to Saint-Cyran, this would be forty years. [39] Actuarial science had progressed far enough by then so that average life expectancy of each age could reasonably be predicted. However, it is a mistake to think that the actuarial tables composed for calculating life rentes were based upon the average life expectancy of the whole population. Again, according to Saint-Cyran, those tables were always calculated upon the life expectancy of elite classes in the population—always higher than for the general population. This would diminish the importance of the Genevan girls being selected because of the salubrious climate of their city-state or the gentle conditions of life of their

37. The evidence Luethy gives for this secret extension of the Loan of Holland is AN P 6028. One finds a bundle of eight notebooks of receipts attached to a larger bundle in which the contents are too far deteriorated to be opened. But the notebooks are in good condition. On the outside of each notebook is written the date "du 31 octobre 1776," but there is no explanation of what that date means. There is an outer covering leaf on which is written in manuscript, on a torn printed page from the office of the *payeur principale de la tréasorie nationale:* "Rentes viagères sur une tête, Lettres patentes du 12 juin 1771 ... dernier cahier de la jouissance du 1 fevrier 1776." The receipt is a printed form in which a notary (whose signature appears on the receipt) has filled in the following information in manuscript: the name of the person making the subscription, the life or "head" on which the rente is constituted, the amount of the subscription, the date on which the "enjoyment" begins, that is, February 1, 1776, and the date of the receipt: "Fait à Paris, le 29 jour du fevrier 1776." On the lower part of nine of the receipts the following is written also by the notary: "La quittance ci-dessus enregistrée en exécution de l'arrêt du conseil du 14 septembre 1776." It is hardly conceivable that Necker could have persuaded several notaries, on October 31, to backdate these receipts to February 29. It was stipulated in the original letters patent of June 1771 that the "enjoyment" of the rente would begin on the first of the month in which the rente was subscribed. If they were in fact subscribed on the last day of February, there was nothing illegal in having the purchaser benefit for the entire month of February. The minister of finance at that time was Turgot.
38. "Lettre à M. Necker, directeur général des finances," *Collection complète de tous les ouvrages,* I, 30ff.
39. Saint-Cyran, *Calcul,* pp. 30-31.

sex and their station in society, the upper bourgeois class. Those conditions were calculated in the actuarial tables; in general, all lives selected had such advantages. [40] Yet, it remained true that if a greater proportion of rentes were placed upon lives younger than forty rather than over that age, the government would be the loser. Saint-Cyran did not think that, in general, this occurred:

According to this calculation [that forty years is the median age for life rentes offered at all ages] if the loan were filled in greater part by very young persons, the borrower would have made a bad deal; but also it must be considered that there are good reasons why a great number of life rentes are [placed on lives] that are no longer young. Ordinarily it is only after the first youth that a person contracts for life rentes, because prior to that time one is not master of his property, or one is not at liberty to dispose of it in that way, and furthermore one hardly decides upon such investments until he has chosen his station in life.[41]

Saint-Cyran obviously thought that most purchasers of life rentes had them constituted on the purchaser's own life rather than on some third party. The great amount of criticism of the *viageriste* in the eighteenth century gives some evidence for this. The investor in life rentes was considered egotistical, selfish, unmindful of his relatives who would not inherit his fortune upon his death. Yet many of the same critics who denounced the *viageriste* for his egotism also denounced the rampant speculation in life rentes. Obviously they could not have it both ways. Either the investor in life rentes was contemptible because he had placed the rentes on his own life, and the income from the rentes would cease with his life, or he had placed his rentes on some other life, and his heirs would continue to enjoy that income after his death; that is, until the death of the lives on which the rentes had been constituted. If these were Genevan maidens destined to live 70 more years after the rentes were constituted on them, then the heirs of the *viageriste* could have no complaint.

It would appear that the proportion of the entire life rente debt of the government at the end of the *ancien régime* that was based on young lives has been grossly exaggerated. It was only a fraction of the 100.6 million livres of life rentes existing on the first of January 1793. The scope can be seen in the "republicanizing process" carried out under the direction of Joseph Cambon in 1794. Cambon revised the life rente debt on the basis of a loan of perpetual rentes at 5 percent. The rentes constituted on the lives that had reached fifty-two years in 1794 suffered no diminution; those based on lives with ages of

40. *Ibid.*, p. 18. Saint-Cyran did admit, however, that the average life expectancy of the Genevan girls on whose lives "consolidated" rentes were based, as described in the *Liégeoise*, was somewhat longer than that of the average rentier (*Calcul*, p. 29). This work was based upon the longevity tables of Antoine Deparcieux, Buffon, and the Dutch scientist Kersebloom. Published in 1779, it was adopted by the French Academy of Science as its authorized table on actuarial science. See the Auckland papers, British Museum, Add. MSS 34,417, fols. 20-35.

41. Saint-Cyran, *Calcul*, p. 31.

forty to fifty-one were reduced 8 percent; those between thirty and forty, 20 percent; those between twenty and thirty, 28 percent; and those between six and twenty suffered a 32-percent reduction. The total amount of rentes placed on one life, 66.6 million livres, was reduced to 56.3 million livres by this operation.[42] (All the rentes based on the Genevan formula were constituted on one life. Those constituted on two or more lives did not interest the Genevan bankers.) Of course, 10 million livres annually was an important saving. It was by no means negligible that the royal government had paid that sum because of the excessive numbers of young lives upon which the rentes were constituted. But it was hardly catastrophic. Furthermore, it would appear that Necker's share of that overpayment calculated by Cambon must have been small. According to Luethy's figures, the amount of Necker's four major loans subscribed to by Genevan bankers was not more than 15 percent.[43] Even so, it is not certain that all that sum was placed on young lives.

The total amount of life rente loans raised by Necker can be verified roughly, although an exact figure is difficult to establish for two reasons. First, the original loan edict is not a safe guide, because the actual subscription to the loan varied from the amount indicated in the edict. Usually the actual subscription surpassed the figure originally authorized; but in one case, the life rente loan of March 1781, the initial subscription was considerably less than authorized in the edict. Secondly, it was an accepted practice for finance ministers to make an extension of a loan granted by an edict passed previously, sometimes many years before. This type of loan could be made without a special edict, on mere authorization of the king, and was not subject to registration by the Parlement. Thus, one can find that a particular loan has become mysteriously swollen in a subsequent *Compte rendu*. An example that we have seen was the Loan of Holland issued by abbé Terray in June 1771.

Despite these handicaps, a fair approximation of Necker's life rente loans can be attempted. It will be remembered that the lottery loan of January 1777 was constituted partly in perpetual and partly in life rentes, the latter amounting to 1 million livres, with an initial capital of 9.8 million livres (despite the edict that had fixed it at 6 million livres). In addition there were four major life rente loans issued by Necker. The first was in November 1778, constituting life rentes of 4.5 million livres, with a capital of 48.36 million livres. The second loan, constituting 6.57 million livres of rentes, came a year later in November 1779, bringing a capital to the treasury of 67.12 million livres. The third loan, the largest of Necker's life rente loans, was issued in February 1781. It was constituted, apparently by the time of Necker's resignation in May, for 7 million livres of life rentes, bringing in a capital of 76 million livres.[44] Necker's last loan, the edict

---

42. *Archives parlementaires de 1787 à 1860,* ed. Marcel Reinhard and Marc Bouloiseau, 1st ser. (1787-1799) (Paris, 1968), LXXXVII, 122-123.

43. Luethy, *La Banque protestante,* II, 508-509, 512.

44. The figures for these loans are taken from Cambon's table of life rente loans cited in n. 42, above.

announcing 3 million livres of life rentes, was issued in March 1781. Contracts amounting to a capital of 37.3 million livres were delivered to the royal treasury by the minister of finance to be sold to the public. In contrast to earlier loans, these rentes were not eagerly subscribed to by the public. When Joly de Fleury came to the *contrôle général,* he withdrew 11.4 million livres worth of contracts, so that the loan was constituted initially at 2.2 million livres of life rentes and a capital of 25.8 million livres.[45] The withdrawn contracts were probably sold to the public in 1783 by Fleury's successor, Lefèvre d'Ormesson.

There were three smaller life rente loans to be added to Necker's account: a loan by the Order of the Saint-Esprit in life rentes for the king, amounting to 142,144 livres and a capital of 2 million livres; a life rente loan of the city of Paris for the king, of 208,171 livres with a capital of 3 million; and a loan of August 1780 for 210,854 livres with a capital of 2.2 million.[46] The total amount of Necker's life rentes thus came to 22 million livres with a capital of 234.4 million livres.[47] These loans were issued over a period of four years and five months. During that time the life rente debt was being extinguished at about the rate of a million and a half livres per year. The edict of the loan of January 1777 stated that the life rente debt at that time was 43 million livres. According to the "Study of the King's Debt as of January 1, 1782," the life rente debt was 58.3 million livres.[48] That would mean that Necker's net addition to the life rente debt was only 15.3 million livres.

The total amount of the life rente debt outstanding on January 1, 1789, was 101,687,938 livres.[49] The proportion of Necker's life rente loans in the debt of

45. The capital received by the royal treasury from the loan of March 1781 is given in "Etat de tous les emprunts fait par le gouvernement depuis le 1 janvier 1777, époque de la guerre, jusqu'à et comprise 1781," BN MSS Joly de Fleury, 1437, fols. 23ff, fol. 266. The amount of life rentes constituted during 1781 is given in another copy of the same document, which contains more details, found in AN F[30] 110A.

46. The latter loan is taken from Cambon's table. The figures for the loans of the city of Paris and the Saint-Esprit are taken from "Etat de tous les emprunts," fol. 23.

47. Luethy gives figures of 385.8 million livres for the capital and 31 million of rentes as the total of Necker's life rente loans (*La Banque protestante,* II, 467), but he does not show how he arrives at those figures. A frequent error is to include the extension made by Calonne of the loan of March 1781 as part of Necker's loans. This was 52.6 million livres in capital added in 1786. In addition, it has been seen that 11.4 million livres were added to the figure given in my table of loans sometime in 1783. The total capital and the rentes for the loan of March 1781 given in the tableau of life rentes of the Hôtel de Ville in 1789, and by Cambon's table in 1793, include those extensions (in the latter, 89,828,106 capital and 8,727,376 rentes). But even with that addition, Luethy's figure of 385.8 million is nearly 100 million livres more. The only life rente loan he mentions that I have not included (other than the supposed extension of the Loan of Holland) is the life rente loan of the comte d'Artois. This prince had contracted a debt of about 1 million livres in life rentes, representing a capital of 10 million livres. The finance minister had no responsibility for this loan until it was assumed by the royal treasury in December 1783, under Calonne's ministry. See BN MSS Joly de Fleury, 1436, fol. 21.

48. "Etat de tous les emprunts," BN MSS Joly de Fleury, 1437, fols. 23ff.

49. Reprinted in Marion, *Histoire financière de la France,* I, 472-473.

1789 can be precisely determined except for his last loan, that of March 1781, due to extensions made on it by his successors. Not counting that loan, it can be seen in the table of 1789 that the total of life rentes derived from Necker's first ministry was 17.7 million livres. Since the March 1781 loan was initially 2.2 million livres, it is evident that his share of the life rente debt of 1789 was less than 20 percent.

It is difficult to see why Necker should have been subjected to so much abuse by historians because of his life rente loans. They were raised to meet the exigencies of a major war, as was also the life rente loan of Joly de Fleury of January 1782, which added 12 million livres initially to the life rente debt. But Calonne, in full years of peace, added nearly 20 million livres to the life rente debt, and Loménie de Brienne, during his brief ministry, added 16 million livres.[50] If it was the life rente which "brought about the ruin of the monarchy," it is not clear why Necker should be singled out for special blame.

Was it because Necker's life rente loans were offered at more onerous terms for the royal treasury than those of his predecessors and successors? This was definitely the opinion of Marion, who fully endorsed Mirabeau's assertion that Necker's loans must be considered the most costly, the most badly organized, and the most ruinous which France had ever been forced to pay. But a reading of the loan edicts preserved by the Paris Chamber of Accounts from the beginning of the Seven Years' War to the outbreak of the French Revolution does not support such a judgment. Necker's life rente loans were certainly offered at no more onerous terms for the royal government than any of the above; and with the notable exception of the loan of February 1781, they were somewhat more advantageous than the average. Marion severely castigated Necker for offering life rentes at 10 percent on one life "at all ages," maintaining that this had not been habitual in the previous reign, where the interest rate was altered according to the age of the person on whose life the rente was constituted.[51] It is true that this was done up to and including the life rente loan of 1754. After that date it became the usual practice to offer the rente "on one life at all ages."[52]

Necker's life rente loan of November 1778 was offered at 10 percent on one life and 8.5 percent on two lives, without distinction of ages; the loans of

50. In 1786, Calonne, by his own admission, made an extension of the loan of March 1781 of 52.6 million livres in capital, and an extension of the loan of January 1782 of 36.3 million livres; see his *Requête au roi: Adressée à sa majesté par M. de Calonne* (London, 1787). These loans, added to his life rente loan of December 1783 (for 100 million livres capital) and December 1785 (for 5.9 million), would make a total capital of 194.6 million livres added to the life rente debt during his ministry. Lomenie de Brienne's first life rente loan of May 1787 added a capital of 66.9 million livres; his loan of November 1787 authorized a capital of 120 million livres, but only 100 million had been constituted before his resignation ("Compte général des revenues et des dépenses fixes au premier mai, 1789," AN AD IX 552, p. 56), making a total of 166.9 million for his ministry.

51. Marion, *Histoire financière de la France*, I, 295.

52. The loan edicts from 1757 through 1764 can be found in AN AD IX, 94; those from 1765 through 1770 in AN AD IX, 95; those from 1771 through 1777 in AN AD IX, 96.

November 1779, February 1781, and March 1781 were offered at 10 percent on one life, 9 percent on two lives, 8.5 percent on three lives, and 8 percent on four lives, all without distinction of ages. Except for the loan of February 1781, Necker's loans were subject to the tax on government securities amounting to one-tenth of the proceeds (the *dixième d'amortissement*). This tax, promulgated by an edict of 1764, had the effect of lowering the interest rate by 1 percent on all government loans subjected to it. If the finance minister should be apprehensive about the success of his loan he could declare it exempt from the *dixième.* This was done by Terray for the Loan of Holland and by Necker for the loan of February 1781. Also exempt from the *dixième* were Fleury's loan of January 1782, Calonne's of December 1783, and Loménie de Brienne's of May 1787.[53]

In the work by Saint-Cyran published in 1779 on the calculation of life rentes, table six computed "the life rentes which must be paid for each 100 livres of rentes offered at all ages" by converting them into perpetual rentes at 5 and 6 percent. For Necker's loans, the equivalent figures Saint-Cyran gave for life rente loans converted into 6-percent perpetual rentes are informative. For one life, the equivalent rate was 8.63 percent; for two lives, 7.23 percent.[54] The three loans of November 1778, November 1779, and March 1781 were all subject to the *dixième,* so the actual rate was 9 percent on one life; for two lives the interest was 7.5 percent on the first loan and 8 percent on the latter two. It can be seen that for these three loans the average rate in perpetual rentes was only slightly above 6 percent, very similar to the interest rate on Necker's lottery loans.

The February 1781 life rente loan was exempt from the *dixième,* so the rate was 1 percent higher. It appears in retrospect that this loan was a miscalculation on Necker's part. He mentioned in the *Compte rendu* that the royal government felt it necessary to offer the next loan at more advantageous terms for investors. He seemed to think the credit situation critical and was concerned about whether he could succeed in raising the necessary money for the military campaigns of 1781. But the government's credit was much better than expected. In building it up he had wrought greater than he knew! The loan was quickly subscribed to and soon oversubscribed. To put a damper on the rush of investors, Necker closed the February loan and issued his fourth major life rente loan, in March 1781, which was subjected to the *dixième.* This did cause the investment market for rentes to slacken, as we have seen. Writing in November of the same year, Isaac Panchaud could see nothing to criticize in the three life rente loans subject to the *dixième,* but he did remark that the February loan "was needlessly offered at 10 percent on all ages."[55]

53. The life rente loans exempt from the *dixième* can be seen in the table of 1789 published by Marion; see n. 49, above.

54. The exact rate was given by Saint-Cyran in livres, sous, and deniers: for one life, 8 livres, 12 sous, 8 deniers; for two lives, 7 livres, 5 sous, 8 deniers. I have converted the sous and deniers into percentages.

55. Panchaud, *Réflexions sur l'état actuel du crédit,* p. 44.

Nevertheless, this one extravagance does not alter the general picture of Necker's wartime loans. The average interest rate of his loans must have been around 6 percent. We have seen that nearly one-third of the total was borrowed at the standard interest rate of 5 percent. The lottery loans averaged slightly over 6 percent. The life rente loans, with the exception of that of February 1781, also averaged slightly above 6 percent when converted to perpetual rentes according to Saint-Cyran's table. That author pointed out that the income of the life rentier subject to the *dixième* tax included both interest and amortization, and therefore this was a much stiffer tax for the rentier than for other categories of investors. The *dixième* was intended to be a tax on interest income alone. This is only one more reason to think that Necker's life rentes were not the "gilt-edged" investments they are so often said to have been.

Six percent was not a cheap rate of interest. The average rate for the British government was certainly less. Necker himself would have liked to see it lower, and one of the goals of his reform was to bring about a reduction for both the government and the private sector of the economy. But under the circumstances none of his loans, with the possible exception of the life rente loan of February 1781, can seriously be criticized. The widely held notion that his loans were ruinous, even catastrophic, for the royal government, cannot stand up under investigation and must be seen as the invention of his enemies. Furthermore, Necker claimed that he had provided for the costs of his loans by economy in administration. How valid that claim was will be the subject of the next chapter.

TABLE 1

Table of Loans During Necker's First Ministry

(in livres tournois)

	Capital	Rentes
I. Perpetual rentes (without definite period of amortization):		
Lottery loan of January 1777	18,000,000	720,000 (4%)
Loan of Saint-Esprit, February 1777	9,257,120	462,856 (5%)
Loan of City of Paris, August 1777	7,828,580	391,429 (5%)
	35,085,700	1,574,285
II. Life rentes (government's obligation ends with life on which they are constituted):		
Lottery loan of January 1777	9,800,000	1,090,000
Loan of Saint-Esprit, February 1777	2,042,880	142,144

Table of Loans During Necker's First Ministry
(in livres tournois)
(Continued)

	Capital	Rentes
Loan of city of Paris, August 1777	2,971,420	208,171
Loan of November 1778	48,365,000	4,519,213
Loan of November 1779	67,150,000	6,571,798
Loan of August 1780	2,216,000	210,854
Loan of February 1781	76,085,900	7,051,539
Loan of March 1781	25,800,000	2,214,540
	234,431,200	22,008,259

III. Royal treasury loans, capital amortized according to terms of loan edict:

City of Genoa, 1776, 1777	7,500,000	
Lottery loan of December 1777	25,000,000	
Lottery loan of October 1780	36,000,000	
Clergy, 1780	14,000,000	
Saint-Esprit, 1780	3,321,143	
	85,821,143	

IV. Loans of the *pays d'états* for the king, amortized:

Burgundy, 1778, 1779	24,200,000	
Languedoc, 1776, 1778, 1779, 1780	48,000,000	
Provence, 1776, 1779	5,437,000	
Artois, 1780	3,000,000	
Brittany, 1779, January 1781	8,535,000	
	89,172,000	

V. Loans from officials and financiers, amortizable at time of abolition of office, interest continues to be paid until debt has been completely liquidated:

| Taxi franchise (*privilège des fiacres*) | 5,500,000 | |
| Addition to surety bonds of employees of *fermes* and *régies* | 24,000,000 | |

Table of Loans During Necker's First Ministry
(in livres tournois)
(Continued)

	Capital	Rentes
Advances from financiers of *fermes* and *régies* (not anticipations)	5,000,000	
Administrators of gunpowder *régie*	1,000,000	
Chamber of Accounts, Provence	1,000,000	
Loan for repurchase of hundredth tax on offices for eight years	7,000,000	
The *fermes* of Sceaux and Poissy	2,000,000	
	45,500,000	
VI. Increase in amount of anticipations during Necker's ministry	40,000,000	
Total of all loans	530,010,043	

Source: The complete list of Necker's loans was given by baron de Staël in Necker, *Oeuvres complètes,* III, 1-5. This is a reliable source except for the life rente loans. On the latter de Staël listed the figures contained in the original loan edicts, which did not always correspond to the amount actually subscribed. My principal source for the life rente loans is the *tableau* of Cambon, (n. 46). But Cambon included the later extensions of the loan of March 1781; my figure for that loan is taken from the manuscript of Joly de Fleury (n. 49). On other than life rente loans, the latter document matches the figures given by de Staël, with one exception: the document of Joly de Fleury gives the figure of private loans from officials at 62.1 livres rather than de Staël's figure of 45.5. On the other hand, the former document did not list the increase of anticipations, as did de Staël. I have followed the latter on those two items.

Chapter IX

AMELIORATION

By November 1778 Necker had achieved a balance of ordinary expenditures with ordinary revenue. Then his task was to maintain that balance in the face of steadily mounting ordinary expenditures caused by war loans. As Napoleon remarked to his secretary soon after the *coup d'état* of 18 Brumaire: "It is not enough to be in the Tuileries, Bourrienne, we must remain here." If Necker were to meet the new ordinary expenditures through administrative reforms, he would have to carry the battle boldly into some of the most powerful and sacrosanct fortresses of the *ancien régime.* He was determined, but the question was how far the king and Maurepas would support him.

The magnitude of his task can be judged retrospectively by the money he borrowed for the royal government and the increased fixed charges which it incurred. In his literary debate with Calonne during the Assembly of Notables in 1787, after the controller general had told the Assembly that there was a discrepancy of 56 million livres in the various items given in the *Compte rendu* of 1781, Necker published his April memorial showing exactly how he had paid for his loans by savings through administrative reforms, which he called amelioration. He admitted that he had borrowed a total of 530 million livres for the king during his ministry. The average annual cost, including interest and amortization, was 8-3/8 percent. This meant an addition of about 44,400,000 livres to the fixed charges to be paid annually by the royal government. But there had to be added to that sum the 24-million deficit in Clugny's *Compte rendu* of 1776. Also to be added was an increase of ordinary expenditures, unrelated to the war loans, of nearly 15 million livres. (The latter included the three million livres' additional deficit that he believed to be in the *Compte rendu* of Clugny.) This meant that Necker had to increase the ordinary, annual income by 83.4 million livres in the four-and-a-half years of his financial ministry. In his April memorial he spelled out in twenty-nine articles exactly how he had achieved that goal.[1] Are we to look upon these as "imaginary calculations" as asserted by Marion, or are Necker's claims supported by evidence?[2]

1. "Mémoire au mois d'avril, 1787," *Oeuvres complètes,* II, 185-196.
2. Marion, *Histoire financière de la France,* I, 321, n. 1.

The table of ameliorations at the end of this chapter (Table 2) shows that the largest single group was due to improvements in new contracts that Necker drew up with the companies of *fermes* and *régies.* These were the companies of financiers who contracted with the government to collect the tax revenue, operate the postal service, and administer the domain, the royal lottery, and other enterprises. The word "financier" had a meaning in the *ancien régime* that it no longer has today: it referred to a person with a private fortune who contracted with the government to perform some task in which he handled the government's money. For that reason, the financier was a *comptable,* one who was required to submit his accounts to a chamber of accounts for verification, or "purification," as it was called. Another word often used for the same class of people was *traitant:* one who contracted with the government to perform a service for profit.

The financiers took a prominent part in the libel campaign begun in 1780. They alleged that Necker was intent on destroying the financiers as a class and replacing them with persons of his own ilk, forcing the government to become dependent on the international community of bankers for its short-term loans. This charge is sometimes repeated in historical works, but it can hardly be taken more seriously than other supposed similarities between Necker and his famous predecessor, John Law. Necker could not do without the financiers, as he freely admitted. He increased anticipations by 40 million livres during his ministry. He negotiated other long-term loans with them, such as the 30-million-livre loan he contracted with the farmers general before leaving office in 1781—negotiations that were completed by his successor, Joly de Fleury.

In his *Compte rendu* of 1781 Necker spoke rather highly of the farmers general, indeed of the entire class of *traitants.* They were no longer the disreputable Turcarets of Le Sage's famous comedy, which had reflected the popular opinion of them earlier in the century. Necker did not try to destroy the financiers as a class. He wanted to diminish government dependence on them, eliminate the onerous terms of their contracts, and reduce the mass of capital they furnished the government for their "charges," and for which they received excessive rates of interest. He compared them to a variety of weed that only grows luxuriantly in a swamp with an unhealthy climate. It was when the king's finances were in critical condition that the financiers were able to write those onerous conditions into their contracts. Also, he believed the financiers needed more supervision by the finance minister than in the past. He thought there was some truth in the complaints of the great remonstrance of 1775 about them. "I reproach the financiers," he wrote in the *Administration of Finances,* "for their tendency to accept too easily the ideas of despotism and of severity.... The desire to collect taxes without any obstacles lends itself easily to inspiring fear and terror in the taxpayers."[3]

3. *Oeuvres complètes,* V, 356. See also Adam Smith's similar criticism of tax farmers in *The Wealth of Nations,* p. 854.

He considered abolishing completely the system of contracting with the financiers and adopting a purely bureaucratic system for the collection of taxes and for other parts of administration that were entrusted to *fermes* and *régies.* Could these functions be assigned to heads of bureaus receiving only a fixed salary? Such a regime required bureaucrats that were efficient, able, dedicated, loyal public servants. But those qualities were not cultivated in a government like the French monarchy, where favor rather than merit so often determined appointments. The social and moral environment did not ensure efficient bureaucratic administration. Therefore it was necessary to appeal to the self-interest of the administrator, to contract with him in such a way as to link his duty to his selfish private interest. The system of venality of office and contract did this.[4] Necker intended to retain the system of venality, but to purify it of its abuses. Too often in the past, offices had been created simply as a fiscal expedient, to acquire the capital of the purchaser of the office. Necker wanted to eliminate useless offices and to make new contracts with the *traitants* that would be more favorable to the interests of the government.

To evaluate the libelists' charges against Necker's handling of the financiers, we need only look at the terms of the contracts he made with them, whether their capital was reimbursed when their offices were abolished, and whether interest was paid regularly on their capital that remained with the government. With Necker's goal of "reform without despotism," existing rights or government promises, even if detrimental to its interests, could not be summarily abolished. For this reason Necker delayed reform of the Royal General Farms until the Laurent David lease expired in 1780 and it was time to draw up a new one. In some cases, particularly with respect to *régies,* where the financiers had not assumed any risk, Necker did set aside contracts and replaced them with new ones because the terms could not be considered an injustice to the financiers. But throughout his reform of the *fermes* and *régies,* scrupulous legality was always observed. Necker also had a humane concern for those whose offices were abolished. They were given special preference for new appointments.

The contracts with financiers created either a *ferme* or a *régie.* In the eighteenth century there was considerable discussion about the relative merits or disadvantages of the two types of contract as far as the royal finances were concerned. It was usually assumed in the popular mind that the *ferme* was much more onerous to the king's interests than the *régie,* an impression seemingly confirmed by the spectacular fortunes of tax farmers. According to a typical *ferme* contract, the farmers engaged themselves to pay a fixed sum periodically to the government, regardless of the income derived from the tax source leased to them. The farmers assumed the risk of whatever fluctuations the enterprise might be subject to; if the yield of tax revenue, for example, was less than the fixed price of the lease, the farmers suffered a loss; if the tax harvest was more lucrative than the fixed price in the lease, the farmers reaped the profits.

4. *Oeuvres complètes,* IV, 233-234.

Throughout the eighteenth century the income from the indirect taxes mounted steadily, so few farming companies suffered a loss. After the Laurent David contract with the farmers general expired in 1780, it appeared that the farm's profits amounted to 55.5 million livres in the six years. All this was income over and above the various emoluments, salaries, and interest payment on their capital. Tax farming was detested because people believed the profit motive impelled the ruthless exaction of revenue from the source farmed.

The *régie* contract differed from the *ferme* in that the income from the enterprise was not assigned to the financial company but remained government property. The *régisseurs intéressés* were so called because when the proceeds surpassed a fixed sum they shared in the surplus. Otherwise their emoluments were limited to the interest payments on their capital, their salaries, and commissions from the money collected. Unlike the *fermiers,* the *régisseurs* assumed no risk, and their share of the profits, that is, the income above a fixed price, was a much lower rate than the farmers usually had. Yet the profit motive was supposedly still strong enough to impel them to exact the greatest possible amount of revenue from the tax leased out to them.

As a result of Necker's reforms, the difference between the two types of contract was greatly mitigated. In the Nicolas Salzard contract, which he signed with the company of the General Farms in 1780, the king's share of profits was significantly increased at the expense of the farmers. In 1784, Necker wrote that the distinction between the two types of leases had become largely grammatical. "The king says to the *regisseurs:* 'You can have a certain proportion of the revenue which surpasses a certain sum.' He says to the *fermiers:* 'The king will have a certain proportion of the revenue which surpasses the fixed price of the lease.' "[5]

Necker's first reorganization took place in April 1777, two months before his appointment as director general of finances. The decree-in-council of April 3, 1777, consolidated five separate *régies* into a single one known thereafter as the *régie générale.*[6] The new General Administration was to begin on the first of October of that year. It was to consolidate the *régies* that had collected different categories of indirect taxes: those known as "reserved rights," which originally were extraordinary war taxes deriving mostly from the entrance taxes to cities imposed in 1758, but which had become quite ordinary; the tax on legal records (*droits de greffe*); the tax on mortgages (*droit d'hypothèque*); those excise and sales taxes levied in Flanders (*les quatres membres de la Flandre maritime*); the *régie des droits réunis,* which collected excise taxes on leather, gold, silver, and iron products and on tallow and starch; and finally, the excise tax on paper and cardboard products. The capital value of these offices and the *croupes* attached to them was 26 million livres. This money was to be refunded in cash to their holders in October. A new company of twenty-five administrators, who were to be selected from the former *régisseurs,* would replace the suppressed *régies.* The

5. *Ibid.,* p. 235.
6. *Ibid.,* III, 128.

capital value of these new offices would amount to 10 million livres, and the interest rate would be paid on this capital at the rate of 5 percent, a lower rate than in the abolished *régies*. All *croupes,* of which there had been 300 in the former administration, were to be eliminated. They had not been in most cases gratuitous pensions but represented capital for the financing of the office. Even so, this type of *croupe* was undesirable from the standpoint of good administration and control by the finance minister.

The economy this achieved was due to the reduced number of administrators, a lower interest rate on their capital, reduced profits of administrators, and extinction of the *croupes*. In his April memorial, Necker claimed a savings of three million livres annually by the creation of the *régie générale* and the suppression of superfluous offices in the administration of the royal domain.[7] In view of the substantial number and the capital value of offices suppressed, this seems a reasonable claim.

The royal domain had been a fertile field for the creation of offices for purely fiscal reasons. It was probably the most negligently managed department of the royal government. Originally the most important source of the king's income in the medieval period, it had deteriorated in the eighteenth century largely due to leases of domain lands to favorites, known as *engagists*. The terms were usually detrimental to the king and highly advantageous to the *engagist*.

In 1777, administration of the royal domains and forests was shared by two financial companies, often with overlapping functions. One was a *régie* consisting of twenty-five *régisseurs* who collected the taxes and feudal dues from the domain. But they shared this function with sixty-four receivers general of the domain and forests; and beneath these were a host of lesser offices expanding almost in geometric proportion. The *régie* had been leased to the firm of Jean Berthaux in 1774 during the administration of Turgot. The lease was to run for nine years, from 1775 to 1783. Formerly this administration had been under a *ferme* contracted with the syndicate of Nicolas Sausseret in 1773 for a period of thirty years. Turgot transformed it into a *régie* and achieved a considerable benefit for the king because Terray had contracted on terms so highly disadvantageous.[8] But Necker found much still left to be done. In August 1777 appeared the king's edict setting aside the Berthaux contract at the end of the year and announcing the formation of a new *régie* of eighteen *régisseurs* to administer the royal domain beginning January 1, 1778. The new administrators were to be appointed by the king. Later in 1777 the contract was awarded to the firm of Jean-Vincent René for nine years. The finance of the offices of the twenty-five *régisseurs* that were abolished, amounting to 6 million livres, was to be reimbursed in January 1778 "in cash." The August edict stated that all *croupes* in the old contract were to be abolished.

This was only the beginning of the elimination of the venal offices in the

7. See Table 2, at the end of this chapter.
8. Pierre Roux, *Les Fermes d'impôts sous l'ancien régime,* p. 375. Turgot achieved a savings of 3.5 million livres, according to Roux.

administration of the royal domains and forests. The preamble of the August edict announced that the new *régie* would assume the duties of the sixty-four receivers general whose offices were to be abolished, as well as the numerous lesser offices. A total of 506 offices were eliminated in this holocaust, with a capital value of over 8 million livres. The new administration would appoint public servants by commission rather than restore venal offices in the lower ranks, introducing a bureaucratic structure similar to that of the General Farms. The only venal officers remaining were those at the top, the eighteen new *régisseurs*. The preamble stated:

We have thought that 18 persons, chosen primarily from among the receivers-general of the domain and the present directors of the *régie* can perfectly well perform all the duties attributed to the 64 offices of receivers of the domains and the 25 directors. At the same time we believe it equally unnecessary to leave standing the 64 offices of controllers of the domains and forests, the 152 offices of *receveurs-particuliers* of the domains and forests, the 152 offices of the receivers of fines in the *maîtrises d'eau et forêt,* and the 49 offices of general guards and collectors of the same fines.[9]

The preamble also referred to one of Necker's foremost concerns in the realm of social welfare. The prisons, prior to 1773, had been supported by funds from the royal domains and forests. In that year, abbé Terray detached them from this administration and placed them under the supervision and financing of municipalities. Evidently this did not improve the quality of the prisons, which by all accounts were atrocious under the *ancien régime.* The edict of August 1777 called attention to their unsatisfactory condition, and said that savings of 300,000 livres a year from this reorganization would go for construction of more adequate prisons.

In 1777, two other important administrative reorganizations were carried out by Necker, in the postal and stagecoach service and in the royal lottery. Both administrations were legacies of the discredited financial ministry of Necker's predecessor, Bernard de Clugny. The latter had drawn up a new *ferme* contract for the postal and stagecoach service in which scandalous gifts were distributed. Terms of the contract were liberal for the *fermiers* and highly unfavorable to the king's interests. The nine-year contract was to begin on January 1, 1777. While Necker was hesitant to break leases with farmers where they had assumed risks, the terms of Clugny's lease were so clearly undeserved that Necker felt it not unjust to set it aside and refund the money to the farmers.

According to the decree-in-council of August 17, 1777, the postal *ferme* was converted into a *régie.* The preamble stated that the farmers of the postal service were making profits out of all proportion to the risk or the work involved. The *régie* established by this act was to begin on January 1 the following year and run six years. It would be granted to six administrators who would provide a

9. Necker, *Oeuvres complètes,* III, 112.

capital of 800,000 livres each, receiving interest on it at 5 percent and a salary of 15,000 livres per year. They would be given one-half of all income above 10,400,000 livres a year. Since the income never reached that figure in the next six years, all the profits went to the king. Necker estimated the annual increase in revenue from this reform at 2.4 million livres.

The reorganization of the postal service required new negotiations concerning the *ferme* of the government stagecoaches (*messageries*), which was a subsidiary of the dissolved *ferme* of the postal service. Clugny had converted the *régie* of Turgot into a *ferme* and granted the farmers lenient terms so characteristic of his administration. The farmers were held to a fixed price of only 1 million livres a year, though rival companies had offered to take the contract for 2 million and 1.8 million livres. In November 1777, Necker renewed the lease with the same company but with 1.8 million livres as the fixed price. This meant a gain of 800,000 alone. Later he converted the *messageries* into a *régie*. Necker estimated the total improvement of this lease at 1.5 million livres in his April 1787 memorial.[10]

One of the most unhappy legacies of the brief financial ministry of Bernard de Clugny was the institution of a royal lottery as a means of revenue. There had been smaller lotteries operated by the Hôtel de Ville, the Royal Military College, and religious communities, which were all suppressed by the decree-in-council of June 30, 1776, establishing the royal lottery.[11] This callous exploitation of human weakness, which brought ruin to poor families, was denounced by the philosophes, the encyclopedists and the enlightened humanitarian community in general. Necker never passed up an opportunity to deplore it, as he did in the *Compte rendu* of 1781. Yet, like the *gabelles* and the tobacco monopoly, it had become a financial prop that could not be removed in wartime. But it was possible to reduce administrative costs, for Clugny had set up an organization top-heavy with administrators enjoying exaggerated emoluments and high rates of interest. According to the *Espion anglais,* the intendant of the lottery, one Mesnard de Conichard, maintained a sumptuous mansion of 40 rooms "as many large as small" costing 200,000 livres. The writer estimated that the new establishment paid out about 1.2 million livres in pensions, and another 800,000 was spent for the furnishing of buildings and apartments of the 12 *régisseurs*.[12]

According to several reports of the incident, Necker called the twelve directors to a meeting and told them: "The king has found many abuses in your administration; he does not accuse anyone, but he finds that you are too many by half. The king leaves it to you to reform yourselves; you may choose six of your number to continue the work of administration."[13] Whatever their recommendations might have been, a decree-in-council of June 1777 reduced the

10. *Ibid.,* pp. 174-175.

11. Marcel Marion, *Dictionnaire des institutions de la France aux XVIIe et XVIIIe siècle* (Paris, 1923), pp. 342-343.

12. *L'Espion anglais,* IV, 239.

13. Soulavie, *Mémoires historiques et politiques,* IV, 34.

number of administrators from twelve to six. They were placed under the direction of a commissioner appointed by the king in place of the former intendant. Salaries were reduced, interest on the capital of the offices was cut to 5 percent, and *croupes,* which had infested the administration of Clugny, were forbidden. The royal lottery after this reform yielded an annual revenue of 7 million livres for the royal treasury. No income from this source had been included in the *Compte rendu* of Clugny in 1776 since it had not been established early enough in the year. Therefore, Necker could count the 7 million livres from this source as new revenue, however regretfully.

One final minor amelioration achieved before the great reforms of 1780 was the reorganization of the *régie* for the supply of troops and their transportation in metropolitan France. This had been performed by a company of nineteen *régisseurs.* By a decree-in-council of October 3, 1778, the number of *régisseurs* was reduced to eight, who were to take charge of the new administration for convoy and supply of troops beginning at the first of the year, 1779. As in all such reforms, the new personnel would be chosen from those whose offices were suppressed. The capital of the suppressed offices would be reimbursed, and *croupes* were forbidden in the new company.[14]

Such was the amelioration claimed by Necker during the first two years of his ministry, 1777 and 1778. In 1779 France was engaged in full-scale war with Great Britain, and the director general of finances was definitely worried that spring. This had already been noted in the memorial he wrote to the king urging the suppression of the treasuries in the royal households.[15] It appeared to Necker that 80 million livres of extraordinary income must be found. He thought it probable that new taxes amounting to 20 or 30 million livres would have to be raised to guarantee the loans necessary for 1779 alone. As it turned out, in 1779 it was not 80 million livres but 116.4 million that was required by the three spending departments: war, navy, and foreign affairs. In the following year, 1780, it could be foreseen that extraordinary expenditures would reach 150 million livres.

If the correspondence of Metra can be relied upon, Necker was on the point of submitting his resignation in March 1779. It was either this, or strike out even more boldly at the abuses and waste in the administration of the royal finances. Much more was possible, but it would require affronting more powerful interest groups than he had yet done. He had not touched the company of the General Farms, since their lease did not expire until 1780. But already he had studied the possibility of a wide-reaching reform in the collection of taxes and had submitted his plan to the royal council in a meeting in mid-March 1779. The plan was vehemently opposed by the secretary of state for the navy and colonies, Gabriel de Sartine. The debate was a violent one; but at the end the king supported Necker, according to Metra's entry of March 16:

14. Necker, *Oeuvres complètes,* III, 188.
15. See p. 114 above.

Mr. Necker was on the eve of offering his resignation, but his ambition has proved to be stronger [than his desire to resign]. The last council meeting witnessed a crisis. Mr. de Sartine treated him [Necker] harshly. [The argument] had to do with the reorganization of the General Farms whose lease will soon expire, and is up for renewal. The director general let go with his heavy guns: "I do not know any other way; I have no other resource." "In that case, do what you want to," said the king, and the council meeting ended.[16]

Early in the summer, public opinion was greatly excited by the expected invasion of England or, alternatively, Ireland by the French army. The entrance of Spain into the war seemed to assure naval superiority for such an operation. Patriotism ran high, and Necker believed this would permit him to issue his second major loan of life rentes. This was done by the edict of November 1779, exactly a year after his first loan. To his relief it was easily subscribed, and his position seemed secure for the moment.

During 1779 he appeared to have the undiminished confidence of the king and of Maurepas. But he had incurred the deep enmity of Sartine. Coming from the conservative magistrate class, with many years of service in government posts, Sartine could only tolerate the Genevan as an efficient house steward, whose duty was to raise money but not to meddle in other matters. The director general's pretension to scrutinize expenditures in the interest of economy went entirely against the grain of both civilian and military chiefs of the departments of navy and war. The minister of war, the prince de Montbarey, who came to this position in 1777 after the death of the comte de Saint-Germain, was considered something of a nonentity who owed his appointment to the intervention of Madame de Maurepas. A conservative aristocrat (his title was derived from the German Empire), Montbarey had little taste for bankers and none at all for Genevans. But he had little weight in council meetings, and his influence was even more tarnished by a liaison with an opera girl that he tried unsuccessfully to keep secret.[17]

Fortunately, Necker did enjoy the support of the individual who, next to Maurepas, was the most powerful minister in the government, the comte de Vergennes. The architect of French foreign policy during the American War, Vergennes appreciated the importance of building government credit. Judging from his correspondence, he looked with considerable admiration on the Genevan's handling of the royal finances. In a letter to Armand Marc, comte de Montmorin, French ambassador to Madrid in 1777, Vergennes gave a favorable report on the financial situation. Referring to the "dilapidation" of the previous reign, he said that matters had not greatly improved in the first years of the new reign, but that "we are now entering a new period which seems to promise real hope." He described Necker's policy of balancing ordinary expenditures by ordinary revenue through reform. He said that these reforms had achieved a

16. Metra, *Correspondance secrète,* VII, 331.
17. Montbarey, *Mémoires,* II, 240ff.

considerable increase in revenue, which seemed to assure an income superior to expenditure for the following year (1778)–unless, he added, war should break out between France and England. He was particularly impressed by the strength of royal securities on the *bourse*.[18] Two years later in a letter to Montmorin, in December 1779, Vergennes again returned to the subject:

Mr. Necker has just issued a loan of sixty million livres in life rentes and it has been subscribed to within a week. . . . We have to give credit to the director general; he has managed finances in a way we have hitherto scarcely had an idea of in France. He prepares his loans by economies and amelioration which enable him to dispense with raising new taxes. If he can finish the war without departing from that system, he will be a very great man in his own domain.[19]

Necker seems to have staked his reputation on being able to continue this policy. During the remainder of 1779 he prepared the great reforms of 1780, the boldest of his first ministry. They were to affect all the financiers who collected the royal revenue, both direct and indirect, the administration of the royal households, and the royal domain.

The regulation of January 9, 1780, announced that the entire apparatus for collecting indirect taxes was to be reorganized, including the Royal General Farms, the *régie générale,* and the *régie* of the domain. The purpose was to attach similar tax collecting functions under the same administration in the interests of greater efficiency and economy. The *aides* (primarily the sales and excise taxes on liquors) were to be detached from the General Farms and placed under the *régie générale.* The General Farms would retain the salt tax (*gabelles*), the tobacco monopoly, and the customs duties (*traites*), all with similar problems of administration.

They were tax revenues which had to do with importation or exportation of foreign or national merchandise, and the defense of exclusive privilege, either at the frontier of the kingdom or at the barrier of the capital, or at provincial boundaries which were still foreign or reputed to be such.[20]

The elaborate apparatus of the General Farms existed to enforce this type of tax levy, which required vigilance against smugglers. The *aides* did not require this particular type of administration, and it was more rational to place it under the *régie générale,* which collected taxes similar to the *aides.*

The economy here was due to the fact that income from the *aides* tended to fluctuate the most widely of all tax revenue. Consumption of the products tapped by this tax tended to vary according to the prosperity of the population. It was a high-risk tax for the tax farmer, and the company of the General Farms

18. Vergennes to Montmorin, April 12, 1777, quoted in Henri Doniol, *Histoire de la participation de la France à l'établissment des Etats-Unis d'Amérique.* 6 vols. (Paris, 1888-1889), II, 260-261.

19. Vergennes to Montmorin, December 17, 1779, quoted in *ibid.,* IV, 493.

20. Necker, *Oeuvres complètes,* III, 140.

had made the most of this situation by demanding extremely favorable terms in the lease it signed for all the taxes it collected. In effect, the government was paying the General Farms a heavy insurance premium against loss on this one item in the lease. The yield from the General Farms' other sources was fairly steady and regular. Therefore, Necker was able to negotiate a "two-price system" for the lease. The first price was fixed low enough to eliminate risk to the *fermiers*. The "rigorous price," as it was called, was fixed at 122,900,000 livres annually, which the General Farms committed itself to furnish to the government at fixed intervals. Between this price and the superior or "hoped-for price" of 126 million livres, the company would not receive any share of the tax harvest. Beyond the "hoped-for price" the General Farms would receive half the yield and the king the other half. As it turned out during the six-year lease, the proceeds never failed to reach the superior price, and the king always received some profit beyond that price.

According to Necker's April 1787 memorial, the king regularly received 1.2 million per year in profits above the superior price of the Salzard lease, but this also included the profits above the fixed price of the other two leases, those with the *régie générale* and the administration of the domain. It was a modest profit, but so was that of the General Farms. The total profit above the fixed price in the Laurent David lease for the six-year period (1774–1780) was 55.5 million livres, of which the king received only 13.5 million livres. Obviously the company of the General Farms suffered a tremendous reduction in profit, and its income now tended to approach that of *régisseurs*, that is, an interest payment on their capital advanced to the government, plus their salary, and only a moderate chance of profit if the yield went above the stipulated price. One historian of the tax-farming system of the *ancien régime* has asserted that, with the lease of Nicolas Salzard negotiated in 1780, "the system of tax farming disappeared almost completely to give place to a system of *régie intéressée*, because the farmers received a salary along with a certain percentage of the profits."[21]

There were other important benefits for the king in the Salzard lease. The system of *croupes* was entirely eliminated. About one-third of the Laurent David lease profit had gone to *croupiers*. Roux published the list of beneficiaries, which included some significant names in view of the libel campaign launched against Necker in 1780. The intendant Sénac de Meilhan received 15,000 livres annually from his brother's position in the General Farms; the mother received another 15,000 livres; Sénac got another 18,000 livres from the *fermier* Marchand de Varennes.[22] The number of *fermiers* was reduced from sixty to forty members in the company. Interest on the capital advanced by each was reduced from what it had been in the previous lease. In the latter, the *fermiers* received 10 percent on the first 1 million livres advanced to the government and 6

21. Pierre Roux, *Les Fermes d'impôts*, p. 381.
22. *Ibid.*, pp. 627-628.

percent on the remaining 560,000 livres, or a total of 133,600 livres in interest payments for each *fermier*. Added to that was a salary of 24,000 livres and an office expense account of 4,200 livres, making a total income of 161,800 livres for each of the "sixty pillars" under the Laurent David contract, or a total of 9,708,000 annually. In contrast, the individual *fermier* under the Salzard lease received 5 percent interest on the first million livres advanced to the government and 7 percent on the next 560,000 livres, or a total interest payment of 89,200 livres, to which was added a salary of 30,000 livres. This made a total of 119,200 livres annually for each *fermier,* or 4,768,000 for the forty members who now made up the company, a savings of 4,940,000 livres yearly.

There were other smaller economies achieved in the Salzard contract with the General Farms. A long-standing custom required the company to make a gift to the controller general of 300,000 livres for the six-year period. After drawing up the Laurent David contract in 1774, abbé Terray pocketed the entire amount. He was induced by Turgot to return all but the first year's portion of 50,000.[23] Turgot himself declined this *pot-de-vin,* but his immediate successors, Clugny and Taboureau des Réaux, did not. Necker never accepted any of the Laurent David gift, turning it over to the royal treasury, and such gifts were expressly eliminated in the Salzard contract. The General Farms agreed in return for its abolition to donate 10,000 livres annually to the hospital for poor patients from the parishes of Saint-Eustache and Saint-Roch. The other two companies also donated 6,000 livres each to the same cause.

After the beginning of the new administration, it appeared that the finance minister intended to supervise the company of the General Farms much more closely than had been customary in the past, when it was allowed almost complete autonomy. He prodded the *fermiers* to make economies in administration amounting to another 1,023,600 per year. Furthermore, he was always aware of the grievances against the harshness of the *commis* of the General Farms, those which had been expressed, for example, in the great remonstrance of the Court of Aides of 1775. In a letter to the *fermiers* in September 1780, he called attention to abuses in the treatment of those arrested for suspected smuggling. He ordered them to send him a list of all cases every three months, and a list of those still detained, with information about each one. Necker also gave attention to the selection of personnel, and required the *fermiers* to send him information about the employees of the General Farms, including such matters as their "zeal and intelligence." Furthermore, he required the administration of the General Farms to send him regular accounts of its operations.[24]

The amelioration of the General Farms in 1780 was only the beginning of the reform, in Necker's plans. He would have liked to reduce the capital of each of the *fermiers* below the figure that he found it under the Laurent David lease, but the financial circumstances of the time did not permit reimbursement for this item. This was to be one of his first measures in the postwar period. Also, he did

23. *Ibid.,* p. 375.
24. Necker, *Oeuvres complètes,* III, 165-171.

not think forty *fermiers* were necessary. In the *Administration of Finances* (1784), he wrote that twenty capable persons would be sufficient. For the other two companies, he thought fifteen administrators for each was all that was needed. Although profits of the *fermiers* were greatly reduced in the Salzard lease, Necker believed in 1784 that they could be further reduced. Finally, he was very much concerned about the mass of anticipations. It was not true, as the libel literature of 1780 was to claim, that Necker wished to do without the short-term credit of the financiers and substitute bankers for them. But he attempted in 1780 to keep anticipations below 100 million livres. If the sum exceeded that level it would be impossible to keep the interest rate of anticipations at 5.5 percent, to which he attached the greatest importance.

Despite limitations of his 1780 reform, it is significant that Necker succeeded in negotiating such a treaty with the company of the General Farms. It indicates that government finances could not have been as critical as Necker's enemies claimed then, or as historians have generally thought since. If they were, the financiers could have exacted much stiffer terms at the expense of the king than they did in the Salzard lease.

Similar terms were made in 1780 with the *régie générale* and the administration of the royal domain. Both leases stipulated a fixed price of 42 million livres. In a financial statement sent to the king, Necker summarized the gains achieved in the total reorganization of the indirect taxes.[25] Based on the lease prices alone, and subtracting costs of administration, there was an amelioration of 13,700,000 livres in the king's ordinary revenues, the largest single item achieved in Necker's reform ministry. In addition, he estimated profits from all three companies that went to the king at 1.2 million livres. It can be seen in the table of *Comptes rendus* in the Appendix that the upward thrust of income from the indirect taxes was unabated throughout the remainder of the *ancien régime.* In the next lease, called the Mager contract, negotiated by Calonne in 1786, the "superior price" of the General Farms was raised from 126 to 150 million livres, and of the other two companies from 42 to 50 million each.

After completing the new contracts for the collection of the indirect taxes, Necker turned his attention to those officials who collected the direct taxes. An edict of April 1780 abolished all forty-eight receivers general and replaced them by a company of twelve administrators who would remit the funds they received from the direct taxes into a single *caisse.* The *caisse* of the receivers general would be managed by a cashier general appointed by the minister of finance, holding his post by commission. The twelve administrators of the company would advance a capital of 1 million livres to the government and receive an annual interest of 5 percent, or 50,000 livres, together with a salary of 25,000 livres. It was a much more drastic reform than that carried out for the General Farms. The editor of the *Encyclopédie méthodique: Finances,* an ardent supporter of the director general, wrote:

25. "Finances, fermes et régies," AN F[30] 110A, no. 2.

It may well be imagined that this great operation did not win the assent of the financiers.... But all enlightened people, all friends of the fatherland, applauded with delight. How could one not fail to acclaim a reform which saved annually two million livres and accelerated the circulation [of money].[26]

Only six months after Necker's resignation in May 1781, his successor restored the forty-eight receivers general. In numerous memorials contained in the manuscripts of Joly de Fleury, it was argued that the savings were not as great as claimed by Necker, that the work was too heavy for the twelve administrators, that it was necessary to have alternates so that the accounts of more than one fiscal year would not have to be handled by the same person. Every argument was marshalled except the real one for restoration of the offices: to acquire the capital that would come to the royal treasury by their sale. In 1784 Necker took cognizance of all these arguments against his reform. He called attention to the fact that the receivers general resided in Paris and that all they had to do turn the tax revenue over to the cashier general. In fact, that single commissioner could have done all the work. He pointed out that the Discount Bank, which also had twelve directors, handled a much greater volume of money, twice the amount of the receivers general, and that the directors all had full-time jobs in addition. The same was true of the directors of the Bank of England.[27]

Necker's reforms in the revenue-collecting agencies of the government were certainly productive of savings. But he still looked upon the spending departments, where waste and prodigality were unchecked, as most in need of reform. It was here that he hoped to make the most progress toward paying the cost of the war loans by "amelioration." Consolidation of the treasuries in those departments was motivated first by a desire to establish "order." An important economy was achieved by reducing the number of treasuries. But, after all, the great decisions on spending were not made by the treasurers. It was rather the *ordonnateurs,* the chiefs of the major divisions within the departments of the navy and war and the royal households, and of course the secretaries of state, who spent the money. There was little hope that Necker could persuade Montbarey and Sartine to allow him to scrutinize their expenditures, especially in wartime. But he evidently attempted to do so, for abbé de Véri commented about the quarrel between the director general of finance and the chiefs of the two military departments. "The military spirit is not inclined toward economy as is that of the man of the pen," he remarked complacently. As usual, he was severe in his judgment of Necker:

He would not have been wrong if he had limited himself to saying: the royal treasury has only such and such a sum to give; take it and do the best you can

---

26. *Encyclopédie méthodique: Finances,* III, 460. The reform shortened the time period required to get the tax money into the royal treasury. In his April 1787 memorial, Necker estimated that this reform of the receivers general, together with that of the treasuries in the departments of war, navy, and royal households, had achieved an amelioration of 3.5 million livres.

27. Necker, *Oeuvres complètes,* IV, 220ff.

with it. But he wants to tell them that they can do better than they do with the money received, and that they always make bad bargains [with the suppliers].[28]

There was one major spending department that was just as hostile to economy as the military departments, and Necker believed it necessary to move against it early in 1780. The royal households presented a spectacle of waste of taxpayers' money that could be less easily tolerated in wartime than that of the military services. The secretary of state for the king's domestic household was Jean-Antoine Amelot de Chaillou, another appointee of Maurepas who had replaced Malesherbes in May 1776. Like the secretary of state for war, Amelot was also considered a nonentity, but fortunately for Necker he was not fundamentally hostile to reform or to the director general himself. In any case, he did not oppose the dramatic shakeup in the administration of the king's household that Necker carried out in January 1780, strongly supported, it appears, by the king if not by Maurepas.

It will be remembered that in the declaration of December 22, 1776, providing for the liquidation of debts of the king's household, Necker had requested the chief *ordonnateurs* of the department to send him proposals for economizing in their respective sections, and that this request was ignored.[29] The edict of October 1778 requiring all accountable officers to submit monthly statements of their operations was deliberately flouted in the king's household, where treasurers were ordered by their chiefs not to comply with it. The response of the king and Necker to this insubordination was to abolish the treasurers' offices and create a single one, to be appointed by the minister of finance, for the households of the king and queen. This solved the problem of accounting for the expenditures of the department, but did not strike at the heart of the problem of limiting the expenditures themselves, which were still left to the decision of the *ordonnateurs.*

It was not the secretary of state for the king's household who made most of those decisions. They were rather the prerogatives of certain *grands* to whom earlier kings had transferred the right to appoint officers in the royal households. Examples were the prince de Condé, grand master of the king's household, the duc de Coigny, first esquire of the king, and the prince de Lambesc, grand esquire of the household. The key administrators under their authority in the king's household were ten intendants and controllers general in charge of the various sections: the king's table, stables, hunting equipment, and so forth.

Backed by the king, Necker abolished this administrative system early in 1780. In a first edict published in January concerning the king's household, it was explained in the preamble that the king desired to reduce household expenditures. To accomplish this, the offices alienated by his predecessors were to be restored to the domain of the crown and brought under the administration of the *parties casuelles,* that is, the administration in charge of offices and their

28. *Journal de l'abbé de Véri,* II, 391, 172-173.
29. See Chapter VII.

financing. The following passage was evidently an attempt to mollify the *grands* for this sacrifice:

We shall maintain our great officers in the honorable right of receiving and transmitting our orders and watching over their execution. But called as they are to serve us in the provinces and in our armies, and being unable to devote full time to the details of finance and economies which require a constant and assiduous attention, we have thought they would not be offended to see that part of the administration taken from their noble functions near our person. And we have too much proof of their zeal and attachment not to be certain that they will second the generous plans which we have formed to maintain order in our finances and to convince our subjects of our desire not to resort to more taxes until we have examined every resource that order and economy can yield.[30]

On the same day a second edict was published, suppressing ten offices of intendant and controller general in the king's household and forming a general bureau to take over their functions. This bureau was to consist of five members holding their posts by commission from the king, and two magistrates from the Paris Chamber of Accounts. The finance minister was permitted to attend meetings of the bureau, which was now to assume the functions of the *ordon-nateurs* for the king's and queen's households. The general bureau was also enjoined to study the royal households and recommend to the finance minister how expenditures could be trimmed, the same task that Necker had sought to impose on the former *ordonnateurs*.

That the new regime took this mandate somewhat more seriously is indicated in the edict of August 1780, which abolished 406 offices in the section of the king's household called *la bouche du roi,* that is, having to do with the king's dining service. All 406 officers were honorific butlers, waiters, tasters, and so on. Those of high rank performed their duties only on ceremonial occasions. The lesser ranks may have done more work, but the king's table probably was as well served after the suppression of those 406 offices as before. The total capital of the offices was 8,786,000 livres. The preamble of the edict of August stated that the capital would be reimbursed within five years, interest at 5 percent being paid on all capital that was not reimbursed. Terms were definitely not harsh for the dispossessed officeholders. They were to keep their privileges, and were assured pensions if they had served over twenty years in the household, or if their fathers had served. There was no official record or *brevet* of the origin of the offices; they seemed to have existed from time immemorial. Yet the decision of the king and of Necker was to reimburse the full amount of the capital claimed by the officers.[31]

Comments by the publicists of the day indicate that the *grands* did not take this reform of the royal households with as good grace as hoped. Metra reported

30. Necker, *Oeuvres complètes,* III, 213-214.
31. *Ibid.* pp. 218-229.

that the prince de Condé would not forgive Necker the loss of revenue incurred by the suppression of his charge of grand master of the household. [32] This although a new military office was created for him, that of colonel general of infantry, with a salary of at least 500,000 livres annually. Bachaumont reported near the end of February:

. . . it appears that Mr. Necker is not finding it easy to carry out his reform of the king's household. The prince de Condé, the prince de Lambesc, the duc de Coigny and others have presented memorials sustaining their respective rights. Madame de Brionne [sister of the duc de Choiseul] has turned on all her charms, but it is said she was coldly received by the king. [33]

Indeed, the king was standing firmly behind his finance minister in 1780. In September, Metra reported that the duc de Coigny, "who enjoys great credit, is moving heaven and earth to keep the director general from touching the 'little stable' "; but the king was supporting Necker. "I wish to put order and economy in every part of my household," Metra quotes the king as saying on one occasion during his toilet, "and those who have anything to say against it I will crush like this glass." Thereupon the king let drop a glass goblet from his hand which shattered into a thousand pieces. The duc de Coigny left, muttering: "It's better to be nibbled at than smashed." [34]

The abbé de Véri, as usual, believed that suppression of the 406 offices was only one more example of the Genevan's penchant for currying popular favor without producing any important results. He noted that it would cost the treasury 8 or 9 million livres to reimburse the officers. "The economy of the new administration of the kitchen, offices, and wine cellars will not amount to two million a year, the reimbursement will prevent the royal treasury from enjoying any relief for several years." [35]

In his April 1787 memorial Necker claimed a saving of 2 to 2.5 million livres annually through reform of the royal households. This might seem a negligible sum to the abbé de Véri, who scorned details. But a banker who had earned his own fortune might look at the matter differently from an abbé who lived on an income of over 200,000 livres annually drawn from church prebends. [36] If there were a sufficient number of small savings, each one paltry in itself, the result might add up to an amount sufficient to pay the cost of the war loans.

The amount and sources of amelioration based upon the April memorial are summarized in Table 2, at the end of this chapter. Necker listed twenty-nine separate items to show how he had achieved a total saving of 84 million livres in the annual ordinary budget during the years of his first ministry. He explained

32. Metra, *Correspondance secrète*, IX, 322-323.

33. Bachaumont, *Mémoires secrets*, XV, 71.

34. Metra, *Correspondance secrète*, X, 207.

35. *Journal de l'abbé de Véri*, II, 352.

36. René de la Croix, duc de Castries, "L'Abbé de Véri et son journal," *Revue de Paris* (November 1953), p. 78.

that he had to rely upon his memory for a number of items since he did not have access to records in the *contrôle général.* For this reason there might have been some errors of detail in his April memorial. But it would appear probable that those figures were a faithful reflection of his first ministry. The evidence available in published edicts, in statements of accounts both published and unpublished, is consistent with the figures in Table 2. For example the revenue from indirect taxes that was increased due to Necker's new contracts with financial companies all appear in the tableau of *Comptes rendus* in the Appendix. It can be seen that the ordinary revenue from 1774 to 1788 increased from 361,880,429 livres in gross revenue to 472,415,549 livres. And this indicates only the amelioration on the revenue side of the accounts. Furthermore, Necker's reform policies were generally abandoned after his resignation in 1781. Many offices abolished by him were restored by Joly de Fleury. Yet, that worthy magistrate did believe in, and pursue, a policy of economy and of balancing the ordinary expenditures with ordinary revenue. But during Calonne's ministry from 1783 to 1787 even the policy of economy was thrown to the winds.

In evaluating Necker's fiscal policy there is a special source of evidence that deserves attention. As mentioned previously, incompetent financial administration was an important reason for France's defeat in the Seven Years' War.[37] As might be expected, the British government closely watched France's financial administration during the American War. British diplomats and espionage agents on the continent sent a steady flow of reports on the subject to London, some of which are preserved today in the Auckland papers in the British Museum. One collection is entitled: "Extracts and substance of letters from Amsterdam, Paris, and Brussels on Mr. Necker's private expedients to support the credit of France."[38] The sources of information were varied; some came from the international banking community, including a "Mr. Haller," possibly the partner of Girardot, Haller and Company. In transmission to London some information was obviously garbled. For example, it was reported that Italian bankers (rather than Genevan) had devised a formula for placing rentes on the lives of young girls. Also, when referring to Necker's life rente loan of November 1779 it was asserted that his terms for rentes placed on three lives "appeared extravagant." This was probably a reflection of a false idea often propagated by the libelists that Necker's life rentes offered on three and four lives were actually a revival of the onerous and discredited *tontines* that Terray had abolished in 1771. In reality, the amount placed on three and four lives was negligible.[39]

For the most part these letters of British agents reported the "expedients of Mr. Necker" in a manner that reflected favorably on the Genevan. One agent wrote that Necker's principles "were carried out with firmness and discretion,

37. See Chapter V.
38. British Museum, Add. MSS 34,417, fols. 20-35.
39. See the table of Joseph Cambon, reported to the National Convention in 1794, in *Archives parlementaires de 1787 à 1860,* LXXXVII, 117.

without commotion and almost without notice." The November 1779 loan of life rentes was

filled in fourteen days and double that sum would have had equal success, such is the change of confidence people have in M. Necker's economy. They talk of the new reforms to be brought forward next month which will enable him to go on smoothly without more than an annual loan of fifty to sixty million. The Farmers-General are to be reduced in number, the croupiers and assistants to be suppressed.[40]

Necker's prestige as a finance minister of uncommon ability was as high in the enemy country as it was generally throughout Europe. In the absence of creditable evidence to the contrary, there seems to be no reason for skepticism about any of his "ameliorations."

TABLE 2
Table of Amelioration, 1776-1781

Source of Ameliorations	Annual Savings in Livres Tournois
I. Reorganization of *fermes* and *régies*.	
(5) The organization of the *régie générale* in 1777 and the suppression of superfluous offices in the administration of the department of domain and forests	3,000,000
(6) The reorganization of the three companies in 1780: the farmers-general, the *régie générale,* and the administration of the royal domain	13,700,000
(7) The king's share of profits from the above three financial companies.	1,200,000
(10) The reform of the postal administration	2,400,000
(16) Reform of the *régie* of powder by Turgot, which was not included in the *Compte rendu* of Clugny in 1776	800,000
(27) Restoration by Necker of the *régie* for stagecoaches	1,500,000

40. British Museum, Add. MSS 34,417, fols. 20-35.

TABLE 2
Table of Amelioration, 1776-1781
(Continued)

	Source of Ameliorations	Annual Savings in Livres Tournois
(28)	Reform of the administration of military supplies for convoys	1,200,000
	Total	23,800,000

II. The government's obligations were being continually amortized during Necker's ministry, this being an
important aspect of his credit policy. Whenever the
government was liberated from a debt for which it
had to make payments in 1776, as recorded by the
Compte rendu of Clugny, that amount could be
added to the list of ameliorations.

(1)	The reimbursement of rescriptions of the receivers general, which had been suspended in 1770, during 1776 and 1777 freed the government of obligation in Clugny's *Compte rendu* of 1776	4,200,000
(2)	Amortization of capital on rentes paid by the *taille*	1,800,000
(3)	Reimbursement of pensions	1,100,000
(4)	Other miscellaneous reimbursements	1,500,000
(20)	The amortization of life rentes due to natural causes during six years, 1776-1781 inclusive, and also amortization of exigible loans during the same period. Estimated by Necker as between 9 and 10 million livres. Carried here as	10,000,000
	Total	18,600,000

III. Increase of revenue from direct taxes through natural
augmentation or by reforms.
(9) Increase of revenue (presumably from the
second *brevet* of the *taille* before 1780) and
from the capitation to raise money for

TABLE 2
Table of Amelioration, 1776-1781
(Continued)

Source of Ameliorations	Annual Savings in Livres Tournois
fodder and supplies for military convoys and for local police and the coast guard	3,500,000
(12) Increase of revenue from the *vingtième* in the *pays d'élection* due to Necker's reform of 1777.	1,800,000
(13) Increase of revenue from the *vingtième* from *pays d'états*, princes of the blood, frontier clergy, and the Order of Malta.	900,000
(14) Reduction of amount permitted for writing off the *vingtième* tax (these had usually been favors granted to high-ranking aristocrats like the duc de Duras at Bordeaux).	800,000
(15) Increase in revenue from administration of the *vingtième* in Paris and the capitation of the court	700,000
Total	7,700,000
IV. (11) A large claim was made by Necker for his reform of pensions, particularly in the payment of those in arrears, which had been a heavy liability in the *Compte rendu* of Clugny. Also included in this figure was liquidation of debts-in-arrears of the king's household	7,200,000
V. (18) Income from the royal lottery founded by Clugny was not included in his *Compte rendu,* as already noted, and after Necker's reform of the administration it yielded annually	7,000,000

VI. The following are a broad range of administrative reforms in several departments, including the suppression of numerous offices considered superfluous.

TABLE 2
Table of Amelioration, 1776-1781
(Continued)

Source of Ameliorations	Annual Savings in Livres Tournois
(8) Suppression of the offices of numerous treasurers in several departments during 1778 and 1779, and the 48 receivers general in 1780. This increased the annual revenue by	3,500,000
(17) The profit from the mint had been granted to individuals as a favor under the name of *sur-achat;* Necker discontinued the practice, yielding a saving of	500,000
(21) Suppression of offices in the king's house- hold and other economies achieved in that department are estimated by Necker as from 2 to 2.5 million livres. Carried here as	2,500,000
(22) Reform of the foundations for beggars	300,000
(23) Economy in administration of the lieuten- ant general of police in Paris.	300,000
(24) Economy in administration of department of foreign affairs.	1,000,000
(25) Income from a tax Clugny had placed on communities but that was not carried in his *Compte rendu* of 1776	1,200,000
(26) An annual expenditure in the *Compte rendu* of Clugny for "acquisitions and exchanges," concerning the transfer of royal domain lands. They were in fact nothing but favors given to *grands*, which Necker discontinued. . .	1,500,000
(29) The final article given by Necker included a large variety of savings achieved by reduction or abolition of gratifications, in the reduction of the item of expenditure called "unfore- seen expenditures," which were often due to ill-considered concessions granted to cour-	

TABLE 2
Table of Amelioration, 1776-1781
(Continued)

Source of Ameliorations	Annual Savings in Livres Tournois
tiers. One example of this category may have been Necker's discovery of the pension paid to Maximilien Radix de Sainte-Foy long after it had expired	6,000,000
Total	16,800,000

VII.   (19) The final category of the "free gift of the clergy," which Necker included as an ordinary revenue, not previously counted as such. This matter will be discussed in Chapter XIV . .   3,400,000

Sources	Amelioration Totals	Livres Tournois
I		23,800,000
II		18,600,000
III		7,700,000
IV		7,200,000
V		7,000,000
VI		16,800,000
VII		3,400,000
Total		84,500,000

Note: The twenty-nine articles are arranged in seven categories (designed by roman numerals). The arabic number in parenthesis is the number given by Necker.

Chapter X

EXPERIMENTATION

The absorbing concern for raising money to finance the fleet and the far-flung military operations of the American War certainly was the primary task Necker faced during his first ministry. Yet it would be wrong to think that this eclipsed everything else. The general nature of his thought on reform has been described earlier.[1] What did Necker accomplish in matters not directly concerned with financing the war?

As readers of the *Eloge de Colbert* were aware, its author did not take a restricted view of the responsibilities and scope of the office of finance minister. "The entire well-being of the people" was directly related to the administration of finances. This encompassed the economy in its various aspects: agriculture, commerce, and manufacturing. It also included what we now call social welfare, that is, the amelioration of the condition of the poorer classes, "the most numerous of the king's subjects" for whom Necker had expressed such eloquent concern in his book on the grain trade. Most of these subjects were directly affected by the fiscal policies of the government, and the improvement of their lot depended upon fiscal reform alone. But there was also the class at the very bottom of the social order, whose condition could not be alleviated. There were the people reduced to beggary through circumstances such as illness or bad luck, the physically and mentally disabled, the aged, orphans, and foundlings; and there were the most wretched of all in the eighteenth century, the inmates of prisons.

These matters had become of increasing concern during the century, and had attracted attention before Necker's ministry. Turgot was by no means indifferent to such problems both during his intendance at Limoges and while controller general. According to a modern authority on public policy toward social welfare in the eighteenth century, Turgot originated a new concept of work-relief for the unemployed. Theretofore, beggars and idle persons had been rounded up forcibly and detained in "depots" where no attempt was made to distinguish the involuntarily idle from the congenital beggars. Turgot believed that most of those detained would prefer to work. As intendant of Limoges he

1. See Chapter VI.

instituted charitable workshops for the unemployed and encouraged other intendants to follow this example when he became controller general. Men were put to work cleaning streets and excavating for public building projects, for example. Women were employed in spinning and weaving. Yet this new institution was rather unevenly applied in the kingdom. It required the initiative and sympathetic support of the intendant. Financing was haphazard because the local community and private charity were expected to provide the funds. Furthermore, Turgot's humane outlook was not generally shared by the *économistes,* who tended to think that families of the sick, aged, and otherwise unfortunate members of society should take the responsibility for their welfare. Beggars should be forced to return to the place of their birth and the local parish required to care for them. Even hospitals were frowned upon because the *économistes* thought it more efficient that the sick be cared for in their own homes.[2]

Of all the ministers of Louis XVI, Necker was the most keenly affected by the suffering of the poor. His concern was so often expressed in his writings that, together with his inspections and legislation while minister, and from what is known of his character by the testimony of Henri Meister, there is hardly any reason to doubt the genuineness of his feeling. "The class of privileged men who are born surrounded by wealth guaranteed them by laws of inheritance—what pity should they not have toward those unfortunate ones!" he exclaimed in *On the Administration of Finances.*[3] Necker was the first minister to insist unequivocally and forcefully on the duty of the government to assume responsibility for social welfare.[4] "It is for the government," he wrote in the *Administration of Finances,* "interpreter and repository of social harmony, to do for this numerous and disinherited class all which order and justice will permit." He listed specific measures the government could carry out. It could mitigate the rigor of laws governing private property (*anciennes conventions*); it should recognize its duty and responsibility toward the unfortunate; it should be considerate of the poor in its fiscal policy; it should initiate public works to provide work-relief for the unemployed; and it should make allocation from its regular budget for social welfare.[5]

His strategy for implementing reform in this area was typical of his other reforms. It was to avoid sweeping, revolutionary, and uniform programs that could get off to a flying start and then soon lose momentum. Rather, he began cautiously by instituting "pilot plants" in order to gain experience. Then, by various techniques of administrative prodding, coaxing, publicity, and persuasion, he would get others in powerful positions to imitate the example. As in

2. Camille Bloch, *L'Assistance et l'état en France à la veille de la révolution* (Paris, 1908), pp. 207-208.

3. Necker, *Oeuvres complètes,* V, 377.

4. Bloch, *L'Assistance et l'état,* p. 218.

5. *Oeuvres complètes,* V, 3, 378-379.

most reforms of this nature, Necker expected the new provincial administration to become the chief imitators, even experimenters, throughout the kingdom. But his first steps were to implement and supervise with persistence the pilot plants.

Like Turgot, Necker became interested in the policy of work-relief for beggars. In the generality of Soissons he found a public-spirited and humanitarian priest whom he engaged to establish an institution at the city of Soissons which in effect converted the system of beggars depots into charitable workshops. Three of the depots, located in various parts of the generality, were consolidated into a single establishment at Soissons. Here glass-polishing and weaving were introduced. Discipline was less severe than in the depots, and incentives were given the workers to acquire skills. Pay scales were drawn up for that purpose, and those willing to work and learn in order to rise out of their condition were given every encouragement. The often harsh treatment meted out to beggars by the local police marshals was restrained. In the city of Châteauroux, Suzanne Necker took the initiative in 1778 for establishing a charitable bureau that became the model for other cities. The bureau took charge of and directed all the city's welfare activities. Persons truly needy and not simply lazy or apathetic were listed. Food, clothing, and medicine was distributed to them. A school for spinning was set up for girls of poor families and for orphans. Finally, the city government was persuaded to set up a workshop for beggars. At Paris the lieutenant general of police, Lenoir, supervised the establishment of a spinning factory that employed women. Some priests took charge of its business affairs, marketing the products of the workshop.[6]

In the area of social welfare, Suzanne Necker found a role that must have been unprecedented for wives of ministers. Not that strong personalities were unknown among the latter, but usually their interests were absorbed in such matters as getting special favors for their friends and relatives. Madame de Maurepas was particularly noted for this role, and according to abbé de Véri, even Necker (who detested this sort of influence) had to bow on occasion to her imperious will.[7] At the beginning of his ministerial career, Necker and his wife had an understanding that she would not receive any solicitations for favors, pensions, or appointments to positions in the government. The journalists of the time mention several incidents in which Suzanne returned such requests to their senders with the note that she could not receive them, but sometimes she suggested they write directly to her husband.[8] In the words of Camille Bloch, "she became his unofficial minister for social welfare." Whether it was her own frail health and experience with illness that led Madame Necker into the particular area of hospital reform can only be conjectured. Whatever the reason, if the name Necker is a landmark in Paris today it is not because of Jacques (for

6. Bloch, *L'Assistance et l'état*, pp. 221-224.
7. *Journal de l'abbé de Véri*, II, 64.
8. Metra, *Correspondance secrète*, V, 376-377.

whom only a tiny street in the Marais can be found bearing his name), but because of Suzanne and the hospital she founded.

The word "hospital" had a somewhat wider meaning in the *ancien régime* than today. It was not only an establishment to care for the sick (this was called a *hôtel-dieu*) but also an orphanage for foundlings and a refuge for the aged, for the blind and crippled, for beggars, and even for criminals. The institution known as the General Hospital in Paris was an administration having five separate major establishments under its authority. There was the Bicêtre, which had about 4,000 male inmates—criminals, poor, elderly, insane, epileptics—all whose condition made them incapable of working. The Saltpêtrière contained 7,000 women with the same infirmities, plus the delinquents and criminals. There was another establishment for foundlings, and one for supplies. The chief medical hospital, the *Hôtel-Dieu*, was under a different administration. There were about 700 such hospitals in the kingdom in 1784, having a revenue of around 20 million livres annually. The *Hôtel-Dieu* at Paris received about one-fourth of this money.[9]

When the Neckers first began to visit hospitals they found scenes beyond description. Administrators were indifferent to such elementary matters as separating patients with contagious diseases from the others. Patients were piled upon the same bed, different types of cases indiscriminately; there was no thought of public hygiene or sanitation, of adequate ventilation or heating. It was no wonder hospitals had such an evil reputation that only the poor and helpless suffered themselves to be taken there.

When Necker raised the matter with the administrators he met the most vexing obstacles that can be put up by minds steeped in routine. It was necessary, they said, to build new hospitals, at a cost clearly beyond the royal treasury. Necker felt the problem was not money, but nonchalant and indifferent administration. The hospitals often had ample endowments, chiefly in land. This property was badly cared for and yielded low income. Necker saw that if they would sell their lands and property not needed for the operation of the hospitals they could invest in rentes of the king at a much higher rate of return. An edict of January 1780 permitted them to do this, and he strongly encouraged them to act on it.[10] Some proceeds were to be used for new construction and for remodeling existing structures. Necker was dealing with the hospital administrators in the manner that so offended the military services, telling them how to make better use of the funds they had.

The administrative reform of the hospitals was undertaken by Suzanne Necker. In the summer of 1779 a small *hôtel-dieu* in the parish of Saint-Sulpice in the left bank was destroyed by fire. Madame Necker had just received a large donation from the archbishop of Paris, money awarded him in a lawsuit. The money was to be used in her charitable enterprises. "She has in this realm as vast

9. Necker, *Oeuvres complètes,* V, chap. 24.
10. Isambert et al., eds., *Recueil général des anciennes lois,* XXVI, 257-262.

projects as her husband has in his," noted Bachaumont. "The prelate has given her his support, even though she is a heretic," he added somewhat ungraciously.[11] Madame Necker then persuaded the parish priest of Saint-Sulpice to build a new hospital along the experimental lines that she had worked out, using the gift she had received from the archbishop.

The Hospice de Charité, as it was called, for it was to be placed at the service of the indigent, was to serve both the parishes of Saint-Sulpice and Gros-Caillou. It was a small establishment with only 120 beds. Every unnecessary expenditure was eliminated. The rule was to be only one patient per bed. The dormitories were carefully ventilated, service was quiet and well-organized; strict hygiene was invoked, diets and drugs carefully watched. Modern hospital routines were established; a physician accompanied by the nurses, all of whom were nuns of the order of Saint-Vincent de Paul, saw each patient twice daily. Most important, in Necker's estimation, was the demonstration that efficient hospital care need not be costly. Writing about this "model hospital" in 1784, he said that with 128 beds (as it then had) it could care for 1,800 patients yearly. This was sufficient for the needs of both parishes if it were limited to the poor. The cost per patient per day was about 17 sous. Only one full-time resident physician, a surgeon, an intern, fourteen "sisters of charity," and five orderlies constituted the hospital staff. "It can be seen that this number has no proportion to what would be required if each patient were treated in his own home or shelter, at great distances from each other."[12]

It was hoped that a much wider scope could be given to the new techniques of hospital administration, which were much publicized by the director general. Brochures describing the Hospice de Charité were printed and copies sent to each of the intendants, who was requested to send one to each hospital in his generality.[13] In Paris, the innovation in hospital administration did attract attention. Visiting foreign, as well as French physicians, paid their respects to the model hospital at Saint-Sulpice. In August 1777, Necker formed a special commission to investigate all hospitals in Paris. From this commission's work came a number of reforms, although not as many as Necker had hoped. The chief medical hospital, the *Hôtel-Dieu,* was simply overcrowded. Necker proposed that small hospitals be established for each parish, or at best, groups of parishes. His ideas were considered too revolutionary by the administration of the *Hôtel-Dieu.*[14] It was not until April 1781, less than a month before his resignation, that he succeeded in getting a decree-in-council passed providing for some reforms in the *Hôtel-Dieu.* There was to be a single bed provided for each of 3,000 patients. They were to be segregated in separate wards according to

11. Bachaumont, *Mémoires secrets,* XIV, 169.

12. Necker, *Oeuvres complètes,* V, 405.

13. Archives départmentales, Marne, C 174.

14. Marcel Fosseyeux, *L'Hôtel-Dieu au XVIIe et au XVIII^e^siècle* (Paris, 1912), pp. 267-268.

type of illness. The hospital Saint-Louis was to be reserved for contagious diseases.[15]

The callous indifference with which the sick and the poor were treated in that day was well illustrated by two of Necker's reforms. The Bicêtre and the Saltpêtrière did not have medical facilities. Inmates who became ill were sent to the *Hôtel-Dieu* in open carts regardless of the season—which frequently caused their death. Necker required that the two hospitals establish their own infirmaries; according to Bloch, only the Saltpêtrière had one by 1790. About 2,000 newborn infants per year were abandoned. The usual practice was to deposit them with the stagecoach service, which could do nothing but take them to Paris, where the only foundling hospital was located. Nine out of ten infants perished either during this journey or as a result of it. Necker forbade the transport of foundling children, who were to be taken to the nearest hospital, the government making good the cost if it exceeded the budget of the hospital.[16]

In propagating more humane ideas and improved methods of hospital administration, Necker did not overlook the help of openminded and intelligent physicians. Near the end of Turgot's ministry the controller general had set up a commission of physicians to correspond with provincial physicians on how to combat epidemics among both humans and animals. (The latter had been a major preoccupation during Turgot's brief ministry.) In August 1778, Necker transformed this commission into the Royal Medical Society, charged to correspond with foreign as well as provincial physicians. The conservative Faculty of Medicine vehemently protested this act, for the commission was composed of young physicians who were open to the newer methods of the profession and sympathetic to the efforts of the Neckers in the area of public health.[17]

The opposition is illustrated by an incident reported by Bachaumont in September 1779. The Conciergerie prison was under the jurisdiction of the Parlement of Paris. Visiting the infirmary of the prison, Madame Necker was shocked by the conditions she found and protested to the architect of the Parlement, the responsible official. She requested permission to correct them herself; her request was referred by the architect to the dean of the Grande Chambre of the Parlement, one Pasquier. "This magistrate," wrote Bachaumont, "was furious, and issued the most severe instruction to oppose the enterprise of the wife of the director general." Bachaumont added that "this incident has only placed the latter in an even worse position with the Parlement."[18] It appears, however, that Madame Necker eventually won. The declaration of the king of August 30, 1780, regarding the reform of prisons stipulated that for the

15. Isambert et al., eds., *Recueil général des anciennes lois*, XXVII, 11-16.
16. *Ibid.*, XXVI, 7-10.
17. Bloch, *L'Assistance et l'état*, pp. 238-239.
18. Bachaumont, *Mémoires secrets*, XIV, 186.

Conciergerie "there would be a new infirmary, spacious and ventilated, where all sick prisoners would be on a separate bed, and it is ordered that all dispositions be taken which humanity and order require."[19]

The administration of criminal law was largely outside the purview of the finance minister, the secretary of state for the king's household and the keeper of the seal having more direct responsibility. Yet even here Necker must have made his influence felt in such matters as the law abolishing the use of torture in criminal investigations.[20] He did have responsibility for administration of the prisons. Conditions of prison life in the eighteenth century were horrible by all accounts. The prisons were small, crowded, and pestilential. Necker found prisoners thrown together indiscriminately—men and women, children, suspects awaiting interrogation, those imprisoned for debt along with vicious criminals. Most notorious were the underground cells (*cachots*), damp, without fresh air or sunshine, where prisoners were chained in isolation. The prisoners were no longer let out on contract to a *ferme* of jailors as formerly, but were still prey to various forms of exploitation and abuse by the prison guards and administrators.

Necker's principal prison reform was his declaration of August 1780 providing for the construction of a new prison at the Hôtel de la Force, also his new regulation for prison administration, enacted after his resignation. The new prison was built in an area ten times that of the two prisons it replaced, the Petit Châtelet and For-l'Evêque, both of which were destroyed. It was to be used only for debtors. The Grand Châtelet was remodeled and the *cachots* were eliminated. The new regulation introduced such modern methods of prison administration as segregation of inmates according to sex, age, and type of crime. A barracks way of life was introduced, including regular hours for dining in common and for sleeping. There was an attempt to eliminate petty graft and abuse of prisoners by guards, although with what success is not known.[21]

Like all reformers who concern themselves with the problems of crime, Necker's attention was drawn to the question of prevention as well as what to do with those convicted. So many of those arrested and sentenced were implicated in salt and tobacco smuggling that he yearned for the war to end so he could implement his plans to reform those monopolies. But there was one breeding ground for crime that could be remedied at little cost to the government: urban life even in that age had many traps for the unwary. Particularly, young men from the provinces could fall into the clutches of the vice rings and find themselves in a moment defrauded of their money. They would take their other possessions to the pawn shops, where usurious rates of interest, as much as 30 or 40 percent, would only complete their ruin. What they required was a friendly hand to steady them from their moment of imprudence and get them back on their feet. Government-sponsored loan companies called monts-de-piété had

19. Isambert et al., eds., *Recueil général des anciennes lois*, XXVI, 376-377.
20. *Ibid.*, pp. 373-379.
21. Necker, *Oeuvres complètes*, V, chap. 25.

existed in other European countries and in the conquered provinces in northern France, but it was Necker who introduced them to Paris. Letters patent of December 9, 1777, founded a Mont-de-piété to be under the supervision of the lieutenant general of police and administered by the General Hospital. Money in small sums was loaned at 10 percent interest per annum based upon possessions turned over to the bank by the borrowers. The government guaranteed to make good any losses, but in fact, the Paris Mont-de-piété seems to have prospered.[22]

As administrator of the royal domain lands, Necker had an opportunity to intervene in an area of human relations that was a prominent subject of concern for the eighteenth-century reform movement. Reformers of that day called it "feudalism," but modern historians designate it "manorialism," the rights and powers of the manorial lord or seigneur who owns a fief over the peasant population living on it. Serfdom, with serfs under the personal authority of the landlord, had disappeared from most of France before the eighteenth century. But residues of this medieval servitude still persisted in some provinces of eastern France: in the duchy of Burgundy, in Franche-Comté, and in the Nivernais. The peasant subject to it could not marry or sell or bequeath property without the consent of the seigneur. If he had children to inherit the land he cultivated, they could do so only if they remained living on it. A more extreme type of serfdom also existed, giving the seigneur the right to tax the serf no matter where he might be in the kingdom. All property gained by the serf even long after he had left the manor still belonged to the seigneur, who could claim it on the death of the serf through an old law called *droit de suite*. The edict of August 1779, written by Necker, abolished this *droit de suite* throughout the kingdom. All other types of personal servitude were abolished on the royal domain; that is, the king gave up whatever such personal rights he may have had over peasants on the domain lands, including lands leased to the *engagists*. The preamble of the edict exhorted all other seigneurs, whether noblemen or religious communities, to follow the example of the king. Certain legal reforms were also made so that the process could be facilitated.[23] Evidently the seigneurs did not follow this good example with alacrity, for personal servitude was not finally abolished until the August decrees of the National Assembly in 1789.

The quantitative importance of Necker's humanitarian and philanthropic reforms was questioned by his critics at that time as well as by later historians. Abbé de Véri scoffed that "there were no serfs under the laws of *mainmorte* [serf law] in the royal domain."[24] It was simply an easy way to get publicity, claimed the abbé, at no expense. But it appears that Necker was criticized not because his reforms did not go far enough, but because his critics were out of sympathy with them altogether. Véri related the testimony of an elderly peasant in Franche-Comté who maintained that *mainmorte* was preferred by peasants

22. Isambert et al., eds., *Recueil général des anciennes lois*, XXV, 153-158.
23. *Ibid.*, XXVI, 139-142.
24. *Journal de l'abbé de Véri*, II, 238-239.

because the land of deceased serfs was kept within the village rather than falling into the hands of outsiders. On another occasion Véri wrote: "I should like to have engraved in letters of gold that the government is useful only in order to prevent violence between citizens, and that it is always harmful when it meddles to do good."[25] Strict laissez-faire was proclaimed by this cleric, even to the point of opposition to hospitals. "I am convinced," he said, "that the sick person left to nature and the compassion of his neighbor will recover more surely than with the so-called care that he would get in hospitals."[26] Just how much compassion his neighbors could expect from him was problematical. He was opposed to hospitals for the aged and for foundlings. He spoke against relief of any kind for the poor.[27] This recipient of 200,000 livres annually from church lands had no use for Necker's Monte-de-piété. Having observed a similar institution in Rome for ten years, he pronounced it "chimerical to think that this could save young dissipators from ruin."[28]

As for the quantitative limitations of Necker's humanitarian reforms, they may be readily admitted. Much of his first ministry was absorbed in the quest for information and in experimenting with methods and institutions. When the experiment seemed successful, as in the case of Madame Necker's hospital, it was given publicity and others were encouraged to adopt it. But the director general could only use persuasion, for he had renounced despotism no matter how enlightened. Furthermore, an evaluation of the quantitative importance of these reforms must take account of their short existence. The six years following Necker's resignation were generally years of reaction against the reform movement. His reforms depended upon continued supervision, prodding, and encouragement by the minister of finance. He was like the manager of a greenhouse who had brought a variety of plants into existence that required sustained care to thrive.

In Necker's policies and legislation concerning the economy in all its aspects, we find the same diligent search for information and the same experimental approach as in his social welfare policies. His administration was guided by this inflow of information much more than by any economic doctrine. Yet it would appear that the cumulative effect of all his economic measures was to carry him much further along the path of liberalism than might have been expected from his writings before entering the government. Both his written works and his legislation during and after his first ministry show a rapprochement with the goals of the économistes, although he still repudiated their esprit de système.

This can be seen first of all in his handling of the grain trade, so fervently debated in the 1760s and the first half of the following decade. Writing in the Administration of Finances nearly ten years after his treatise on the grain trade

25. *Ibid.,* p. 21.
26. *Ibid.,* p. 292.
27. *Ibid.,* I, 364-370.
28. *Ibid.,* II, 71-72.

published in 1775, Necker thought his earlier work was weak in some respects and certainly "imperfect."[29] What he regretted most was his attempt to set price limits for determining automatically whether to prohibit export of grain. As a result of the experiences of his first ministry he now thought these decisions should be the administrator's, unfettered by such legislative guidelines. So many unforeseen contingencies were involved that the minister of finance should be left entirely free to withhold export in some provinces and not in others, or even to give full liberty to export from the kingdom or to prohibit it, according to the circumstances. But his thinking on the overall question of the grain trade had shifted decidedly in the direction of liberalism. In 1775, he seemed to fear the export of grain, believing that a shortage was a constant menace, and that export should be permitted only in exceptional circumstances. In 1784, he thought just the opposite. "I continue to believe that in France liberty of exportation must be envisaged as habitual and fundamental. But the government must suspend this liberty in certain places and in certain circumstances, or even generally when the facts invite such prudence."[30]

Such was his policy during his first ministry. Yet because of his reputation as an admirer of Colbert, and his apparent opposition to freedom of the grain trade during the Flour War of 1775, historians for a long time assumed that Necker's economic policy must have been governed by the narrowest precepts of mercantilism. Thus the Russian historian of the grain trade, Georges Afanassiev, wrote in 1894 that, while Necker did not revoke any of Turgot's legislation, "even so, the entire spirit of administration was changed, and by measures of detail the entire effect of [Turgot's] reform was destroyed."[31] A review of Necker's acts on the grain trade from 1776 to 1781 does not bear out this judgment.

The fundamental law regarding the commerce in grain remained Turgot's decree-in-council of September 13, 1774. Necker not only left this statute unrepealed but observed its spirit, as can be seen in the grain crisis that surfaced in the summer of 1777. Fortunately, we have a fairly complete dossier of correspondence on this from September 1777 through June 1778. The director of the bureau of subsistence, Michau de Montaran, maintained a file of correspondence both of his own letters and those of Necker to intendants and other officials regarding the grain supply. It is possible to follow Necker's policy on every aspect of this crisis during that period.[32]

The decree of September 1774, which did not restore automatic freedom of grain export to foreign countries, left it to the discretion of the finance minister whenever conditions seemed to make export advisable. In 1776 and in the early

29. Necker, *Oeuvres complètes,* V, chap. 27.

30. *Ibid.,* p. 432.

31. Georges Afanassiev, *Le Commerce des céréales en France au dix-huitième siècle* (Paris, 1894), p. 423.

32. "Correspondance relative aux subsistances tenue par M. de Montaran fils, intendant du commerce et chargé du détail des grains. Commencée le 5 juillet et finie le 26 juin 1778," AN F11* 1. The letters are bound in a register of 440 pages.

months of 1777, the grain supply was such that export was permitted from most of the frontier provinces, although not from Normandy to Flanders. But this changed the following summer. The harvest was not bad in the northern provinces, but in the *midi,* especially in the southwest, it was "below mediocre." Soon after he entered office as director general of finances on June 29, 1777, Necker found a letter on his desk from the intendant of Auch addressed to Taboureau des Réaux. It called the controller general's attention to the poor grain harvest in this generality, and the probability of a severe rise in the price level that could bring popular disturbances. The intendant asked for instructions for coping with the impending crisis. In his reply Necker laid down the guidelines to observe throughout the autumn and winter. He advised the intendant to avoid any act that would tend to alarm the public, for he believed people were prone to panic beyond what was justified by reality. Second, Necker told the intendant to "allow commerce all liberty and security it requires." He should encourage importation by private shippers and exercise great care not to use government funds in a way that would upset the plans of speculators.[33]

Similar instructions were given to other intendants during October. On October 7 Necker wrote the intendant of Bordeaux that it was better for the intendant than for the finance minister to handle the problems caused by a grain shortage. "It has been seen in the past that such action [by the central government] is almost always misinterpreted, badly managed, and your merchants will be discouraged by such competition."[34] When the intendant of Montauban requested a grant of 100,000 livres to cope with the crisis by extending relief to the indigent who could not afford the high price of bread, Montaran made it clear that Necker did not intend for this money to be used in an attempt to lower the price of grain:

The minister asks you not to lose sight of the fact that relief given by the administration should be only to provide what is necessary to maintain public tranquillity and not to cause a lowering of the price of bread, an operation which would be very costly and would deprive the province of those who can procure grain for it by way of private enterprise.[35]

Later that month the intendant of Auch wanted to purchase a reserve of three thousand sacks of wheat in order to "contain the monopolizers and even the merchants." Montaran wrote that this would be contrary to Necker's policy because it would frighten merchants from performing their useful and necessary service. "It is not part of our system for the king to purchase and sell grain; that would be the surest way to discourage merchants and risk incalculable expenditures." On the contrary, merchants should be encouraged to take grain where it is needed.[36]

33. *Ibid.,* fol. 2.
34. *Ibid.,* fol. 53.
35. *Ibid.,* fols. 74-75.
36. *Ibid.,* fol. 99.

Readers of Afanassiev's book would not know that the above principle was expressed repeatedly in this dossier of correspondence. Certainly no one knew better than Necker, with all his experience in the grain trade, how governments can harm operations of merchants. Ignoring these passages, Afanassiev called attention to those instances in which Necker departed from the ideas of the *économistes*. It will be remembered that Necker believed the government had a clear responsibility to intervene in the commerce of grain when free enterprise could not cope with popular disturbances, and when the price of grain approached a level that threatened the subsistence of the popular classes. He believed government intervention could be most effective by regulating the export of grain outside the country. In fact, that was his basic policy through the crisis of 1777–1778, and it was not in violation of the edict of September 1774.

But Necker also believed that the government should control internal marketing when the price reached a critical level. Consequently one can find instances in Montaran's correspondence in which Necker appeared to violate the spirit of the edict of 1774 even though he denied doing so. Writing to the intendant of Grenoble in the summer of 1777 on the right of a private person to tax a local market (the case of the *leyde* of the viscomtesse du Pont to be discussed below) Necker asserted that, when it is necessary to ensure public tranquillity, the government has the right to require merchants to sell their grain in a public marketplace specifically authorized by the king, and that "this was not an infringement on the edict of 1774." [37] In a letter to the intendant of Montauban he alluded to acts of speculators that were detrimental to the public interest because they artificially raised the grain price. He said the law of September 1774 was not intended to permit those activities and cited the letters patent of the following November 2, which implemented the principles of the edict. [38] About the same time he authorized the Parlement of Toulouse to take needed steps to supply the regular markets, saying that he would ask the keeper of the seals to "close his eyes" to any possible violation of the edict of 1774. [39] It would appear that Necker was uncomfortable in that instance, and it is undeniable that here was a clear conflict of principle between himself and Turgot. But such interventions in the domestic commerce of grain were few in number and certainly did not contravene his basic policy, namely, to allow private enterprise as much freedom as possible to cope with the crises.

Necker's export policy in the crisis of 1777–1778 can be followed in detail in the correspondence of Montaran. In late September he received sufficient information about the grain shortage at Bordeaux and the heavy shipments to Spain (which also suffered a poor grain harvest) and England to lead him to prohibit further export from the western and southern provinces. In letters to

37. *Ibid.,* fols. 12-15.
38. *Ibid.,* fols. 58-59.
39. *Ibid.,* fols. 58. Evidently the Parlement of Toulouse had completely reversed its position on this subject from what it had been at the time of the Flour War.

the intendants of La Rochelle and Brittany, Necker explained the government's policy:

Because harvests in the south have not been up to expectations His Majesty wants other provinces to help those areas which have experienced a shortage. At the same time you must reassure merchants that there will be no obstacle placed in the circulation of any type of grain throughout the extent of the kingdom. Nor will there be any restraint of importation of grain and flour from foreign countries, nor of re-export of such grain from the kingdom, which will be exempt from all duties, in conformity to the decrees-in-council of 14 July 1770 and 13 September 1774.[40]

Afanassiev asserted that Necker overestimated the seriousness of the shortage and that his prohibition of export was impulsive and unnecessary and seriously damaged the exporters.[41] This is not borne out in the correspondence of Montaran. The grain crisis continued in the south and caused considerable suffering by the following spring when the supply was at its lowest. Riots broke out in Sarlat and Toulouse, very similar to those of three years before in the Flour War.[42] Necker asked the keeper of the seals, Miromensil, not to deal harshly with the rioters "because they were simply reacting to suffering caused by the grain shortage"—a contrast to the attitude of Turgot, who three years earlier had demanded and gotten exemplary punishment for two offenders. At the same time Necker barred traditional remedies. An attempt of the Parlement of Toulouse to fix the price of bread was set aside by the government.[43] Nor did Necker permit a resort to government stockpiling. A Breton merchant offered to do this in the generality of Bordeaux, but Necker replied:

I thank you for your offer, but it would not be in accord with my way of thinking to propose to His Majesty any stock-piling of grain, but rather to allow commerce to operate in tranquillity, preserving for it the complete liberty which it must enjoy in order to carry out its operations.[44]

The assertion that Necker acted impulsively and without accurate knowledge of the grain situation in the southwest is not borne out by research on the grain trade in the eighteenth century published in recent years. Labrousse's tables show that wheat prices rose sharply following the harvests of 1777, particularly in the southwestern generalities of Montauban, Bordeaux, and Auch. There the price of wheat had fallen to a low of 20 to 22 livres per setier in 1776. The trend was abruptly reversed, reaching a peak of 28 to 30 livres in 1778. It fell again,

40. *Ibid.*, fols. 35-36.
41. Afanassiev, *Le Commerce des céréales en France*, p. 436.
42. AN F[11]* 1, fols. 408-409.
43. *Ibid.*, fol. 193, 234.
44. *Ibid.*, fols. 82-83.

after the favorable harvest in the summer of 1778, to 18 to 20 livres per setier.[45]

The correspondence of Montaran preserved in the Archives Nationales ends abruptly in June 1778. But other documents sent to him are in the manuscript collection of Joly de Fleury at the Bibliothèque Nationale. One indicates that the 1778 summer harvest was fortunate, and that export was restored to most frontier areas. By 1780, however, the grain commerce was being seriously impeded by the war.[46]

Throughout his first ministry Necker sought to free domestic commerce and manufactures from the many restraints imposed by the *ancien régime*. The intricate network of internal customs duties between provinces—that which Colbert had abolished in the area of the Five Great Farms—Necker wished to abolish throughout the kingdom. "Necker was the first minister since Bertin to give the single-duty project wholehearted backing," writes J. F. Bosher.[47] But this reform, like the other indirect taxes, had to await the end of the war because it was necessary to make up for the lost revenue by other means. It was possible, however, to make thorough studies and have plans ready to put into effect as soon as the state of the royal finances permitted. Necker set up a bureau to revise customs duties and placed it under baron Guillaume-François Mahy de Cormeré, who became an expert on this subject as was Montaran on the grain trade. Like Montaran, Cormeré was completely dedicated to Necker's fiscal policies.

Other trade restraints had lingered from the feudal age: rights of private landowners to levy tolls on goods passing along rivers and roadways. As early as 1724 a commission had been set up to study these rights, called *péages*. Many tributes exacted by landowners were found to be without sufficient title. According to a study made of *péages*, that commission suppressed 3,521 of them that were without title, leaving only 2,054 by 1779.[48] In that year, by a decree of August 15, 1779, Necker gave a new direction to the commission. No longer was it simply to verify titles; it would prepare the way for the abolition of all *péages* by determining what the repurchase price would be. "Originating for the most part in the misfortunes and confusion of ancient times," stated the preamble, "they create so many obstacles to the facility of exchange, that powerful incentive for agriculture and for industry."[49] A distinction was made

45. Ernest Labrousse et al., *Histoire économique et sociale de la France,* 2 vols. Vol. II: *Des Derniers Temps de l'âge seigneurial aux préludes de l'âge industriel (1660-1789)* (Paris, 1970), p. 402, fig. 37.

46. "Mémoire sur le départment des subsistences confié à M. de Montaran, May 1781," BN MSS Joly de Fleury, 1448, fol. 51.

47. Bosher, *The Single Duty Project,* p. 103.

48. Jeanne Bouteil, *Le Rachat des péages au dix-huitième siècle d'après les papiers du bureau des péages* (Paris, 1925), pp. 27ff.

49. Necker, *Oeuvres complètes,* III, 419.

between those tolls in which capital had been invested by the toll owners into roads, ferries, and canals, and those which had no other basis than their feudal origin. In a year the commission had verified 1,104 titles, and the head of the bureau indicated that the remainder probably would not stand up under serious investigation. Some progress was even made toward the repurchase of road and waterway tolls. According to Bouteil, twenty-six *péages* were eliminated during 1779 at a cost to the treasury of 1,007,659 livres.[50]

Similar to the *péages* were those rights of private persons to exact dues for the use of marketplaces. These were generally called rights of *minage* or *leyde*. No special study has been made of them as in the case of the *péages,* but there is evidence that they were being eliminated. Turgot set up a commission to investigate them in 1775. In the summer of 1777 Necker was confronted with a case at Grenoble on the rights of a vicomtesse du Pont to levy charges on all transactions at the chief marketplace of that city. Some merchants had set up another marketplace outside the city limits to carry on their transactions. The Parlement of Grenoble ruled against them and enforced the rights of the vicomtesse. Necker wrote to the intendant explaining his views on the matter. Private property rights must be respected, and he approved the act of the Parlement. When owners of such rights have invested in the construction of market facilities it is legitimate for them to levy a charge. But even if legitimate, he said, such rights hinder commerce and the government should negotiate for their repurchase. This was done with Madame du Pont, although it was a long process and not completed until months after Necker left office.[51]

With regard to manufactures, Necker recognized the merits of the argument of Vincent de Gournay in favor of free enterprise and the ending of excessive government regulation. This admirer of Colbert was by no means a Colbertist if that term meant a minute and vexatious control of industry. In 1778 Necker persuaded Dupont de Nemours to enter the government and to take charge of the commission investigating the regulation of manufactures. According to Georges Weulersse, Dupont was the author of the letters patent of May 1779 announcing a liberal policy regarding manufactures.[52] His preamble stated that "We have seen that regulation is useful to restrain unenlightened cupidity and to insure public confidence." However, the preamble continued, this should not go so far as to inhibit the imagination and the genius of creative and enterprising

50. Bouteil, *Le Rachat des péages,* p. 121.

51. AN F11* 1, fols. 12-15. For the contract between the government and the vicomtesse du Pont, see AN P 2741, "Plumitif de la chambre des comptes," the entry dated December 29, 1781. The contract was concluded on August 28 and September 4 of that year, the government paying Madamme du Pont 32,400 livres in life rentes. In Afanassiev's discussion of this affair he mentioned only that Necker defended the right of the vicomtesse, and that this was an example of his opposition even to internal freedom of the grain trade! See *Le Commerce des céréales en France,* pp. 424, 452.

52. Georges Weulersse, *La Physiocratie sous les ministères de Turgot et de Necker, (1774-1781)* (Paris, 1950), p. 300.

individuals, nor to "resist the succession of fashions and the diversity of tastes."[53] The goal of economic policy here was a compromise between what is necessary for the protection of consumers and the indisputable advantages of free enterprise. The letters patent of May 1779 announced the end of royal monopolies and the practice of designating certain industries as "royal industries" that were competitive with others. Regulations governing size and combinations of ingredients would be discontinued. Only accurate labeling of products was required. "All textiles of national manufacture can circulate without distinction freely throughout the kingdom and be offered for sale, so long as it has the official lead seal." It was not yet laissez-faire, but a liberalization of previous legislation. Furthermore, it was only a beginning. This act announced that a more comprehensive statute governing manufactures was to be drawn up, and manufacturers were invited to send information and suggestions on its provisions.

This was typical of Necker's entire reform. The chief administrator called on the king's subjects to offer advice on how they should be governed. Such was the basic thought behind the establishment of the provincial assemblies and provincial administrations, the most significant of all Necker's experimental projects.

53. Necker, *Oeuvres complètes,* III, 443.

Chapter XI

TAX REFORM AND THE
PROVINCIAL ASSEMBLIES

Although Necker's aim was to finance the war without raising taxes, he was always ready to do so if it appeared that amelioration would fall short of meeting the war costs. This was often stated in preambles of his loan edicts. His reluctance to raise taxes was due to the system's inequities; if they should have to be raised in an unreformed system it would simply compound those injustices. Therefore, his apprehension that taxes might have to be increased led him to push reform of the direct taxes without awaiting the war's end. The purpose was not so much to increase the revenue as to reform the system so that taxes could be more easily raised when and if necessary.

Some important tax laws were to expire during the war years, and Necker had the disagreeable task, for him, of continuing them. The levying of municipal taxes (*octrois*) had been an emergency wartime measure of the Seven Years' War. In 1765 Laverdy had apologetically decreed their continuance until 1778. By the declaration of August 2, 1777, Necker extended these taxes until December 31, 1787. The second *vingtième* was due to expire in 1781. By an edict of February 1, 1780, Necker extended it another ten years, to expire in December 1790. Despite his quarrel only two years before with the *parlements* over his reform of the *vingtième,* there was little opposition to this extension. In fact, the Parlement of Paris heaped praise upon the Genevan for his fiscal policy.[1] His "ameliorations" were exactly what the magistrates had long called for, asserting that the government could meet its extraordinary needs by putting its fiscal house in order.

The trouble between the director general and the Parlement occurred during the summer and fall months of 1777 before Necker had been able to demonstrate his reform program. It was the eruption of a long-standing quarrel between the administrative monarchy and the sovereign courts over the nature of the *vingtième* tax. The magistrates looked upon this levy as an extraordinary tax to be tolerated only in wartime or an emergency. They contested the legality of a proportional tax based upon a certain percentage of the taxpayers' income. The king, they said, must specify his needs and collect a definite sum. At the end of

---

1. Egret, *Necker: ministre de Louis XVI,* p. 82.

the Seven Years' War the *parlements* accepted the continuation of the first and second *vingtièmes* only if the tax rolls would remain stationary, where they were in 1763. With the quasi-royal revolution of 1770 and the suppression of the *parlements,* it was possible for the controller general, Terray, to proceed with the revision of the tax rolls of 1763. His edict of November 1771 permitted the intendants, administrators, and controllers of the *vingtième* to verify the rolls and bring them up to the level of the actual income of the proprietors.

As with the *taille,* the most perplexing problem for the administration of the *vingtième* was to find out the exact value of the lands and the owners' annual income. Ideally, the total landed wealth of the parish should be surveyed, and then each proprietor's wealth assessed. This had been the goal of Bertin's proposed cadastral survey in 1763, which the *parlements* firmly rejected. According to them the only permissible method was for the administrators of the *vingtième* to rely upon the individual declarations of the proprietors. Since Terray was convinced that many declared their income far below the actual sum, he refused to rely upon them. In his correspondence with intendants he listed some useful criteria for assessing income independently of the declarations. There were the tax rolls of the *taille* for those subject to that tax; the local assessments for maintenance of parish churches and poor relief, which all classes paid; the records for payment of church tithes; the officially registered leases between proprietors and renters: "All these means will give you some general knowledge. They will not be free of many errors, which it will be necessary to discover and correct over a period of time."[2]

As for the anguished outcries of landed proprietors that they were being subjected to inquisitorial investigations by the intendants and the controllers of the *vingtième,* Terray protested:

The spirit of despotism is not at all what animates the ministers of the king. They are seeking to repair the damage which the resistance of the *parlements,* pushed to the extreme limit, has brought about, forcing the administrators of the finances to use such ruinous expedients as continual loans at onerous terms, and excessive anticipations, means destructive of the finances and in the end, a hardship on the subjects of the king. Now that those unjust modifications [of 1763] no longer exist, the assessment of the *vingtième* can be carried out in proportion to the income from landed property.[3]

Such was the voice of "enlightened despotism." Tax reform was to be done by the administrators alone. There was no place in Terray's plans for participation by the taxpayers themselves, as had been proposed in the remonstrance of the Court of Aides of 1775, and which was provided for in the reform program of both Turgot and Necker.

With the end of the Terray ministry in 1774 and the restoration of the *parlements,* the process of verifying the rolls of the *vingtième* was bound to

2. Laugier, *Un Ministère réformateur sous Louis XV,* p. 211.
3. Quoted in Marion, *Histoire financière de la France,* I, 268.

become more difficult because the landowners now had sympathetic and power-ful listeners. Turgot continued Terray's policy of supervising the intendants' verifications of the tax rolls. He was probably the author of a memorial that initiated the policy Necker was to adopt in his decree-in-council of November 2, 1777. This was an undated manuscript entitled "Instruction of the controller general," which was distributed to the administrators of the *vingtième*.[4] It directed the controllers in the *élections* to form a commission in each parish to survey the revenue of all parish land. This commission was to consist of the syndic of the parish, the collectors of the *taille,* and three proprietors chosen by the parish assembly. Its first task was to survey all lands of the parish. Next it would appraise the tax rolls of the individual proprietors subject to the *ving-tième*. The commission would do this in the presence of each proprietor or his agent, so an opportunity for contradiction and presentation of evidence was given the taxpayer.

The "Instruction" asserted that the king did not wish to increase total revenue from the *vingtième*; that the taxpayer should not be assessed more than one-twentieth (or two-twentieths as the case was) of his revenue; and that the "tax must be partitioned among the contributors in proportion to their respec-tive revenues." Thus, it was essentially a tax of repartition and not truly proportional. The rate of 10 percent was simply the maximum that could be levied on any taxpayer. In addition to the "Instruction," Turgot was probably the author of a much more detailed guide for the use of these commissions in fulfilling their task of appraising the land and income of the parishes.[5]

How widely these methods were carried out by the administrators of the *vingtième* is not known. Turgot, as already noted, issued no new legislation on the subject. The most important measure in the above documents was the principle that assessment would be done by a commission rather than by an individual, the controller of the *vingtième*. It is likely that this was intended to quell the rising chorus of protest by irate landowners whose cause was taken up by the *parlements*. In the summer of 1777 the Parlement of Paris ordered an investigation in all the generalities within its jurisdiction on the activities of the controllers, and how they assessed and collected the two *vingtièmes*. It evidently found many shocking cases of "ministerial despotism" and use of "inquisitorial" methods to pry into private affairs of landowners in order to revise their tax rolls. It was evident that the Parlement was accumulating an elaborate dossier for a coming showdown with the royal government. The situation was potentially

4. Georges Lardé, *Une Enquête sur les vingtièmes au temps de Necker: Histoire des remontrances du parlement de Paris (1771-1778)* (Paris, 1920), p. 8. Lardé believes the document was written in 1776 but does not say that the author was Turgot. It would appear probable that Turgot wrote it because it refers to the new tax for financing road work based upon the *vingtième*. Therefore, it must have been written sometime between the enforced registration of that act by the Parlement of Paris in February 1776 and Turgot's fall from power on May 12 of that year.

5. *Ibid.,* pp. 11-17.

dangerous. It was over the *vingtième* and its administration that the serious confrontation occurred during the Seven Years' War. Necker saw the peril and grasped the nettle. The course he chose was to continue the process of verification of tax rolls initiated by Terray, but also to take heed of the protests regarding the arbitrary assessments and harassing treatment of property owners by agents of the *vingtième*.

These were the guidelines in the decree-in-council of November 2, 1777, "concerning the repartitioning of the *vingtième* and suppressing the *vingtième* of industry in the towns, villages, and countryside."[6] The preamble reminded the king's subjects that the *vingtième* was a tax proportional to the revenue of the taxpayer. Yet it noted that "the poorest class of the king's subjects are the ones who pay the *vingtième* in the most exact proportion." The reason for this, the preamble continued, was the immutability of the tax rolls, which, despite the evident increase in land values and landed income, remain what they were in 1749, 1741, and even in 1734. Revaluation had taken place in some parishes, but the process was too slow. To maintain the rolls at a fixed level, the preamble said, would be "to substitute a fixed subsidy for a proportional tax." If the tax rolls remained immutable this would favor the wealthier proprietors, "who need it least," since land values are constantly rising and "the king's revenue should follow the increase, at least at a certain distance." By not paying in proportion to the increased value of their properties, the landowners shifted the burden to the poor and postponed the time when the government could lighten the burden on that class. Furthermore, if events should force the government to raise the *vingtième* tax, these injustices would be all the more aggravated.

But the November 2 decree also recognized the complaints about the arbitrary revision of rolls. It ruled that no tax roll could be altered by an individual assessor or controller. The tax rolls would be made up by a commission, established in each parish, consisting of the syndic of the parish, the collectors of the *taille*, and three proprietors to be named by the parish assembly to which all citizens subject to the *vingtième* could attend. The commission would also consist of the controllers of the *vingtième*. If the commissioners disagreed about a roll, that would be included in the *procès-verbal* the controller would send to the intendant. The latter could, if advisable, order a new assessment by the parish commission. The decree stated that once this process had been completed, the tax rolls of the *vingtième* could not again be revised for twenty years. This would guarantee that proprietors' assessments would not be changed continually.

Necker's decree obviously only codified what Turgot had earlier worked out, as far as administering the *vingtième* was concerned. Other important provisions in the decree of November 2, 1777, should also have pleased the *économistes*. The *vingtième* of industry, that is, the tax on income other than landed income—such as wages and salaries, profits, "the fruits of work and intelligence"—was abolished in the small towns (*bourgs*), in the villages, and in the

6. Isambert et al., eds., *Recueil général des anciennes lois,* XXV, 146-151.

countryside. The reason was stated to be the difficulty in assessing the tax, which required an inquisitorial inspection into private affairs that was considered intolerable in that age. In the large cities the tax was collected by the corporations of artisans and merchants and therefore was not so objectionable. But the decree declared that even in the cities the *vingtième* of industry would eventually be abolished. "General plans for reform must be implemented by degrees, in order to make their execution easier and more solidly based," the preamble read, an unmistakable sign of Necker's authorship. The principal reason for the abolition of this tax was economic. Businessmen, manufacturers, and merchants would be encouraged to move from large cities to smaller towns. A certain kind of land use was encouraged by a provision in which leases for money-rent (rather than in kind, as in the *métayage* system where the renter shared the crop with the proprietor) would be automatically reduced one-fifteenth of their value for purposes of assessment. Land which was not rented, but cultivated directly by the proprietor, would be taxed more lightly than rented land.

Despite the reasonableness of the decree, the magistrates of the Parlement of Paris attacked again, reiterating the principle that the king did not have the right to levy a proportional tax on his subjects. "In the absence of the States-General representing the nation, the king must rely upon the personal declaration of the individual landed proprietor." The remonstrance repeated the principle of "the free gift," that the only legitimate tax is a subsidy based upon the demonstrated need of the government. It denied that the poor paid the *vingtième* in a more exact proportion than the wealthy. And the new method of assessment would not work, the magistrates asserted, because the controller would dominate the commission.[7]

The government reply to the remonstrance firmly rejected its constitutional claims.[8] The king did have legitimate authority to levy a proportional tax. Yet, some attempt was made toward conciliation. The decree-in-council of April 26, 1778, reduced the assessment of the value of the leases from one-fifteenth to one-twelfth, and this same rate was extended to all lands the proprietor cultivated directly. Also, roads, dikes, and other capital investments in land would receive a reduction. The Parlement of Paris was not mollified and again remonstrated. But the king's reply of May 2, 1778, seems to have ended the matter. In the summer the young firebrand in the Parlement's Chamber of Inquests, Duval d'Eprésmesnil, attempted to rekindle the quarrel, but without success.[9] Necker went ahead with his reform, and the complaints about the *vingtième* from landowners declined rapidly. In 1784 Necker wrote that the council of finance received less than ten complaints after the reform had been implemented.[10] In

7. Jules Flammermont, ed., *Remontrances du parlement de Paris au XVIIIᵉ siècle*, 3 vols. (Paris, 1888-1898), III, 394-413.

8. *Ibid.*, pp. 414-422.

9. Lardé, *Une Enquête sur les vingtièmes*, p. 74.

10. Necker, *Oeuvres complètes*, IV, 396.

its initial remonstrance the Parlement had claimed to have public opinion on its side, as evidenced by the widespread complaints about the assessments of the *vingtième*. If this were a fair gauge of public opinion, then Necker obviously won the contest. The outcome gave some credence to his strategy in dealing with the sovereign courts. "The Parlement," wrote Cardinal de Bernis earlier in the century, "is strong only with the voice of public opinion. . . . The *parlements* must give way as soon as they are abandoned by the public."[11]

But if Necker won the battle with public opinion, how successful was his reform of the *vingtième* in other respects? The purpose of the reform was not necessarily to increase revenue from this source, although an augmentation of 1,800,000 livres was achieved during his ministry.[12] But did the poorest class continue to be those "who paid the *vingtième* in the most exact proportion?" This is more difficult to determine. The taxpaying habits of the aristocratic society of the *ancien régime* were deeply rooted in tradition and custom. They could not be changed at once by decree, as Necker was well aware. This is why he believed the best method for reform of the *ancien régime* lay with the provincial assemblies and the administration under their supervision. Through the *procès-verbeaux* of these institutions, it is possible to follow up the fate of this reform as well as others during and after Necker's first ministry. These documents provide some of the most interesting and revealing evidence available on the reform of the *ancien régime*.

The importance Necker attached to the new provincial assemblies and the administrative bodies set up by them (intermediate commissions) in the provinces of Berri and Haute-Guienne can be seen in the events surrounding his resignation in May 1781. He insisted on removing the intendant of Moulins, who had refused to install a provincial assembly in the province of the Bourbonnais. He also insisted that the Parlement of Paris be forced to register the edict setting up this assembly. On the other issues he might have made concessions, but not on this. On no other of his innovations had he placed such great hopes for the regeneration of public life by tapping the great unused reservoir of patriotism, public spirit, and talent that he believed existed in the notables of the provinces.

The two provincial assemblies that he did succeed in setting up in 1778 and 1779 illustrated his method and style of reform. Schemes for similar institutions had been publicized since the time of Fénelon, but they varied considerably in organization and goals. Some were nostalgic dreams of restoring the old monarchy of estates that preceded the absolute monarchy; each province would have institutions as did Brittany, where the royal government would have to negotiate

11. Quoted by Jean Egret, *Louis XV et l'opposition parlementaire* (Paris, 1970), p. 230.

12. Augustin Rioche, *De L'Administration des vingtièmes sous l'ancien régime* (Paris, 1904), p. 108. The following figures are given: in 1778 there was a slight diminution of the yield of the *vingtièmes* from what they had produced in 1776; in 1779 there was an increase of 447,000 livres; in 1780, an increase of 78,000 livres; in 1781, 399,000 livres; and in 1782, 364,000 livres.

a yearly "free gift" and where all noblemen would have an automatic right to sit in the assembly. The latter would be organized according to medieval notions, the three estates deliberating and voting in separate chambers and the vote counted by order. Moreover, according to the old assemblies of estates, each deputy had the right, if not of a complete veto as in the Polish Diet, at least to have his minority vote and views inscribed in the minutes. A deputy to these medieval assemblies did not ordinarily have full powers to commit his constituency to any decision of the assembly that was not authorized in his mandate.[13] In contrast, Necker's assemblies were modern, deliberative bodies, and they retained very little of the traditional estates; naturally, they found little favor with those who were hoping for a restoration of the old type.

At the opposite extreme were plans for a very restricted and manageable system of assemblies such as in most physiocratic schemes.[14] These were to be agents of "enlightened despotism" by helping the monarchy overcome traditional aristocratic resistance to reform. The assemblies were to be small and carefully supervised by the administrative monarchy. They were to consist only of landed proprietors who would apportion the single tax on land but would have no other important function. The "municipalities" described by Dupont and, presumably, Turgot were not so extreme, but tended in that direction rather than toward aristocratic estates. As for Necker's assemblies, "they resemble mine as much as a windmill resembles the moon," Turgot remarked scornfully to Dupont. There were important differences, but they were not necessarily to the discredit of the Genevan. Turgot and Dupont envisaged a complete blueprint from the parish assembly to the great national municipality. Necker's method was to initiate a tentative and cautious plan in which most details were to be worked out by the provincial assembly, based on its experience. Turgot's municipalities were to be established all at once; Necker began with a single province, waiting until public opinion and the local situation made it opportune to introduce them in other provinces, a method Turgot found "puerile."[15]

Yet, in practice the two projects had much in common. Some historians see a major contrast in Turgot's elimination of the traditional three estates, basing representation exclusively on land ownership, whereas Necker retained the traditional estates. In reality, there was little difference between the two plans in this respect. The deputies of Necker's assemblies were actually landed proprietors, and he always referred to them as such. The number of deputies of the third estate was to be equal to that of the other two orders combined, the famous "doubling principle" used in the elections of 1789 for deputies to the States-General. Unlike the latter body, however, deliberation in the provincial

13. Emile Lousse, *L'Organisation corporative du moyen âge à la fin de l'ancien régime* (Louvain, 1943).

14. Pierre Renouvin, *Les Assemblées provinciales de 1787* (Paris, 1921), p. 18.

15. *Oeuvres de Turgot,* ed. Schelle, IV, 624.

assemblies was in common and the vote counted by head, a procedure that had been customary in the estates of Languedoc. All these provisions practically eliminated the significance of the privileged orders in Necker's assemblies. In fact, according to one historian, if Turgot's project had ever gone beyond the planning stage his municipalities would have used a numerical majority of deputies from the privileged orders rather than the doubling principle in Necker's assemblies.[16] This is quite plausible in view of the minimal representation accorded urban property by Turgot and Dupont. In contrast, Necker's assemblies required that at least one-fourth of the deputies be both urban and nonnoble. Anyway, the important matter for Necker was not the social status or economic basis of the deputy, but his ability, knowledge, and zeal for public service. Of course, Necker shared the prevalent bias of that day which required deputies to be "men of substance," of independent economic means. It was believed that property and character went together, that this is what insured the independence of the deputy from outside influence.

Both Turgot's and Necker's schemes were reform measures, by no means reactionary or revolutionary. The authority of the absolute monarchy was to remain intact. Turgot feared that the assemblies could become revolutionary and, according to abbé de Véri, hesitated to implement them for that reason. In this respect, the "timid Genevan," as Necker is so often called, proved the bolder reformer. There can be no question but that on this as well as other aspects of reform he accomplished more than did his supposedly more brilliant predecessor.

The new institutions set up in Berri and in Haute-Guienne were in fact radical changes in administration at the provincial level. While the absolutism of the king was untouched, that of the intendant in the province came to an end. He continued to exercise "police power" in the generality, but the administration of finances, social welfare, public works, and economic improvement were taken out of his hands by the provincial assembly and the intermediate commission, which governed as the executive branch of the provincial government. The intendant appeared before the assembly in its opening and closing ceremonies of each session to present the king's orders. He could seek admission at any time he believed the king's business called for his presence. But he did not take part in the regular deliberations of the assembly or the intermediate commission. The president of the latter body (who was also the president of the assembly and the foremost prelate in the province) was actually the chief administrative officer in the provinces of Berri and Haute-Guienne. Some intendants accepted the reform; others, angered by their greatly reduced powers, joined the ranks of Necker's enemies.

The assemblies were to be given a large measure of autonomy, both in their organization and in a broad area of reform: transportation, industrial and

16. L. de Lavergne, "Les Assemblées provinciales en France avant 1789," *Revue des deux mondes,* 34 (July 1861), 39.

commercial development, and the problems of social welfare and public health, as well as fiscal reform. Necker did closely observe the sessions in Berri and Haute-Guienne. He sent a memorial to Bourges on November 1, 1778, with suggestions on the organization and procedure of the assembly, but the deputies themselves were to form a committee on this matter and make their own recommendations to the king. [17] Sometimes Necker prodded the assembly, as when he insisted that the *corvée* be abolished in Berri. At other times he used a restraining hand, as when he reminded the assembly of Haute-Guienne that the granting of the *abonnement* for the *vingtième* did not mean they could negotiate the amount. Like all his experiments, the provincial administrations required his continued attention if they were to realize their goals. After Necker's resignation in 1781, the provincial administrations of Berri and Haute-Guienne were not abolished in the reaction that followed. But his successors were indifferent if not suspicious toward them, and the authority of the intendants was largely restored in the two generalities.

The foundation deed for the first provincial administration, that of Berri, was promulgated on July 12, 1778. The territories to be governed by the new regime were all included in the generality of Bourges. The old provincial name of Berri was revived to designate the new administration. The generality evoked the absolute powers of the intendant; the name of the province suggested the principle of self-government. The lengthy preamble of the decree-in-council announced the king's intentions in establishing the new administration. Many themes of Necker's April 1778 memorial were repeated in the act—except, of course, the unflattering remarks he had made about the intendants, their subdelegates, and the *parlements*. The preamble made clear that the new administration for Berri was the first of its kind, that others would eventually be established in all generalities of the *pays d'élections*. The king explained that the war had prevented tax reductions he had hoped for at the beginning of his reign. But the new provincial administration would be able to carry out needed reforms "by calling upon the proprietors of the province to bring an end to arbitrary assessment and to assure justice in the partition of the tax burden." Because of the diversity of the regions in wealth, soil, habits and character, uniform laws of direct taxation passed by the royal government were not advisable. "It is preferable," said the preamble, "to allow each province to determine how it can best raise the quota of tax revenue assigned to it by the royal government." The existing system of tax administration was too overcentralized. There was too large a gap between the immense task imposed upon the finance minister and his capability of dealing with it effectively.

His Majesty cannot remain unaware that by having all details of the finances converge at the center, the disproportion between this immense task and the

17. Auguste-Théodore, baron de Girardot, *Essai sur les assemblées provinciales et en particulier sur celle du Berry* (Bourges, 1845), pp. 48-52.

measure of time and strength of the minister whom he has honored with his confidence, either extends too far the intermediate authorities, or submits important interests to hasty decisions; while these same interests, left to the examination of local administrations wisely selected, would be almost always better known and balanced.[18]

It was explicitly stated in the preamble that the purpose of the new institution was not to raise more revenue. The province would pay no more direct taxes than in the past. The benefits of this reform were to redound to the taxpayers themselves, and particularly the poorer classes.

Why was Berri chosen for the first experiment? The preamble explained that Berri was one of the most economically backward of all the provinces, yet had the greatest potential for progress if brought under enlightened and energetic administration. It was wealthy in natural resources. Its agriculture needed only the new ·methods of farming to increase production. The population of the province was about one-half million. It paid a total of 8 million livres in taxes, having a per capita taxation of slightly less than 16 livres. It had the lightest per capita rate for the *taille* of all the generalities in the kingdom. Only 2.5 million of the 8 million livres came from direct taxes, the remainder being indirect. The generality of Bourges was within the provinces of the *grandes gabelles* and the *pays d'aides.* It was under the regime of the personal *taille,* and its roads were built and maintained by the *corvée.*

The king sent letters to sixteen proprietors of the province directing them to assemble at Bourges on October 5 to select the other thirty-two members of the assembly. Of the forty-eight members thus selected, twelve were to be from the provincial clergy, twelve noble proprietors, twelve bourgeois of the cities, and twelve nonnoble landowners from the countryside. The first assembly was opened on November 10, 1778, presided over by the archbishop of Bourges, Phélypeaux de la Vrillière, a relative of Maurepas. The assembly, after the opening ceremonies, set up four committees to investigate and make proposals concerning rules of procedure, tax reform, agriculture and commerce, and public works.

If one can judge from the *procès-verbeaux* of these sessions, Necker's wager that the notables in the provinces would second his own reform projects was amply borne out. There were many divergent ideas expressed; numerous projects were presented both in committees and in the assembly as a whole. There was open discussion and a weighing of alternatives for each question. The assembly seemed to attract the kinds of persons Necker hoped to see in the provincial administrations. His strongest ally was the archbishop of Bourges, who joined with him at Versailles in February 1780 to persuade the king (and no doubt Maurepas) that it was essential to remove the intendant of Bourges, who was stubbornly opposed to abolition of the *corvée.*[19] One of the most prominent

18. *Collection des procès-verbeaux de l'assemblée provinciale du Berri,* 2 vols. (Bourges, 1787), I, v-xiii.
19. Lavergne, "Les Assemblées provinciales," pp. 404-405.

liberal nobles of the province was the duc de Béthune-Charost, who had abolished seigneurial *corvées* on his own estates in 1770 and was known for his philanthropic activities.[20] The comte du Buat, although a conservative aristocrat, was a specialist in problems of tax reform and was influential on the tax committee that took charge of that part of reform.

The chairman of the tax committee was none other than abbé de Véri, whose benefices were located in the province of Berri. The monastery of Saint-Satun of which he was titular abbott no longer existed, and he had no pastoral duties, but that did not prevent him from continuing to receive the ample endowments originally assigned to that monastery. Véri was a close friend and advisor of Turgot, as well as of Maurepas. Turgot and the *économistes* had formed Véri's opinion of Necker. But now that he was intimately involved in Berri's administration he had an opportunity to consult with Necker and to become acquainted with him personally. He described in his *Journal* entry of February 5, 1779, his first conference with the director general of finances:

I found his reasoning precise and to the point. I found him flexible in his thinking, not attached to unimportant details, nor too wrapped up in his ideas, and with a good heart [*l'âme bonne*]. I admit that a rather puerile desire for glory and popular acclaim led him to decide somewhat lightly on the creation of provincial assemblies. He formed that of Berri without knowing what he would do with it, and without having examined the obstacles he would find in the existing legal forms.[21]

Véri's *économiste* convictions would account for his inability to understand a policy of experimentation rather than of a blueprint imposed all at once. Otherwise, his assertion that Necker did not know what he was going to do with the assembly in Berri would be nonsense in view of what has already been seen. Surprisingly, Véri proved to be one of the notables who seconded Necker's intentions in forming the assembly. The abbé supported those who wanted to replace the *corvée* with money allocations for road construction and maintenance. As chairman of the committee on tax reform, he reported to the assembly on November 20 the results of the deliberations of that committee; in doing so he expressed the consensus of the committee rather than his own ideas. The report was and still remains an illuminating commentary on the fiscal system of the *ancien régime* and the necessity for reform.

The evils in the administration of the *taille* were laid before the assembly in stark clarity. The collectors chosen by the local parish assembly were saddled with the burden of both assessing and collecting the *taille*, and were collectively and legally responsible for turning over to the receiver of the *élection* exactly the amount assessed. If they could not collect that amount, they had to borrow it on their own account and hope to be reimbursed the following year by having

20. *Ibid.*, p. 403.
21. *Journal de l'abbé de Véri*, II, 173.

the shortage reimposed on the parish *taillables.* Since no one ever volunteered to be collector, the job was made compulsory for any *taillable* called to serve. Collectors were changed each year, but even so, a one-year appointment could be disastrous. It required two years for the collection of a fiscal year to be completed. About half the time of the collectors was taken up in attempting to collect the *taille* from unwilling and hostile taxpayers. The collectors-assessors had nothing to go by in levying the rates except their own opinion of the wealth of their fellow parishioners. One does not have to read Balzac's "scenes of provincial life" to imagine what the clash must have been between the collectors, who were trying to appraise their neighbor's wealth in the dark, and the *taillables.* "In the shock of these quarrels," said Véri, "it is not venturing too much to say that it is the poorest people who are always the victims."[22] In any case, taxpayers resisted the assessment and the collection because not doing so exposed them to higher assessments. Collectors naturally followed the line of least resistance and tended to be lenient to those who threatened to cause the most trouble. The "cocks of the parish" were often let off lightly, and the defenseless poorer members had to make up for their delinquence. Litigation was frequent among *taillables* who took their cases to the courts alleging unjust assessments. Yet the justice available to them was so expensive that the bribes paid to the judge could be larger than the total amount of the surtax.

It is noteworthy that Véri condemned the method of collection of the *taille* but said nothing about exemptions from it as a problem for reform. He believed these exemptions did not apply to noble and church lands that were leased to farmers, who paid the tax out of income that would otherwise have gone to the proprietors. The exemptions applied only in those cases where the noble or clerical proprietors exploited their lands directly, and then with restrictions which, according to Moreau de Baumont, greatly mitigated the extent of exemptions from the *taille.*[23] For these reasons, the assembly of Berri believed the *taille* was the direct tax which had the least number of exemptions. This was an important matter when the replacement for the *corveé* was discussed.[24]

The evils in the system of assessment and collection were patent and agreed upon. What to do about them was more difficult. The tax committee insisted that earlier measures to correct these evils had been inadequate. The *taxe d'office* of the intendant and his subdelegates only attempted to repair damage already done. This was a practice introduced early in the century whereby the intendants assumed the right of correcting tax rolls made up by the collectors of the parish, either by mitigating or adding to the burden placed on individual *taillables.* But this only substituted the arbitrariness of the intendants for that of

22. *Collection des procès-verbeaux,* I, 72.
23. Moreau de Beaumont and Poullin de Viéville, *Mémoires concernant les impositions,* V, 55. A special study is needed on the subject of exemptions to the *taille.* According to Moreau de Beaumont, the edict of July 1766 greatly restricted the exemptions. Marion scarcely mentions this act in any of his works.
24. Necker, *Oeuvres complètes,* V, 7-8.

the collectors. Earlier in the year, by the declaration of April 23, 1778, Necker had sought to reform the procedures by which *taillables* could obtain remedy at law in cases of unfair assessment.[25] The complainants could appeal to the court of the *élection* on unstamped paper, in a simple *mémoire,* without having it notarized by an attorney. The committee on taxation applauded this reform, but felt it was inadequate because litigants still had to travel to the seat of the *élection.* It also doubted the capacity of those courts to decide such cases.

Numerous projects for reform of the *taille* were examined by the committee. Most suggested some form of the proportional *taille* implemented in the generalities of Limoge, Paris, and Châlons. This consisted essentially of making an exact assessment of all property and "faculties" subject to the *taille,* rather than leaving it to the "souls and consciences" of the hapless and often ignorant collectors. The most elaborate reform of this type had been carried out in the generality of Paris by the intendant, Bertier de Sauvigny. Official registers of property were made up in each parish by oral declarations of the *taillables* in a parish assembly. Surveys were carried out only in cases of disagreement. A sliding scale was made for the parishes depending upon their degree of wealth, so that assessment became almost automatic. Necker gave high praise to the work of Bertier de Sauvigny in his *Compte rendu* of 1781 and evidently believed that this was the solution to the problem of assessment.[26] Yet, paradoxically, the reform of Bertier, which seemed the administrator's ideal of perfect equity, was not very popular in the generality of Paris, as the parish *cahiers* of 1789 were to reveal. It seemed that many peasants feared public disclosure of their property, preferring to take their chances in the traditional system of obscurity. In the face of the physical difficulties of the assessment of all property, and the suspicions of the peasants about any innovation, the assembly at Bourges seemed to hesitate about reforming the *taille.* It would be preferable, they decided, to take up first the administration of the *vingtième,* which did not offer so many bristling problems. If the experiment with the *vingtième* should work out satisfactorily, perhaps the same methods could be used for the *taille.*

For the immediate future the committee recommended that the *taille* collection system be changed. Instead of relying upon amateur and variable personnel for assessment and collection, expert appraisers would be appointed in each parish. They would receive the same commission as had the collectors, 6 deniers per livre. Taxpayers would be required to bring their tributes to the new officials, rather than having the collectors visit each household. The reform made the expert appraisers at the parish level similar to receivers of the *élection* and the receivers general of the generality: their positions and duties were permanent, and they would not be collectively liable for the quotas assigned the parishes.

25. Isambert et al., eds., *Recueil général des anciennes lois,* XXV, 267-279.
26. Necker, *Oeuvres complètes,* II, 89-90.

On the *vingtième,* the taxation committee won assembly approval of the reform it would propose to the king. The *vingtième* was easier to reform because it was assessed on farm land alone (the act of November 1777 having abolished the *vingtième* of industry), and the principle of collective liability did not operate. The decree-in-council of July 12 establishing the Berri assembly had stated that the king would grant a fixed sum (*abonnement*) for the province of Berri. The assembly formally requested that this sum be set at its current assessment. This would remove the suspicion that the assembly was a covert scheme to increase revenue. The assembly then accepted the committee's recommendation that each parish be given a fixed quota that could not be altered in future years. The parish assembly would be left free to apportion the burden among its members in the same way that local expenses for repair of churches and presbyteries were allocated. That is, each local assembly, which would consist of proprietors subject to the *vingtième,* would select expert notables (*prudhommes*) who would preside over the assessment of the *vingtième* on each property in the parish, in the presence of the owners themselves. Other than the above stipulation, each parish was to be free to carry out the task according to its own judgment. The intendant and his agents, the controllers, thus were completely eliminated from administration of the *vingtième.* The local assemblies were to be given three years to complete the assessment on individual landowners. Then the rolls would remain stationary for six years. The assembly of Berri was somewhat more strict in the supervision of these rolls than provided for by the decree-in-council of November 2, 1777, which was now superseded in this province.[27]

The inhabitants of Berri were now free from the vexatious agents of the *vingtième* sent out by the intendant's office. But how well did the reform work? The king granted the *abonnement* as he had promised, and the quota was fixed permanently in each parish. Beyond that it is difficult to know. In the session of October 1783, held nearly two-and-a-half years after Necker's resignation, it appeared from the *procès-verbal* that the local assemblies were not functioning very satisfactorily. The committee on taxation reported that "out of 723 parishes in the province, scarcely 230 have bothered to make up the new rolls, and what is more unsatisfactory, is that these rolls are badly done."[28] But the tone of the committee's report was far from discouraged. The explanation it gave for the large number of parishes failing to comply was the lack of capable persons at the local level to assume the functions of the "notable experts."

A third *vingtième* had been imposed on the other two *vingtièmes* by Necker's successor, Joly de Fleury, in the summer of 1782. Necker had wanted to avoid this, knowing it would hinder tax reform. In addition, the powers of the intendant over the provincial administration and its intermediate commission

27. *Collection des procès-verbeaux,* I, 77-80, 103, 145ff.
28. *Ibid.,* II, 56-57.

had been greatly strengthened by Joly de Fleury, also contrary to Necker's intentions. The remedy that the tax committee in 1783 chose to enforce its legislation on the *vingtième* was to propose that the intermediate commission name a "repartitioning commissioner," who would go to the delinquent parishes, summon an assembly of local landowners, and form the tax rolls. If the taxpayers refused to assemble or to declare their property holdings, the intermediate commission should then make up the rolls without their participation. Thus, the new provincial government seemed forced into the same quandary and the same tactics of those of abbé Terray and his intendants.[29]

With respect to the *taille,* the threat that increased taxes might become inevitable led Necker to take a step early in 1780 that has often seemed puzzling to historians but was actually quite consistent with his views on·taxation. By the declaration of February 13, 1780, the king announced that any future increase of the *taille* would require the formal registration of the *parlements.*[30] Without such a formal edict the *taille* would be fixed at the level of 1780, which was itself exactly the sum of the preceding year. This applied not only to the second brevet of the *taille* but also to the *capitation* for the *taillable.* The preamble noted that these two direct taxes had increased out of all proportion to the other taxes in recent years. The reason was clear. Procedures for increasing the other taxes, namely the *vingtièmes* and the *capitation* of the non-*taillable* required the registration of the *parlements.* It was easy for the financial administration to raise the second brevet at will. In 1772, the second brevet was 9,404,279 livres. In 1780, it had risen to 24,284,463 livres. This had come about primarily in the administration of abbé Terray. Henceforth, such a progression would not be possible.[31]

Fixing the rolls of the *taille* did not mean they could not be reduced, either by the usual procedure of granting relief in hardship cases (*moins imposés*) or if the yield from the *capitation* of the non-*taillables* should make possible a reduction. The two-brevet system was ended and the *taille* was now consolidated into a single brevet. This reform included the *taille* for the *pays d'élections* and the *pays conquis.* The preamble referred to plans to reform indirect taxes when the war ended and said that a ceiling on the *taille* was needed because of the possibility of a momentary interruption of income from these sources. This meant that the *taillables* ran the risk of having to make up the difference. In reality, Necker's motives may not have been fully stated in the preamble. Moreau de Beaumont believed this was a temporary measure pending the fundamental reform of the *taille* that Necker expected the provincial assemblies to carry out. The best encouragement he could give these new assemblies was to fix the upper limit of the tax quotas definitively, so that *taille* could be reformed

---

29. *Ibid.,* p. 64.
30. Isambert et al., eds., *Recueil général des anciennes lois,* XXVI, 270-274.
31. Moreau de Beaumont and Poullin de Viéville, *Mémoires concernant les impositions,* V, 35.

in the same way that the *vingtième* was reformed in Berri, that is, by fixing the *abonnement*. It would, he hoped, lessen the peasants' innate distrust of any tax changes.

At the opening of the Berri assembly in September 1780, the president of the intermediate commission reported "a fortunate event" in regard to the *taille*. Explaining the provisions of the February 13 declaration, he said that uncertainty about the assessment of the *taille* each year had made it difficult for the committee on taxation to get more information about the taxpaying abilities of the *taillables*. Now he thought it possible to acquire the information necessary for a reform.[32]

In October 1780 the assembly at Bourges abolished Berri's *corvée*, substituting for it a monetary tax levied on the parishes based upon the *taille*, and the *capitation* in the cities.[33] The assembly also took an interest in agricultural, commercial, and industrial progress. Space does not permit a discussion of these activities of the assembly of Berri, or of the second provincial assembly established by Necker in Haute-Guienne in 1779. The problems were somewhat different in that province from what they were in Berri. But Necker felt that the record of accomplishments in reform of the second assembly was even better than that of Berri.

It is not possible here to give a final evaluation of these assemblies. As the preceding discussion shows, the notables took seriously their new duties. It is surely an error to say that Necker's assemblies were "reactionary." Undoubtedly some members were, but there was an important progressive and public-spirited element in both assemblies. The actual accomplishment may have seemed unimpressive compared to that of the National Assembly. But, then, Necker's provincial administration in Berri and Haute-Guienne was only a beginning. Its significance lay in its promise. This was the most important part of the liberal reform program as contrasted to the reform of enlightened despotism.

32. Lavergne, "Les Assemblées provinciales," p. 408.
33. *Collection des procès-verbeaux*, I, 220-221.

Chapter XII

THE EMBATTLED REFORMER

Among the private papers left by baron Pierre-Victor de Besenval, which were published after his death by the vicomte de Ségur, was one written in 1780 entitled, "Anecdote of Louis XV; Reflections on Mr. Necker." The anecdote was related to Besenval by the duc de Choiseul when the latter was the foreign affairs minister in the government of Louis XV. One day when the minister and the king were riding in a carriage on a hunting trip, the king asked Choiseul to estimate what the carriage had cost the government. Upon reflection, Choiseul said that he supposed the price of the carriage would be about five or six thousand francs (livres). However, he added, since purchases of the king's household were usually made on credit, this would perhaps make the price as much as eight thousand francs. "You are wide of the mark," said the king, "this carriage cost thirty thousand francs." Choiseul was so shocked that he suggested to Louis XV that such abuses in the purchasing departments of the royal household be corrected and offered to give his attention to the matter. The king replied:

My dear friend, thefts in my establishment are enormous, but it is impossible to stop them. Too many people, and especially the powerful, are implicated in them to flatter oneself by thinking the matter could be remedied. Every minister who has served me has entertained the idea of putting my household in order, but, appalled by the difficulties in carrying it out, they abandoned it. Cardinal Fleury was very powerful; he was the master of France. He died without effecting any of the plans he had formed on the subject. So believe me, don't allow it to worry you; leave an incurable vice alone.[1]

What prompted Besenval to record the above anecdote was the appearance of the royal edict of January 1780 initiating the reforms of the king's household described in Chapter IX above. Besenval was astounded that a person like Necker would attempt to do what cardinal Fleury and Choiseul had renounced:

It is extraordinary that what the most accredited ministers did not dare to undertake has just been effected in the edict of the month of January, 1780, by

1. Pierre-Victor de Besenval, *Mémoires*, ed. Alexandre de Segur, 2 vols. (Paris, 1821), I, 425-426.

a simple citizen of Geneva, Mr. Necker, an isolated individual, without support, precariously occupying a place from which his religion, his foreign birth, and the prejudices of the nation might seem to have excluded him, and who has in his favor only a marked unselfishness. His firmness of character, his views on economy, have so conciliated public opinion that the beginnings of his administration have seen a marked strengthening of credit. However, this credit is based only on the confidence he has been able to establish; it has enabled him by a policy of retrenchment of expenditures to raise the stock quotations of government notes, to sustain the immense expenditures of the war without additional taxes, a war as costly as it has been badly managed. These results should certainly do honor to him, and earn him a favorable opinion. But they will not make him an idol of the French, whose lively intelligence [*génie*] avidly seizes every impression, but which is inconstant because it lacks reflection and principle.[2]

Reading this, one might suppose that this distinguished general and courtier would have supported Necker's reforms, and would have sought to counter those traits of national character he so lucidly described. But not at all; he turns out to be a partisan of the unreformed *ancien régime*. While admitting that he was not personally acquainted with Necker, and that he knew nothing of financial administration, Besenval judged Necker to be nothing more than a good house steward (*intendant de maison*), whose administrative reforms "smelled more of the banker than of the statesman." He supposed that the king would not always be economy-minded but would "sometimes behave like a monarch"–the behavior of Louis XV evidently being the kingly norm. Besenval admitted that "depredations of the great lords who are the cause of the expenditures in the king's household, are enormous, revolting," yet he thought Necker's edict would only irritate them without bringing any remedy. "If one does not crush at the first blow but only produces pained outcries, the hope of being able to evade the reforms fastens upon the imagination."[3]

It was sadly true that the more successfully Necker reformed the flagrant abuses of the central administration of finances, the more enemies he made among the powerful at court. As his provincial assemblies alienated the intendants and the *parlements* who saw in them rivals to their own authority, Necker's reforms of the financial institutions of the royal government aroused against him two other powerful classes, the financiers and the *grands*. Financiers were offended by the assault on useless venal offices and the terms of new contracts more favorable to the royal government than to themselves. The *grands* were thwarted in their pursuit of pensions, sinecures, and various other benefactions from the royal treasury. They included members of the royal family, princes of the blood, peers of the realm, and other aristocratic families whose prestige was such that it was no light matter to stand between their interests and the royal treasury.

2. *Ibid.*, pp. 426-427.
3. *Ibid.*, p. 428.

Necker had hoped to influence those closest to the king as he had the king himself. The young queen seems to have been persuaded of the importance of economy, and she remained a strong supporter of the Genevan throughout his first ministry.[4] Necker was highly esteemed by her relatives in Vienna, Marie Theresa and Emperor Joseph. The role Marie Antoinette had played in bringing down Turgot was severely criticized by them, and this may have induced a change of conduct on her part. But Necker was much less successful with the king's two brothers, and this failure ultimately doomed his reform ministry. The older brother, "Monsieur," comte de Provence, had a pronounced antipathy for the Genevan from the start and harbored in his household some of Necker's most implacable enemies, including Cromot du Bourg, erstwhile candidate for the position of controller general. With the younger brother, the comte d'Artois, Necker seemed to enjoy good relations at first. But sometime in 1780 this situation altered drastically, and the household of Artois also became a nest of Necker's foes, with the young prince openly heading the anti-Necker faction. The explanation was simple: The finances of this prince were becoming clouded. He had constantly asked the king for more money, but as long as the king was influenced by Necker's arguments on the necessity of economy, the comte d'Artois's solicitations were resisted. "An 'N' should be removed from the king's title [king of France and Navarre]," the young prince was quoted as saying. When he heard the pun the king retorted: "He is right. I am avaricious of the property of my subjects."[5]

In the spring of 1790, the National Constituent Assembly published the famous *Red Book,* a record maintained by the council of finance on the secret expenditures of the royal government since the beginning of the reign of Louis XVI. In the excited state of public opinion of that time, the divulgences of the *Red Book* took on the dimensions of an enormous scandal. Necker was still finance minister (his third ministry), and he sought to explain to the public why certain expenditures were made secretly. But it was difficult and embarrassing to explain the enormous sums granted in this way to the two brothers of the king. In a pamphlet published on the subject, Necker wrote:

The part of the expenditure of the Red Book which has fixed public attention is rightly the extraordinary assistance given to the princes, the brothers of the king; these were considerable sums in the king's view also. But since during my first ministry I constantly resisted these requests, since my actions in this respect, generally known, deprived me of favor which would have been precious to me, it

4. The Austrian ambassador, Mercy-Argenteau, wrote to Marie Theresa on April 17, 1780, that "of all the king's ministers the director Necker is the one for whom the queen has the highest regard and consideration." Mercy-Argenteau, *Correspondance secrète entre Marie-Thérèse et le comte de Mercy-Argenteau,* III, 422. The editors point out (p. 7) that the story given by Metra of Necker offering the queen a subsidy from his own purse is completely without foundation.

5. Metra, *Correspondance secrète,* VIII, 136.

should be permitted to me more than another to make the following observations: That the princes were placed at the age of sixteen at the head of a very extensive administration; that the households of the princes under the late king were managed in an extravagant and expensive manner, and a great number of venal offices were attached to them; that the princes had to choose intendants for their affairs at a period of life when one is not yet acquainted with men; finally, that the princes, raised from childhood in an atmosphere of luxury of a great monarchy, easily spent each year more than their revenue . . . that these debts, I say, could gradually become very enormous, and once contracted, the king had to be very sensitive to the fear of exposing his brothers to dishonor and their creditors to drastic ruin.[6]

Relations between Necker and the princes were not only strained because of his resistance to their importunate demands for extraordinary secret funds, but also because he did not intend to exempt their appanage lands and households from his reforms. These consisted primarily of suppression of useless offices. Turgot had abolished the receivers of the *taille* in the *élections* in 1775, substituting for them a single receiver for all direct taxes in each *élection*. But he did not extend that reform to the appanage lands of the princes. It was Necker who did so in a royal declaration of August 14, 1777.[7] In February 1780 he eliminated useless treasurer offices in the households of both Provence and Artois, consolidating them into a single treasurer for each household.[8] It appears from comments made by Bachaumont and the bookseller Hardy that early in April Necker undertook a much more thorough reorganization of the two households, but no confirmation of this appears in collections of royal acts or in the records of the Chamber of Accounts.[9] However, his reform of the receivers general affected the princes of the blood because it deprived them of their right to sell those offices that collected the direct taxes on their appanage lands. There is ample evidence to indicate that the young princes were incensed by these measures.[10] It was at this time, in April 1780, that the first libel pamphlet against Necker was distributed in Paris.

As Necker intimated in his comments above on the *Red Book,* it was not so much that the king's two brothers were greedy, but that they were young and inexperienced, and liable to fall under the influence of unsavory characters. Some of Necker's most deadly enemies came from the same social class as

6. Jacques Necker, *Observations de M. Necker sur l'avant-propos du livre rouge* (Paris, 1790), p. 8.

7. Isambert et al., eds., *Recueil général des anciennes lois,* XXV, 93.

8. AN P 2518. "Mémorial du chambre des comptes," fol. 188-193.

9. Bachaumont, *Mémoires secrets,* XV, 130; Sebastien Hardy, "Journal du Libraire Hardy," BN MSS Fonds français, 6683, fol. 271.

10. Mercy-Argenteau wrote the Empress in the letter cited above (n. 4) that "the comte d'Artois had a very animated discussion of this matter with the director general of finances, who replied to him respectfully but with much firmness." He added that the king was strongly supporting Necker, as was the queen, who was beginning to show less indulgence for the antics of her brother-in-law.

himself, that is, from a bourgeois background. But they had advanced to wealth and power by currying the favor of the *grands*. Such a person was Maximilien Radix de Sainte-Foy, who became superintendent of the household of the comte d'Artois in September 1776.

The career of Sainte-Foy was a fascinating contrast to that of Necker. A protégé of Choiseul-Praslin, cousin of the eminent minister of Louis XV, Sainte-Foy was made first secretary in the foreign affairs ministry during the Seven Years' War. It was while serving in that post that he claimed to have given secret information to Necker about the Canadian notes and said he was cheated by the Genevan out of his agreed-upon share of the profits. When Choiseul-Praslin left foreign affairs to become secretary of state for the navy, Sainte-Foy also went to that department. With the financial assistance of his father, he purchased one of the four offices of treasurer general of the navy for a capital value of 800,000 livres. He held this office in alternate years, 1764, 1766, 1768, and 1770— enough to enable him to amass a gigantic fortune. With the fall of the Choiseuls in 1770, Sainte-Foy sold his office. But because he had been the original discoverer of the charms of Madame du Barry, and it was as his mistress that she first came to the attention of Louis XV, naturally Sainte-Foy did not share in the disgrace of the Choiseuls. He was given a substantial pension through the influence of Madame du Barry and was appointed French minister to the court of Zweibrücken. There he initiated the young German princelet into the fashionable, extravagant dissipations of the gilded youth of the day. In a period not notable for austere morals, Sainte-Foy acquired a reputation as a spectacular rake. He spent lavishly, maintaining such palatial residences as a château on the river-front at Neuilly. Horses, carriages, one of the foremost art collections of the time, beautiful mistresses—everything that Parisian life could offer the wealthy sybarite was in the possession of Maximilien Radix de Sainte-Foy.[11]

It was natural that after his return to Paris from Zweibrücken, Sainte-Foy would gravitate into the social milieu of the comte d'Artois, where, according to the complaint of the court historiographer, J. N. Moreau, "all decent people passed as pedants, all those who amused [the prince] and procured him pleasure were alone fêted."[12] By letters patent of September 24, 1776, the comte d'Artois united the offices of superintendent of the domains and finance to that of superintendent of buildings, manufactures and gardens, and placed the office on Radix de Sainte-Foy. As administrator, the latter exacted the utmost tribute possible from the hapless peasants living on the appanage lands of the prince. Nevertheless, by 1780 Artois was clearly facing bankruptcy. The king permitted his brother to issue life rentes amounting to 875,882 livres and perpetual rentes of 55,651 livres.[13] After Necker's resignation in May 1781, there was less resistance to the importunate demands of the household of Artois. During 1782

11. Charles Leroux-Cesbron, *Gens et choses d'autrefois* (Paris, 1914), pp. 103-123.

12. Jacob-Nicolas Moreau, *Mes Souvenirs,* 2 vols. (Paris, 1898-1901), II, 205.

13. BN MSS Joly de Fleury, 1436, fol. 36-37.

the prince's affairs became increasingly tangled. Although he received three million livres per year from the royal treasury to maintain his establishment and an additional 568,000 livres from his appanage lands, still he was running a yearly deficit of 549,000 livres. He was permitted to issue another life rente loan. His total capital debt was 25,844,274 livres.[14]

Where did the money go? The household existed only to maintain the prince in a "state of splendor" befitting the youngest brother of the king; it provided no other useful function for the state or the taxpayers. Like the queen, Artois was inordinately fond of gambling, and some money paid gambling debts. Suspicion began to surface, too, that much of the household's income was being used to maintain not only the splendor of the prince, but that of his chief administrator, Radix de Sainte-Foy. The Parlement of Paris as early as 1778 acquired information about malversation of funds in the household of Artois and in December of that year arrested Antoine Le Bel, first secretary of the household.[15] Le Bel complained that he was a scapegoat for those higher up, and implicated Sainte-Foy.

It was not easy for the Parlement to lay hands on a person so firmly protected by the comte d'Artois. In May 1781, fire destroyed the house of one Nogaret, treasurer of the Artois household, and financial records were lost in the fire.[16] A month later Metra reported that Radix de Sainte-Foy was suspected of embezzling 5 million livres from the household's treasury. In the summer of 1782, the Parlement finally presented an indictment against him listing eight separate cases of wrongdoing. "Most of these accusations," writes a modern historian, "were based on precise facts and indisputable documents."[17] In July 1783, Sainte-Foy fled to England just as the Parlement ordered his arrest. But the comte d'Artois was not one to abandon a good friend. He insisted that the king present to the Parlement letters of extinction erasing all charges against Sainte-Foy; the king did so, over the Parlement's protest. In 1784 Sainte-Foy returned to Paris and resumed his style of life. In later years he became a boon companion of such famous rakes as the comte de Mirabeau and Talleyrand, both of whom shared his contempt for the "virtuous Genevan."[18]

Sainte-Foy's hostility is understandable because Necker was the chief obstacle to acquiring more royal funds for the prince's household. But the animosity had more personal reasons. When Necker reorganized the pension system, he examined in great detail existing pensions. He found that sometime before the death of Louis XV, through the influence of Madame du Barry, Sainte-Foy had

---

14. *Ibid.*; Maximilien Radix de Sainte-Foy, *Mémoire à Monseigneur le comte d'Artois sur l'administration de ses finances* (Paris, 1781). (BN L^f 15.8.)

15. André Doyon, "Maximilien Radix de Sainte-Foy (1736-1810)," *Revue d'histoire diplomatique*, 80, no. 3 (1966), 260.

16. Metra, *Correspondance secrète*, XI, 252.

17. Doyon, "Maximilien Radix de Sainte-Foy," p. 264.

18. Leroux-Cesbron, *Gens et choses d'autrefois*, pp. 120-123.

received the entire capital value of his pension in a single payment; but, through some oversight, he continued to be paid 8,000 livres per year as formerly. Necker noticed the discrepancy and discontinued the pension. Whereupon Sainte-Foy complained to Maurepas, and the latter sent him on to the director general of finances. It was a stormy meeting. Necker not only refused to restore the pension but demanded that Sainte-Foy return the money given to him by mistake. Severely shaken by the interview, Sainte-Foy is said to have returned to his mansion at Neuilly and gone to bed with a high fever.[19]

The libel campaign against Necker that began late in April 1780 was well concerted, and had support from highly-placed sources. Bachaumont noted on April 29 that "there has been published and distributed within the last few days a 'Letter of Mr. Turgot to Mr. Necker' which has caused a devilish noise."[20] A few days later the same writer reported: "It appears certain that the pamphlet against Mr. Necker was written under the auspices of the comte d'Artois, who had it printed at the Temple, and on the day it came out, His Royal Highness himself distributed it." It was in the same entry that Bachaumont mentioned the supposed affair on the Canadian notes, and the charges by Sainte-Foy that Necker had cheated him out of his share of the profits in 1762. It seemed evident that the household of Artois was the source of the pamphlet. A few days after that a second brochure appeared, this time in the form of a "comparative table" in which a summary of the acts of John Law appeared on one side and those of Jacques Necker on the other.[21] The message was clear: the Genevan was pursuing exactly the same operations as his Scottish predecessor, and it was obvious that France was on the same road to financial catastrophe!

This was only the beginning. More followed in the summer and fall months of 1780. Bachaumont, generally hostile to Necker, observed the pamphlet campaign with intense interest and summarized the contents of all brochures for his readers. With respect to the first one, he wrote: "All the operations of this minister [Necker] are successively described, and one cannot deny that if there is a great deal of bitterness, there is also much cogent and reasonable discussion." But he also added that "one must be wary of the author, who there is reason to believe is a financier, or a great partisan of that class."[22]

It was apparent even to Bachaumont, whose standards of criticism were not exacting, that the author of the pamphlets could not be Turgot. All the libels were either published anonymously or given an author recognized as fictitious. The authorship of some is still uncertain, as in the case of the *Liégeoise,* published on September 12, which there is reason to believe was written by Gabriel Sénac de Meihan.[23] A century later the memoirs of J. M. Augeard were

19. The incident is recorded by both Metra and Bachaumont, and seems to have been notorious. Metra, *Correspondance secrète,* XI, 177-178; Bachaumont, *Mémoires secrets,* XVII, 117-118.

20. Bachaumont, *Mémoires secrets,* XV, 153-154.

21. *Ibid.,* pp. 164-165.

22. *Ibid.*

23. See Chapter I.

published, identifying some writers. Augeard himself claimed authorship of the first two pamphlets mentioned above and also those published later entitled: *On the Administration of Mr. Necker by a French Citizen.* Augeard was a farmer general, and also held the office of "Secretary of the *Commandements* in the queen's household." He was, according to his own report, on close terms with Maurepas, who he says often sought his advice on financial matters.[24]

Whoever the authors were, even though there was some variation in literary style, the contents of the libels were alike. The most serious allegation against Necker was that his true motives were divulged neither in the preambles of his legislative acts, nor in his memorials written for the king, nor in his two books published before 1776, but were in fact quite inconsistent with the ideas and sentiments expressed in them. The real purpose of the reforms carried out from December 1776 through early 1780, the pamphlets charged, was to crush the traditional class of financiers and replace them by an international clique of bankers whose interests were sordidly mercenary and had nothing to do with "order, good faith, and the wretched condition of the poorer classes of His Majesty's subjects." Far from serving the king unselfishly without any financial remuneration, Necker was adding to his fortune because he was still a secret partner in the bank of Girardot, Haller and Company and was using his position as finance minister to further the interests of his bank. Necker's avowed motives for reducing the power of the financiers were turned against him by the self-proclaimed spokesmen of that class. The director general had wished to free the government from excessive dependence on the financiers for short-term loans (anticipations), for this gave them the opportunity to exact higher commissions, and to exact them more often during the year than necessary. This, said the author of *Letter of Mr. Turgot to Mr. Necker,* was exactly what the latter and his bankers were doing. It was claimed that 130 million livres worth of short-term loans had been made to the government by Necker's bank. It was for this reason that the royal government could not dismiss the Genevan without bringing down the credit structure of the government. The commissions exacted by Necker's bank were swollen by the same kind of circulation the *Liégeoise* alleged in the case of his financing the Company of the Indies' purchase of Spanish piasters. The writer of the *Letter of Mr. Turgot* claimed that the above-named short-term loans were negotiated four times a year by drawing first on the bank in Geneva, then from Geneva through London, and from London through Holland. In this way four commissions were charged the government by those international bankers when only one was necessary.[25]

It was not only that the bankers were controlling the government and making exorbitant profits at it. Readers of the *Letter of Mr. Turgot,* the *French Citizen,* and the *Liégeoise* were told that the entire structure built up by these non-French bankers was exactly like that of another foreign Protestant who had gained control of the country's finances, John Law. The ghost of the "System"

---

24. J.-M. Augeard, *Mémoires secrets* (Paris, 1866), p. 94.
25. *Lettre de M. Turgot à M. Necker,* in *Collection complète de tous les ouvrages,* I, 14.

was most insistently evoked in the pamphlet that followed the *Letter of Mr. Turgot*. It listed all the legislative acts of John Law on one side and, corresponding exactly to them, the acts of Necker arranged in the same numerical order on the opposite side of the table. Numbers five and ten were typical: "No. 5: Decree in council of May 2, 1716, which permitted Law and Co. to establish The Bank." Opposite side: "Decree in council of September 22, 1776 [*sic*], which permitted a company to establish a public bank under the title of Discount Bank." And "No. 10: The rescriptions [of the receivers general] were converted into bank notes [by Law]." Opposite: "It is believed that the rescriptions will be discredited, and that it is desired to replace them with the notes of the Discount Bank."[26]

The paper money issued by John Law found its counterpart, according to the libelists, in the "black notes" issued by the Discount Bank. These notes were said to be reaching alarming proportions. Over 100 million of them had been issued, and they were being given forced circulation by the government. They were, in effect, paper money just as under the System, so it was said. Not only was the Discount Bank issuing a flood of "black notes" without backing, but that institution was the vehicle of foreign bankers to market the long-term war loans of the government. Necker's policy of financing the war through loans was not really to shelter the taxpayers from hardship, according to *Turgot,* the *French Citizen,* and the *Liégeoise,* but to make enormous profits through exorbitant terms on the loans. The bank of Girardot, Haller and Company was always given advanced, privileged information about forthcoming loans, always bought up the subscriptions using the credit of the Discount Bank at 4 percent, and marketed them through the international clientele at more than double that rate. The Girardot, Haller bank was making huge profits without ever using its own money! This was exactly what Necker had found the financiers were doing with the king's money. That the terms of Necker's loans were onerous for the king's government was a standard allegation of all the libels. The *Liégeoise* disclosed for the first time that certain Genevan bankers were placing life rentes on the young lives of "thirty Genevan girls" whose longevity would surely bankrupt the royal government!

Having raised the frightening specter of another Mississippi bubble, the writers of the pamphlets went on to demolish one by one all the proud achievements of Necker's three years at the helm of the royal finances. His emphasis on economy was suitable for a small republic like the city-state of Geneva, but totally unfitted for a great monarchy, just as the vaunted talents of the director general (hard work, close attention to details) were the virtues of subalterns, of first secretaries, but hardly of great ministers. Just to show the director general of finances that he could beat him at his own game if need be,

26. "Tableau comparatif de ce qui s'est passé en 1716, 1717, etc., et ce qui s'est passé en 1776, 1777, 1779, 1780," in *ibid.,* vol. I. The Discount Bank was established by Turgot on March 24, 1776. See Isambert et al., eds., *Recueil des anciennes lois,* XXIII, 442-446. Of course, the rescriptions of the receivers general were not altered in any way by Necker.

Mr. Turgot turned his attention to the ameliorations. He found that Necker's claims of economy by reorganizing the *fermes* and *régies* was "despicable charlatanry" and proceeded to give exact figures showing no gain at all for the king's revenue. All that was accomplished was the ruin of financiers and their families, loyal subjects of the fatherland, who, unlike bankers, were proprietors of landed estates and therefore good patriots. Despite the most solemn promises in the preambles of his edicts that all suppressed offices would be reimbursed in cash, Necker "had not reimbursed a single office." The suppression of offices was a disaster for the royal government because it deprived it of needed credit. Somewhat inconsistently it was also stated in the *Mr. Turgot* that Necker had borrowed 130 million livres worth of anticipations from receivers general "up to March, 1781."[27] Officers who retained their posts were also victims of the ruthless director general, who forced them to add supplements to their surety bonds, or make forced loans, such as the "repurchase" of the tax on offices for a period of eight years by paying a lump sum equal to six years of the tax.

As for Necker's boast of having financed the war without raising taxes, this also was sheer charlatanry. It was not true, in the first place, said the libelists, because Necker did raise taxes secretly and illegally. The author of the *Liégeoise* stated the case for all:

But what is this inconceivable pretension of continuing the war without taxes, and this even stranger pretension that in fact you have not taxed, when by simple fiat you have forced up all the old taxes? It is known with what excess you have carried the *vingtièmes* wherever you have dared; the Parlements have certainly felt it, and have made representations, but you have not feared to substitute everywhere the arbitrary authority of your office for the immutable will of the law; *vingtièmes, capitation, taille,* all have been pushed to the extreme; and the people whom you have forced to make loans despite themselves, do you suppose they have not been taxed? And the unfortunate ones whose offices have been suppressed without reimbursement, they have not been taxed? What an astonishing abuse of words! But we are beginning to see things clearly. You will soon be at the end of your miserable resources and it will be necessary finally to have recourse openly to taxes.[28]

In this passage, Necker was condemned at the same time for raising taxes secretly and for not raising them openly and "legally." If he had raised taxes of 50 million livres per year in the latter way at the beginning of the war, they would have yielded 200 million livres by the end of this fourth year of war. It had cost the king 200 million livres all because of Necker's fear of losing his place!

As for his claim of ameliorating the finances, not only was this insulting to the king and the *grands,* it had seriously harmed the war effort, maintained the

27. *Collection complète de tous les ouvrages,* I, 30-31.
28. *Lettre à M. Necker, Directeur-Général des Finances,* in *ibid.,* vol. I, essay no. 6, pp. 44-45.

Liégeoise. That writer claimed that Necker had refused to grant loans to the Americans, that he was secretly working for the defeat of France and had treasonable relations with Lord Stormont, his good friend, the former British ambassador to France.

Not even Necker's humanitarian reforms, not even Madame Necker and her hospital were spared by the libelists. The edict on the sale of real property of hospitals was nothing but a device to raise money by loans for the government. As for the new model hospital of St. Sulpice, the *Liégeoise* had heard on good authority that patients were never given any food, only medicine. No wonder it was so economical!

Because many of Necker's contemporaries believed, like Bachaumont, that if there was much exaggeration in the libel literature there was also much truth, and since many historians have appeared to agree with this view, it is necessary to take these brochures seriously. Indeed, the image of Necker that appears in most secondary histories today, even college textbooks, is derived in considerable measure from the libels.[29] Reputable authors have cited lengthy tracts from the brochures as worthwhile evidence. Of course, the fact that the pamphlets were intentional libels need not rule them out as evidence. Nor would the obvious "big lies" in the style of Nazi propaganda necessarily render them valueless. Few pieces of historical evidence come down to us pure and unalloyed. But the libels alone would not be sufficient to substantiate any charges they brought against Necker, especially if other independent evidence contradicts them.

It is certain that the comparison of Necker's administration to the System of John Law was not simply an exaggeration but totally false, and the attempt to arouse the latent fears of a new financial catastrophe was the sheerest demagoguery. The "black notes" of the Discount Bank were freely convertible into hard money, and perfectly safe. They were accepted by the public on a voluntary basis, and were not given forced circulation. The founder of the Discount Bank, Isaac Panchaud, became a financial advisor of Joly de Fleury in the summer of 1781 and immediately sought to expand the scope of its operations. His criticism of Necker's administration of the bank was exactly the opposite of that of the libelists. Panchaud believed that the control of the Discount Bank by Parisian bankers was too conservative. The notes of the bank circulated only in Paris and not in the provinces. In a memorial written in August 1781, Panchaud sought to persuade the finance minister to order all the treasuries, including the receivers of the direct taxes in the provinces, to accept Discount Bank notes in order to expand their circulation. The Parisian bankers tended to restrict the Discount Bank to their own use, so that it did not discount commercial paper as

29. See, for example, the discussion of Necker in Leo Gershoy, *The French Revolution and Napoleon* (New York, 1964), pp. 92-94. This book was first published in 1933 and has probably been the most commonly used textbook on the subject in American colleges for a generation.

originally intended. The number of depositors and the amount on deposit could be greatly increased. In this respect also, the bank served only the bankers, whereas it should also allow merchants to maintain their accounts.

Panchaud was constantly opposed in his schemes for monetary reform by the arch-conservative director of the royal treasury, Jacques Marquet de Bourgade, who also wrote memorials to the finance minister taking issue with the ideas of Panchaud, which he generally believed too adventurous and unsuitable for France. On the Discount Bank, Bourgade defended the status quo. He recognized the value of the bank but feared any extension of its operations because of the general distrust of bank note circulation in the French public. He defended the bankers' control of the Discount Bank and argued that its primary function was to serve the banks. He alluded to the dangers of the Discount Bank being unable to convert its notes readily into specie, and said that in the past it had been forced to call upon the royal treasury for assistance.

In his reply to Bourgade, Panchaud said that this had only happened twice: First, at the time of Necker's resignation (May 19, 1781), there was an "unfounded fear" that the notes would not be honored and there was a "run" on the Discount Bank. But this crisis was not serious, and the treasury received interest for its assistance, so it was not a detriment. Later, in August, there had been an imprudent amount discounted, which left the bank momentarily short of funds to redeem notes. But these were insignificant events that in no way called into question the basic soundness of the institution. Panchaud rebutted the defense Bourgade had offered of banker domination of the administration of the Discount Bank:

The bankers were called to the Administration on April 8, 1778. At that time the Discount Bank had only about one million livres of notes in circulation. It was expected that this would produce a great effect. However, six months later the bank notes were only 1,760,000 livres, and in the month of April 1779 there were only about 2,800,000 livres worth of notes in circulation. It was only during the month following when Mr. Necker began to feed into the Discount Bank the two million livres of money which he had left in the royal treasury for a long time without interest, that the bank notes began to rise to four and five million livres. It was only in March and April 1780, two years after the admittance of the bankers to the administration, Mr. Necker having given orders to the royal treasury and the General Farms to keep notes at all times in their treasuries, that the sum [of bank notes] was increased to 8, 10 and 12 million livres. It was not finally until April and May 1781, three years after the accession of the bankers, and due to the stimulation of the loans opened by the royal treasury that the notes of the bank finally reached up to twenty and twenty-three million livres. From that figure it has successively lowered to sixteen or seventeen million livres where they are today.[30]

Panchaud used the above information to demonstrate that the Discount Bank, if left to bankers alone, would not expand its operations. It was rather

30. BN MSS Joly de Fleury, 1434, fol. 17b-18.

government initiative that could give the bank the scope he thought it should have. He proposed that the finance minister expand a policy that Necker had initiated on a limited scale, by ordering the different treasuries throughout the kingdom, and particularly the receivers of tax revenue at the *élection* level, to receive notes of the Discount Bank in payment for taxes. Panchaud vigorously denied Bourgade's charge that he advocated forced circulation of these notes. He repudiated any thought of paper money being forced on the public. But as long as these notes were freely convertible to hard money they were perfectly safe. "Eighteen million livres of notes are not going to make a great impression amid 1,800 million livres in specie that circulated in the country. Even if the amount of notes were doubled or even tripled, there would still be no danger."[31]

It will be seen that, according to Panchaud, notes in circulation in the spring of 1780 totaled about 12 million livres, in contrast to the 100 million asserted by the libels. The capital subscription of the stockholders of the Discount Bank was initially 12 million livres, and the bank's assets also included the same amount of bills of exchange. There could be no question about its soundness.[32]

As for the allegation that the bank of Girardot, Haller and Company had issued about 130 million livres worth of short-term loans, there is no evidence whatever. The financiers who did grant short-term credit (anticipations) to the government are well known, and the sums they granted are recorded.[33] That the Girardot, Haller bank marketed long-term loans appears probable. There was widespread complaint about Necker's relying upon the banks for marketing the loans. Ordinary citizens who wanted to invest in his loans were often disappointed to find the loan so quickly closed, taken up within a few days by bankers.[34]

One of the persistent complaints in the pamphlets was that Necker had not reimbursed "a single office" of those that he had suppressed. An account in the documents on the *Compte rendu* preserved at the Château de Coppet refutes this. In 1781, the total capital value of all offices liquidated or in the process of liquidation was 64,730,164 livres. Of this amount, 19,216,720 livres had been reimbursed, leaving a sum of 45,513,453 livres to be paid in the future. But interest at the rate of 5 percent, or 2,275,672 million, was being paid annually on this debt.[35]

31. *Ibid.*, fol. 19b.
32. Necker, *Oeuvres complètes*, V, 527.
33. Bosher, *French Finances*, pp. 96-97.
34. Hardy, BN MSS Fonds français, 6683, fol. 227.
35. "Pièces justificatives du compte rendu," Château de Coppet, G 11-21: "Offices supprimés dont les intérêts sont payés au Trésor royal." Necker considered the reimbursement of the capital of an office an extraordinary, not an ordinary, expenditure. This figure of 19.2 million livres must represent only the offices paid up in 1780. According to P. J. B. Nougaret, the royal treasury reimbursed 20 million to the intendants of finance and other officers on November 1, 1777; *Anecdotes du règne de Louis XVI*, 3 vols. (Paris, 1776-1780), III, 214.

The publicists of the time gave rapt attention to the pamphlet attack. Metra, Bachaumont, Linguet, and others dwelt at length on the libels and reported the reaction of the director general to them. There seems little doubt that Necker was grievously wounded by the onslaught. According to a well-known phrase of Madame de Staël, he thought public opinion was "almost divine." His enemies knew that nothing could hurt him more than to sully his reputation and denigrate his achievements as minister of finance. Of course, he had considered the matter and discussed it in the *Eloge de Colbert*. The able minister will often be subjected to abuse by publicists, but he must pay no attention to the libels and look upon them as "fire which will purify his heart as it does gold, which causes grosser metals to separate from it." Now, in the summer of 1780, he found it difficult to ignore the libels for two reasons.

First, under the *ancien régime,* those in power could protect themselves from libelists by *lettres de cachet.* Early in his ministry Necker had used this weapon, and he even had a libelist placed in the Bastille, according to one report by Metra.[36] This was in late September 1777, when Necker was at the height of his influence at court, both with the king and with Maurepas. A year later it appeared that his position had altered.

One of Necker's important reforms, which earned him the deep enmity of some *grands,* was his attempt to end the despoiling of the king's domain lands by those called *engagists,* who had leased the lands by contracts that were highly favorable to their own interests and detrimental to the king's. To build up the wealth and income of the domain lands was no less an opportunity than improving the economic position of the hospitals. One approach was to scrutinize carefully the contracts with the *engagists,* and to require the land to be returned to the domain if the titles were questionable. This policy brought Necker into direct confrontation with his erstwhile colleague in the affairs of the Company of the Indies, Louis de Brancas, comte de Lauraguais. The father of the count was required to restore an engaged land to the domain. Lauraguais was a gifted scholar and brilliant polemicist, a redoubtable person to antagonize. In October 1778 he published a satirical letter heaping ridicule upon "this Genevan who wants to govern France gratuitously."[37] It was the kind of satire, wrote Bachaumont, that "too often in France is the prelude to disgrace [of a minister]." The king was furious at Lauraguais and wanted to put him in the Bastille. Maurepas, on the contrary, was delighted by the brochure and intervened to protect Lauraguais. He did keep him from the Bastille, but was unable to prevent his exile from Paris for the winter. It was apparent that Maurepas, always sympathetic to the *grands* when their interests were involved, was willing to defend those who attacked Necker, but only when it could be done secretly.

When the second libel was published in May 1780, comparing Necker's administration to that of John Law, the director general sought permission from

36. Metra, *Correspondance secrète,* V, 189.
37. Bachaumont, *Mémoires secrets,* XII, 128-130.

the king to discuss and refute the pamphlet in a council meeting. But the king did not wish to take time for it and insisted on proceeding to more important matters. "You have many enemies here," the king is reported to have told Necker on several occasions, "but you need not worry. I will defend you." This was not very satisfactory assurance from Necker's standpoint, because one reason the libels received such great publicity was the failure of the government to act against them. In the *ancien régime* this did not mean toleration of dissident views, but that someone in power was permitting the libels to be published and distributed. At what time Necker became aware that Maurepas was secretly protecting the libelists is uncertain. Early in 1781 Madame Necker approached Maurepas, without the knowledge of her husband, and asked him to use the power of the government to prevent further dissemination of the pamphlets. By that time Necker knew of the mentor's role in the libel campaign and informed his wife, but not before she had taken the false step that must have greatly titillated the elderly courtier's famous sense of humor.

The second reason Necker could not remain aloof from the pamphlet campaign was that many intelligent observers were puzzled by his fiscal policies. Remembering the serious financial difficulties of the Seven Years' War, they found it hard to believe that the war could be financed without a substantial rise in tax revenue. It was well known that extraordinary expenditures for the war in 1780 had surpassed 150 million livres, a matter Necker himself had revealed in the preambles of his loans and referred to in his *Compte rendu* in January 1781.[38] Could his ameliorations be so substantial as to pay for the costs of his war loans? Among the skeptics was the abbé de Véri, who, of course, was confident that he knew more about the royal finances than the Genevan with his petty preoccupation with details. In the fall of 1780, Véri told Necker that "no new tax levy would be sufficient" and yet he had not raised taxes at all. Necker replied, according to Véri, that "all the loans I have made are assured funding, and I am prepared to prove it in a council meeting." Véri's opinion was unchanged by the conversation. "Charlatanism does have its successes," he wrote in his diary at the end of October, after seeing the lottery loan of 36 million livres quickly subscribed to by investors. The abbé was greatly puzzled by the ease with which Necker's loans were marketed.[39]

It may have been this conversation and the disbelief that he must have seen on the abbé's face that led Necker to consider the advisability of publishing the *Compte rendu.* The new procedures of accounting laid down in the declaration of October 17, 1779, had now been in operation long enough to make possible a complete accounting of the ordinary revenue and expenditures. He had planned to present a statement to the king shortly after the beginning of the year. Since

38. Notably in the preamble of the life rente loan of March 1781. See AN AD 97, no. 5. It is pointed out that extraordinary expenditures for 1780 amounted to 150 million livres and that the same amount would also be needed in 1781. *Compte rendu au Roi,* in Necker, *Oeuvres completès,* II, 20.

39. *Journal de l'abbé de Véri,* II, 392-393.

he had embarked upon an audacious policy of taking the public into his confidence, why not publish this account? What better way to reassure his friends and sympathizers, to persuade the skeptical, and to silence his enemies? Yet the project was fraught with dangers that must have given him pause. It would be a break with the tradition that such accounts were for the king's eyes alone. It might give his enemies an additional weapon to use against him, for nothing could be easier than to muddy the waters in such an intricate and complex subject. It would be necessary to be well prepared for such attacks by having in his possession accounts from each department approved and signed by officials independent of his control. This would be necessary anyway when presenting the account to the king, and possibly to the council of state.

But how would his colleagues view such a move? Would they not see it as a demagogic maneuver to win public opinion to his side in his quarrels with other ministers in the royal council? This also must have given Necker pause. The long-strained relations between himself and Sartine reached a climax in October 1780. The result was a triumph of the Genevan banker over the secretary of state for the navy. But it was won at the cost of further deepening the rift between himself and Maurepas. By the end of the year foreign policy concerns came to engross Necker, and his single foray into diplomacy must have seriously damaged his relations with the secretary of state for foreign affairs, the comte de Vergennes, who had been one of his strong supporters. It is necessary to turn to that matter before resuming the story of the *Compte rendu.*

Chapter XIII

NECKER'S PEACE INITIATIVE

The personal differences between Necker and Sartine were well known to the public because they were often commented upon by journalists. Metra and Bachaumont reported stormy scenes at council meetings between the director general of finances and the secretary of state for the navy. Sartine continually demanded greater appropriations, and insisted that funds be delivered promptly to his department by the finance minister. Necker insisted on having some information about how the money was spent. Waste and inefficiency in the department was notorious. Even Vice-Admiral d'Estaing chafed at it, and was instrumental in the ousting of Sartine. The duc de Chartres was disaffected from Sartine for other reasons, but this gave Necker an important ally in his quarrel with the naval secretary over financial management of the department.[1]

Sartine had strenuously opposed Necker's reorganization of the treasuries in the naval department, which had eliminated all but one. The single treasurer general who remained, Baudard de Sainte-James, was a loyal ally of Sartine and one of the wealthiest financiers of France. According to Necker's edict of October 18, 1778, treasurers were no longer permitted to issue notes on their own credit without authorization of the director general of finances. This rule was systematically ignored by the naval department, to Necker's increasing annoyance. Early in October 1780, he learned that Baudard de Sainte-James had issued four million livres of such notes without authorization. He complained to Maurepas, who promised to look into the matter. Immediately after this conversation, Necker discovered that the treasurer general had issued 17 million livres more of those notes and, under instructions from Sartine, tried to conceal it from Necker. "It was a bombshell as much unexpected as incredible," Necker wrote to Maurepas.[2] The additional 21 million livres worth of naval notes had a significant impact on the overall credit situation of the government. In fact, it later upset Necker's plans of holding the interest rate for anticipations at 5.5 percent. Due to the unauthorized issue of naval notes, the cost of anticipations in 1781 was to be 6 percent.

1. Ségur, *Au Couchant de la monarchie,* II, 281.
2. AN K 161, no. 12.

Necker let it be known to Maurepas and the king that he could no longer serve as finance minister under those conditions. "Which one shall we dismiss, Sartine or Necker?" the king asked Maurepas. Maurepas was stricken with an attack of gout and was unable to travel to Versailles when the crucial decision was made. Necker was able to present his case against Sartine; powerfully assisted, according to Véri, by the queen, he won the king to his side of the dispute.[3] Sartine was dismissed and replaced by the marquis de Castries, a friend of Necker's. Maurepas was not greatly attached to Sartine, and was kept informed by Necker of the proceedings of the council meeting. Yet the circumstances of the dismissal indicated to Maurepas that his paramount influence over the king was being threatened. In December 1780 the secretary of state for war, the prince de Montbarey, resigned voluntarily. He had been a close ally of Sartine and hostile to Necker. His successor, the marquis de Ségur, was a friend of Necker's. This was a more direct blow to Maurepas, whose wife had been a staunch protector of Montbarey. Furthermore, the mentor had opposed the nomination of Ségur. Thus the appointment of Necker's supporters to the two military departments was heavily offset by the rapid deterioration of his relations with Maurepas.[4]

When called upon by the king to explain his acts, Sartine replied that the 21 million livres of notes were to be used for secret naval operations that could not be divulged to Necker. The director general was, after all, a foreigner whose anglophilism was well known. It was in the interest of military security that the issue of naval notes was concealed from him. Sartine repeated one of the pamphlet libels, that Necker had treasonable relations with English friends, particularly the former British ambassador to France, Lord Stormont. It is known that Necker did send a communication to Stormont in July 1780, for it was mentioned in the minutes of a Cabinet meeting at London.[5] The contents of this communication remain unknown but probably expressed the desire of the French government to open negotiations with the British government. About the same time, Maurepas wrote a letter to a friend in the British government and expressed in no uncertain terms his own desire to enter into peace negotiations.[6] The Spanish government had already initiated peace talks with the British. Both the king and Vergennes were ardently longing for an end to the conflict. "We are at the point," Vergennes wrote to Montmorin at Madrid, "where we must hazard everything to win gloriously, or at least succumb with honor. This war has dragged out too long; it is truly a war between treasuries [*une guerre d'écus*], and there is reason to fear that if it continues we will not be the last to become exhausted."[7]

3. *Journal de l'abbé de Véri*, II, 395-396.
4. *Ibid.*, p. 415.
5. George III, *The Correspondence of King George the Third*, ed. John Fortescue, 6 vols. (London, 1927-1928), V, 106. The communication from Necker to Stormont is mentioned in minutes of the cabinet meeting on August 3, 1780.
6. *Ibid.*, p. 104, letter of the king to Lord North, July 30, 1780.
7. Doniol, *Histoire de la participation*, IV, 516.

Peace talk was in the air in the summer and autumn of 1780, and there was nothing unusual about Necker's peace feeler, if such it was. That year had been gloomy both on the battle fronts and in relations between the allies. Spanish interests could not easily be harmonized with those of France and even less with the American ally. The Spanish navy was dealt a devastating blow in January by the British fleet. The Americans suffered serious military defeats in South Carolina and Georgia, losing the key port city of Charleston. The British still held New York, and it seemed unlikely that they could be expelled from American soil by military means. The French government was formally committed by the treaty of 1778 to continue the war until the independence of the American colonies was assured. Yet, Vergennes did not think that commitment was inconsistent with seeking an armistice and beginning peace negotiations.[8] But he did not believe the French government should take the initiative, and no doubt would have protested if he knew of the Necker and Maurepas letters, Vergennes feared that a French initiative would be a sign of weakness. To avoid such an impression, he wanted to persuade the Russian and Austrian governments to mediate between the belligerents and to initiate negotiations. Vergennes disagreed with Spanish policy, which was to propose a peace settlement in which each side kept permanently the territory in its possession at the moment of the cease fire (the principle of *uti possidetis*). The French foreign minister thought this was clearly contrary to France's treaty obligations to the Americans.[9]

Necker's attitude toward the war throughout his first ministry has already been mentioned. He thought the sooner it could be ended without discrediting the king or the nation the better. He was anxious to get on with his reform program, for which the war was an unwelcome interloper. About the American cause, he was rather reticent. He was not well acquainted with Americans. Benjamin Franklin was a dinner guest at the Necker house on occasion, but no friendship or intellectual intimacy developed. Franklin as well as Jefferson in later years were friends of physiocrats and therefore probably no great admirers of the Genevan banker.

Furthermore, the monetary policies of the Continental Congress could not have helped win Necker's sympathy to the American cause, so contrary were they to his own fiscal ideas of "prudence, order, and good faith." In 1780 the American Congress practically repudiated the paper money it had issued since the beginning of the war by fixing its value at one-fortieth the gold dollar. Vergennes wrote in a letter to La Luzerne, French envoy at Philadelphia, that "this operation dealt a severe blow to those French merchants who had the courage to trade with the Americans at the beginning of their rebellion."[10] This indeed wiped out much of the American debt, but Congress was unable to

8. *Ibid.,* p. 529.
9. *Ibid.,* p. 510.
10. *Ibid.,* p. 415.

borrow money thereafter outside the country at less than 33 percent interest.[11] Necker did not relish the monetary policies of the Spanish government any more than those of the American. One issue of notes by Madrid seemed so dubious to him that he refused to allow the Discount Bank to accept them.[12] The Spaniards were highly indignant, but Necker's position was understandable. He had not struggled to rebuild the credit of France in order to have it frittered away by allies.

In view of these considerations there was nothing surprising or scandalous about Necker's seeking a way to open peace negotiations. The only question is whether he was willing to go further than Vergennes and get the king to agree to a settlement that would be contrary to treaty obligations by leaving some of the thirteen colonies under British rule. Since he was accused of pursuing this policy by his enemies at the time, and since this accusation has been repeated by some present-day historians, it is necessary to examine his single known diplomatic foray in December 1780.

As a banker Necker had formed a wide circle of acquaintances in the international banking community. Among them was Thomas Walpole, cousin of the more famous Horace Walpole. Convinced that the British government had embarked upon a ruinous course by attempting to subjugate the colonies, Walpole was anxious to serve as mediator in getting a peace parley started. Before leaving London en route to Paris on banking business in October 1780 he had an interview with the prime minister, Lord North, to see if he could make use of his contacts in Paris to explore the possibility of opening negotiations. Neither North nor King George wished to encourage Walpole, who after all belonged to the political opposition. Nevertheless, Walpole had sufficient self-confidence to seek out Necker and give him the impression that North was anxious for peace. Relying upon that source, Necker sent a secret dispatch to the British prime minister dated December 1, with the approval of Maurepas and the king, setting forth his own ideas on how peace negotiations might get started:

We both desire peace. Why could we not initiate negotiations which would then be carried on by our respective foreign ministers? This would not infringe upon their responsibility. We would only initiate negotiations, or explore the possibility of negotiations to see if the time is ripe. . . . But His Majesty must insist, as does the king of England, that the peace must be honorable, and I fully realize that is where the difficulty begins. . . . I say frankly that my first thought is that a truce of greater or less duration in which the belligerents in America would maintain what they possess would be a reasonable solution.[13]

The peace feeler did not produce the hoped-for reaction. King George replied that peace would come only when the French government ceased helping the

11. Duc de Castries, *La France et l'indépendance américaine*, p. 240.

12. Doniol, *Histoire de la participation*, IV, 472-73.

13. Necker's letter of December 1, 1780, is preserved in the North papers and was published in 1854 by Philip Henry Stanhope, Lord Mahon, in the latter's *History of England*

rebels.[14] With that response it appeared doubtful that an armistice could be reached without further military developments. It was necessary to plan for another year of war, another costly campaign in America. Necker shouldered the task of raising the money, which he succeeded in doing by the end of March 1781. The military campaign was planned by the marquis de Castries and succeeded brilliantly at Yorktown in October. By that time Necker had fallen from power and was no longer involved in the further diplomatic events of the American War.

Except for his July letter to Lord Stormont, the secret letter sent by Necker to Lord North on December 1, 1780, was the only known diplomatic intervention of the Genevan banker in the American War. This message did suggest the principle of *uti possidetis* as a basis for initiating an armistice; but nothing in it indicated that Necker planned this to be the final basis of the settlement. His concern that the final settlement must be honorable for his king suggests that he did not contemplate departing from the provisions of Article 11 of the Treaty of 1778, namely that the complete independence of the American colonies would be guaranteed by France. Furthermore, he recognized that he was not an experienced diplomat and that his only rôle was to help initiate negotiations. It may be noted also that King George did not interpret Necker's message as an offer to compromise on the issue of independence. He wrote to Lord North on December 18:

Within these few Minutes I have received Lord North's letter accompanying the Secret he has received from Mr. Necker; it shews France is certainly in greater difficulties than we imagined or She would [not] by Such various Channels seem to court Peace; no one has more inclination or interest in wishing so desirable an event as myself provided it can be obtained on honourable and Solid terms; with France it [is] easily to be settled if She would desist from encouraging Rebellion and not add to Her insults by wanting to affect Independency which whether under its apparent name, or a truce is the same in reality; till She gives up that view I do not see how Peace can be a safe measure.[15]

Some historians assert that Necker did intend to establish a permanent peace on the basis of *uti possidetis,* and that this would have partitioned the colonies, leaving New York, Charleston, and other areas under British rule.[16] But the

---

from the Peace of Utrecht to the Peace of Versailles, 7 vols. (London, 1836-1854), vol. VII, appendix, pp. xiii-xv. The copy that Necker kept was displayed in the Château de Coppet in 1955. See *Necker et Versailles: Château de Coppet, 7 mai–14 avril, 1955* (Coppet, 1955), no. 350. Necker indicated in a marginal note that he had sent this letter to Maurepas and that it was approved by the king before being sent to Lord North.

14. George III, *The Correspondence of King George the Third,* V, 163.

15. *Ibid.*

16. Richard B. Morris, *The Peacemakers: The Great Powers and American Independence* (New York, 1965), p. 106. Sanche de Gramont, *Epitaph for Kings* (New York, 1967), pp. 310-311.

evidence is not convincing. It rests entirely upon what Richard B. Morris calls "the Mountstuart-Necker negotiations."[17] It is apparent from Morris' own discussion that there was never any direct communication either oral or written between the French finance minister and the British diplomat, Viscount Mountstuart, who was sent to Turin by the British government in December 1779. The "negotiations" were between one Paul-Henri Mallet, who was known as a scholar but never had any official position in the Genevan or any other government. It may be questioned whether the conversation and letters of this rather vain, self-important Genevan, who had selfish personal motives for thrusting himself into the diplomatic scene, should be dignified by the word "negotiations."

On his way to Turin in the winter of 1779 Mountstuart did stop at Paris. He wrote to his superior in the Foreign Office, Lord Hillsborough, about his impressions of the French scene. He did not meet Necker personally but commented at length about his financial operations and his "character."

I have been told and from the best authority, that this gentleman's character is so well established throughout the Kingdom, not only for ability but excessive probity, that was it necessary to lay on a Tax it would be submitted to without a murmur, and should other resources fail, that the means are already found to raise a very considerable sum in that manner without destroying the Nation.[18]

In the summer of 1780 Mountstuart asked and received permission from Lord Hillsborough to journey to Geneva in order to escape the hot season in the Po valley, ostensibly out of consideration for his wife's health. It was at Geneva that the British diplomat met his erstwhile traveling companion Paul-Henri Mallet, who had recently returned from Paris and claimed to have had extensive conversations with his old school friend, now the director general of finances. According to Mountstuart's account, this conversation was indeed compromising to Necker's historical reputation. As he described it in a letter to Hillsborough dated September 18, 1780:

He [Mallet] certainly betrays confidential opinions—opinions which, should they ever be known, might greatly prejudice M. Necker, if not undo him, with his royal master, who now openly supports him against every attempt a very strong party, headed by the Queen and assisted by M. de Sartine and the Prince de Montbarey, can devise to get him removed.[19]

Mountstuart added that, according to his informant, Sartine and Montbarey were spending enormous sums, not only for their military departments, but to build up their own private fortunes; and so they wanted the war to continue. Sartine, it was said, was maintaining the favor of the queen by transferring to her private use large sums received by him for the navy. Mallet reported Necker as

17. Morris, *The Peacemakers*, p. 111.
18. Mountstuart to Hillsborough, December 18, 1779, British Museum, Add. MSS 36,802, fol. 18-19.
19. *Ibid.*, fols. 205-214.

saying that he was at the end of his resources for financing the war. "The taxes must grow heavier and France was never less in a condition to bear the oppressive load which threatened her." All this was to "support a war he never had nor could approve." Necker wished the British success in taking Charleston, for "every step they gained in America was a step toward peace in Europe." Mountstuart's letter to Hillsborough continued his account of what Mallet had told him:

Monsieur Necker occasionally said many more things, all tending to the same purpose, and on my Friend asking him whether it might be possible to devise something short of the independence of America, he replied: "I wish it might." Monsieur Mallet then observed that he had often turned his thoughts that way, and that he could not see why a proposition of this kind might not be adopted, that some one province, for example, New England, should be declared independent, and the others obliged to return to their ancient allegiance. Monsieur Necker expressed his approbation of the idea, but seemed to decline entering into any explanation on that head.

Mallet told Mountstuart that he would be willing to go to Paris and open discussions with Necker on behalf of the British diplomat. Mountstuart himself was in favor of peace negotiations. The son of Lord Bute, who had initiated the peace talks in 1762 that had ended the last war, Mountstuart felt that the war was ruining the British nation. "We are not in a situation," he wrote Hillsborough, "to carry on a war which is destructive in every part, and which each hour preys more and more on our vitals, and if of much longer duration, must inevitably terminate in total ruin and Destruction, though the laurels of victory should adorn our enterprise." He requested Hillsborough's permission to follow up on Mallet's offer, although he pointed out the dubious character of his informant. Mallet was asking that the British king grant him a life pension in return for his services. Mountstuart expressed some reservation about the reliability of his interlocutor:

I must add that when I pressed him hard, and began to talk seriously on Monsieur Necker's inclination to peace, he grew frightened, and wanted to retreat, not indeed from his offer of going, but he wished to *seem* alarmed at the consequences of having so freely related what had passed in private, friendly conference. . . . He said more than once that though worth the trial, he did not think it probable such a step would be attended with success; it was rather improbable but we agreed that Treaties had often taken rise from more trifling circumstances.

Hillsborough attached even less value to the proffered services of this would-be diplomat and told Mountstuart to refuse the offer of his "Genevan friend."[20] The British government was not interested in pursuing his ties with Necker. Mountstuart and Mallet exchanged some letters in October and November, the

20. Hillsborough to Mountstuart, British Museum, Add. MSS 36,801, fols. 126-128.

Genevan scholar offering his own version of what was happening in the French government. He wrote that Necker was heading a peace party in opposition to the war party of Sartine and Montbarey. The replacement of these ministers by Castries and Ségur meant the triumph of the peace party and greatly increased the prospects for negotiations. Castries and Necker had won Maurepas over to their side. In such circumstances the Genevan scholar no doubt had visions of being asked to go to Paris and contact Necker. That life pension was within grasp! But the call from Turin never came.[21]

Such were the "Mountstuart-Necker negotiations." There is no evidence whatever, even in the correspondence of Mountstuart and Mallet, that Necker had initiated the contacts between his former school friend and the British diplomat at Turin, or even had any knowledge of them. As for Mallet's account of conversations with Necker, there is little to corroborate it from other sources. The allegation that Necker intended to partition the American colonies places great weight on the testimony of Mallet as reported by Mountstuart. That so much of what he told Mountstuart was palpably false does not enhance the reliability of that source. It was not true that the queen supported Sartine in the naval secretary's quarrel with Necker; quite the opposite. It is certain that the queen, and probably Vergennes, favored the dismissal of Sartine.[22] Nor was it true that Necker was leading a "peace party" in opposition to a "war party" supported by the queen, Sartine, and Montbarey. The prince de Montbarey was as opposed to the war as anyone in the council, being as contemptuous of Americans as he was of Genevans.[23] On the other hand, both Castries and Ségur, whom Necker supported and who in turn were admirers of the Genevan banker, ardently favored continuing the war to an honorable conclusion. The ministerial shakeup in October and December was not due to a difference of opinion over foreign policy. It was simply because of the incompetence and wastefulness of the dismissed ministers. But it must be said on their behalf that no other source has ever accused them of diverting funds into their own pockets, and the story that Sartine gave enormous sums to the queen is completely without foundation. It appears that the Genevan scholar had little sound information on French government affairs and made up for it with a fertile imagination. It is no wonder that Hillsborough was not favorably impressed.

There is nothing to indicate that Necker was displeased with his government's negotiating posture in December and January, or that he believed France should have made further concessions to get peace talks started. The failure to reach a

21. British Museum, Add. MSS 36,803, fols. 56-60, 145, 202; Add. MSS 38,744, fols. 31-37.

22. Doniol, *Histoire de la participation*, IV, 489-490. Doniol indicates that Vergennes was dissatisfied with Sartine and favored his replacement by Castries. But Ségur, relying upon Véri, gives a contrary view for Vergennes. See Ségur, *Au Couchant de la monarchie*, II, 292.

23. Montbarey, *Mémoires*, II, 296-297.

cease-fire was clearly the decision of the British monarch. There is no evidence that Necker thought otherwise. During the events leading up to his resignation on May 19, 1781, foreign policy was never an issue. He did ask the king to admit him to the High Council. This request was based on his often-expressed belief that the council needed to be advised of the financial and economic situation in the country when making great decisions on foreign policy. It would be gratuitous to assume that he intended to become a dictator and force an end to the war that would have been dishonorable to the king and the nation. He would have had to become a dictator because no one else in the ministry would have followed him in that course, neither Vergennes, Castries, nor Ségur.

Looking back on the scene after 200 years, Americans should have some feeling of gratitude toward the Genevan banker rather than reproach for his lack of enthusiasm for the American cause. His management of the royal finances unquestionably enabled France to win the American War, in contrast to her defeat in 1763. Several participants and observers in the American War expressed the opinion that it was a "war of *écus*" like the previous one. King George wrote to Lord North in September 1780 that "the finances of France as well as Spain are in no good situation; this War like the last will prove one of Credit."[24] In 1776 Turgot had opposed French intervention in America because "the first cannon shot would bankrupt Your Majesty's government." This prophecy was belied by Necker. Whatever his own private feelings about that war, in serving his king and the French nation he also served the cause of American independence.

Yet there has been a firm conviction in the historiography of the French Revolution that events proved Turgot to be right in the long run. It is often said that France's participation in the American War eventually brought about her bankruptcy, and that the Genevan banker had cleverly concealed from the king and the French public the true situation of the finances in the *Compte rendu*, which he published in February 1781. The justice of that verdict is seriously open to question.

24. George III, *The Correspondence of King George the Third*, V, 136.

Chapter XIV

THE *COMPTE RENDU*

Early in February 1781, the bookseller-diarist Hardy noted that "the director general of finances seems more firmly anchored in the king's favor than ever." The king assured Necker that he was pleased that he had so many enemies because "if you had fewer, your merit would be less." On February 15 Hardy mentioned the publication of the new life rente loan and quoted extensively from its preamble in his journal. He noted also that "next Monday or Tuesday there will be published an account rendered to the king by Mr. Necker of all his operations since His Majesty deemed fit to confer upon him the administration of the finances." The reason for this unusual event, said Hardy, "was to close the mouths of his enemies and obliterate the impression made by their libels; the work to be published by the said Mr. Necker is a kind of defiance."[1]

On Monday, February 19, the *Compte rendu* was published and began its celebrated career. It was printed both at the royal printing shop and at the establishment of the bookseller Panckoucke, located in the Hôtel Thou in the Saint-André-Des-Arts quarter. The duc de Cröy witnessed the throng that besieged the printing shop:

You never saw such a crowd. Three thousand copies at a time were printed, and they were snapped up instantly. Soon 20,000 copies were sold. There was good reason to run there. Never before had one seen the finances of the kingdom laid bare, the king giving an accounting, so to speak, and a very faithful accounting, to his people.[2]

The *Compte rendu* fell on such fertile soil that even Necker must have been astonished at the eagerness with which the public seized upon the treatise, noting minutely every figure in the account, toting up the sums of revenue and expenditure, seeing how much the king spent for favors and pensions, and what the royal households cost, and exactly what tribute was levied upon the people. According to Metra, "there has never been a printed work which has had a

---

1. Hardy, BN MSS Fonds français, 6683, fols. 404, 410.
2. Emmanuel de Cröy, *Journal inédit du duc de Cröy: 1718-1784,* ed. vicomte de Grouchy and Paul Cottin, 4 vols. (Paris, 1906), IV, 230.

success comparable to that of the *Compte rendu* of Mr. Necker."[3] Soon 100,000 copies were sold, at three livres per copy, which made a handsome profit for the publisher, Metra noted. Royalties to the author were all turned over to Madame Necker for her hospital work.

The enthusiasm was not limited to France. The book was translated and published in English, Dutch, German, Danish, and Italian. The Duke of Richmond, a member of the opposition in Great Britain and an admirer of the Genevan, purchased 6,000 copies to distribute in England. Foreign statesmen and sovereigns took note of the work. Emperor Joseph wrote the Austrian ambassador at Paris that "if the figures are exact, this book is infinitely interesting; just as it would be a miserable expedient if its purpose is only to bolster credit in order to facilitate the marketing of the loan."[4] But he told the ambassador to congratulate the director general on the publication of the account, and to mention that the emperor himself had thought of doing the same thing in his own government.

Not all comment was favorable. Archduke Leopold of Tuscany was a convert to physiocratic ideas, and like all members of the sect he took a dim view of the Genevan and his *Compte rendu*.[5] Bachaumont noted that the book was bound in the bright blue paper used for children's fairytales, and so the mockers were calling it "the blue story" (*conte bleu*).[6] It was evidently going to be a matter of the greatest importance for Necker's reputation that the figures were exact and above reproach.

But there was much more than figures in the treatise. Necker surveyed for the king (and the public) everything he had accomplished during his ministry. He expressed his ideas on reform and summarized what had been accomplished, and what he hoped to accomplish when the war ended. The book was written in an informal style, somewhat similar to a present-day "fireside chat" by a president, although Necker was formally addressing the king. It was admittedly an *apologia* for his entire ministry, in which pride was not lacking. He wondered if the publication of an accounting of the royal finances should not become a permanent institution:

The obligation of putting his administration in broad daylight would have an influence on the first steps a finance minister would take in his ministerial career. It is darkness and obscurity which favors nonchalance; publicity, on the contrary, can only become an honor and a reward in so far as one has felt the importance of his duties and has exerted himself to fulfill them. Such a *compte rendu* would enable each person who makes up your councils to study and follow the situation of the finances, important knowledge which must be

3. Metra, *Correspondance secrète*, XI, 129.

4. Comte de Mercy-Argenteau, *Correspondance du comte de Mercy-Argenteau avec l'empereur Joseph II et le prince de Kaunitz,* ed. A. d'Arneth and J. Flammermont, 2 vols. (Paris, 1889-1891), I, 27.

5. *Ibid.*

6. Bachaumont, *Mémoires secrets,* XVII, 72.

considered in all great decisions. . . . At the same time the hope of publicity would make him even more indifferent to those obscure pamphlets which attempt to disturb the peace of the administrator, and whose authors, secure in the knowledge that a man of elevated soul would not deign to grapple with them in the arena, take advantage of his silence by disturbing some minds with lies. . . . Finally, what is worthy of most serious consideration, such an institution could have the greatest influence on public confidence.[7]

Specifically, he suggested that every five years the finance minister appear before the other ministers and present his documentation for his figures, and then have the account published. "I dare to think that after a man of my character would have desired such a verification, no one who comes after me should be offended by being required to submit to the same rule."[8] The statement is disconcerting in its lack of modesty, and the libels that proliferated in the months following the publication of the *Compte rendu* taunted him about his "character" and "elevated soul." He evidently assumed that the public was well aware that he served the king without any emolument whatever, even declining the free box seat at the opera, and no doubt the public was aware of it.

But the occasional flashes of vainglory should not obscure from history the importance of the ideas in the *Compte rendu*. The principles of moderate reform (summarized for the most part in Chapter VI) generated strong public support. It is probable that the *Compte rendu* was more widely read and more influential than the *Contrat social* of Rousseau. Necker's brief treatise of 1781 became the political handbook for a generation, as far as public administration of the finances were concerned. Rabaut-Saint-Etienne wrote that it "produced the effect of sudden light in the midst of darkness."[9] The future marshal of the Grand Army, Auguste-Frédéric de Marmont, learned to read from a copy of the *Compte rendu* his father gave him. Sainte-Beuve wrote that Marmont "retained from his father this wellspring of political principles which, after so many quite different events and ideas, were never to leave him."[10]

Important as the *Compte rendu* was in its own time, it did not become a classic. No new editions were printed after 1781, except for its inclusion in Necker's complete works published in 1820 by baron de Staël. Historical works that mention it today usually deride it.[11] What appears to have discredited the *Compte rendu* was its figures. Near the beginning of the treatise Necker wrote:

At this moment I hasten to announce to Your Majesty that as a result of the diverse reforms which he has permitted me to enact, and by the extinction of some rentes and retirement of certain debts, the actual state of his finances is such that despite the deficit of 1776, despite the enormous expenditures for the

7. *Compte rendu au roi,* in *Oeuvres complètes,* II, 1-2.

8. *Ibid.,* p. 16.

9. Jean-Paul Rabaut-Saint-Etienne, *Précis de L'Histoire de la Révolution française,* rev. ed. (Paris, 1821), pp. 101-102.

10. Sainte-Beuve, *Causeries du lundi,* VI, 4.

11. For example, Luethy, *La Banque protestante,* II, 519.

war, and the interest payments for loans to sustain them, the ordinary revenue of Your Majesty exceeds at this moment his ordinary expenditures by 10,200,000 livres.[12]

At the end of the pages describing his reforms, one finds the accounts. First is the "statement of the Items of Revenue brought to the Royal Treasury for the Ordinary Year." There follow thirty-one items of revenue; for each item is given the gross amount received by the revenue-receiving company or administration, the amount it spent for the king's affairs, and the net amount it turned over to the royal treasury. Second is the "Statement of Expenditures Payed by the Royal Treasury for the Ordinary Year," consisting of forty-nine items. Notes and explanations accompany many of these items of ordinary expenditure, such as the fact that the royal treasury now pays for pensions, which causes a reduction from what was heretofore the ordinary sum paid to the military services by the treasury. Next follows a shorter, summary account of the revenue received by the royal treasury and its expenditures, in the same numerical order as the preceding table. The totals given in this table are: revenue, 264,154,000; expenditures, 253,954,000. It would appear that this is the only account seen by some historians, who allege that the *Compte rendu* did not include the sums retained and spent by the receiving departments.[13]

According to Charles Gomel, a historian whose two-volume work on the financial causes of the French Revolution was published in 1892-1893, the figures given by Necker in the *Compte rendu* were "absolutely false."[14] From this source the message has passed into the history books of the twentieth century. Even authors sympathetic to the Genevan and his reform ministry desert him on the *Compte rendu,* which they find indefensible.[15] "The ordinary expenditures," wrote Gomel, "were in excess of the ordinary revenue, and an enormous deficit existed because of the extraordinary expenditures."[16] More than that, Gomel asserted in effect that the *Compte rendu* was a fraud. "He [Necker] drew up an ideal account of revenue and expenditure which did not correspond to the facts of any definite fiscal year, and he arrived at a surplus of 10 million livres in revenue. People took him at his word."[17]

It was just because Necker knew that he could not be taken at his word that he went to great pains to validate with great thoroughness every item in the *Compte rendu.* He expected the libelists to attack his treatise, and the assault was not long in coming. The Genevan had prepared for it. He explained near the beginning of the treatise why he chose his method of accounting. Revenue items were those reported to the treasury and verified by the revenue-receiving

12. *Oeuvres complètes,* II, 12-13.

13. Again for example, Luethy, *La Banque protestante,* II, 519.

14. Gomel, *Les Causes financières de la révolution française,* I, xxviii.

15. For example, Ségur, *Au Couchant de la monarchie,* II, 361-362; Roux, *Lex fermes d'impôts,* pp. 390ff.

16. Gomel, *Les Causes financières de la révolution française,* I, xxviii.

17. *Ibid.,* p. xxvii.

departments, signed by the first secretary of that department. The spending departments had submitted their accounts, which were incorporated into the *Compte rendu.* That information was known to a great number of officials in the spending department. When the *Compte rendu* was sent to the king it was accompanied by these documents (*pièces justificatives*), which validated every item. Necker was prudent enough to take a copy of each of these documents for his own files. When the exactness of his accounts was challenged by the treasurer of the household of the comte d'Artois, Antoine Bourboulon, Necker asked and received permission to refute Bourboulon's account by presenting his documents before a council of ministers.[18] When Calonne impugned the *Compte rendu* before the Assembly of Notables in 1787, Necker wrote the controller general and the king asking permission to show his documents. "Since I prepared the *Compte rendu* with the greatest care, I am perfectly confident of its accuracy; and I have in my possession the documentation for each article that is susceptible of verification."[19]

Neither Calonne nor the king were interested in seeing his documents. Nor have historians who have written about the *Compte rendu* shown curiosity about them. Yet the same documents that Necker wrote about and described in his April 1787 memorial are located today in the Château de Coppet near Geneva. Thousands of visitors who have filed through the library of the château must have seen the small wooden box on the table with the inscription: "Pièces Justificatives du Compte Rendu au Roi par M. Necker au Mois de Janvier 1781." Inside are eight folders of documents arranged by letter from A to H. File F is entitled, "Statement of items of revenue turned into the royal treasury for the ordinary year." File G is entitled, "Development concerning the account of expenditures (p. 110 of the *Compte rendu*)."

One would like to be able to say that every item of the *Compte rendu* has its justificatory document intact. Unfortunately, six of the thirty-one items of revenue and ten of the forty-nine items of expenditure are missing. The most important of the former concern the free gift of the clergy, the king's share of the profits from the *régies* and the General Farm, and the extinction of rentes. The other three are of negligible importance. The total amount of the missing documents is 6,820,000 livres. The remaining twenty-five items, amounting to 257,334,000 livres, do have their *pièces justificatives,* and they leave nothing to be desired. Each gives the same figure as the published *Compte rendu,* although in exact numbers rather than round numbers. Every item gives details of the account and is signed by the responsible official. For example, the first item, "General revenue from the receivers of the *pays d'élections*," gives the breakdown in twelve articles of the 19,049,180 livres spent by the receivers general. It indicates exactly what amount was received from the *taille,* its accessories, the

18. See Chapter XV.
19. *Mémoire publié par M. Necker au mois d'avril 1787 en réponse au discours prononcé par M. de Calonne devant l'assemblée des notables,* in Oeuvres complètes, II, 161-162.

capitation, and the *vingtièmes.* The document is "signed and certified correct by Harvoin" and dated January 25, 1781. All other items of revenue are signed and dated in the same manner. The signer of the document was the first secretary in the financial company that collected the revenue.

Of the ten missing expenditure items, three are important. Most regrettable is the absence of number 5, the expenditure of the navy and colonial department, one of the most discussed in the debate between Necker and Calonne in 1788. Also, the expenditure for anticipations (number 16) and the unforeseen expenditures (number 49) are missing, and they too were much disputed. The other seven are negligible. The total amount of the missing items is 40 million livres out of the total expenditures by the royal treasury of 253,954,000 livres. But the documents for the remaining thirty-nine items have the same thoroughness as those for revenue, indeed they are even more detailed. These documents do not have signatures at the bottom, but other evidence indicates that they come from departments outside the ministry of finance. The first item is entitled, "War department. Expenditures ordered by the Marquis de Ségur for the ordinary service of the year 1781." The department of foreign affairs contains an autographed letter by Vergennes stating that the ordinary expenditures for his department will be 8,525,000 livres, the amount given in the *Compte rendu,* and another letter to Dufresne saying that the department is asking an additional 4 million livres for extraordinary expenditures.

Despite the gaps, the Coppet documents on the *Compte rendu* constitute an irrefutable vindication of Necker. That is, they conclusively prove the accuracy of his figures on the ordinary revenue and expenditure for 1781. Some historians who claim that the *Compte rendu* was "totally false" do so on the basis that it was not the kind of document they think it should have been—which Necker never intended it to be. The most common complaint is that he did not include the extraordinary costs of the war, but passed them over in silence, "leaving them to his successors."[20] It is certainly true that the extraordinary costs of the war were running at the rate of about 150 million livres per year at the time the *Compte rendu* was published, a fact that Necker never tried to conceal; indeed, he mentioned it in the *Compte rendu.* But if he had published an account of both ordinary and extraordinary accounts, would the result have been a deficit? Such an account was Joly de Fleury's "Situation of the Finances for the year 1783." No deficit was indicated in that account, rather a surplus of about 34 million livres.[21]

According to practice, then, if one included the extraordinary expenditures on the debit side, one included the extraordinary income on the opposite side. That would be, for the most part, money from loans. When he resigned in May 1781, Necker submitted a statement to the king indicating the money assured in the treasury to meet the costs of the war for the remainder of 1781. This

20. Luethy, *La Banque protestante,* II, 519.
21. BN MSS Joly de Fleury, 1442, fol. 53.

document is also in the wooden box at Coppet.[22] The total revenue for the last eight months would come to 367.4 million livres. The expenditure would be 302.9 million livres, allowing a surplus of 64.5 million in the treasury to begin the next year. Both the revenue and the expenditure were itemized. The former included cash in the treasury when the statement was submitted in May, namely, 70 million livres; the income from the two life rente loans of February and March and other income from royal treasury loans, totaling 108.2 million livres from loans; 88.45 million livres from anticipations; and 15.85 million from loans from the *pays d'états.* The expenditures also were itemized: war department, 67.35 million livres; navy, 96 million; bonuses for the lottery of 1777, 4.6 million.

That there was sufficient money for the 1781 campaign is confirmed in the manuscripts of Joly de Fleury, although the amount remaining to begin the new year was less. When he took office in May, the new finance minister was nervous about the financial situation. He was concerned, as we have seen, by the slowness of the March life rente loan on the bourse, and he withdrew over 10 million livres of rentes that had been offered for sale. He felt also that Necker's statement underestimated somewhat the expenditures that would be needed. But results of the year proved these fears unfounded, as a document written in 1787 in the Fleury manuscripts confirms: "Despite those errors, almost impossible to avoid in a projection of the finances, Mr. de Fleury found money in the royal treasury sufficient for all the expenses of the campaign of 1781."[23]

When Calonne attacked the *Compte rendu* in 1788 he asserted that Necker's successor found the treasury practically empty and had to search desperately for extraordinary means to meet war costs. He was driven to such desperation, said Calonne, that he extended the old loan of Terray of February 1770 (that issue of 4-percent perpetual rentes) by 70 million livres. He had to raise a total of 141 million livres from May to the end of the year.[24] In his rebuttal, Necker pointed out that Joly de Fleury did negotiate more loans, but these were primarily to meet the needs of 1782, not 1781. Indeed, of the loans he negotiated, only 34,359,276 livres was received by the royal treasury in 1781. Of that sum the greatest part was the 30-million-livre loan made with the farmers general that Necker himself had initiated and Joly de Fleury completed.[25] Necker's assertions on this matter are confirmed in the manuscripts of Joly de Fleury, both as to revenue received by the royal treasury from his loans and the fact that most of his loans negotiated in 1781 were to provide for the needs of the following

22. File E, "Apperçu de la situation des finances pour les huit derniers mois, 1781."

23. BN MSS Joly de Fleury, 1432, folio 154; see also "Mémoire particulier sur la situation des finances pour l'année 1782," dated March 1782, in AN F[30] 110A, which confirms that there was in the treasury on January 1, 1782, the sum of 56, 132,000 livres.

24. Charles-Alexandre de Calonne, "Pièces justificatives," in *Réponse à l'écrit de M. Necker* (London, 1788), p. 31.

25. *Nouveaux éclaircissements sur le compte rendu,* in *Oeuvres complètes,* II, 515-521.

year.[26] As for Calonne's allegation about the 70-million extension of the loan of February 1770, nothing is more clearly false. In fact, it is disproved by his own financial statement sent to Louis XVI after his fall from the ministry in April 1787.[27] These 4-percent notes had been consistently worth 60 percent of their face value on the bourse, and the finance minister would have had to issue 40 percent more than the 70 million if he were to realize that sum in effective receipts. That would mean an extension of 98 million livres from May to December 1781. No such extension appears in any other account of the royal debt.[28]

The conclusion to the above observations is that if Necker had presented in the *Compte rendu* the extraordinary as well as the ordinary revenue and expenditure, it would have shown a surplus of around 60 million livres. But he believed this kind of account was not nearly as useful for analyzing the financial posture of the government as what he published. His reasoning has already been explained.[29] The wealth of the royal government consisted in its annual fixed revenue, drawn mostly from taxation. Regular income should cover the interest and amortization costs of loans. This was the guarantee to creditors that the government could continue to pay interest and reimbursements of capital in the peace following the war. In his April 1787 memorial he explained again these principles:

It is necessary to recall, first of all, the purpose and motive of the *Compte rendu*. It was not intended to present the king with a speculative tableau of diverse extraordinary expenditures which could result from the continuation of the war. The purpose was simply to present to His Majesty a positive statement of his ordinary revenue and expenditures, a statement which must always be the basis for all important decisions of the government. The king believed that giving publicity to the state of his finances would have a favorable influence on the government's credit; and that in a period when the country seemed surprised

26. BN MSS Joly de Fleury, 1442, fol. 103, 214. According to this source, the amount received from loans made by Joly de Fleury was 34,482,000 livres in 1781. This is close to the figure given by Necker in the preceding footnote: 34,359,276 livres. In a memorandum written by Jacques Marquet de Bourgade, an advisor of Joly de Fleury, dated October 7, 1781, it was estimated that additional loans amounting to 160 million livres should be planned for the needs of 1782 (BN MSS Joly de Fleury, 1434, fols. 187-193). Marion mistakenly wrote that this document referred to the needs of 1781 and indicated a shortage of 160 million livres for that year (Marion, *Histoire financière de la France*, I, 340-341). But it is clear that Bourgade was referring to the needs of 1782. The title of the document in question is "Mémoire et observation sur le détail que le ministre se propose de faire dans son rapport au roi des besoins et des secours de l'année prochaine pour justifier de la nécessité du rétablissement des receveurs généraux des finances," dated October 7, 1781.

27. Charles-Alexandre de Calonne, *Requête au roi: Adressée à sa majesté par M. de Calonne, ministre d'état* (London, 1787), p. 102. Calonne admitted here that he had himself extended the loan of 1770 by 20 million livres during the years 1784-1786.

28. Necker, *Nouveaux éclaircissements sur le compte rendu*, in *Oeuvres complètes*, II, 519-523.

29. See p. 122 above.

that the needs of war had not yet given occasion for the establishment of new taxes, His Majesty believed it desirable to make known by the rapport existing between his ordinary revenue and ordinary expenditures that there was a surplus sufficient to pay for loans needed for the campaign of 1781.[30]

What military and diplomatic contingencies might develop in the year were not precisely foreseeable, and there is no reason to suppose that Necker, had he remained in the ministry, would not have considered the decision that Joly de Fleury made in July: that is, that the probability of the war continuing until 1783 made it necessary to find new sources of ordinary revenue through taxation. At other times during his first ministry he believed it would be necessary to raise taxes, but he managed to find new sources of revenue through amelioration. New taxes, he said, should be imposed if necessary, but they should be the last resort, after all possibilities of economy had been exhausted.

Necker's critics, both in his own day and among historians, say that he should have raised taxes in preference to borrowing. The argument is unrealistic. Even with new taxes, it would have been necessary to borrow, given the time lag for tax revenue to come into government coffers. Furthermore, it would have been foolish as well as impossible to attempt to raise taxes high enough to pay 150 million livres per year of war expenditures. British financial policy, always Necker's model, did not attempt to meet war costs out of current revenue. A present-day historian of British finances writes that

... the cost of eighteenth century war was mainly borrowed and not paid out of current revenues. ... In other words, the actual practice [of the British government] was not unlike the doctrine attributed to Necker when Director-General of Finances in France: "Pour les dépenses permanentes, les taxes ordinaires; pour les dépenses exceptionelles, l'emprunt."[31]

Criticism of Necker's *Compte rendu,* to be fair, must be based on a view of it as the type of document he intended it to be: an accounting of the king's ordinary revenue and expenditures. In Necker's own time there was never any thought of doing otherwise. The libelists in 1781, including Calonne, claimed that the *Compte rendu* gave those figures incorrectly. It was only many years after Necker's death that a new basis was introduced for discrediting it, the *état au vrai* for 1781, discussed below.

The financial history of Charles Gomel was not based upon original research. Gomel did not delve into the archives or manuscript sources, or try to compare different financial accounts of the *ancien régime.* To justify his accusation that the *Compte rendu* was "totally false," he was content to refer his readers to an earlier financial history, that of Antoine Bailly, published in 1830.[32] Bailly was not a historian, but an inspector of finances in the government of Charles X. His

---

30. Necker, *Oeuvres complètes,* II, 200-201.
31. Binney, *British Public Finance,* p. 106.
32. Antoine Bailly, *Histoire financière de la France,* 2 vols. (Paris, 1830).

two-volume history of French finances is a mediocre work of history. Long tracts are taken from other printed sources, such as the work of Veron de Forbonnais. Unfortunately, the volumes of Forbonnais, which were excellent, ended at the year 1721. After that date Bailly's authorities rapidly dwindled in respectability, coming to rest upon long passages from the polemical and preposterous essay of Auget de Montyon, published anonymously in 1812. Bailly was not interested in historical research. He knew nothing of the collection of *Comptes rendus* by Mathon de la Cour, or other published *Comptes rendus,* except that of 1781. But as inspector of finances, he did have access to a type of document known as the *état au vrai* for the fiscal year. He referred to the *état au vrai* of 1781 only in a footnote. It was almost as an aside that he gave the figures, which, through Gomel, have passed into many historical works of the twentieth century:

One can see by the extract from the *état au vrai* of 1781 how much the real operations of that fiscal year differed from the sketch presented by Mr. Necker. According to the *Compte rendu,* the public revenues were supposed to be 430 million, from which were deducted the charges assigned to different *caisses* amounting to 166 million; thus, there remained to the royal treasury 264 million. The expenditures which the treasury had to pay were evaluated at 254 million, thus presenting a surplus of 10 million.

According to the *état au vrai,* on the contrary, the impositions and taxes realized during the fiscal year 1781 produced, with 12 million of accidental receipts, the sum of 436,900,000 livres. The payments effected on the expenditures of the same fiscal year, including the *acquits de comptant* of 92 million, arose to 526,600,000 livres. Therefore the excess of payments over the resources of the fiscal year, or the real deficit, was 89,700,000 livres. In addition, the anticipations acquitted in 1781 had exceeded the funds of preceding fiscal years which had been assigned to their payment by 121,250,000 livres; and there had been paid for the reimbursement of loans, 7,800,000 livres. The result is that between income [resources] and expenditures paid in 1781 under the ministry of Mr. Necker there was a difference of 218,730,000 livres.[33]

A deficit of over 218 million? No minor error of arithmetic on Necker's part! But what do these terms and figures mean: *acquits de comptant,* the 121 million livres of anticipations, the reimbursement of 7.8 million livres on loans? They are not to be found in Necker's *Compte rendu* of 1781 or in any other *Compte rendu* of the reign of Louis XVI. What kind of an account was the *état au vrai* upon which Bailly's figures are based?

In an appendix of his second volume, Bailly printed extracts from the *état au vrai* of 1785.[34] It is clear from this that he was actually using a document furnished by the guardian of the royal treasury to the council of finance for a fiscal year; but this was done many years after that year had passed. The

33. *Ibid.,* II, 236.
34. *Ibid.,* 287-294.

document was explained to Joly de Fleury by Moreau de Beaumont shortly after the former became finance minister in 1781.[35] It was limited to the operations of the royal treasury. According to Moreau de Beaumont's description, the accounts presented by the guardian consisted of three parts: the expenditures by *acquits patents,* the expenditures by *acquits de comptant,* and the *état au vrai* itself. The first expenditures were called "ordinary," and they were distinct from the second type, paid by *acquits de comptant.* The latter were not sent to the Paris Chamber of Accounts as were the "ordinary" expenditures. They were, in other words, secret expenditures authorized by the king. This is quite a different usage of "ordinary" and "extraordinary" than employed in Necker's *Compte rendu.* It means only those expenditures verified and scrutinized by the Chamber of Accounts, as distinguished from the secret expenditures that were not. The different use of those terms appears occasionally in the financial statements and can be perplexing until one becomes aware of it.

In the third document, the *état au vrai,* were gathered together the "totality of revenues and expenditures." The revenue was accounted for under eleven chief categories, such as income from the farmers general, the receivers general (but limited to the *taille*), the *capitation,* the *vingtième,* and other smaller sources of income. The ninth and tenth categories are especially important to notice. The ninth, called "extraordinary income," included all income from loans; the tenth, called "treasury funds," were anticipations, but not those negotiated by the government for that year. Rather, these were the allotments made to that fiscal year from the anticipations negotiated with financiers in several preceding years. Expenditures were divided into the categories already noted, the *acquits patents* and the *acquits de comptant.* But there were other categories of expenditure which Moreau de Beaumont said were "entirely fictitious," such as the reimbursements of government rentes not by payment but by conversion into different types of rentes.

In Bailly's excerpts of the *état au vrai* for 1785 we find total revenue balanced with total expenditure, instead of a deficit. This was accomplished by the handling of anticipations. The expenditure side of the ledger included *acquits patents* amounting to 305,663,200 livres, *acquits de comptant* amounting to 136,684,800 livres, and a third major category called "extraordinary operations for the fiscal year 1785." This consisted of two parts: first, the expenditure of that year derived from the income from anticipations of several preceding years, or 222,475,000 livres; second, the money spent in 1785 by way of anticipations drawn on future years, specifically, 1786 and 1787. This was 185,128,500 livres, making a grand total of 849,952,000 livres for expenditures.

On the other side of the ledger, the total receipts of the royal treasury for 1785, we find that the total income received from the various *caisses* of

35. "Mémoire sur le trésor royal et sur les comptes que rendent les gardes du trésor," BN MSS Joly de Fleury, 1443, fols. 222-237.

financiers was 356,723,800 livres. This was the ordinary income, consisting of the *vingtièmes* (59,386,500 livres), *capitation* (23,872,100 livres), revenue from domain and forests (408,800 livres), "free gift of the clergy" (18,000,000 livres), *régie* of posts (15,999,800 livres), and so on. It can be quickly seen that none of those items have anything to do with a *Compte rendu*. One may check them with the tableau of *Comptes rendus* given in the Appendix. Furthermore, the document of Bailly indicates that those figures represent income derived not just from 1785, but from several previous years also.

But those were the "ordinary" items of revenue. The *état au vrai* also listed as extraordinary income the revenue from the royal lottery (14,522,100), the *marc d'or* (the tax on offices), and loans amounting to 105,133,000 livres. A final category of extraordinary revenue consisted of anticipations assigned to 1785 from previous fiscal years, amounting to 101,318,800 livres, and those assigned to 1785 from anticipations drawn on the years 1786, 1787 and 1788, amounting to 201,609,200 livres. All this came to a total of revenue for 1785 of 849,951,700 livres.

The deficit for each year was not given in the *état au vrai* but was calculated by Bailly, freely drawing from other sources to supplement his figures. He wrote that in 1785 the actual expenditure, not counting anticipations, exceeded the ordinary income by 78.3 million livres, a figure not indicated in the *état au vrai*. To this deficit was added 27.3 million livres for pensions not listed in the *état au vrai*. Then there was an item called the "restes of 1785," an arrears of indebtedness that by decision of the National Assembly on July 1, 1791, was added to the expenditures of the fiscal year 1785! Thus, concluded Bailly, there was a total deficit in that year of 177.6 million livres.

Hardly anything could be more arbitrarily arrived at than the deficits of Antoine Bailly. Yet his figures for 1781 have passed into the history books as definitive on Necker's *Compte rendu*. The author of the volume devoted to the reign of Louis XVI in the Lavisse history of France, Henri Carré, obviously relied upon Bailly's figures, though without citing him:

Since [Necker] fixed the receipts at 264 million livres and the expenditures at 254, he found a surplus of receipts of 10 million. The reality was quite different . . . the receipts arose to 436,900,000 livres, and the expenditures to 526,000,000 livres, so that there was a deficit of 89,700,000 livres, and, since it was necessary to reimburse 129,100,000 livres of loans and anticipations in that fiscal year, the excess of expenditures over receipts totalled 218,800,000 livres.[36]

36. H. Carré, P. Sagnac, and E. Lavisse, *Louis XVI (1774-1789), in Histoire de France illustrée depuis les origines jusqu'à la révolution*, ed. Lavisse, 9 vols. (Paris, 1900-1911), IX, pt. 1, p. 88.

The same figures have been accepted as authoritative in other works.[37] Yet there is no reason to trust them. Bailly used the *états au vrai* of other years to calculate the deficit. His method was never consistent. He asserted that Necker issued loans in 1781 alone that amounted to 236 million livres, all of which was received in the treasury, and that Joly de Fleury issued and received another 190 million the same year. That would make 426 million livres in loans for 1781 alone, clearly a sum not supported by any document.[38]

It will be remembered that the *état au vrai* for a fiscal year was drawn up by the council of finances several years later. The reason was the tardiness of the king's payments for many expenditures, and the similar straggling in of the regular income from taxation. It was certain, for example, that 32 million livres would be received from the *capitation* for 1781. But it would not all come in during the calendar year. Anticipations was the means by which the royal government was able to spend that revenue. Hence, the confusing distribution of anticipations over several fiscal years and the similar distribution of income. Perhaps only one-fourth that amount from the *capitation* would be actually received in the calendar year, the other three-fourths would be spent, but in the form of anticipations. The latter were a flexible way to make ends meet. At the final conclusion of the *état au vrai* years after the fiscal year in question, anticipations could be juggled around from one fiscal year to the other in order to reach a balance between total expenditure and total revenue. Necker referred more than once to this old system of accountability. In the April memorial he wrote:

The entanglement of one fiscal year into the other does not mean that each year does not have its own revenue and its own expenditures; the effective accounts of the royal treasury which are rendered to the Chamber of Accounts are composed of the extraordinary as well as the ordinary accounts, of money payments as well as payments in notes and of fictitious articles of pure accountability.[39]

It is apparent that the final account of revenue and expenditures of a fiscal year were made up independently of the person who was finance minister that year. At the time of the publication of the *Red Book* by the National Assembly, which revealed the secret expenditures (*acquits de comptant*) made by the royal government during each year of the reign, Necker wrote that, according to an ancient system of accountability of the operations of the royal treasury (he was probably referring to the *états au vrai*), it was possible for a finance minister to assign *ordonnances de comptant* to some anterior fiscal year. "The result of this process, prescribed by the rules of accountability of the royal treasury, is that an

37. For example, Ségur, *Au Couchant de la monarchie,* II, 362; and Gershoy, *The French Revolution and Napoleon,* p. 93.

38. Bailly, *Histoire financière,* II, 236-37.

39. *Oeuvres complètes,* II, 208.

account relative to one year often includes expenditures not ordered by the minister in office that year."[40]

These old rules of accountability are still mysterious, but it is clear that they did not contain the "real situation" of a fiscal year, and that they were a fallacious basis for impugning the *Compte rendu*. It appears that they simply recorded the amount of money actually received by the royal treasury during the year without regard to any system of accounting. For example, the Assembly of the Clergy met in 1785 and granted 18 million livres to the royal government, the figure which appears in the *état au vrai*. But in a *compte rendu* only one-fifth that sum would be assigned to 1785, since the clergy made its "free gift" once every five years. According to contract, the *régie* of the postal service turned over to the government each year around 11 million livres. The figure given in the *état au vrai* for 1785, nearly 16 million livres, obviously represents income belonging to other years.

Not all who have written about the finances of the *ancien régime* have been misled by the *états au vrai*. Léon Bouchard, also an inspector of finances in the 1880s, wrote that there was no attempt in the *états au vrai* to budget the finances of a fiscal year.[41] Analyzing the *Compte rendu* of abbé Terray for 1774, Edgar Faure dismissed the *états au vrai* because "they inextricably mix the idea of budgeting with treasury operations."[42] It is significant that Marcel Marion did not base his attack on Necker's *Compte rendu* on the *états au vrai*, and that he never mentioned Bailly at all in his own financial history of France.

Marion was no less convinced than Gomel that the *Compte rendu* was "totally false," but he evidently saw the fallacy of Bailly's work, and he attacked Necker from quite a different base. He accepted everything Calonne said about the *Compte rendu* before the Assembly of Notables in 1787, and also the work that Calonne published in London the following January.[43] Calonne had been active in the libel campaign against Necker. In the spring of 1781 his pamphlet (unsigned, of course), entitled *The Whys*, interpellated the director general on points of form and substance: Why did he use the particular form of *compte rendu* based upon the reports of the different *caisses* and departments? Why did he not include as an expenditure the interest charges on the new life rente loans; why did he include as a regular revenue the free gift of the clergy; why the inclusion of the peacetime income from the Domain of the Occident, which in wartime produced no revenue at all?[44] Practically all the points of the indictment against the *Compte rendu* that Calonne presented later were in this essay of 1781. Paradoxically, while denouncing the director general for concealing a deficit in the ordinary accounts, the writer of the *Whys* took issue with the policy of balancing ordinary expenditure through retrenchment and economy.

40. Necker, *Observations de M. Necker sur l'avant-propos du livre rouge*, p. 24.

41. Léon Bouchard, *Système financier de l'ancienne monarchie* (Paris, 1891), pp. 467-468.

42. Edgar Faure, *La disgrâce de Turgot*, pp. 152-153, n. 1.

43. *Réponse à l'écrit de M. Necker publié en avril, 1787.* (London, 1788).

44. *Les Comments*, in *Collection complète de tous les ouvrages*, II.

Such a policy, he said, was inconsistent with the grandeur of the throne and of France, which was not a poor country but enormously wealthy and which could afford great expenditures.

The *Whys* indicated clearly enough the policy its author would follow when he became controller general in November 1783. Economy was thrown to the winds, as were the accounting procedures initiated by Necker in October 1779. Gigantic new loans were floated each year. Rumors circulated of enormous favors granted to *engagists* of royal domain lands. The households of the princes and the queen were now unconstrained. The Parlement of Paris was becoming restive. Why all those new loans after the end of the war?[45] In 1784, Necker's lengthy treatise on the administration of finances in France appeared. It was generally viewed as an attack on the "gay economy" of his successor.

In 1786 the third *vingtième*, strictly a wartime tax measure, was due to expire, and the controller general was in trouble. The government's credit had plummeted. Something drastic was needed. In November, Calonne explained the situation to the king and asked him to convene an assembly of notables before which he could submit an elaborate reform program. This would enable the government to increase tax revenue in order to close the enormous gap between ordinary expenditure and revenue, now at about 112 million livres. Was he ready to admit that the gay economic policy was a mistake, and that it was time to think of trimming expenditures? Not at all. The fault lay with his predecessors, and chiefly the Genevan banker. If Necker had increased taxes by 50 million livres a year the government would not be in its present predicament. He specifically attacked Necker's *Compte rendu:*

At the time of Mr. Necker's retirement from the ministry the annual fixed expenditures had no relation whatever to the opinion which he wished to create; and if the illusion of a surplus of 10 million livres when there was in actual fact, according to the *comptes effectifs,* a deficit of 46 million which one could even estimate at 75 million, had the momentary effect of charming the public, it has at the same time occasioned the greatest evil by having misled the [financial] administration for so long.[46]

Calonne's address of February 22, 1787, before the Assembly of Notables made a profound impression on the public. Was it possible that the "virtuous Genevan," so long considered the model of ministerial honesty, had actually deceived the public? There was wavering even among those most sympathetic to Necker's reform ideas. The Archbishop of Toulouse, Loménie de Brienne, who was emerging as the leader of the opposition to Calonne in the Assembly of Notables and who had been a strong supporter of the Genevan, said that a discrepancy of even 5 million livres between the *Compte rendu* of 1781 and the actual situation would be a severe blow to Necker's reputation.

45. Flammermont, *Remontrances du parlement de Paris,* III, 640-649.
46. Calonne's November 1786 *mémoire* to the king was printed in his *Réponse à l'écrit de M. Necker,* pp. 166-167.

Necker was living in retirement on his estate at Saint-Ouen near Paris. When he heard rumors that Calonne was planning to attack the credibility of the *Compte rendu,* he wrote to the controller general asking permission to examine his accounts and to explain what divergences there might be between Calonne's figures and those of the *Compte rendu.*

Since I prepared the *Compte rendu* with the greatest care, I am perfectly confident of its accuracy; and I have in my possession the documentation for each article that is susceptible of verification. I believe, sir, that I am in a position to ask that you either do not alter in any manner the confidence in the exactitude of the account, or that you permit me to clarify any doubts you may have about it. I request this not only in my own interest, but also for reasons to which a minister of finance could not be insensible. For one cannot doubt that the sanction accorded by the king to the account I presented him in 1781 . . . has served for a long time as a basis for public confidence.[47]

Calonne replied haughtily that his accounts had been carefully drawn and were approved by the king; therefore, they were not subject to revision. He attempted to soften the blow to Necker's pride by saying that his corrections of the *Compte rendu* were based upon *comptes effectifs,* the actual results of the payments and receipts of the royal treasury as shown by treasury records after the fiscal year had ended; if there was a disparity between the *comptes effectifs* and what had been predicted at the beginning of the year it should be no disgrace to the author of the *Compte rendu.* It is obvious that this was hardly in keeping with the opinion Calonne had expressed in his memorial to the king the previous November. Necker was not mollified by it and wrote the king, earnestly asking permission to appear before the Assembly of Notables or any other council in the presence of Calonne and to defend the *Compte rendu* as he had at the time of Bourboulon's attack upon it. The king refused. Furthermore, in view of the excited state of public opinion since the convening of the Assembly of Notables, the king ordered Necker to refrain from any public statement about the affair. Necker's indignation was too great to be bridled, however, and in April he published his defense, beginning with the sentence: "For five years I served the king with a devotion that knew no bounds."[48]

Calonne's attack on the *Compte rendu* in the Assembly of Notables had rested on the premise that the deficit in 1776 was 37 million; that the service charges on the loans made during Necker's ministry had increased the ordinary expenditures by 44 million; that the ameliorations amounted to only 17 million. Therefore, it was clear from this rough calculation alone that the deficit must have been around 64 million livres in 1781. Necker's defense was to stipulate in twenty-nine articles the various ameliorations accomplished during his ministry, amounting to 84 million livres. This was clearly more than enough to balance the deficit of 24 million livres of 1776 and the increased service charges on the

47. The letters between Necker and Calonne were printed in Necker's April *Mémoire, Oeuvres complètes,* II, 161ff.
48. *Ibid* . p. 159.

public debt, which Necker estimated at 45 million livres. In an appendix of his April memorial Necker also answered all the objections brought against details of his *Compte rendu*.

Louis XVI was irritated by Necker's disobedience in publishing the memorial and exiled him from Paris for a time. But it was an embarrassing situation, because the notables obviously had more faith in the veracity of the Genevan than in the controller general. The Assembly naturally wanted more information. Would the controller general let a committee of the Assembly examine the *comptes effectifs* that he said disproved the *Compte rendu?* Calonne explained that this would not be feasible:

It is necessary to be very well-versed in this part of the administration, and know accounting to the most minute detail in order to distinguish in the accounts and *états* what belongs to each fiscal year, and what can make up the ordinary balance; that receipts as well as expenditures are distributed over several fiscal years; that there are fictitious expenditures (*ordonnances*) which are only for regularizing the accounts, so that even at this moment one is signing them dated from 1775; in sum, it is very difficult to be certain on the situation of each year.[49]

It was not a very satisfactory answer to a deliberative assembly. If that was the situation, why was the controller general so certain of the 56 million livres' error in the *Compte rendu* of 1781? Evidently the king must not have been able to make much of those accounts either. Only the controller general could decipher them, and the notables would have to be content with that. It was quite a different position from that of the Genevan, who was so anxious to show his documents to the notables but could not without the king's approval.

Which other witnesses would be useful? The Assembly learned of reports that Necker's successor, Joly de Fleury, was convinced the *Compte rendu* was accurate. Calonne had heard otherwise. His wife's uncle was Marquet de Bourgade, director of the treasury in the ministry of Joly de Fleury. From him Calonne was informed of a document drawn up in the *contrôle général* in July 1781, to justify the imposition of a 10 percent surtax on indirect taxes.[50] It maintained that the *Compte rendu* was in error by about 25 million livres and stipulated at which items. They were the same items mentioned in the brochure the *Whys*. Certain that he had an ally in Joly de Fleury, Calonne wrote him early in April, asking if he believed the *Compte rendu* was exact. The reply from the former finance minister was disappointing:

I tell you frankly that I do not believe there was a deficit at the time I was entrusted with the finances. Your uncle may have believed it, but he was unable to persuade either myself or Mr. de Maurepas. Anyway it is easy to see if either

49. Public Record Office, London, PC 1, 124, fol. 61. There are several cartons of Calonne's documents contained here, but few are related to his financial ministry. The bulk are derived from his career as leader of the émigrés. The *comptes effectifs* are not here.

50. "Mémoire d'observation sur le compte rendu par M. Necker au mois de Janvier, 1781," BN MSS Joly de Fleury, 1438, fol. 217-218.

he or I were in error. As to what concerns my administration, far from there being a deficit caused by loans, which were not as massive as you say, it is notorious that the revenue of the king was augmented by the surtax on indirect taxes and the third *vingtième*.[51]

After Vergennes's death early in the year, Louis XVI felt cast adrift with no firm anchor he could trust. The keeper of the seals, Hue de Miromesnil, took Vergennes's place as principal advisor. He had been unsympathetic toward Necker and was inclined to believe Calonne's version of the quarrel. Joly de Fleury had the good sense to send a copy of his letter to Miromesnil, who showed it to the king. It profoundly shook the confidence of both in the controller general. Miromesnil suggested calling a conference on the origins of the deficit. The two guardians of the royal treasury could be present and perhaps clarify the documents Calonne had submitted to the king.[52] Louis XVI decided instead to dismiss Calonne, and fired Hue de Miromesnil a week later!

Calonne fled to London to escape the wrath of the Parlement of Paris, who sought to try him for abuse of power. But he did not give up the argument. His *Reply to the Writing of Mr. Necker*, setting forth in great detail his case against the *Compte rendu*, appeared in January. In the appendix were eighteen "justificatory documents" offered as evidence. They consisted of the *Compte rendu* of abbé Terray for 1774, Turgot's for 1776, Necker's for 1781, the "Situation of the Finances," by Joly de Fleury for 1783, and Calonne's own *Compte rendu* for 1787. All his predecessors' accounts were corrected, based upon the *comptes effectifs* of those years. But the *comptes effectifs* themselves remained mysterious. Only one or two at the most of the justificatory documents could remotely resemble a *compte effectif* of the royal treasury.[53] Posterity, like the Assembly of Notables, was required to take the former controller general at his word.

In the summer of 1788, prior to beginning his second ministry in the government of Louis XVI, Necker replied to Calonne in *New Clarifications on the Compte rendu*.[54] Laboriously, item by item, he went over every issue between himself and Calonne, producing signed affidavits from officers in the General Farms or other departments of the financial administration. Calonne never responded. He explained that he would early in 1789, but his reply was not forthcoming.[55] That was the end of the debate over the *Compte rendu*, as the momentous events of 1789 overwhelmed both the reform movement and the financial difficulties of the prerevolutionary period.

51. Joly de Fleury to Calonne, April 5, 1787, printed in Pierre Chevallier, ed., *Journal de l'assemblée des notables de 1787* (Paris, 1960), p. 121. The original can be seen in AN K 163. It will be remembered that Maurepas died in November 1781, so it was during that year that the conversation between Bourgade, Joly de Fleury, and Maurepas took place.

52. Miromesnil to Louis XVI, April 5, 1787, Chevallier, ed., *Journal*, p. 119.

53. See my article "Necker's *Compte rendu* of 1781: A Reconsideration," *Journal of Modern History*, 42, no. 2 (June 1970), 161-183, a discussion of the literary debate between Necker and Calonne in 1788.

54. *Oeuvres complètes*, II, 243-602.

55. Charles-Alexandre de Calonne, *Motif pour différer jusqu'à l'assemblée des états généraux la réfutation du nouvel écrit [par] M. Necker*, (n.d., n.p.), BN L^b 39.536.

It is difficult to understand why posterity should have concluded that the *Compte rendu* was "totally false," when the proof of its accuracy exists today at the Château de Coppet and these documents are largely confirmed by the manuscripts of Joly de Fleury. Nor is it clear why Calonne's *comptes effectifs* should be considered the final word when they are not available; indeed, they are as mysterious as Bailly's *états au vrai.* Calonne's tactic of discrediting the *Compte rendu* on the basis of the *comptes effectifs* was fallacious in principle. The fact that the clergy did not meet in 1781 and made no contribution to the royal treasury that year did not mean it was improper to divide the "free gift" of 1780 into five equal parts since the gift was granted once every five years. One-fifth that sum was considered by Necker to be part of the ordinary income for 1781. Unlike the Genevan banker, Calonne did not seem to be accustomed to accounting principles.

Furthermore, he was inconsistent in his use of the *comptes effectifs* of the royal treasury to discredit not only Necker's *Compte rendu,* but all those of his predecessors during the reign. As any businessman knows, cash received and spent in the year will not tell him whether he is solvent. A large sum spent for insurance, for example, in one year may have acquitted that expense for several years. As Necker pointed out in the *New Clarifications,* to compare the *comptes effectifs* of the royal treasury with the *Comptes rendus* is to compare two entirely different financial documents. They could hardly ever match on any one item of either expenditure or income. Yet Calonne corrected only certain items in the *Comptes rendus* published in his *Reply to Necker,* leaving the impression that the uncorrected items were in harmony with the *comptes effectifs,* which was highly improbable.

A final inconsistency in Calonne's attack on the *Compte rendu* of 1781 was to condemn the Genevan for certain practices that he used himself in his account to the Assembly of Notables in 1787. He said Necker's account erred in giving naval department expenditures at the figure authorized by the king for ordinary expenditures, when in fact the amount spent exceeded that figure by 6 million livres. But Calonne did the same in 1787. He blamed Necker for giving the superior price of the leases with the General Farms and the two *régies,* rather than the "rigorous price." But he did likewise in his own *Compte rendu.* He also included as an ordinary income the prorated gift of the clergy, although this was omitted in the version he published in his *Reply to Necker.*[56]

That Necker's *Compte rendu* of 1781 was "utterly false" is one of the most firmly entrenched beliefs in historical writing about his first ministry. Yet in view of the evidence available, that opinion is no longer tenable. It is the most unjust libel that his enemies succeeded in foisting upon posterity.

56. The version submitted to the Assembly of Notables can be seen in BN MSS Fonds français, 23617, fol. 174. It has been published in Chevallier, ed., *Journal,* p. 134.

Three months after the publication of the *Compte rendu,* Necker's reform ministry came to an end. His resignation, submitted to the king on May 19, 1781, followed a libel campaign of increasing ferocity. The director general was accused of subverting the ancient monarchical institutions of France, and it was even said that he deserved to be tried for treason and put to death.[1] The absurdity and "extreme malevolence" of these libels was commented upon even by those journalists who were not sympathetic to Necker or his reform program.[2] The pamphlets were printed anonymously and distributed without charge. It was clear that the writers enjoyed protection in high places.

As Necker had expected, the *Compte rendu* itself became a major target. The pamphleteers gave their readers the impression of being well-versed in the intricate details of the royal finances. When one of them revealed his identity to the Paris lieutenant general of police as Antoine Bourboulon, intendant of finance in the household of the comte d'Artois, Necker believed he could no longer remain silent. The brochure of Bourboulon had circulated in manuscript for some weeks before it was published. The writer claimed to have found errors in Necker's *Compte rendu* amounting to over 35 million livres.[3] The director general asked the king's permission to confront his accuser before the royal council and go over every article attacked by Bourboulon. The king appointed a commission of three ministers to carry out this verification: Maurepas, Vergennes, and Miromesnil. According to Marmontel, the verification was carried out and Necker succeeded in vindicating his account.[4] Auget de Montyon, in his brochure published in 1812, denied that such a meeting took place and said that Necker had had to be satisfied with a personal letter from himself on behalf of the comte d'Artois (Montyon was chancellor of his household at that time) disavowing the pamphlet of Bourboulon.[5] But it is certain that the meeting of

1. Egret, *Necker: ministre de Louis XVI,* p. 175.
2. Bachaumont, *Mémoires secrets,* XVII, 166-167.
3. Antoine Bourboulon, *Réponse du sieur Bourboulon au compte rendu au roi par M. Necker* (London, 1781). A manuscript copy exists in AN K 892.
4. Marmontel, *Oeuvres complètes,* II, 216.
5. Egret, *Necker: ministre de Louis XVI,* p. 176.

the three ministers did take place and that Necker vindicated his *Compte rendu* in their presence, because he referred to this event in his April 1787 memorial.[6]

In August 1781, some three months after his resignation, Necker was indignant to read in the *Courrier de l'Europe* an article stating that the reason for the recent 10-percent increase in indirect taxes was to pay for the loans issued by the royal government the previous February and March.[7] Necker wrote to Vergennes asking him to disavow the article and reminded him of the conference attended by himself, Miromesnil, and Maurepas in which the *Compte rendu* had been verified. According to Necker's April 1787 memorial, Vergennes consulted with Joly de Fleury about the matter and then had the following disavowal published in the September 18 issue of the *Courrier de l'Europe:*

It was according to erroneous information that we stated in the 24th of August issue of our journal that the recent increase in taxes was for the purpose of paying for the life rentes which had been issued some time before, since the costs of those loans was sufficiently provided for by diverse economies or ameliorations in the finances, as the edicts for those loans had announced.[8]

Since Necker was powerless at that time, Vergennes had no reason to take this particular initiative except out of regard for justice toward the Genevan. As for Maurepas, the letter of Joly de Fleury to Calonne in April 1787 testified that the mentor did not believe the *Compte rendu* was erroneous. Hue de Miromesnil also attended that conference verifying the *Compte rendu* in 1781 and probably it was his advice in April 1787 which led Louis XVI to dismiss Calonne as controller general.[9]

It was not a question of the accuracy of the figures of the *Compte rendu* which turned Vergennes and Miromesnil against Necker in the ministerial crisis of May 1781. Both were conservative ministers of the *ancien régime*, with no sympathy for the reform movement. They had not cared for Turgot's reforms any more than for those of the Genevan banker. The tactic of taking the public into the confidence of the government by publishing the state of the finances was contrary to the practice of the absolute monarchy. Both ministers looked upon Necker as a foreigner whose innovations were incompatible with French tradition. Vergennes appreciated the ability of Necker to raise money. But now that the funds for the campaign of 1781 were assured, it was possible to do without the encumbrance of this ambitious and energetic individual who insisted on supervising the expenditures of all departments. The initiative taken by Necker in approaching the British government the previous December was probably keenly resented by the foreign minister. Both Vergennes and Miro-

6. Necker, in *Oeuvres complètes,* II, 206-207.

7. This article was based evidently upon the memorandum found in the manuscripts of Joly de Fleury (MSS Fonds Joly de Fleury, 1438, fols. 217-218), written in July presumably by Marquet de Bourgade. This is the same document referred to above in Chapter XIV.

8. Necker, "Mémoire au mois d'avril," *Oeuvres complètes,* II, 208.

9. See Chapter XIV.

mesnil helped to persuade the king that even the royal dignity itself was being compromised by the demands put forth by the Genevan in mid-May. "He does have a tendency to pull the covers over to his side of the bed," the king admitted.[10]

Only Castries and Ségur remained staunch supporters of the Genevan. This may have been due not only to personal friendship but to the fact that they were "Choiseulists," as was Necker. For the figure of that minister of Louis XV loomed larger than ever in the background as Maurepas suffered from increasingly severe attacks of the gout and it was evident he could not long remain at his post. Marie Antoinette and the government at Vienna still hoped for the return to power of the sponsor of the Franco-Austrian alliance.

The household of the elder of the king's two brothers, the comte de Provence, was no less active in the intrigue that led to Necker's disgrace than the household of Artois. Cromot du Bourg, superintendent of finances of the household of Provence, had mischievously published Necker's secret memorial written to the king in 1778 in order to persuade him of the desirability of instituting provincial assemblies. It appears that Provence had heard about the memorial and asked Necker if he could see it. Necker sent him a copy in the safekeeping of a trusted aid, Valdec de Lessart. The latter unfortunately allowed himself to be persuaded to leave it with Provence for a few hours, long enough for a copy to be made, so that it could be published at the opportune moment by the prince's household.[11] The remarks Necker had made to the king about the magistrates and the intendants were uncomplimentary enough, and would have been embarrassing even if reported accurately. But in the spectacular publicity given to the memorial, Necker's statements were grotesquely distorted. It was said that he wished to carry out another holocaust of the courts like that of Chancellor Maupeou's. The purpose of the provincial assemblies, so it was reported, was to replace the *parlements* in order to remove all barriers to despotism. The new assemblies would be easily managed and corrupted by the minister.[12]

The memorial was published just as Necker had succeeded in getting the approval of the king and the council for another provincial assembly in the generality of Moulins. The Parlement of Paris now bristled at the prospect of more such assemblies and withheld its registration of the edict. The intendant of Moulins insolently refused to obey Necker's order to set up the assembly in the Bourbonnais. This was the most direct and flagrant challenge to his authority so far, and Necker made the fateful decision to present to the king a list of conditions for continuing as director general of finances.

10. The quotation comes from the unpublished journal of abbé de Véri as quoted in Ségur, *Au Couchant de la monarchie*, II, 397.

11. *Ibid.*, pp. 381-384.

12. Egret, *Necker: ministre de Louis XVI*, p. 175.

The key person in the situation was the mentor. The king was genuinely attached to both Maurepas and Necker, and it was shattering when he realized he would have to dismiss one or the other. His attachment to Maurepas was a far warmer and more personal bond than to the Genevan, whose firm management of the finances he admired, and whose policy of economy he strongly endorsed. Maurepas's dislike of Necker was purely personal rather than due to differences of policy. He sometimes admitted facetiously that, while he governed the king, his wife governed him; and Madame de Maurepas had become violently hostile to Necker after Montbarey's resignation the previous December. Nothing illustrates so dramatically the contrast between the reform-minded ministers of the *ancien régime* and their conservative opponents. Madame de Maurepas knew and cared nothing about the fundamental social and economic problems of the *ancien régime* that so urgently called for reform. Her purview was limited to the small coterie of relatives and friends whom she attempted to place in prominent positions in the government, however worthless they might be—as was certainly true of the prince de Montbarey. As for Maurepas, he was titular head of the Council of Finance, and Necker's failure to mention him in the *Compte rendu* was said to have given him mortal offense. Maurepas was the first to coin the pun about the "blue story" that spread rapidly in the households of the princes. According to some reports the mentor was asked if the *Compte rendu* were true and he replied, "It is as true as it is modest," bursting into a fit of hilarity.

Confronted by a mocking and frivolous superior in the ministry, by the insubordination of the intendant of Moulins, and by the hostility of the sovereign courts and the conservative ministers in the government—and also seeing Bourboulon not only remaining at his post in the household of Artois but attending official functions as if nothing had happened—Necker decided it was necessary to get an unequivocal demonstration of support by the king or resign. Three separate requests were presented by Necker to Maurepas around the middle of May. First, he asked to be admitted as a permanent member of the High Council, which required the rank of minister. Necker had taken part in many informal council meetings in the presence of the king, but he was not allowed to attend the more formal High Council, where final decisions on great matters were taken. Maurepas appeared to think that Necker's religion would be an insurmountable barrier to the High Council and suggested that he become a Catholic. Necker protested that "Sully did not go to mass and he had the right of entrance to the High Council." The mentor was only amused by that argument: so the Genevan compared himself to the great Sully! In addition, Necker stipulated that he would resign unless the edict establishing the provincial assembly for Moulins were registered by the Parlement, which the king could force it to do, and also that he be given the right to supervise the expenditures of the war and naval departments, to which both Ségur and Castries had agreed.[13]

13. Ségur, *Au Couchant de la monarchie,* II, 409-410.

Maurepas refused to present Necker's demands to the king, and suggested that he ask the queen to act as intermediary. The next day, during an hour-long conference, Marie Antoinette sought to dissuade Necker from presenting his resignation; but she finally consented to deliver his message to the king. It was late in the afternoon, and shadows crept into the rooms of the château at Versailles. Fortunately for Necker, he did not see the tears in the queen's eyes, which would have caused him to lose all self-control, so deeply moved was he during the interview.[14] On Saturday, May 19, Necker learned from Maurepas that the king had refused his requests. His great gamble had failed, and he was stunned—so much so, according to one account, that when he turned to leave Maurepas' room, he could not find the door handle and had to be led out by a servant.[15]

The next day was Sunday, and the news spread rapidly in Versailles and Paris. There had been rumors that Necker was on the way out of the ministry. Yet the announcement was received with consternation by the public. There was no doubt that his popularity had withstood the vehement libel campaign against him, indeed, had continued to grow because of it. In Paris, especially, there was widespread dismay over the fall of the Genevan. According to the writer in Grimm's *Correspondance,* "One would have thought there was a public calamity . . . people looked at each other in silent dismay and sadly pressed each other's hand as they passed."[16] Metra wrote that "those people who have reasons for hating reforms and the reformer, and particularly the financiers, are the only ones who rejoice."[17]

The event caused a sensation abroad also. The Austrian chancellor, Kaunitz, labeled the dismissal of Necker as "pure folly." Emperor Joseph instructed his ambassador to see if Necker would be interested in serving the Austrian government.[18] A British informant in Paris reported to London that the news of Necker's resignation caused a sharp drop in Company of the Indies stock on the Paris bourse, and that it also raised the discount rate for rescriptions of the receivers general and had caused a run on the Discount Bank. "The best men," he reported, "consider M. Necker's retreat a fatal stab to the credit of France, and to the independence of America."[19] He reported also that the audience at the Comédie-Française were so loud in their disapprobation that additional guards were called in, an incident confirmed by other sources. Several reports also mentioned that Bourboulon was roundly hissed by the crowds in the

14. Baron de Staël, "Notice sur M. Necker," in Necker, *Oeuvres complètes,* I, clxxvi-clxxvii.

15. Egret, *Necker: ministre de Louis XVI,* p. 178.

16. Grimm, *Correspondance littéraire,* XII, 511.

17. Metra, *Correspondance secrète,* XI, 266.

18. Mercy-Argenteau, *Correspondance secrète du comte Mercy-Argenteau avec l'Empereur Joseph II et le prince de Kaunitz,* I, 40-43.

19. George III, *The Correspondence of King George the Third,* V, 238.

gardens of the Palais Royal and had to leave precipitously to escape being thrown into the pond.

There is hardly any question that Necker was the most widely respected by the public of any minister of the *ancien régime,* and that he had the greatest following. Whether he might have prevented the upheaval of 1789 is, as has been said, a false question. But that does not mean that the history of the reform movement is not an interesting subject in its own right. Nor does it free historians from their obligation to present major actors on the historical stage in a just light insofar as the evidence available permits.

Necker's first ministry has not been well understood, as some writers in recent years have pointed out. For too long he has been the butt of the polemicists. Historians are, in a sense, custodians of the reputations of the great men and women of the past. It is their responsibility to enter sympathetically into the mind of the historical figure, to interpret it, and to judge his acts accordingly. As Boissy d'Anglas noted as early as 1821: "Necker, of all states-men, has been treated with the greatest injustice. Many have spoken about him; few have known him, and even fewer have wanted to know him."[20] Only in recent years has there been an indication of a change in the historical writing about Necker from what it was in 1820. The rehabilitation of the Genevan banker is long overdue.

20. François-Antoine de Boissy d'Anglas, *Essai sur la vie . . . de M. de Malesherbes,* 3 vols. (Paris, 1819-1821), II, 254.

Appendix

TABLE OF *COMPTES RENDUS*

Selected Items of Ordinary Income
for the Royal Government

In view of the importance given to finances in bringing about the collapse of the *ancien régime* it is strange that so little attention has been given to the actual figures. One exception has been in the work of Frédéric Braesch, who made a detailed study of Loménie de Brienne's *Compte rendu* for 1788 and of Necker's for 1789 and 1790. Similar statements for earlier years are by no means as detailed but they do exist. Mathon de la Cour published several in 1788 at Lausanne. I have found others in the archives and in manuscript collections. In fact, some kind of statement exists for every year of the reign of Louis XVI except the years 1780, 1784, and 1785. Further research may fill those gaps. These accounts vary considerably in the amount of data they yield and the manner in which it is presented. But I believe it will be possible to present eventually a fairly complete table of *Comptes rendus* for the reign of Louis XVI.

In the meantime, the following illustrates the usefulness of such a table. In the first three *Comptes rendus* it has been necessary to combine some figures. For example, before the establishment of the *régie générale* in 1777, those accounts listed the income from the different *régies* rather than giving a single figure.

TABLE OF COMPTES RENDUS

Selected Items of Ordinary Income for the Royal Government

Year	General Farms	Régies	Domains and Forests	Postal Services	Royal Lottery	Total Ordinary Income
1774	155,085,000	20,598,600*	8,356,912*	7,700,000	–	361,880,429
1775	154,497,396*	19,329,600*	9,506,231*	7,700,000	–	370,167,398
1776	154,697,396	24,037,280*	9,503,972*	7,700,000	–	377,542,027
1781	126,000,000	42,000,000	42,000,000	11,120,000	7,000,000	427,530,571
1787	150,000,000	51,800,000	50,000,000	11,700,000	9,600,000	474,047,639
1788	150,106,875	51,000,000	50,340,000	13,100,000	9,860,000	472,414,549

Source: The account for 1774 was compiled by Terray, the next two by Turgot, the one for 1781 by Necker, and that for 1787 by Calonne. All were published in Charles-Joseph Mathon de la Cour, *Collection de comptes rendus*, 2d ed. (Lausanne, 1788). The last account, compiled by Loménie de Brienne, was published in 1788: *Compte rendu au roi au mois de mars, 1788, et publié par ses ordres* (Paris: Imprimérie royale, 1788).

*These figures are not in the original documents but are from my own addition.

BIBLIOGRAPHY

A. Primary Sources

1. Manuscripts

Archives départementales (AD), France

Gironde. Series C: correspondence of Necker with the intendant, 1776–1781. C 93–97; 3138.

Marne. Series C: intendance of Champagne. C 174, 1041, and 1046.

Puy-de-Dôme. Series C: correspondence of Necker with the intendant of Auvergne. C 180–185.

Archives nationales (AN), Paris

Col. C^2 46, 47, 105, 106. Documents on the Company of the Indies.

F^4 1082–1088. Diverse accounts of the royal treasury.

F^{11*} 1 and F^{11} 265. Documents on the grain trade.

F^{30} 110A, 110B, and 111. Central administration of the finances.

G^1 6, 7, and 54. Documents on the *fermes* and *régies*.

H^1 1600. Provincial assemblies.

K 161, 163, 681, 885, 892, and 899. Diverse letters and memorials.

P 2507–2521. Memorials of the Chambre des Comptes, 1774–1781.

P 2739–2741. Official copy of the *plumitif* of the Chambre des Comptes, 1774–1781.

P 3656. Trésor royal, 1781.

P 6028. Rentes of June 1771.

Château de Coppet, Switzerland

Pièces justificatives du compte rendu au roi par M. Necker au mois de janvier, 1781.

Bibliothèque nationale (BN), Paris

MSS Fonds Joly de Fleury. 1432, 1434–1444, 1448–1450. Collection from his financial ministry.

MSS Fonds francais: 6680–6683, journal of Hardy; 6877–6879, papers of President de Lamoignon; 8019–8020, archives of Marquet de Bourgade; 14086–14090, "Reflections on Finances"; 22043, "Observations d'un homme d'état sur le compte rendu de Necker"; 23617, Calonne's *Compte Rendu* of 1787.

MSS Fonds francais, nouv. acquis. 22111. Journal of Lefebvre d'Amécourt.

British Museum, London

Additional MSS 34, 413–417. The Auckland papers.

Additional MSS 36, 801–803; 38, 774. Correspondence of Viscount Mountstuart.

Public Record Office, London
PC 1 124, 125. Collection of Calonne's manuscripts.
State Papers, 92/82–83. Correspondence of Viscount Mountstuart.

2. *Printed Documents*

Almanach Royal. Paris: d'Houry, 1776–1781.
Archives parlementaires de 1787 à 1860. First ser. (1787–1799), vol. 87. Edited
    by Marcel Reinhard and Marc Bouloiseau. Paris: Centre national de la recher-
    che scientifique, 1968.
Boislisle, Arthur Michel de. *Chambre des comptes de Paris: Pièces justificatives
    pour servir à l'histoire des premiers présidents, 1506–1791.* Nogent-le-
    Rotrou: Gouverneur, 1873.
Collection des édits, déclarations et arrêts du conseil d'état. (BN F 23628–30.)
Collection des procès-verbeaux de l'assemblée provinciale du Berri. 2 vols.
    Bourges: 1787.
Collection Rondonneau, archives nationales. (AN IX 94–97, 375, 385, 389, 490,
    491, 509, 522, 554, and 570.)
Compte général des revenus et des dépenses fixes au 1 Mai, 1789. (BN L^f
    76.124.) Paris: 1789.
Compte rendu au roi au mois de Mars 1788 et publié par ses ordres. (BN L^b
    39.534.)
Flammermont, Jules, ed. *Remontrances du parlement de Paris au XVIIIe siècle.*
    3 vols. Paris: 1888–1898.
George III. *The Correspondence of King George the Third from 1760 to
    December 1783.* Edited by Sir John Fortescue. Vol. 5: 1780 to April 1782.
    London: Frank Cass, 1967.
Isambert, François André; Jourdan; Decrusy, eds. *Recueil général des anciennes
    lois françaises.* 29 vols. Paris: 1822–1827. Reprinted Farnborough, Hants.,
    England: Gregg Press, 1966.
[Malesherbes, Chrétien-Guillaume Lamoignon de.] *Protest of the Cour des Aides
    of Paris: April 10, 1775.* Edited by James H. Robinson. Translated by Grace
    Reade Robinson. Philadelphia: P. S. King, 1899.
Martens, George Frédéric de, ed. *Recueil des principaux traités d'alliance, de
    paix, de trêves . . . depuis 1761 jusqu'à présent.* 8 vols. 2d ed. rev. Göttingen:
    Dietrich, 1826–1835.
Mathon de la Cour, Charles-Joseph. *Collection de comptes rendus: Pièces au-
    thentiques, états et tableaux concernant les finances de France, depuis 1758
    jusqu'en 1787.* 2d ed. Lausanne: 1788.
*Procès-verbal des séances de l'assemblée provinciale de Haute-Guienne tenue à
    Villefranche.* 5 vols. Villefranche: 1779–1786.

3. *Printed Books, Memoirs, Journals, and Pamphlets*

Augeard, Jacques-Mathieu. *Mémoires secrets de J. M. Augeard.* Paris: H. Plon,
    1866.
Bachaumont, Louis Petit de. *Mémoires secrets pour servir à l'histoire de la
    république des lettres en France depuis 1762 jusqu'à nos jours.* 36 vols.
    London: J. Adamson, 1777–1789.
Besenval, Pierre-Victor de. *Mémoires.* 2 vols. 2d ed. Edited by Alexandre de
    Ségur. Paris: F. Buisson, 1805.

Boissy d'Anglas, François-Antoine de. *Essai sur la vie, les écrits et les opinions de M. de Malesherbes adressé à mes enfants.* 3 vols. Paris: Truettel et Würtz, 1819–1821.

Bourboulon, Antoine. *Réponse du sieur Bourboulon au compte rendu au roi par M. Necker.* London: 1781.

Calonne, Charles-Alexandre de. *Discours prononcé par M. de Calonne dans l'assemblée des notables tenue à Versailles le 22 février 1787.* Versailles: P. D. Pierres, 1787.

———. *Motif pour différer jusqu'à l'assemblée des états généraux la réfutation du nouvel écrit [par] M. Necker.* N.p., n.d. (BN L^b 39.536.)

———. *Réponse à l'écrit de M. Necker publié en avril, 1787.* London: T. Spilsbury, 1788.

———. *Requête au roi: Adressée à sa majesté par M. de Calonne, ministre d'état.* London: T. Spilsbury, 1787.

Château de Coppet. *Necker et Versailles: Exposition, 7 mai–14 août, 1955.* Coppet: 1955.

Collection complète de tous les ouvrages pour et contre M. Necker. 3 vols. Utrecht: 1781.

Coppons, President de. *Examen de la théorie et pratique de Monsieur Necker dans l'administration des finances de la France.* N.p. 1785. BN L^b 39.6290.

Coquereau, Jean-Baptiste. *Mémoires concernant l'administration des finances sous le ministère de M. l'abbé Terrai.* London: J. Adamson, 1776.

Cröy, Emmanuel de. *Journal inédit du duc de Cröy: 1718–1784.* 4 vols. Edited by vicomte de Grouchy and Paul Cottin. Paris: Flammarion, 1906.

Du Deffand, Marie Anne. *Correspondance complète de la marquise du Deffand.* 2 vols. Paris: H. Plon, 1865.

[Dupont de Nemours, Pierre Samuel.] *Procès-verbal de l'assemblée baillivale de Nemours pour la convocation des états généraux avec les cahiers des trois ordres.* 2 vols. Paris: 1789.

Familiengeschichte des Herrn von Necker, Königl. Französischen Staatsministers; Nebst beyläufigen Bemerkungen über seinen Karakter und seine Finanzoperationen. Regensburg: 1789.

Gibbon, Edward. "Memoirs of My Life and Writings." Vol. 1 of *The History of the Decline and Fall of the Roman Empire.* New York: Harper, n.d.

Golovkin, Fédor, ed. *Lettres diverses recueillies en Suisse.* Geneva: 1821.

Grimm, Friedrich Melchior. *Correspondance littéraire, philosophique et critique par Grimm, Diderot, Raynal, Meister, etc.* 16 vols. Edited by Maurice Tourneux. Paris: Garnier, 1877–1882.

Hermann, J. *Zur Geschichte der Familie Necker.* Berlin: Gaertner, 1886.

Knies, Carl Gustav, ed. *Correspondance inédite de Dupont de Nemours et du marquis de Mirabeau avec le margrave et le prince héréditaire de Bade.* 2 vols. Heidelberg: 1892.

Le Trosne, Guillaume-François. *De L'Administration provinciale et de la réforme de l'impôt.* Basel: 1779.

Loménie de Brienne, cte. Athanase-Louis de, and Etienne-Charles Loménie de Brienne, *Journal de l'assemblée des notables de 1787.* Edited by Pierre Chevallier. Paris: C. Klincksieck, 1960.

Marmontel, Jean-François. *Oeuvres complètes de Marmontel.* 19 vols. rev. ed. Paris: Verdière, 1818–1820.

Meister, Jacques-Henri. *Mélanges de philosophie, de morale et de littérature.* 2 vols. Geneva: J. J. Pashoud, 1822.

Mercy-Argenteau, Florimond-Claude de. *Correspondance secrète du comte de Mercy-Argenteau avec l'empereur Joseph II et le prince de Kaunitz.* 2 vols. Edited by A. d'Arneth and J. Flammermont. Paris: 1889–1891.

———. *Correspondance secrète entre Marie-Thérèse et le comte de Mercy-Argenteau.* 3 vols. Edited by A. d'Arneth and A. Geffroy. Paris: 1874.

Metra, François. *Correspondance secrète, politique et littéraire, ou mémoires pour servir à l'histoire des cours, des sociétés et de la littérature en France depuis la mort de Louis XV.* 18 vols. London: J. Adamson, 1787–1790.

Mirabeau, Honoré-Gabriel de Riqueti, comte de. *Lettres du comte de Mirabeau sur l'administration de M. Necker.* N.p.: 1787.

Montbarey, Alexandre-Marie, prince de. *Mémoires.* 3 vols. Paris: Eymery, 1826–1827.

[Montyon, Antoine-Jean Auget de.] *Particularitiés et observations sur les ministres des finances les plus célèbres depuis 1660 justqu'en 1791.* Paris: Le Normant, 1812.

Moreau, Jacob-Nicolas. *Mes Souvenirs.* 2 vols. Paris: E. Plon, Nourrit, 1898–1901.

Moreau de Beaumont, Jean-Louis, and Poullin de Viéville. *Mémoires concernant les impositions et droits en Europe.* Vol. 5. Paris: J. C. Desaint, 1787–1789.

Morellet, abbé André. *Examen de la résponse de M. N[ecker] au mémoire de M. l'abbé Morellet sur la Compagnie des Indes.* Paris: Desaint, 1769.

———. *Mémoire sur la situation actuelle de la Compagnie des Indes.* Paris: Desaint, 1769.

———. *Mémoires de l'abbé Morellet.* 2 vols. 2d ed. Paris: 1882.

Necker, Jacques. *Observations de M. Necker sur l'avant-propos du livre rouge.* Paris: Imprimerie royale, 1790.

———. *Oeuvres complètes de M. Necker publiées par M. le baron de Staël, son petit-fils.* 15 vols. Paris: Treuttel et Würtz, 1820–1821.

———. *Réponse au mémoire de M. l'abbé Morellet sur la Compagnie des Indes.* Paris: Imprimerie royale, 1769.

———. "Sur La Législation et le commerce des grains." In *Mélanges d'économie politique.* Ed. Gustave de Molinari. Vol. 2. Paris: Guillaumin, 1848.

Necker, Madame (S. Curchod de Nasse). *Mélanges extraits des manuscrits.* 3 vols. Paris: C. Pougens, 1798.

Nougaret, Pierre-Jean-Baptiste. *Anecdotes du règne de Louis XVI.* Paris: J. F. Bastien, 1778.

Panchaud, Benjamin [Isaac]. *Réflexions sur l'état actuel du crédit de l'Angleterre et de la France.* N.p.: 1781.

[Pidansat de Mairobert, Mathieu-François]. *L'Espion anglais.* 10 vols. London: J. Adamson, 1779–1784.

Radix de Sainte-Foy, Maximilien. *Mémoire à Monseigneur le comte d'Artois sur l'administration de ses finances.* Paris: 1781. (BN L^f 15.8.)

[Rousselot de Surgy, Jacques-Philibert.] *Encyclopédie méthodique: Partie finances.* 3 vols. Paris: Panckoucke, 1784–1787.

Saint-Cyran, Paul-Edmé Crublier de. *Calcul des rentes viagères sur une et sur plusieurs têtes.* Paris: 1779.

Ségur, Louis-Philippe de. *Mémoires: Ou Souvenirs et anecdotes*. 3 vols. Paris: A. Eymery, 1825–1826.

Sénac de Meilhan, Gabriel. *Le Gouvernement, les moeurs, et les conditions en France avant la Révolution*. Edited by M. de Lescure. Paris: Poulet-Malaisis, 1862.

Smith, Adam. *An Inquiry into the Nature and Causes of the Wealth of Nations*. Edited by Edwin Cannan. New York: Modern Library, 1937.

Soulavie, Jean-Louis. *Mémoires historiques et politiques du règne de Louis XVI, depuis son mariage jusqu'à sa mort*. 6 vols. Paris: Treuttel et Würtz, 1801.

Staël, Auguste de. "Notice sur M. Necker." In Jacques Necker, *Oeuvres complètes de M. Necker* . . . Vol. 1. Paris: Treuttel et Würtz, 1820.

Staël-Holstein, Anne-Louise-Germaine de. *Mémoires sur la vie privée de mon père, suivies des mélanges de M. Necker*. Paris: 1818.

Tilly, Alexandre de. *Mémoires de Tilly pour servir à l'histoire des moeurs de la fin du XVIIIᵉ siècle*. 3 vols. Paris: 1828.

Turgot, Anne-Robert-Jacques de. *Oeuvres de M. Turgot: Précédées et accompagnées de mémoires et de notes sur sa vie, son administration et ses ouvrages*. Edited by Pierre-Samuel Dupont de Nemours. 9 vols. Paris: Delance, 1808–1811.

———. *Oeuvres de Turgot et documents le concernant, avec biographie et notes*. Edited by Gustave Schelle. 5 vols. Paris: F. Alcan, 1913–1923.

Véri, Joseph-Alphonse de. *Journal de l'abbé de Véri*. Edited by Jehan de Witte. 2 vols. Paris: J. Tallandier, 1928–1930.

Voltaire, François Marie Arouet de. *Oeuvres complètes*. 52 vols. Paris: Garnier, 1877–1885.

B. Secondary Works

Afanassiev, Georges. *Le Commerce des céréales en France au dix-huitième siècle*. Translated from the Russian. Paris: A. Picard, 1894.

Andlau, Béatrice d'. *La Jeunesse de Madame de Staël (de 1766 à 1788) avec des documents inédits*. Geneva: Droz, 1970.

Bailly, Antoine. *Histoire financière de la France depuis l'origine de la monarchie jusqu'à la fin de 1786*. 2 vols. Paris: Moutardier, 1830.

Binney, John Edward Douglas. *British Public Finance and Administration, 1774–1792*. Oxford: Clarendon Press, 1958.

Bloch, Camille. *L'Assistance et l'état en France à la veille de la révolution*. Paris: A. Picard, 1908.

Bosher, J. F. *French Finances, 1770–1795: From Business to Bureaucracy*. Cambridge: At the University Press, 1970.

———. "Jacques Necker et la réforme de l'état." *Rapport annuel de la Société historique du Canada* (1963), 162–175.

———. "The *premier commis des finances* in the Reign of Louis XVI." *French Historical Studies*, 3, no. 4 (1964), 475–495.

———. *The Single Duty Project: A Study of the Movement for a French Customs Union in the Eighteenth Century*. London: Athlone, 1964.

Bouchard, Léon. *Système financier de l'ancienne monarchie*. Paris: Guillaumin, 1891.

Bouteil, Jeanne. *Le Rachat des péages au dix-huitième siècle d'après les papiers du bureau des péages.* Paris: 1925.

Braesch, Frédéric. *Finance et monnaies révolutionnaires: Recherches, études et documents.* 3 vols. Nancy: Roumegoux, 1934.

Braudel, Fernand, and Ernest Labrousse, editors. *Histoire économique et sociale de la France.* Vol. 2: 1660-1789. Paris: Presses universitaires de France, 1970.

Cahen, Léon, "Le Pacte de famine et les spéculations sur les blés." *Revue historique,* 152 (1926), 32-43.

———. "Le prétendu pacte de famine." *Revue historique,* 176 (1935), 173-216.

Callatay, Edouard de. *Madame de Vermenoux: Une Enchanteresse au XVIIIe siècle.* Paris and Geneva: 1956.

Carré, Henri. "Le Premier Ministère de Necker." *La Révolution française,* 44 (1903), 97-136.

Carré, Henri; Pierre Sagnac; and Ernest Lavisse. *Louis XVI (1774-1789): Histoire de France illustrée depuis les origines jusqu'à la révolution.* Edited by Ernest Lavisse. Paris, 1900-1911. Vol. 9, pt. 1. Reprinted: New York: AMS Press, 1969.

Castries, René de la Croix, duc de. "L'Abbé de Véri et son journal." *Revue de Paris* (November 1953), 76-93.

———. *La France et l'indépendance américaine: Le Livre du bicentenaire de l'indépendance.* Paris: Librairie académique Perrin, 1975.

Chapuisat, Edouard. *Necker (1732-1804).* Paris: Librairies du Recueil Sirey, 1938.

Conan, M. J. "La Dernière Compagnie française des Indes: Privilège et administration." *Revue d'histoire économique et sociale,* 25 (1939), 37-58.

Cramer, Marc. "Les Trente Têtes genevoises et les billets solidaires." *Revue suisse d'économie politique et de statistique,* 83 (1946), 109-138.

Darnton, Robert. "The Memoirs of Lenoir, lieutenant de police of Paris: 1774-1785." *English Historical Review,* 85 (1970), 532-559.

Doniol, Henri. *Histoire de la participation de la France à l'établissement des Etats-Unis d'Amérique.* 6 vols. Paris: Imprimerie nationale, 1886-1899.

Doyon, André. "Maximilien Radix de Sainte-Foy (1736-1810)." *Revue d'histoire diplomatique,* 80, no. 3 (1966), 231-274.

Dull, Jonathan R. *The French Navy and American Independence: A Study of Arms and Diplomacy, 1774-1787.* Princeton: Princeton University Press, 1975.

Durand, Yves. *Les Fermiers généraux au XVIIIe siècle.* Paris: Presses universitaires de France, 1971.

Egret, Jean. *Louis XV et l'opposition parlementaire: 1715-1774.* Paris: Armand Colin, 1970.

———. "Malesherbes: Premier Président de la cour des aides (1750-1775)." *Revue d'histoire moderne et contemporaine,* 3 (1956), 97-119.

———. *Necker: Ministre de Louis XVI: 1776-1790.* Paris: H. Champion, 1975.

Faure, Edgar. *La Disgrâce de Turgot.* Paris: Gallimard, 1961.

———. "Les Bases expérimentales et doctrinales de la politique économique de Turgot." *Revue historique de droit français et étranger,* 39, ser. 4 (1961), 255-295, 382-447.

———. "Turgot et la théorie du produit net." *Revue d'histoire économique et sociale*, 39 (1961), 273–286; 417–441.

Girardot, Auguste-Théodore, baron de. *Essai sur les assemblées provinciales et en particulier sur celle du Berry: 1778–1790.* Bourges: Vermeil, 1845.

Glagau, Hans. *Reformversuche und Sturz des Absolutismus in Frankreich: 1774–1788.* Munich: R. Oldenbourg, 1908.

Gomel, Charles. *Les Causes financières de la révolution française.* 2 vols. Paris: Guillaumin, 1892–1893.

Grange, Henri. *Les Idées de Necker.* Paris: C. Klincksieck, 1974.

———. "Turgot et Necker devant le problème des salaires." *Annales historiques de la révolution française*, 29 (1957), 19–33.

Grosclaude, Pierre. *Malesherbes: Témoin et interprète de son temps.* 3 vols. Paris: Fishbacher, 1961.

———. "Morale et politique dans la pensée de Jacques Necker." *Revue des travaux de l'Académie des sciences morales et politiques*, 121, ser. 4 (1968), 25–44.

Harris, Robert D. "French Finances and the American War: 1777–1783." *Journal of Modern History*, 48, no. 2 (June 1976), 233–258.

———. "Necker's *Compte rendu* of 1781: A Reconsideration." *Journal of Modern History*, 42, no. 2 (June 1970), 161–183.

Haussonville, Othenin d'. "Le Salon de Madame Necker." *Revue des deux mondes*, 37 (1880), 47–98; 38 (1880), 63–106; 42 (1880), 790–828.

Jobez, Alphonse. *La France sous Louis XVI.* 3 vols. Paris: 1877–1893.

Jolly, Pierre. *Necker.* Paris: Presses universitaires de France, 1951.

Kraus, Berta. *Das Okonömische Denken Neckers.* Vienna: 1925.

Lardé, Georges. *Une Enquête sur les vingtièmes au temps de Necker: Histoire des remontrance du parlement de Paris (1777–1778).* Paris: Letouzey et Ané, 1920.

Laugier, Lucien. *Un Ministère réformateur sous Louis XV: Le Triumvirat (1770–1774).* Paris: La Pensée universelle, 1975.

Lavaquery, Eugène. *Necker: Fourrier de la revolution: 1732–1804.* Paris: Plon, 1933.

Lavergne, L. de. "Les Assemblées provinciales en France avant 1789." *Revue des deux mondes*, 34 (1861), 36–66, 392–428.

Legohérel, Henri. *Les Trésoriers généraux de la marine: 1517–1788.* Paris: Editions Cujas, 1965.

Leroux-Cesbron, Charles. *Gens et choses d'autrefois.* Paris: J. Tallandier, 1914.

Logette, Aline. *Le Comité contentieux des finances près le conseil du roi (1777–1791).* Nancy: 1964.

Luethy, Herbert. *La Banque protestante en France de la révocation de l'édit de Nantes à la révolution.* 2 vols. Paris: SEVPEN., 1961.

———. "Necker et la Compagnie des Indes." *Annales, Economies, Sociétés, Civilisations*, 15 (1960), 852–881.

Marion, Marcel. *Dictionnaire des institutions de la France aux XVIIe et XVIIIe siècle.* 1923. Reprinted Paris: Picard, 1972.

———. *Histoire financière de la France depuis 1715.* 6 vols. Vol. 1. Paris: A. Rousseau, 1914–1929.

———. *Les Impôts directs sous l'ancien régime, principalement au XVIIIe siècle.*

Paris: E. Cornely, 1910.

———. "Turgot et les grandes remontrances de la cour des aides (1775)." *Vierteljahrschrift für Social und Wirtschaftsgeschichte,* 1 (1903), 303–313.

Matthews, George T. *The Royal General Farms in Eighteenth-Century France.* New York: Columbia University Press, 1958.

Montcloux, Hte. de. *De la Comptabilité publique en France.* Paris: 1840.

Morris, Richard B. *The Peacemakers: The Great Powers and American Independence.* New York: Harper & Row, 1965.

Ozanam, Denise. *Claude Baudard de Sainte-James: Trésorier général de la marine et brasseur d'affaires (1738–1787).* Geneva: Droz, 1969.

Palmer, Robert R. *The Age of the Democratic Revolution.* Vol. 1: *The Challenge.* Princeton: Princeton University Press, 1959.

Pange, comtesse Jean de. "Necker en Angleterre: Le Mystérieux Voyage de 1776." *La Revue littéraire, histoire, arts et sciences des deux mondes* (April 1948), 480–499.

Rioche, Augustin. *De L'Administration des vingtièmes sous l'ancien régime.* Paris: A. Rousseau, 1904.

Ritter, Eugène. *Notes sur Madame de Staël, ses ancêtres et sa famille.* Geneva: H. Georg, 1899.

Roux, Pierre. *Les Fermes d'impôts sous l'ancien régime.* Paris: Rousseau, 1916.

Sainte-Beuve, Charles-Augustin. *Causeries du lundi.* 15 vols. 3d ed. Paris: Garnier, 1850–1862.

Ségur, Pierre-Henri, marquis de. *Au Couchant de la monarchie.* 2 vols. Paris: Levy, 1913.

Sivers, Fr. von. "Necker als Nationalökonom." *Jahrbücher für Nationalökonomie und Statistik,* 22 (1874), 17–27.

Stanhope, Philip Henry, Lord Mahon. *History of England from the Peace of Utrecht to the Peace of Versailles.* 7 vols. London: 1836–1854.

Stourm, René. *Les Finances de l'ancien régime et de la révolution.* 2 vols. Paris: Guillaumin, 1885.

Tarrade, Jean. *Le Commerce colonial de la France à la fin de l'ancien régime: L'Evolution du régime de "l'exclusif" de 1763 à 1789.* 2 vols. Paris: Presses universitaires de France, 1972.

Vacher de Lapouge, Claude. *Necker économiste.* Paris: M. Rivière, 1914.

Vührer, Adolphe. *Histoire de la dette publique en France.* 2 vols. Paris: Berger-Levrault, 1886.

Weber, Henry. *La Compagnie française des Indes (1604–1875).* Paris: A. Rousseau, 1904.

Weulersse, Georges. *La Physiocratie sous les ministères de Turgot et de Necker (1774–1781).* Paris: Presses universitaires de France, 1950.

———. *Le Mouvement physiocratique en France de 1756 à 1770.* 2 vols. Paris: F. Alcan, 1910.

INDEX

Abonnement, 184, 189, 191
Académie française, 46
Academy of Science (French) 129n
Acquits de comptant, 226, 227, 229
Acquits patents, 227
Administrative monarchy, 73, 102, 176, 182
Afanassiev, Georges, 169, 171-72, 174n
Aides, 85, 146, 185
Aiguillon, Emmanuel-Armand, duc d': ministry of, 59; mentioned, 37, 101
Alembert, Jean Le Rond d', 5, 38, 46
Amelot de Chaillou, Jean-Antoine, 151
American colonies: plans to partition, 212, 215; independence of, 240. See also Britain, colonies
American War: French finances and, 117-36 passim, 154, 160; French intervention in, 119, 212, 216; mentioned, 84, 87, 117
Anticipations, 71, 72, 110, 138, 149, 177, 199, 208, 223, 227-29
Antoine, Michel, 105n
Anville, duchesse d', 101
Ardascheff, Pavel, 94n
Artois, Charles-Philippe, comte de: finances of, 131n, 194-97; relations with Necker, 195n; role in libel campaign, 198; mentioned, 107, 221, 236, 238, 239
Assembly of Notables (of 1787): Calonne's attack on the Compte rendu of 1781 during, 230-35 passim; mentioned, 82, 98, 137. See also Notables
Auch, generality of, 170, 172
Auckland papers, British Museum, 154
Augeard, Jacques-Mathieu, 6, 100, 198

Bachaumont, Louis Petit de, 10, 15, 62, 153, 164, 165, 195, 198, 202, 205, 208, 218
Bailly, Antoine, 225-35 passim

Bank of England, 27, 121, 150
Bastille, 205
Baudard de Sainte-James, Claude, 111, 208
Baudeau, Nicolas, abbé, 62
Beggars, 158, 160-62, 163. See also Social welfare
Bernis, François-Joachim de Pierre, cardinal de, 181
Berri, province of. See Provincial assemblies
Berthaux, Jean, 141
Bertier de Sauvigny, Louis-Jean, 188
Bertin, Henri, 69, 92, 177
Besenval, Pierre-Victor, baron de, 88, 192-93
Béthune-Charost, Armand-Joseph, duc de, 186
Bicêtre. See Hospitals
Black notes. See Discount Bank
Bloch, Camille, 162, 165
Boissy d'Anglas, François-Antoine, 241
Bonstetten, Charles-Victor, 44
Bordeaux, generality of, 91n, 170, 171, 172
Bosher, J. F., 173
Bouchard, Léon, 230
Bourbonnais, province of. See Provincial assemblies
Bourboulon, Antoine, 221, 232, 236, 239, 240
Bourdieu and Chollet, 12, 13
Bourges, generality of, 92, 184, 185, 191
Bourse, 146, 223, 240
Bouteil, Jeanne, 174
Boutin, Charles-Robert, 12
Brienne, Etienne-Charles Loménie de. See Loménie de Brienne
Brissot de Warville, Jacques-Pierre, 96, 98
Britain (Great): Necker's admiration for, 56, 87, 96; model for physiocrats, 59; credit and taxation in, 68-69, 120, 121, 124, 134; colonies of, 102; debt of, 119; plans to invade, 145; fleet of, 210;